Family and Succession Law in South Africa

Family and Succession Law in South Africa

Third Edition

Jacqueline Heaton
Anneliese Roos

This book was originally published as a monograph in the International Encyclopaedia of Laws/Family and Succession Law.

Founding Editor: Roger Blanpain
General Editor: Frank Hendrickx
Volume Editor: Walter Pintens

Wolters Kluwer

Published by:
Kluwer Law International B.V.
PO Box 316
2400 AH Alphen aan den Rijn
The Netherlands
E-mail: international-sales@wolterskluwer.com
Website: lrus.wolterskluwer.com

Sold and distributed in North, Central and South America by:
Wolters Kluwer Legal & Regulatory U.S.
7201 McKinney Circle
Frederick, MD 21704
United States of America
Email: customer.service@wolterskluwer.com

Sold and distributed in all other countries by:
Air Business Subscriptions
Rockwood House
Haywards Heath
West Sussex
RH16 3DH
United Kingdom
Email: international-customerservice@wolterskluwer.com

Printed on acid-free paper

ISBN 978-94-035-1661-5

e-Book: ISBN 978-94-035-1662-2
web-PDF: ISBN 978-94-035-1663-9

Printed in the United Kingdom.

The Authors

Jacqueline Heaton lectures Family Law at the University of South Africa. She is one of the editors of the *South African Law Journal* and a former editor of the *Annual Survey of South African Law.* She is also a former Rapporteur of the Family Law Committee of the International Law Association. She is the author of several books, chapters in books and articles in law journals on the Law of Persons, Family Law, and Child Law.

Professor Anneliese Roos lectures Law of Succession and Data Privacy Law at the University of South Africa. She is the author of a casebook on the Law of Succession and chapters on Data Privacy Law in three books. She has published articles on the Law of Succession and Data Privacy Law.

The Authors

Table of Contents

Table of Contents

List of Abbreviations

§1. Common Terms

RACAP	Register on Adoptable Children and Prospective Adoptive Parents

§2. Legislation

Constitution	Constitution of the Republic of South Africa, 1996
interim Constitution	Constitution of the Republic of South Africa 200 of 1993

§3. Common Cited Law Reports

AD	Reports of the Appellate Division of the Supreme Court of South Africa
All SA	All South African Law Reports
BCLR	Butterworths Constitutional Law Reports
Buch	Buchanan's Reports
Buch AC	Buchanan's Appeal Cases, Cape Appeal Court
CPD	Reports of the Cape Provincial Division
CTR	Cape Times Reports
EDC	Reports of the Eastern Districts Courts of the Cape
EDL	Reports of the Eastern Districts Local Division
JOL	Judgments Online
Menz	Menzies' Reports
NLR	Natal Law Reports
NPD	Reports of the Natal Provincial Division
Off Rep	Official Reports, Reports of the High Court of the South African Republic
OPD	Reports of the Orange Free State Provincial Division
PH	Prentice-Hall Weekly Legal Service
Roscoe	Roscoe's Reports

List of Abbreviations

SA	South African Law Reports
SC	Cape Supreme Court Reports
TS	Reports of the Transvaal Supreme Court
TPD	Reports of the Transvaal Provincial Division
WLD	Reports of the Witwatersrand Local Division

Preface

The Law of Persons, Family Law and the Law of Succession are viewed as three distinct fields of law in South Africa. In this monograph, the discussion of these three fields of South African law was nevertheless cast in the classification mould prescribed by the publishers and editors of the Family Law and Succession series of monographs. Further, although some of the terms used in the prescribed outline and the model monograph for this series of monographs have different meanings or are no longer the most up-to-date terms in South African law, an attempt was made to follow the prescribed classification and outline as closely as possible. To avoid glaring omissions of important South African legal rules, the authors were, however, compelled to deviate from the prescribed outline in some areas.

Jacqueline Heaton and Anneliese Roos,
Pretoria,
April 2019

General Introduction

§1. General Background of the Country (Demographic Data)

I. Introduction

1. South Africa occupies the southern tip of the African continent. It has common boundaries with Namibia, Botswana and Zimbabwe to the north and Mozambique and Swaziland to the north-east. The total national territory of South Africa is 1,219,090 km^2, making the country approximately one-eighth the size of the United States of America, twice the size of France and three times the size of Germany.[1] Cape Town is the legislative capital of the country and Pretoria the administrative capital.

2. The country has been occupied by humans since the Stone Age. The first known modern human occupants of South Africa were the Khoi and the San people. The indigenous population expanded when African groups moved into southern Africa from the north.[2]

White people first arrived in South Africa in the fifteenth century when Portuguese seafarers, en-route to India, visited the South African coast. The first White settlement was established in 1652 when Jan van Riebeeck occupied the Cape of Good Hope in order to run a halfway station for the trading fleet of the Dutch East India Company (*Verenigde Oost-Indiesche Companje*). British occupation replaced Dutch occupation in 1795. The first British occupation lasted until 1803, when the Dutch again took over for a brief period. A second British occupation followed between 1806 and 1910. During this time, several thousand British settlers moved to South Africa, and a number of Afrikaner pioneers moved into the interior of the country. The pioneer expeditions have become known as the Great Trek (*Groot Trek*). The Afrikaner pioneers settled in various parts of the interior and established *Boer* or *Voortrekker* Republics, each with its own legislature.[3]

---

1. E. Tibane (ed.), 'Land and Its People', *2017/18 South Africa Yearbook* 1 (Government Communication and Information Service 25th ed. 2018).
2. R.W. Johnson, *South Africa: The First Man, The Last Nation* 1–17 (Weidenfeld & Nicolson 2004); N. Worden, *The Making of Modern South Africa: Conquest, Segregation and Apartheid* 7–9 (Blackwell Publishing 3d ed. 2000).
3. For more detail on the periods described in this paragraph, *see* E. Tibane (ed.), 'History', *2017/18 South Africa Yearbook* 1–4 (Government Communication and Information Service 25th ed. 2018); H. Giliomee, *The Afrikaners: Biography of a People* 1–245 (Tafelberg 2003); H.R. Hahlo & E. Kahn, *South Africa: The Development of Its Laws and Constitution* 2–7 (Stevens & Sons Limited,

After two wars between the *Boere* and the Brits, South Africa was unified in 1910 as the Union of South Africa.[4] In 1948, the National Party won the general election in South Africa. Thenceforth, the policy of *apartheid* was implemented and enforced at national level.

In 1961 South Africa became a republic,[5] but, under *apartheid*, several homelands were created in order to exclude the majority of the population from the republic. Some of these homelands received independence[6] and could enact their own legislation, including legislation governing aspects of Family and Succession Law.[7]

The *apartheid* regime came to an end with the coming into operation of the interim Constitution[8] in 1993. The interim Constitution afforded all South Africans citizenship and the right to vote, abolished the homelands, and again unified the whole territory.[9] It also contained South Africa's first Bill of Rights.[10] In 1996 the interim Constitution was replaced by the final Constitution[11] (hereinafter 'Constitution'), which also contains a Bill of Rights.[12] Thus, today, South Africa is a constitutional democracy.

3. South Africa has nine provinces: KwaZulu-Natal (capital: Pietermaritzburg); Western Cape (capital: Cape Town); Eastern Cape (capital: Bhisho); Northern Cape (capital: Kimberley); Free State (capital: Bloemfontein); Gauteng (capital: Johannesburg); North West (capital: Mahikeng (formerly Mafikeng)); Mpumalanga (capital: Mbombela (formerly Nelspruit)); and Limpopo (capital: Polokwane (formerly Pietersburg)).[13]

1960); Johnson, *South Africa: The First Man, The Last Nation*, 30–101; D. Marais, *South Africa: Constitutional Development: A Multi-Disciplinary Approach* 17–150 (Southern Book Publishers Revised 2d ed. 1993); Worden, *The Making of Modern South Africa*, 9–37, 21–72.

4. Union of South Africa Act 1909, s. 4. This Act was enacted by the British Imperial Parliament.
5. Republic of South Africa Constitution Act 32 of 1961.
6. Status of Transkei Act 100 of 1976; Status of Bophuthatswana Act 89 of 1977; Status of Venda Act 107 of 1979; Status of Ciskei Act 110 of 1981.
7. *See*, e.g., Transkei Marriage Act 21 of 1978; Transkei Reciprocal Enforcement of Maintenance Orders Decree 16 of 1990; Venda Dissolution of Marriages on Presumption of Death Act 7 of 1982; Ciskei Customary Law Amendment Decree 23 of 1991. For more detail on the periods described in this paragraph, *see* Giliomee, *The Afrikaners: Biography of a People*, 245–541; Hahlo & Kahn, *South Africa: The Development of Its Laws and Constitution*, 7–9; Johnson, *South Africa: The First Man, The Last Nation*, 101–167; Marais, *South Africa: Constitutional Development*, 151 et seq.; Worden, *The Making of Modern South Africa*, 35–37, 82–164.
8. Constitution of the Republic of South Africa 200 of 1993.
9. Sections 1, 5, 6 and 230(1) read with Schs 1 and 7.
10. Chapter 3.
11. Constitution of the Republic of South Africa, 1996.
12. The current Bill of Rights is contained in Ch. 2 of the Constitution.
13. Constitution, s. 103; Tibane (ed.), *Land and Its People*, 3–8.

4. South Africa is classified as an emerging market and developing economy[14] with medium, but rising, human development.[15] There is wide divergence in the wealth of and population density in the various provinces. For example, although the Northern Cape is the largest province, it has the smallest population and is the poorest of all the provinces. In contrast, Gauteng, which is the smallest province, has a large population, is the most densely populated province and is one of the wealthiest provinces in the country.[16]

5. South Africa is governed by national, provincial and local governments.[17] Legislation is enacted by the central and provincial legislatures.[18] Statutes regarding Family and Succession Law are the domain of the central government, but local councils may issue by-laws on childcare facilities.[19]

II. Demography

6. South Africa is a racially, religiously, linguistically and culturally diverse nation. South Africa's population is approximately 55.5 million.[20] Slightly more than half the population (51%) is female. Some 80% of the population consists of Black/African people. The Black segment of the population consists of various ethnic groups, including the Zulu, Xhosa, Basotho, Tswana and Tsonga. So-called 'Coloured' persons and White persons are the second and third most populous groups in the country, constituting around 9% and 8% of the population, respectively. The White people mainly descend from British, Dutch, French and German ancestors, while the 'Coloured' people have mixed White, African, Indian and Malay ancestry. The Indian/Asian segment of the population constitutes approximately 2.5% of the population.[21]

---

14. International Monetary Fund, 'Country Groups Information', https://www.imf.org/external/pubs/ft/weo/2018/02/weodata/weoselagr.aspx, 30 Jan. 2019.
15. United Nations Development Programme, 'Human Development Indices and Indicators: 2018 Statistical Update. Briefing Note for Countries on the 2018 Statistical Update', 2, http://www.hdr.undp.org/sites/all/themes/hdr_theme/country-notes/ZAF.pdf, 30 Jan. 2019.
16. Tibane (ed.), *Land and Its People*, 5 and 7; Statistics South Africa, *Community Survey 2016 in Brief, Report 03-01-06* (Statistics South Africa 2016), Table 2 and Figure 3; Statistics South Africa, 'Statistical Release P0301.4, Census 2011', Tables 2.1 and 3.1, http://www.statssa.gov.za/publications/P03014/P030142011.pdf, 30 Jan. 2019.
17. Constitution, ss 1 and 40(1).
18. Constitution, s. 43.
19. Constitution, ss 43, 44, 104 and 156 read with Schs 4 and 5.
20. Statistics South Africa, *Community Survey 2016 in Brief, Report 03-01-06*, Table 2. The 2018 mid-year population estimates put the figure at around 58 million: Statistics South Africa, 'Mid-year Population Estimates 2018, P0302', Table 5, http://www.statssa.gov.za/publications/P0302/P03022018.pdf, 24 Mar. 2019.
21. Statistics South Africa, *Community Survey 2016 in Brief, Report 03-01-06*, Tables 3, 4, 8 and Figures 4, 5 and 6. The 2018 mid-year population estimates put the figures at approximately 81% for African people, 9% for 'Coloured' people, 2.5% for Indian/Asian people, and 7.8% for White people: Statistics South Africa, 'Mid-year Population Estimates 2018, P0302', Table 5.

7. South Africa has eleven official languages, namely, Sepedi (also known as Sesotho sa Leboa), Sesotho, Setswana, siSwati, Tshivenda, Xitsonga, Afrikaans, English, isiNdebele, isiXhosa and isiZulu.[22] Of the official languages, isiZulu is the mother tongue of the greatest proportion of the population, namely 24.6%. Isi-Xhosa is the mother tongue of 17% of the population, followed by Afrikaans (12.1%), Sepedi (9.5%), Setswana (8.8%), English (8.3%), and Sesotho (8%). Each of the other languages is the mother tongue of less than 5% of the population.[23] Although English is not the mother tongue of the majority of the population, it is the most widely understood language.[24]

There is a marked difference in the languages spoken within the various provinces. For example, isiXhosa is spoken by the vast majority of the people in the Eastern Cape, while Sesotho is most common in the Free State, isiZulu in KwaZulu-Natal, Afrikaans in the Western Cape and Setswana in the North West.[25]

8. Around 78% of South Africans identify themselves as Christians. The followers of the Islamic and Hindu faiths, respectively, constitute around 1.6% and 1% of the population. The followers of the Jewish religion make up less than 0.1% of the population.[26]

9. The annual population growth rate increased between 2002 and 2018 from around 1% to around 2%.[27]

10. The infant mortality rate is 36.4 per 1,000 live births.[28] The estimated life expectancy for a South African male born in 2018 is 61.1 years and 67.3 years for a female.[29]

Approximately 8.5% of the population is 60 years or older, but the proportion of persons aged 60 and over is estimated to increase to 11% in 2025 and 13% in 2050.[30] Around 8% of the South African population is disabled.[31]

11. The overall population density in South Africa is approximately forty-six persons per square kilometre.[32] Nearly a quarter of the population (24%) lives in the smallest and most densely populated province of the country, namely Gauteng. At approximately 20%, KwaZulu-Natal also has a large population but a much

22. Constitution, s. 6(1).
23. Statistics South Africa, *Community Survey 2016 in Brief, Report 03-01-06*, Table 12 and Figure 11.
24. Tibane (ed.), *Land and Its People*, 3.
25. Statistics South Africa, *Community Survey 2016 in Brief, Report 03-01-06*, Tables 13 and 14.
26. *Ibid.*, Table 15.
27. Statistics South Africa, 'Mid-year Population Estimates 2018, P0302', Figure 7. For statistics on the number of live births recorded each year, *see* the annual P0305 statistics available at www-.statssa.org.za.
28. Statistics South Africa, 'Mid-year Population Estimates 2018, P0302', Appendix 2.
29. *Ibid.*
30. *Ibid.*, Table 6; S.Z. Kalula et al. *Profile and Management of Patients at a Memory Clinic South* 100 Afr. Med. J. 449 (2010).
31. Statistics South Africa, *Community Survey 2016 in Brief, Report 03-01-06*, Figure 18.
32. The population density rates provided in this paragraph were calculated based on Statistics South Africa, *Community Survey 2016 in Brief, Report 03-01-06*, Table 2.

lower population density rate than Gauteng. Some way behind these two provinces is the Eastern Cape with approximately 12.5% of the population. Limpopo and the Western Cape are, respectively, home to approximately 10% and 11% of the population. Mpumalanga has a population of some 8%, while the Free State and North West respectively has a population of some 5% and 6%. Only 2% of the population lives in the Northern Cape, which is the largest province in South Africa.

Nearly two-thirds of the population lives in urban areas, and the rate of urbanization is increasing steadily. In 1990 52% of the population lived in urban areas. By 2018 the figure had risen to nearly 67%.[33]

12. Unemployment stands at more than a quarter of the population, with women suffering more unemployment (29%) than men (26%).[34] The unemployment rate differs markedly between the Black and 'Coloured' population groups, on the one hand, and the Indian and White population groups, on the other. The unemployment rate is around 31% and 22% for Black and 'Coloured' persons, respectively, while it is around 10% for Indian people and around 7% for White people.[35] The number of children involved in child labour declined from 779,000 in 2010 to 577,000 in 2015.[36]

§2. Historical Background of Family and Succession Law

I. Introduction

13. The first legal system which operated in South Africa was customary or indigenous law. The system of law that has come to be known as 'the common law' arrived in the country with the White occupiers and settlers. Because of the occupation of the Cape of Good Hope by the Dutch East India Company, Roman-Dutch law – which is a civil-law system – is at the root of South African common law. Due to subsequent British occupations of the country, South African common law was also influenced by English law – which is a common-law system. What South Africans call 'the common law' is therefore a hybrid or mixed legal system.[37]

Although customary law was the first legal system to operate in South Africa, it was, for a long time, denied full official recognition. The only legal system which

33. Central Intelligence Agency, 'Urbanization', https://www.cia.gov/library/publications/the-world-factbook/geos/sf.html, 30 Jan. 2019.
34. Statistics South Africa, *Quarterly Labour Force Survey, Quarter 3, 2018, P0211* (Statistics South Africa 2018), Tables A and 2. The quarterly surveys are available at www.statssa.gov.za.
35. Statistics South Africa, *Quarterly Labour Force Survey, Quarter 3, 2018, P0211*, Table 2.1.
36. Statistics South Africa, *Survey of Activities of Young People, 2015, P0212* (Statistics South Africa 2015), Tables 12a, 12b, 13 and Figure 34.
37. For more detail on the history of South African law, *see* A.B. Edwards, *The History of South African Law – An Outline* 1 et seq. (Butterworths 1996); Hahlo & Kahn, *South Africa: The Development of Its Laws and Constitution*, 10–28, 51–182, 317–334; T. Humby, L. Kotzé & A. du Plessis (eds.), *Introduction to Law and Legal Skills in South Africa* 101–115 (Oxford University Press Southern Africa 2012); D. Kleyn et al. *Beginner's Guide for Law Students* 26–54 (Juta Law 5th ed. 2018); Marais, *South Africa: Constitutional Development*, 17–46, 69–188, 253.

was fully recognized was the common law as interpreted in case law, and modified by statutory rules. Today, customary law enjoys full recognition alongside the common law.[38]

No system of religious law is officially recognized in South Africa. However, individuals and religious groups constitutionally have the right to freedom of religion and belief, and to practice their religion and/or belief in association with others.[39]

II. Pluralism

14. In a multi-cultural and multi-religious society such as South Africa, pluralism of laws is inevitable.[40] As pointed out immediately above, customary law is recognized alongside the common law, but no system of religious law is recognized. However, Hindu and Muslim marriages receive recognition for specific, limited purposes.[41] Pluralism is therefore very much part of South African Family and Succession Law.

Unification of the various legal systems is unlikely to occur because it would probably unjustifiably limit the constitutional rights to freedom of culture and religion.[42] However, harmonization is being selectively employed. Thus, for example, the legislature and courts have attempted to harmonize the law relating to customary and civil marriages,[43] but these attempts have been criticized as denuding customary marriage law and supplanting it with the law relating to civil marriages.[44] Other examples are the judicial abolition of the separate system for administering the intestate estates of Black persons,[45] and the enactment of the Reform of Customary Law of Succession and Regulation of Related Matters Act 11 of 2009[46] to harmonize customary and common law relating to intestate succession.

38. Constitution, s. 211(3).
39. Constitution, ss 15(1) and 18.
40. On legal pluralism in South Africa, *see* C. Rautenbach, *The Phenomenon of Legal Pluralism*, in *Introduction to Legal Pluralism in South Africa* 5–16 (C. Rautenbach & J.C. Bekker eds., LexisNexis 4th ed. 2014).
41. *See* Part II, Ch. 1, §1 below.
42. Constitution, ss 15, 31 and 36.
43. *See*, e.g., the Recognition of Customary Marriages Act 120 of 1998 and *Gumede v. President of the Republic of South Africa* 2009 (3) SA 152 (CC).
44. C. Himonga, *The Advancement of African Women's Rights in the First Decade of Democracy in South Africa: The Reform of the Customary Law of Marriage and Succession*, Acta Juridica 84 (2005); J. Bekker & G. van Niekerk, *Gumede v. President of the Republic of South Africa: Harmonisation, or the Creation of New Marriage Laws in South Africa?*, 24 SA Public Law 214 (2009).
45. *Bhe v. Magistrate, Khayelitsha (Commission for Gender Equality as Amicus Curiae); Shibi v. Sithole; South African Human Rights Commission v. President of the Republic of South Africa* 2005 (1) SA 580 (CC).
46. The Act came into operation on 20 Sep. 2010.

§3. SOURCES OF FAMILY AND SUCCESSION LAW

I. Introduction

15. South African law has never been codified although portions of the law have been (partly) embodied in legislation. Currently, the main written sources of South African Family and Succession Law are the Constitution, legislation, case law, old texts such as Justinian's *Corpus Iuris Civilis*, the writings of authors such as Grotius, Voet, Van Leeuwen and Van der Keessel on the Roman-Dutch law that was received into South African law,[47] and the writings of modern authors.

16. Discovering the content of customary Family and Succession Law is often difficult, for this body of law is largely unwritten and is subject to ethnic and regional differences. In KwaZulu-Natal, customary law is partly codified in the KwaZulu Act on the Code of Zulu Law 16 of 1985 and the Natal Code of Zulu Law.[48] Further, the Recognition of Customary Marriages Act 120 of 1998 replaced many customary rules regarding customary marriages with ones which are similar or identical to those that govern civil marriages. However, the Act also retained some of the customary rules regarding customary marriages. Thus, for example, it provides that the validity of a customary marriage that was concluded before the coming into operation of the Act must be determined by customary law, and a customary marriage that is concluded after the coming into operation of the Act must be negotiated and entered into or celebrated in accordance with customary law,[49] but it does not set out the relevant rules of customary law.

Case law provides some guidance on the content of customary law, as do publications by authors. However, these sources – especially publications by authors – are frequently criticized as conveying an official, stultified version of customary law which has been influenced by *apartheid* policies and perspectives. Thus, expert witnesses are sometimes used to establish current, living customary law.[50]

II. Constitution

17. The Constitution is the supreme law against which all other legal provisions – including legislation – must be tested.[51] The Bill of Rights in the Constitution applies to all law, and binds the legislature, the executive, the judiciary and all

47. Some of the texts of these authors that are still relevant today are cited in the footnotes of this monograph.
48. Proclamation R151 in *G.G.* 10966 of 9 Oct. 1987.
49. Sections 2(1) and 3(1).
50. On the differences between official customary law and current, living customary law, and the difficulties in ascertaining the true content of customary law, *see*, e.g., *Alexkor Ltd v. Richtersveld Community* 2004 (5) SA 460 (CC); *Bhe v. Magistrate, Khayalitsa (Commission for Gender Equality as Amicus Curiae); Shibi v. Sithole; South African Human Rights Commission v. President of the Republic of South Africa* 2005 (1) SA 580 (CC); *Shilubana v. Nwamitwa* 2009 (2) SA 66 (CC); *Gumede v. President of the Republic of South Africa* 2009 (3) SA 152 (CC).
51. Constitution, ss 8(1), 8(2), 39(1) and 39(2).

organs of state.[52] A provision of the Bill of Rights can also be invoked against a natural or a juristic person 'if, and to the extent that, it [that is, the provision] is applicable, taking into account the nature of the right and the nature of any duty imposed by the right'.[53]

18. The Bills of Rights in the interim and final Constitutions have resulted in wide-ranging and fundamental change to South African Family and Succession Law. The constitutional rights which have been, and will remain, of special significance for Family and Succession Law include the following:

(1) The right to equality, which provides that everyone is equal before the law and has the right to equal protection and benefit of the law, and prohibits direct and indirect unfair discrimination on any ground, including race, gender, sex, pregnancy, marital status, ethnic or social origin, colour, sexual orientation, age, disability, religion, conscience, belief, culture, language and birth.[54]
(2) The right to human dignity.[55]
(3) The right to bodily and psychological integrity, which includes the right to make decisions concerning reproduction.[56]
(4) The right to privacy.[57]
(5) The right to freedom of conscience, religion, thought, belief and opinion. This right does not preclude the enactment of legislation recognizing marriages concluded under any tradition or system of religious, personal or family law, or legislation recognizing systems of personal and family law under any tradition or adhered to by persons professing a particular religion.[58]
(6) The child's rights:
   (a) to a name and a nationality from birth;
   (b) to family or parental care, or appropriate alternative care when he or she is removed from the family environment;
   (c) to basic nutrition, shelter, basic health care services and social services;
   (d) to be protected from maltreatment, neglect, abuse or degradation;
   (e) to be protected from exploitative labour practices;
   (f) not to be required or permitted to perform work or provide services that are inappropriate for a person of his or her age, or place his or her well-being, education, physical or mental health or spiritual, moral or social development at risk;
   (g) not to be detained except as a measure of last resort. If the child is detained, he or she has (in addition to the right to freedom and security of the person, the right to bodily and psychological integrity, and the rights enjoyed by arrested, detained and accused persons) the right to be detained only for the shortest appropriate period of time; to be kept separately from

52. Constitution, s. 8(1).
53. Constitution, s. 8(2).
54. Section 9(1), (3) and (4).
55. Section 10.
56. Section 12(2)(a).
57. Section 14.
58. Section 15(1) and (3).

adult detainees; and to be treated in a manner and be kept in conditions that take his or her age into account;
(h) to have a legal practitioner assigned to him or her by the state, at state expense, in civil proceedings affecting him or her if substantial injustice would otherwise result;
(i) not to be used directly in armed conflict, and to be protected in times of armed conflict; and
(j) to have paramountcy afforded to his or her best interests in every matter concerning him or her.[59]

(7) The right to use the language and participate in the cultural life of one's choice, subject to the proviso that the Bill of Rights may not be infringed in the exercising of this right.[60]
(8) The right to enjoy one's culture, practice one's religion and use one's language with other members of one's community, and to form, join and maintain cultural, religious and linguistic associations and other organs of civil society.[61]
(9) The right not to be deprived of one's property except in terms of law of general application, which law may not may permit arbitrary deprivation of property.[62] This right is said to include the right to dispose of one's property during one's lifetime or at one's death.[63]

A limitation of a right enshrined in the Bill of Rights is justifiable only if it occurs in terms of law of general application and is reasonable and justifiable in an open and democratic society based on human dignity, equality and freedom. Justifiability is determined by taking all relevant factors into account, including the nature of the right, the importance of the purpose of the limitation, the nature and extent of the limitation, the relation between the limitation and its purpose, and less restrictive means to achieve the purpose.[64]

19. The Bill of Rights does not expressly protect the right to family life. Despite the absence of this right, the Constitutional Court has ruled that the right to dignity encompasses and protects the rights of individuals to enter into and sustain permanent intimate relationships.[65] Thus, the right to family life is protected by the constitutional right to dignity.

---

59. Section 28(1) and (2).
60. Section 30.
61. Section 31.
62. Section 25(1).
63. *See* M.J. de Waal & M.C. Schoeman-Malan, *Law of Succession* 4 (Juta 5th ed. 2015) and Part IV, Ch. 2, §6 below.
64. Section 36.
65. *Dawood v. Minister of Home Affairs; Shalabi v. Minister of Home Affairs; Thomas v. Minister of Home Affairs* 2000 (3) SA 936 (CC) para. 36; *see also Harksen v. Lane* 1998 (1) SA 300 (CC) para. 93.

III. Legislation

20. Legislation includes national and provincial Acts; regulations and rules issued under national or provincial Acts; proclamations, norms and standards issued in terms of Acts or regulations; and by-laws issued by municipal councils. It even includes a few old Dutch statutes, such as the Perpetual Edict of 1540 and the Political Ordinance of 1580, some sections of which still apply in South Africa.

21. As indicated above in this chapter, Acts regarding Family and Succession Law are the domain of the central government, but local councils may issue by-laws on childcare facilities. The most important Acts in the field of Family Law are the Marriage Act 25 of 1961, Civil Union Act 17 of 2006, Recognition of Customary Marriages Act 120 of 1998, Matrimonial Property Act 88 of 1984, Maintenance Act 99 of 1998, Maintenance of Surviving Spouses Act 27 of 1990, Divorce Act 70 of 1979, Children's Act 38 of 2005 and Mediation in Certain Divorce Matters Act 24 of 1987. These Acts regulate the conclusion and consequences of civil marriages, civil unions and customary marriages; enforcement of the spousal and parental duties of support; the maintenance claim of a surviving spouse or civil union partner against the estate of his or her deceased spouse or civil union partner; termination of a civil marriage, civil union or customary marriage; matters relating to child law, such as acquisition of parental responsibilities and rights, adoption, foster care, child protection, child-headed households, cross-border child abduction and surrogate motherhood; and the Office of the Family Advocate. Hopefully, in the near future, South Africa will also have legislation governing Muslim marriages and cohabitation outside marriage or a civil union.[66]

Insofar as the Law of Succession is concerned, the most important statutes are the Intestate Succession Act 81 of 1987, Wills Act 7 of 1953, Maintenance of Surviving Spouses Act, Reform of Customary Law of Succession and Regulation of Related Matters Act 11 of 2009, Administration of Estates Act 66 of 1965, Immovable Property (Removal or Modification of Restrictions) Act 94 of 1965, and Trust Property Control Act 57 of 1988. These Acts regulate the devolution of a person's estate in terms of the rules of intestate succession; the formalities for the execution, amendment and revocation of a will; the maintenance claim of a surviving spouse or civil union partner against the estate of his or her deceased spouse or civil union partner; the administration of a deceased estate; the removal of restrictions on the alienation of immovable property imposed by a will; and control of trust property.

66. The draft Domestic Partnerships Bill, 2008 was published for public comment in Gen.N. 36 in *G.G.* 30663 of 14 Jan. 2008, while the draft Muslim Marriages Bill, 2010 was published for public comment in Gen.N. 37 in *G.G.* 33946 of 21 Jan. 2011. In 2018, a division of the High Court declared the continued non-recognition of Muslim marriages unconstitutional, and required the legislature and the executive branch of government to collaborate to rectify the position by 31 Aug. 2020: *Women's Legal Centre Trust v. President of the Republic of South Africa* 2018 (6) SA 598 (WCC).

IV. Treaties

22. Generally, the international and regional instruments South Africa has ratified or acceded to become enforceable when they are enacted into local law by national legislation.[67] Such instruments include the Hague Convention on Protection of Children and Co-operation in respect of Inter-country Adoption and the Hague Convention on the Civil Aspects of International Child Abduction, which have been included in the Children's Act 38 of 2005, and the Hague Convention on the Conflicts of Laws Relating to the Form of Testamentary Dispositions, which has been included in the Wills Act 7 of 1953.[68]

However, it is not only binding international instruments that must be taken into account in South Africa. Both binding and non-binding international law is used for interpretative purposes,[69] because the Constitution requires courts, tribunals and forums to consider international law when they have to interpret the Bill of Rights.[70] Furthermore, when interpreting any legislation, the courts must prefer any reasonable interpretation that is consistent with international law over an interpretation that is inconsistent with it.[71]

V. Jurisprudence

23. The precedent system operates in South Africa. Thus, the binding force of each judgment depends on the place the court that delivered the judgment occupies in the hierarchy of courts. Briefly, the decisions of the Constitutional Court bind all courts, and those of the Supreme Court of Appeal bind all the divisions of the High Court and the Magistrate's Court. Decisions by a particular division of the High Court bind that court and the Magistrate's Courts which fall within the geographical area of that division of the High Court. The decisions of the Magistrate's Courts do not serve as precedents.[72] A court may deviate from a precedent only if it is convinced that the earlier decision is clearly wrong because it was arrived at on a fundamental departure from principle or a manifest oversight or misunderstanding; mere disagreement with the earlier decision does not justify departure from the precedent system.[73]

---

67. Constitution, s. 231(4).
68. Section 3*bis*.
69. *S. v. Makwanyane* 1995 (3) SA 391 (CC) para. 35.
70. Constitution, s. 39(1)(b).
71. Constitution, s. 233.
72. For a detailed discussion of the precedent system, *see* F. du Bois, *Sources of Law: Common Law and Precedent*, in *Wille's Principles of South African Law* 76–92 (F. du Bois ed., Juta & Co 9th ed. 2007); Humby, Kotzé & Du Plessis (eds.), *Introduction to Law and Legal Skills in South Africa*, 134–135; Kleyn et al., *Beginner's Guide for Law Students*, 82–94.
73. *See*, e.g., *Camps Bay Ratepayers and Residents Association v. Harrison* 2011 (4) SA 42 (CC); *Patmar Explorations (Pty) Ltd v. Limpopo Development Tribunal* 2018 (4) SA 107 (SCA).

§4. The Courts Administering Family and Succession Law

I. Introduction

24. The South African court structure is divided into superior and lower courts. Courts at both levels have the power to decide matters relating to Family Law, but lower courts have no jurisdiction in respect of Succession Law.

South Africa does not have specialized Family Courts at either superior or lower court level. The creation of such courts was recommended many years ago. It was recommended that these courts should function at High Court level and that they should have a legal and a social component, follow an inquisitorial procedure, and apply mediation,[74] but the proposed courts were never established.

II. Lower Courts

25. The lower courts are the Magistrate's Courts and certain specialized lower courts. The Magistrate's Courts are divided into District Courts and Regional Courts. District and Regional Courts function only as courts of first instance.[75]

In the past, Magistrate's Courts had jurisdiction to administer the estates of deceased Black persons.[76] The Constitutional Court declared this separate system of administration of the estates of Black persons unconstitutional.[77] All deceased estates are now administered under the supervision of the Master of the High Court.[78]

District and Regional Courts have jurisdiction to deal with many matters relating to Family Law. They can hear most criminal matters, including juvenile-justice cases. Regional Courts have the same jurisdiction as the High Court to decide divorce and nullity cases, cases relating to customary marriages, and matters arising from such cases.[79]

Neither the District nor the Regional Court has jurisdiction in respect of determining a person's mental status, the validity or interpretation of a will or another testamentary document, or the constitutionality of any legislation or any conduct of Parliament.[80]

---

74. Hoexter Commission, *Fifth and Final Report RP 78/1983 Commission of Inquiry into the Structure and Functioning of the Courts* paras 9.4.1–9.4.2. (Government Printer 1983).
75. Kleyn et al., *Beginner's Guide for Law Students*, 323.
76. Black Administration Act 38 of 1927, s. 23 read with the regulations issued under the Act.
77. *Moseneke v. The Master* 2001 (2) SA 18 (CC).
78. *Bhe v. Magistrate, Khayelitsha (Commission For Gender Equality as Amicus Curiae); Shibi v. Sithole; South African Human Rights Commission v. President of the Republic of South Africa* 2005 (1) SA 580 (CC).
79. Magistrates' Courts Act 32 of 1944, s. 29(1), (1A) and (1B) read with Sch. 2 of G.N. 670 in *G.G.* 33418 of 29 Jul. 2010.
80. Constitution, s. 170; Magistrates' Courts Act 32 of 1944, s. 46(2)(a) and (b).

26. The specialized courts which function at lower court level and have jurisdiction in matters relating to Family Law are the Maintenance Courts and the Children's Courts.[81] As their name suggests, the Maintenance Courts decide matters concerning maintenance. The Children's Courts have jurisdiction in respect of an array of child-related matters, including adoptions, child protection, foster care, paternity disputes, care of a child, and contact with a child.[82] Except in the context of adoption, Children's Courts do not have jurisdiction to make an order regarding guardianship of a child.[83] Children's Courts also do not have jurisdiction in respect of matters relating to artificial fertilization; the departure, removal or abduction of a child from the country; applications requiring the return of a child to South Africa from abroad; the age of majority; the contractual or legal capacity of a child; the safeguarding of a child's interest in property; surrogate motherhood; and child-related issues in divorces, customary marriages, maintenance cases or domestic violence cases.[84]

Pilot Community Courts have been established at lower court level. These courts deal only with petty crimes, such as shoplifting, petty theft, petty traffic offences, drunkenness, failure to comply with a lawful instruction of a police officer, common assault, and so forth.[85] Community Courts focus on quick assessment of the accused, and many of them offer restorative justice processes. Many, but not all, of them deal with adults and juveniles and assess young offenders with a view to diverting them from the criminal justice system into suitable programmes.[86]

III. Superior Courts

27. At present, the superior courts consist of fifteen divisions (including six local divisions) of the High Court,[87] a single Supreme Court of Appeal, and the Constitutional Court. The divisions of the High Court are spread throughout the country.[88] They have jurisdiction as courts of first instance in all criminal and civil cases. Each division of the High Court is also the upper guardian of all minors within its area of jurisdiction. As such, it has the power to make any order that is in the best interests

81. Maintenance Act 99 of 1998, s. 3; Children's Act 38 of 2005, s. 42(1).
82. Children's Act 38 of 2005, s. 45(1).
83. Children's Act 38 of 2005, ss 24 and 45(3)(a) and (b); *Ex parte Sibisi* 2011 (1) SA 192 (KZP).
84. Children's Act 38 of 2005, ss 1(4) and 45(3)(c)–(h).
85. M. Lue-Dugmore, V. Karth & J. Redpath, *Petty Crimes that Matter: Evaluating the Western Cape Community Courts* SA Crime Quarterly 27 (March 2005); Department of Justice and Constitutional Development, 'Community Courts', http://www.justice.gov.za/about/sa-courts.html, 30 Jan. 2019.
86. E. Tibane (ed.), 'Justice and Correctional Services', *2017/18 South Africa Yearbook* 11 (Government Communication and Information Service 25th ed. 2018); Lue-Dugmore, Karth & Redpath, *Petty Crimes that Matter*, 28, 30, 31, 32; Department of Justice and Constitutional Development, 'Community Courts'.
87. Superior Courts Act 10 of 2013, s. 6(1) and 6(3)(c).
88. For a list of the seats of the divisions of the High Court (excl. local divisions), *see* s. 6(1) of the Superior Courts Act 10 of 2013. For a list of the current names of all the divisions of the High Court (incl. local divisions), *see* Directive 3/2014 issued by the Office of the Chief Justice. The directive was published in *G.G.* 37390 of 28 Feb. 2014.

of the child.[89] The divisions of the High Court may decide all constitutional matters except for those falling within the exclusive jurisdiction of the Constitutional Court.[90] They also act as courts of appeal and review in respect of cases decided by the lower courts.[91]

The Supreme Court of Appeal has its seat in Bloemfontein.[92] It is solely a Court of Appeal, not a Court of First Instance.[93]

The Constitutional Court is the highest court of the country.[94] Its seat is Johannesburg.[95] It may decide constitutional matters and any other matter which raises an arguable point of law of general public importance which ought to be considered by the Constitutional Court.[96] If a High Court or the Supreme Court of Appeal makes an order that an Act or a section of an Act is unconstitutional, the order must be referred to the Constitutional Court for confirmation.[97]

The Constitutional Court, Supreme Court of Appeal and all the divisions of the High Court have the inherent power to protect and regulate their own process and to develop the common law, taking into account the interests of justice.[98] When a court develops the common law, it must promote the spirit, purport and objects of the Bill of Rights.[99]

---

89. *See*, e.g., *Ex parte Kedar* 1993 (1) SA 242 (W); *Hay v. B* 2003 (3) SA 492 (W); *Soller v. Maintenance Magistrate, Wynberg* 2006 (2) SA 66 (C); *B v. B* 2008 (4) SA 535 (W).
90. Constitution, s. 169(a)(i).
91. Constitution, s. 169(b); Magistrates' Courts Act 32 of 1944, s. 83; Criminal Procedure Act 51 of 1977, ss 302, 304A, 309, 310 and 310A; Maintenance Act 99 of 1998, s. 25(1); Children's Act 38 of 2005, s. 51(1); Child Justice Act 75 of 2008, ss 84 and 85.
92. Superior Courts Act 10 of 2013, s. 5(1)(b).
93. Constitution, s. 168(3).
94. Constitution, s. 167(3)(a).
95. Superior Courts Act 10 of 2013, s. 4(1)(b).
96. Constitution, s. 167(3)(b).
97. Constitution, ss 167(5) and 172(2)(a).
98. Constitution, s. 173. Generally on the South African court system, *see* Kleyn et al., *Beginner's Guide for Law Students*, 319–331.
99. Constitution, s. 39(2).

Part I. Persons

Chapter 1. The Status of a Person

§1. Definition of a Person

28. In South African law, legal personality attaches to either a human being ('natural person') or an association of natural persons that qualifies as a juristic person. Every man, woman and child is deemed to be a person (legal subject), irrespective of how handicapped he or she may be.[100]

The requirements for the beginning of a natural person's legal personality are the following:

(1) Birth must be completed, that is, the bodies of the mother and the child must be completely separated, although the umbilical cord need not have been severed.[101]
(2) The child must live after the separation, even if only for a short period.[102]

Because legal personality begins at birth, a foetus is not a legal subject. However, if it appears that the unborn child would have had certain claims or rights had he or she already been born, his or her potential interests are protected by employing the fiction that he or she was born at the time of his or her conception. This fiction is expressed in the adage *nasciturus pro iam nato habetur, quotiens de commodo eius agitur* which formed part of Roman-Dutch law[103] and still operates

---

100. *Tjollo Ateljees (Eins) Bpk v. Small* 1949 (1) SA 856 (A).
101. *Digesta* 25.4.1.1, 35.2.9.1; *Codex* 6.29.3; J. Voet, *Commentarius ad Pandectas*, trans. with explanatory notes and notes of all South African cases by P. Gane under the title *The Selective Voet Being the Commentary on the Pandects [Paris Edition of 1829] by Johannes Voet [1647–1713] and the Supplement to That Work by Johannes van der Linden [1756–1835]*, 1.5.5. (Butterworth & Co. (Africa) Ltd 1956).
102. *Digesta* 50.16.129; *Codex* 6.29.3.
103. H. Grotius, *Inleidinge tot de Hollandsche Rechts-geleerdheid with Notes by S.J. Fockema Andreae* (L.J. van Apeldoorn ed., S Gouda Quint 3d ed. 1926), *Inleidinge*, 1.3.3, 1.3.4; D.G. van der Keessel, *Praelectiones Iuris Hodierni ad Hugonia Grotii Introductionem ad Iurisprudentiam Hollandicam*, trans. H.L. Gonin in Consultation with D. Pont under the title *Voorlesinge oor die Hedendaagse Reg na Aanleiding van De Groot se 'Inleiding tot de Hollandse Rechtsgeleerdheyd': D.G. van der Keessel* 1.3.4 (P. van Warmelo, L.I. Coertze & H.L. Gonin eds., AA Balkema 1961–1975).

in South Africa today.[104] By means of the *nasciturus* fiction the legal position is kept in abeyance until the child is indeed born or it is certain that the child will not be born (e.g., because of a miscarriage or because the pregnancy has been terminated).[105] Succession is the main field in which the *nasciturus* fiction is applied nowadays.[106]

29. South African law distinguishes between incorporated and unincorporated associations of natural persons. An unincorporated association is not a legal entity distinct from its members and therefore does not have legal personality. However, it is sometimes deemed to have elements of legal personality, such as the capacity to incur liability for tax.[107] In general, the members of an unincorporated entity incur personal liability for the entity's debts.

Associations that are incorporated in terms of legislation or the common law are recognized as juristic (or artificial) persons. Thus, the following entities qualify as juristic persons:

(1) Associations that are incorporated in terms of general enabling legislation, such as companies and co-operatives.[108]
(2) Associations that are created and recognized as juristic persons in specific legislation, such as universities, organizations that are partly owned by the State, and public corporations that are fully owned by the State.
(3) Associations which qualify as *universitates personarum* in terms of the common law. The common-law requirements for the coming into existence of a *universitas personarum* are that the association must have a continuous existence irrespective of a variation in members, it must have the capacity to have rights and duties in its own right, and its object must not be the acquisition of profit.[109]

A trust is not a juristic person; it is a legal institution sui generis.[110]

---

104. The *nasciturus* fiction is sometimes called the *nasciturus* rule. On the difference between the two, *see* J. Heaton, *South African Law of Persons* 26–27 (LexisNexis 5th ed. 2017).
105. *See*, e.g., *Pinchin v. Santam Insurance Co Ltd* 1963 (2) SA 254 (W); *Christian League of Southern Africa v. Rall* 1981 (2) SA 821 (O).
106. *Ex parte Boedel Steenkamp* 1962 (3) SA 954 (O).
107. *Commissioner for Inland Revenue v. Witwatersrand Association of Racing Clubs* 1960 (3) SA 291 (A).
108. *See* the Companies Act 71 of 2008 and Co-operatives Act 14 of 2005.
109. *See*, e.g., *Malebjoe v. Bantu Methodist Church of SA* 1957 (4) SA 465 (W); *Ahmadiyya Anjuman Ishaati-Islam Lahore (SA) v. Muslim Judicial Council (Cape)* 1983 (4) SA 855 (C); *Wiseman v. Ace Table Soccer (Pty) Ltd* 1991 (4) SA 171 (W); *Ex-TRTC United Workers Front v. Premier Eastern Cape Province* 2010 (2) SA 114 (ECB). In terms of s. 8(3) of the Companies Act 71 of 2008, any association of persons carrying on a business for gain must be registered as a company or be formed pursuant to another law in order to obtain legal personality. Non-profit organizations may be incorporated in terms of the Act. If they are so incorporated, they fall within the first category mentioned above, i.e., associations incorporated in terms of general enabling legislation.
110. *See*, e.g., *Commissioner for Inland Revenue v. Friedman* 1993 (1) SA 353 (A); *Land and Agricultural Bank of South Africa v. Parker* 2005 (2) SA 77 (SCA); *Lupacchini v. Minister of Safety and*

§2. CAPACITY

I. General

30. South African law distinguishes between legal capacity (the capacity to have rights and duties), capacity to act (the capacity to perform juristic acts by which rights and duties are acquired or disposed of), *locus standi in iudicio* (the capacity to be a party to a lawsuit), and the capacity to be held accountable for crimes and torts (or delicts, as they are called in South Africa).[111]

All persons have legal capacity, but their legal capacity does not extend equally far. Some natural persons cannot have particular rights or duties at all, or cannot have particular rights or duties at a specific moment. This means that their legal capacity is limited to some extent. Thus, *infantes* (children below the age of 7 years) have no capacity to act, capacity to litigate, or capacity to be held accountable for crimes and delicts, while minors over the age of 7 years and mentally ill persons have limited capacity to act, litigate, and be held accountable for crimes and delicts. Insolvents (bankrupts) and prodigals who have been restrained by court order from administering their estate lack full capacity to act and to litigate. Depending on the degree of their intoxication or disability, persons who are under the influence of alcohol or drugs, and persons who are incapable of managing their own affairs because of a physical or mental disability may also lack full capacity to act, litigate, and be held accountable for crimes and delicts. The limited capacities of the above-mentioned categories of persons are discussed in more detail in Chapters 3, 7, 8 and 9, below.

II. Minority in South African Law

31. A natural person attains majority when he or she reaches the age of 18 years.[112] Majority ensues at the beginning of the day of the person's eighteenth birthday, unless it is to the person's advantage to prolong minority to the precise moment that corresponds to the time of his or her birth.[113]

Security [2011] 1 All SA 138 (SCA). However, certain Acts confer legal personality on trusts for specific purposes, such as taxation: *see* the definition of 'person' in s. 1 of the Income Tax Act 58 of 1962. *See* further Part IV, Ch. 2, §8.

111. Some authors call the first capacity 'passive legal capacity', and the capacity to perform an act which affects one's rights and duties (i.e., the second and third capacities) 'active legal capacity': *see*, e.g., J. Heaton, *The Concepts of Status and Capacity: A Jurisprudential Excursus* in *Boberg's Law of Persons and the Family* 66, 73–74 (B. van Heerden, A. Cockrell & R. Keightley eds., Juta & Co, Ltd 2d ed. 1999); C. Himonga, *Persons and Family: Introduction*, in *Wille's Principles of South African Law* 146 (F. du Bois ed., Juta & Co 9th ed. 2007).

112. Children's Act 38 of 2005, s. 17.

113. Voet, *Commentarius ad Pandectas,* 4.4.1; Grotius, *Inleidinge tot de Hollandsche Rechtsgeleerdheid*, 3.48.9; S. van Leeuwen, *Censura Forensis,* Lugduni in Batavis: S Luchtmans and C Haak, 1741, 1.1.8.4–1.1.8.5, 1.4.43.11–1.4.43.12.

A person who enters into a valid civil or customary marriage before turning 18 becomes a major for all purposes. If the marriage is dissolved by death or divorce before the person reaches the age of 18 years, his or her minority does not revive.[114]

32. Although, generally speaking, South Africans acquire full capacity on their eighteenth birthday, several earlier ages are of legal importance. For example, minors over the age of seven have limited capacity to act, which means that they can, as a rule, enter into contracts with their guardian's assistance.[115] At the age of 12, a child acquires the capacity independently to buy condoms and receive free condoms on request, and he or she may be provided with other contraceptives if he or she requests this, receives proper medical advice, and undergoes a medical examination to determine whether there are any medical reasons why a specific contraceptive should not be provided to him or her.[116] At the same age, a child acquires capacity to consent to medical treatment or an operation if he or she is sufficiently mature and has the mental capacity to understand the benefits, risks, social and other implications of the treatment or operation.[117]

33. In respect of some legal matters a fixed age does not apply. Instead, an individual maturity assessment is employed. Thus, for example, the child's right to be informed of any action or decision in a matter which significantly affects him or her, and his or her right to participate are determined in the light of his or her age, maturity and stage of development;[118] and a pregnant girl of any age can consent to termination of her pregnancy provided that she is able to give informed consent.[119]

III. Child as a Term of Relationship

34. In South African law, the word 'child' is used either to denote a relationship to another person (such as being someone's biological child, stepchild, foster child, or grandchild) or to signify a person below a particular age. In the latter context, 'child' is usually equated with 'minor', that is, a person below the age of 18 years.[120]

35. In the context of relationship for purposes of the Law of Succession, a presumption operated in the past that if a male testator used the word 'child', it referred only to a child born in wedlock (or, in accordance with modern terminology, a child

114. *Cohen v. Sytner* (1897) 14 SC 13.
115. On the capacity to act of an *infans* and a minor *see* Part I, Ch. 3, §2 below.
116. Children's Act 38 of 2005, s. 134(1) and (2).
117. Children's Act 38 of 2005, s. 129(2). The child still needs his or her guardian's assistance to have an operation: s. 129(3)(c).
118. Children's Act 38 of 2005, ss 6(5) and 10.
119. Choice on Termination of Pregnancy Act 92 of 1996, s. 5(1)–(3); *Christian Lawyers Association of South Africa v. The Minister of Health (Reproductive Health Alliance as Amicus Curiae)* 2005 (1) SA 509 (T).
120. *See* e.g. the definition of 'child' in s. 1 of the Children's Act 38 of 2005 and s. 28(3) of the Constitution.

born of married parents).[121] This presumption did not apply to female testators. Thus, if the intention of a testator was unclear, a reference in a mother's will to 'my children' included her children born out of wedlock (children born of unmarried parents), but if the testator was a father, his children who were born of unmarried parents were not included in the phrase.[122] This discriminatory position has fortunately been revoked.[123] Now, birth of unmarried parents is irrelevant when determining a person's relationship to a testator or any other person. The position is the same if a person dies without leaving a valid will.[124]

§3. ABSENTEES

36. The court has the power to appoint a curator to a person who is incapable of managing his or her own affairs because he or she has disappeared[125] or resides in an enemy country during war.[126] Usually, only a *curator bonis* (curator for the person's property) is appointed but, if the need arises, the court may also appoint a *curator ad litem* to represent such a person in legal proceedings in South Africa. An application to place an absentee under curatorship must be brought in the court that has jurisdiction over the area where the person is domiciled or where he or she owns immovable property.[127]

37. If an absentee has disappeared and is suspected to have died, a presumption of death may be pronounced in terms of the common law or, in certain instances, in terms of statute. No fixed term needs to expire before the application can be made.

In terms of the common law, any interested party may approach the division of the High Court that has jurisdiction over the area where the missing person was domiciled to grant a presumption of death in respect of the person.[128] A creditor, the absentee's heir, and the absentee's surviving spouse or civil union partner would, for example, qualify as applicants. The applicant must prove on a preponderance of probabilities that the missing person is dead.[129] The court takes factors such as the absentee's age, the length of his or her absence, whether he or she was engaged in

121. In the past, South African law categorized children as either legitimate or illegitimate. Now, the Children's Act 38 of 2005 refers to a married or an unmarried father, a married or an unmarried mother, a married or an unmarried person, and married parents: *see*, e.g., ss 19–21, 38, 40 and 233. Thus, the terms 'child born of married parents' and 'child born of unmarried parents' are the more up-to-date descriptors. *See also* Part II, Ch. 4, §1 below.
122. *In re Russo* (1896) 13 SC 185; *Hoffman v. Estate Mechau* 1922 CPD 179.
123. Wills Act 7 of 1953, s. 2D(1)(b).
124. Intestate Succession Act 81 of 1987, s. 1(2). On a child's position as an heir or beneficiary, *see* further Part IV, Ch. 1, §2 and §3 and Part IV, Ch. 2, §3 below.
125. *See*, e.g., *Re McKenzie's Estate* 1908 TS 420; *Ex parte Thomson* 1919 CPD 277; *Ex parte Shulman* 1955 (1) SA 514 (W); *Ex parte Pearlman* 1957 (4) SA 666 (N).
126. *Ex parte Kuhr* 1940 CPD 327; *Ex parte Becker* 1943 CPD 164.
127. *Ex parte Derksen* 1960 (1) SA 380 (N); *Ex parte Berry: In re Berry* 1961 (4) SA 79 (D); *Ex parte De Villiers* 1976 (4) SA 576 (O).
128. *Ex parte Maclean* 1968 (2) SA 644 (C).
129. *Ex parte Rungasamy* 1958 (4) SA 688 (D); *Ex parte Rookminia: In re Sardha* 1964 (4) SA 163 (D).

a risky or dangerous business or trade, his or her state of mind, and his or her physical health into account in deciding whether or not to grant a presumption of death.[130]

The Inquests Act 58 of 1959 provides another avenue for obtaining a presumption of death. This avenue is available if it is suspected that the absentee died of unnatural causes. If the presiding officer at the inquest into the absentee's death makes a finding regarding his or her identity and the date of his or her death, this finding is referred to the High Court for review. If the High Court confirms the finding, the effect is the same as if the court had made an order presuming the absentee's death.[131]

38. Once a presumption of death has been ordered, the absentee's estate may be administered and divided among his or her heirs as if he or she were dead. However, the courts have on occasion adopted a cautious attitude and have ordered that the estate may be divided but that the heirs must furnish security for the restoration of the property, or its value, should the missing person return.[132]

A presumption of death under the Inquests Act 58 of 1959 results in the automatic dissolution of the missing person's marriage or civil union on the date that is indicated as the date of the person's death.[133] If the presumption of death is ordered in terms of the common law, the person's marriage or civil union is not automatically terminated. However, the court that orders the presumption of death may simultaneously or subsequently deem the person's marriage or civil union to have been dissolved by his or her death. Such a deeming order is made only if the missing person's spouse or civil union partner applies for it.[134]

As a presumption of death order merely creates a rebuttable presumption that the person is dead, the court that made the order can set it aside if it becomes clear that the missing person is alive. If anyone has received patrimonial benefits as a result of the order, those benefits or their value must be returned. If a beneficiary fails to return a benefit or its value, he or she can be sued by means of an enrichment action.[135]

39. Occasionally, the court refuses to grant an order presuming a missing person's death but nevertheless orders that the person's property can be divided amongst his or her heirs.[136] In such cases the heirs are usually required to furnish sufficient security for the return of the property or its value, should the missing person reappear.[137]

---

130. *See*, e.g., *Ex parte Alexander* 1956 (2) SA 608 (A); *Ex parte Rookminia: In re Sardha* 1964 (4) SA 163 (D); *Ex parte Pieters* 1993 (3) SA 379 (D); *Ex parte Stoter* 1996 (4) SA 1299 (E).
131. Section 18(1), (2) and (2A).
132. *Ex parte Estate Russell* 1926 WLD 118; *Ex parte Davids* 1948 (1) SA 1018 (W).
133. Dissolution of Marriages on Presumption of Death Act 23 of 1979, s. 2.
134. *Ibid.*, s. 1.
135. *Berger v. Aiken* 1964 (2) SA 396 (W).
136. *See*, e.g., *In re Kannemeyer: Ex parte Kannemeyer* (1899) 16 SC 407; *Ex parte Halbert* 1912 CPD 706; *In re Cuthbert* 1932 NPD 615; *Ex parte Davids* 1948 (1) SA 1018 (W).
137. *Ibid.* But contrast *Ex parte Pieters* 1993 (3) SA 379 (D) where the amount to be distributed was so small that the court dispensed with the need for security.

Chapter 2. Registration of Civil Status

§1. The Registrar

40. In terms of the Births and Deaths Registration Act 51 of 1992, the Director-General of the Department of Home Affairs is responsible for registering all live births, stillbirths and deaths that occur in South Africa.[138] The Director-General must also register the birth of every child who is born outside South Africa if either of the child's parents is a South African citizen. The same applies to any death in South Africa and any death outside South Africa of a South African citizen or person who lawfully and permanently resided in South Africa.[139] Registration is achieved by recording the relevant particulars in the population register.[140] The Director-General also keeps a record of marriages and civil unions that are solemnized by South African citizens and persons who are lawfully and permanently resident in South Africa.[141]

41. The Act requires that the Director-General must be notified of a live birth, within thirty days of the birth having taken place.[142] The duty to give notice rests primarily on the child's parents.[143] In the case of an abandoned child, notice is given by a social worker or authorized officer in the Public Service.[144]

In the case of a stillbirth,[145] the medical practitioner who was present at the stillbirth or examined the stillborn child's corpse must notify the Director-General of the stillbirth. If no medical practitioner was present or examined the child's corpse, the duty falls on anyone who was present at the stillbirth.[146] If there is reasonable doubt whether an alleged stillbirth was indeed a stillbirth, the Director-General must report the matter to the police.[147] An inquest is then held in terms of the Inquests Act 58 of 1959.[148]

Every death must be reported to the Director-General irrespective of whether it was due to natural or other causes. If the death was attributable to natural causes, anyone who was present at the death, became aware of it, or is in charge of the deceased's funeral must notify the Director-General.[149] If it is suspected that the

138. Sections 2 and 3. For statistics on the number of live births recorded each year, *see* the annual P0305 figures available at www.statssa.org.za. For statistics on the number of deaths, *see* the P0309 figures that are published periodically at the same website address.
139. Births and Deaths Registration Act 51 of 1992, ss 2, 3, 13 and 19(1).
140. *Ibid.*, s. 5(2); Identification Act 68 of 1997, s. 8.
141. Identification Act 68 of 1997, ss 3 and 8(e). For statistics on the number of marriages and civil unions concluded and the number of divorces granted each year, *see* the annual P0307 figures available at www.statssa.org.za.
142. Section 9(1) read with the definition of 'birth' in s. 1(1) of the Act.
143. Section 9(1).
144. Section 12.
145. A stillbirth is the birth of a child who 'has had at least 26 weeks of intra-uterine existence but showed no signs of life after complete birth': s. 1.
146. Section 18(1) and (2).
147. Section 18(4) and (5).
148. Births and Deaths Registration Act 51 of 1992, s. 16; Inquests Act 58 of 1959, s. 2(1).
149. Births and Deaths Registration Act 51 of 1992, s. 14(1).

deceased died of unnatural causes, the Director-General or the medical practitioner who attended the deceased before his or her death or examined the corpse must report the matter to the police.[150] The matter is then dealt with in terms of the Inquests Act.[151]

The Director-General must also be notified of the solemnization of a civil marriage or civil union. The duty to give notice rests on the marriage officer who solemnized the civil marriage or civil union.[152] Although customary marriages are not solemnized by a marriage officer, these marriages must also be registered. Registration must take place within three months of the date of the wedding.[153] Either spouse may apply for registration of the customary marriage. If neither spouse requests registration, any party who has 'a sufficient interest in the matter', such as a child who was born of the marriage, may request the registering officer to enquire into the existence of the customary marriage, and to register it if it exists or existed.[154] The applicant must furnish the necessary information to enable the registering officer to be satisfied that the customary marriage indeed exists or existed.[155]

§2. Registers and Certificates

42. Once a birth or death has been registered and recorded in the population register, the Director-General issues an official birth or death certificate.[156] The certificate is prima facie proof of the birth or death.[157]

In the case of a civil marriage or civil union, the marriage officer issues a marriage or registration certificate to the couple after they have completed the marriage or civil union register.[158] A duly signed marriage or registration certificate is prima facie proof of the existence of the civil marriage or civil union.[159]

In the case of a customary marriage, a registering officer who is satisfied that the spouses indeed entered into a valid customary marriage registers the marriage and issues a registration certificate to the spouses or the person who requested the enquiry into the existence of the customary marriage.[160] The registration certificate is prima facie proof of the existence of the customary marriage.[161]

---

150. *Ibid.*, ss 14(3), 14(4) and 15(3).
151. *Ibid.*, s. 16.
152. Marriage Act 25 of 1961, s. 29A(2); Civil Union Act 17 of 2006, s. 12(6).
153. Recognition of Customary Marriages Act 120 of 1998, s. 4(3)(b).
154. *Ibid.*, s. 4(5)(a).
155. *Ibid.*, s. 4(2).
156. Births and Deaths Registration Act 51 of 1992, s. 22; Identification Act 68 of 1997, s. 13(1).
157. Births and Deaths Registration Act 51 of 1992, s. 28(2); Identification Act 68 of 1997, s. 13(1).
158. Regulation 5B(1) of the regulations issued under the Marriage Act 25 of 1961; Civil Union Act 17 of 2006, s. 12(3).
159. Identification Act 68 of 1997, s. 13(2); Civil Union Act 17 of 2006, s. 13(2).
160. Recognition of Customary Marriages Act 120 of 1998, s 4(4)(a), (b) and (5)(b).
161. *Ibid.*, s. 4(8).

Chapter 3. Personality Rights

§1. Introduction

43. In respect of the content of this chapter, it should, first of all, be noted that in South African law, the term 'personality rights' does not refer to all the rights a legal person has. The term is reserved for a particular category of rights, namely the rights a person has to his or her personality property. Personality property relates to aspects of a person's personality, such as his or her good name (reputation), honour, personal identity and physical integrity. Thus, the heading of the present chapter is misleading in the context of South African law. It is, nevertheless, used for the sake of consistency among the various monographs on Family and Succession Law in this series. In South African law, the content of the present chapter would have been described as the effect of minority on a person's status.

44. An adult has legal capacity, capacity to act, capacity to litigate and capacity to be held accountable for his or her delicts and crimes unless he or she is mentally ill, insolvent or an interdicted prodigal, or a curator has been appointed for him or her because he or she is disabled or is, for some other reason, unable to administer his or her affairs. Consumption of alcohol and drugs may also have an effect on an adult's capacity. The capacity of adults who do not have full capacity to act, litigate and be held accountable for their delicts and crimes is discussed in other chapters. The present chapter focuses on the capacity of minors.

As is explained in more detail below in this chapter, children who are below the age of 7 years (*infantes*) have no capacity to act, litigate or incur criminal or delictual liability. Minors over the age of 7 years do have such capacity, but their capacity is limited with the result that they cannot enter into legal transactions unassisted.

Minors between the ages of 7 and 18 years are sometimes called '*pupilli*',[162] but they are more commonly simply called 'minors', and the latter term is the one that is used in this chapter.[163]

45. A juristic/artificial person acts through its members or functionaries. Thus, for example, in terms of the Companies Act 71 of 2008, the directors and officers of a company have the power to manage and bind the company. Although there are circumstances in which directors can incur personal liability, the rights and duties that flow from the transactions directors conclude in the name of the company are normally those of the company. A company has the capacity to commit delicts and crimes and may even incur vicarious liability for delicts its directors, officers, servants and agents commit.

---

162. *See*, e.g., C. Himonga, *Children (Minors)*, in *Wille's Principles of South African Law* 173 (F. du Bois ed., Juta & Co 9th ed. 2007).

163. On the preference for the word 'minor' to denote persons between seven and eighteen years of age, *see* J. Heaton, *The Concept of Capacity*, in *Boberg's Law of Persons and the Family* 755 n. 39 (B. van Heerden, A. Cockrell & R. Keightley eds., Kenwyn: Juta & Co, Ltd 2d ed. 1999).

§2. Minors' Contracts

I. General

A. Infantes

46. As an *infans* has no capacity to act, he or she cannot validly enter into any agreement.[164] This rule applies even if the *infans*' guardian assists him or her.[165] The only way in which an *infans* can acquire rights and duties is if his or her guardian acts on his or her behalf.[166] There are, however, certain transactions a guardian cannot conclude on an *infans*' behalf, such as a contract of engagement to marry (betrothal).[167]

Because an *infans* has legal capacity, he or she – not his or her guardian – acquires the rights and duties arising from the legal transactions his or her guardian concludes on his or her behalf.[168]

B. Minors

47. A minor has limited capacity to act. As a rule, he or she can enter into a contract only if he or she is assisted by his or her guardian. However, if a contract is non-onerous in the sense of conferring rights on the minor without imposing any duties on him or her, he or she does not need assistance.[169] For example, a minor may independently accept a donation or enter into an agreement releasing him or her from a debt. Various Acts also create exceptions to the rule that a minor cannot incur contractual liability without his or her guardian's assistance.[170]

48. A minor's guardian has a duty to assist the minor in legal transactions that benefit the minor or to conclude such transactions on the minor's behalf. If the guardian is unable or unwilling to assist the minor, the court may order him or her to do so, or may itself give the required consent.[171] The court will also intervene if a guardian's interests in a particular transaction run counter to those of the minor.[172]

If a minor enters into a contract with the consent of his or her guardian, or if the minor's guardian enters into a contract on the minor's behalf or ratifies the minor's

164. Voet, *Commentarius ad Pandectas*, 26.8.9.
165. A child's parent is normally his or her guardian: *see* Part II, Ch. 6, §3 below.
166. Voet, *Commentarius ad Pandectas*, 26.8.9, 41.2.6; S. van Leeuwen, *Het Rooms-Hollands-Regt with Notes by C.W. Decker & J. Ten Houten* 4.2.2 (Hendrik en de Wed van Dirk Boom, vol. I 1780, vol. II 1783).
167. Children's Act 38 of 2005, s. 12(2)(a).
168. Voet, *Commentarius ad Pandectas*, 26.9.2.
169. *Edelstein v. Edelstein* 1952 (3) SA 1 (A).
170. E.g., in terms of s. 24(2) of the Matrimonial Property Act 88 of 1984, an antenuptial contract a minor entered into without consent is valid in certain circumstances: *see* further Part III, Ch. 4, §3 below.
171. Voet, *Commentarius ad Pandectas*, 26.8.8.
172. *See*, e.g., Voet, *Commentarius ad Pandectas*, 26.8.6; Grotius, *Inleidinge tot de Hollandsche Rechtsgeleerdheid*, 1.7.11; Van Leeuwen, *Rooms-Hollands-Regt*, 1.16.4.

unassisted contract, the minor is contractually liable as if he or she were a major.[173] Unless the minor acted as the guardian's agent, the guardian does not incur personal liability in respect of the contract.[174]

The guardian's consent may be provided expressly or tacitly and may apply to a single transaction or to several. The consent may even be so extensive that it amounts to emancipation of the minor. Emancipation occurs if the guardian grants the minor freedom independently to enter into contracts. This may happen, for instance, if the minor runs his or her own business with the consent of his or her guardian. The degree of legal independence an emancipated minor enjoys is a question of fact that depends on all the circumstances of the case. If the guardian has given the minor 'complete freedom of action with regard to his mode of living and earning his livelihood',[175] the minor is emancipated for all purposes except alienation and encumbrance of immovable property and marriage.[176] The minor's capacity to act is restricted to matters connected with his or her business if his or her guardian has only emancipated him or her for the purpose of that particular business.

49. In some instances the guardian's consent is insufficient to enable the minor to enter into a particular type of contract. Thus, for example, the consent of the High Court or the Master of the High Court is required for alienating or mortgaging the minor's immovable property.[177]

50. If a minor independently enters into a contract which does not fall within one of the exceptions where the assistance of his or her guardian is not required, the contract creates a natural obligation (*naturalis obligatio*) insofar as the minor is concerned. This means that the contract cannot be enforced against the minor or his or her guardian.[178] However, the agreement is not void, for the other party must honour his or her part of the agreement.[179] From the other party's side the obligation is a civil one (*civilis obligatio*), which is enforceable against him or her. As the minor's unassisted contract creates a natural obligation, it can be ratified by his or her guardian or by the minor personally once he or she has attained majority. Ratification converts the natural obligation into a civil one with the result that it becomes fully enforceable against both parties with retroactive effect.[180]

---

173. *See*, e.g., *Skead v. Colonial Banking & Trust Co Ltd* 1924 TPD 497; *Marshall v. National Wool Industries Ltd* 1924 OPD 238; *Wood v. Davies* 1934 CPD 250; *Van Dyk v. SAR & H* 1956 (4) SA 410 (W).
174. *See*, e.g., *Marshall v. National Wool Industries Ltd* 1924 OPD 238; *Ex parte Fortoen* 1938 WLD 62; *Fouche v. Battenhausen & Co* 1939 CPD 228.
175. *Dickens v. Daley* 1956 (2) SA 11 (N) 16G.
176. Administration of Estates Act 66 of 1965, s. 80; Marriage Act 25 of 1961, s. 24.
177. Administration of Estates Act 66 of 1965, s. 80.
178. *See*, e.g., *McCallum v. Hallen* 1916 EDL 74; *Mazzur v. Cleghorn & Harris Ltd* 1917 CPD 291; *Marshall v. National Wool Industries Ltd* 1924 OPD 238.
179. *Edelstein v. Edelstein* 1952 (3) SA 1 (A).
180. *See*, e.g., *Du Toit v. Lotriet* 1918 OPD 99; *Baddeley v. Clarke* (1923) 44 NLR 306; *Fouche v. Battenhausen & Co* 1939 CPD 228; *Perkins v. Danford* 1996 (2) SA 128 (C).

While the minor's minority lasts it is up to the guardian to decide whether the contract should be honoured or repudiated.[181] If the minor has already performed in terms of a contract that is repudiated, he or she may recover whatever he or she has performed, but the value of his or her performance is reduced by the amount by which he or she was unjustifiedly enriched by the other party's performance.[182]

51. A minor who misrepresents himself or herself to be a major, to be emancipated or to have the necessary consent, and who thereby persuades the other party to enter into a contract with him or her incurs liability, but there is no unanimity on the basis of his or her liability. According to some decisions and authors the contract becomes enforceable against the minor because of the misrepresentation.[183] Other authors argue that the minor is liable in delict and must pay damages which compensate the other party for loss he or she suffered as a result of the misrepresentation.[184]

52. A minor can incur liability as a result of entering into an unassisted contract if he or she obtains an unjustified enrichment as a result of the transaction.[185] Liability on the ground of unjustified enrichment arises if one person obtains a patrimonial advantage at the expense of another in the absence of a recognized legal ground justifying the enrichment.[186] Because enrichment liability is not based on contract, the minor's limited capacity to act is irrelevant.

An enrichment claim is limited to the lesser of either the amount by which the enriched person's estate remains enriched at the date of institution of the action or the amount by which the impoverished person's estate remains impoverished at that date.[187] The contract price is ignored. It is the actual value of the asset at the time of institution of the action that is at issue. If the asset was alienated prior to institution of the action, the impoverished party can claim only what is left of the proceeds, unless the proceeds were used for necessaries, such as food, clothing,

181. *See*, e.g., *Rhode v. Minister of Defence* 1943 CPD 40; *Edelstein v. Edelstein* 1952 (3) SA 1 (A).
182. *Baddeley v. Clarke* (1923) 44 NLR 306.
183. *See*, e.g., *Fouche v. Battenhausen & Co* 1939 CPD 228; *Louw v. MJ & H Trust (Pty) Ltd* 1975 (4) SA 268 (T); J.C. de Wet & A.H. van Wyk, *Die Suid-Afrikaanse Kontraktereg en Handelsreg: Volume I: Kontraktereg* 63 (Butterworths 5th ed. 1992).
184. *See*, e.g., A. Cockrell, *Capacity to Perform Juristic Acts: Contracts*, in *Boberg's Law of Persons and the Family* 826 (B. van Heerden, A. Cockrell & R. Keightley eds., Juta & Co, Ltd 2d ed. 1999); Heaton, *Law of Persons*, 95; Himonga, *Children (Minors)*, 181; H. Kruger & A. Skelton (eds), *The Law of Persons in South Africa* 132 (Oxford University Press Southern Africa 2nd ed. 2018); E. Spiro, *Law of Parent and Child* 115 (Juta 4th ed. 1985).
185. *Edelstein v. Edelstein* 1952 (3) SA 1 (A).
186. *See*, e.g., *Nortjé v. Pool* 1966 (3) SA 96 (A); *McCarthy Retail Ltd v. Shortdistance Carriers CC* 2001 (3) SA 482 (SCA).
187. *See*, e.g., T. Boezaart, *Law of Persons* 78 (Juta 6th ed. 2016); Cockrell, *Capacity to Perform Juristic Acts: Contracts*, 811; J. du Plessis, *The South African Law of Unjustified Enrichment* 80–81 (Juta 2012); Himonga, *Children (Minors)*, 181–182; Kruger & Skelton (eds), *The Law of Persons in South Africa*, 129.

accommodation and medical treatment.[188] In the latter event, the cost of the necessaries is used to determine the amount of the enrichment.[189]

53. A minor may escape contractual liability even if he or she validly entered into a contract or his or her guardian validly entered into a contract on his or her behalf. The remedy which offers the minor such escape is *restitutio in integrum.*[190] It can only be invoked if the contract was prejudicial to the minor when it was made.[191] *Restitutio in integrum* entails that all the parties to the contract must be placed in the position they would have been in had they never entered into the contract. Therefore, each party must return everything he or she received under the contract as well as the proceeds or any advantage he or she derived from the contract. Each party must also compensate the other for loss suffered as a result of the contract.[192]

A minor who committed a misrepresentation as regards his or her capacity to act and thereby persuaded the other party to enter into the contract may not claim *restitutio in integrum*;[193] nor may an erstwhile minor who ratified the contract after attaining majority do so.[194]

II. Minors' Marriages and Civil Unions

A. Infantes

54. An *infans* cannot enter into a marriage or a civil union. In the case of civil and customary marriages, the Minister of Home Affairs has the power to consent to the marriage of a boy who is a minor and of a girl who is below the age of 15 years.[195] However, the weight of modern opinion favours the view that this power does not relate to children below the age of puberty because a person below the age of puberty has no capacity to marry.[196] Being below the age of puberty, an *infans* is thus absolutely incapable of marrying.

---

188. *Edelstein v. Edelstein* 1952 (3) SA 1 (A).
189. *See*, e.g., Boezaart, *Law of Persons* 78; Himonga, *Children (Minors)*, 182; Kruger & Skelton (eds), *The Law of Persons in South Africa*, 129.
190. *See*, e.g., *Breytenbach v. Frankel* 1913 AD 390; *Du Toit v. Lotriet* 1918 OPD 99; *Skead v. Colonial Banking & Trust Co Ltd* 1924 TPD 497; *Wood v. Davies* 1934 CPD 250.
191. *See*, e.g., *Van der Byl & Co v. Solomon* (1877) 7 Buch 25; *Skead v. Colonial Banking & Trust Co Ltd* 1924 TPD 497; *Wood v. Davies* 1934 CPD 250.
192. *Wood v. Davies* 1934 CPD 250.
193. *See*, e.g., *Fouche v. Battenhausen & Co* 1939 CPD 228; *Louw v. MJ & H Trust (Pty) Ltd* 1975 (4) SA 268 (T).
194. *See*, e.g., *Wolff v. Solomon's Trustee* (1895) 12 SC 42; *Fenner-Solomon v. Martin* 1917 CPD 22; *Du Toit v. Lotriet* 1918 OPD 99; *Skead v. Colonial Banking & Trust Co Ltd* 1924 TPD 497.
195. Marriage Act 25 of 1961, s. 26(1) read with s. 3(3) of the Recognition of Customary Marriages Act 120 of 1998.
196. *See*, e.g., A. Barratt (ed.), *Law of Persons and the Family* 66 and 67 (Pearson Education South Africa 2d ed. 2017); Boezaart, *Law of Persons*, 86; H.J. Erasmus, C.G. van der Merwe & A.H. van Wyk, *Lee and Honoré Family, Things and Succession* para. 41 (Butterworths 2d ed. 1983); Heaton, *Law of Persons*, 100; J. Heaton & H. Kruger, *South African Family Law* 17 (LexisNexis 4th ed.

As the Civil Union Act 17 of 2006 restricts a civil union to majors,[197] *infantes* are absolutely incapable of entering into a civil union.

B. Minors

1. Civil Marriages

55. A minor has limited capacity to enter into a civil marriage. He or she cannot conclude a valid civil marriage without the consent of all his or her guardians.[198] Usually, both parents are the guardians of a child born of married parents, and the mother is the guardian of a child born of unmarried parents.[199]

If the consent of one or more of the minor's guardians cannot be obtained because the guardian is absent, mentally ill, or in any other way incompetent to consent to the marriage, or if the minor can for any other good reason not obtain the consent of his or her guardian, he or she may ask the presiding officer of the Children's Court to consent to the marriage.[200]

If a guardian or presiding officer withholds consent, the minor may approach the High Court for consent. The court will grant consent if it is of the opinion that the refusal by the guardian or presiding officer is without adequate reason and contrary to the minor's best interests.[201]

Unless the High Court authorizes the marriage, a male minor and a female minor who is below the age of 15 years must also obtain the written consent of the Minister of Home Affairs. Such consent will be given only if the marriage is desirable and in the parties' interests.[202]

56. If a minor marries without obtaining the consent of his or her guardians or the presiding officer of the Children's Court, the marriage is voidable. The minor may approach the High Court for dissolution of the marriage before he or she reaches majority or within three months thereafter. The minor's guardians may also apply for dissolution of the marriage, but they must do so before the minor attains majority and within six weeks from the date on which they become aware of the existence of the marriage. The court may not set the marriage aside unless it is satisfied that doing so is in the minor's interest.[203] If an application for dissolution is not made within the periods mentioned above, the marriage becomes unassailable

---

2015); J.D. Sinclair assisted by J. Heaton, 1 *The Law of Marriage* 367 (Juta 1996); E. Spiro, *Marriage Without the Requisite Permission of the Minister of the Interior*, 23 J. Contemp. Roman-Dutch Law 5 (1960). But contrast H.R. Hahlo, *The South African Law of Husband and Wife* 90 (Juta 5th ed. 1985). The age of puberty is 12 years for girls and 14 years for boys.

197. *See* below in this chapter.
198. Children's Act 38 of 2005, s. 18(3)(c)(i) and (5).
199. *Ibid.*, ss 19–21.
200. Marriage Act 25 of 1961, s. 25(1).
201. *Ibid.*, s. 25(4).
202. *Ibid.*, s. 26(1).
203. *Ibid.*, s. 24A.

and continues to exist until it is terminated by death or divorce. If a minor's voidable civil marriage is dissolved, the court may make any order with regard to the division of the matrimonial property it deems just.[204] If the marriage is not dissolved, the patrimonial consequences are the same as if the minor were of age when the marriage was entered into, and an antenuptial contract in terms of which the accrual system is included is deemed to be valid even though it was concluded without the requisite consent.[205]

If the Minister's consent to the marriage was not obtained, the Minister may ratify the marriage if the marriage is desirable and in the parties' interests and in all other respects complies with the Marriage Act 25 of 1961.[206]

2. Customary Marriages

57. The consent requirements for a minor's customary marriage are the same as those that apply to a minor's civil marriage.[207] As is the case in respect of a minor's unassisted civil marriage, a minor's unassisted customary marriage is voidable on application by the minor or his or her guardians, and if the marriage is dissolved, the court may make any order with regard to the division of the matrimonial property it deems just.[208] However, unlike the position in respect of an unassisted civil marriage which is not set aside, it is unclear what the patrimonial consequences are if an unassisted customary marriage is not set aside.[209]

The Minister of Home Affairs may ratify a minor's customary marriage that was concluded without ministerial consent, provided that the marriage is desirable and in the parties' interests and in all other respects complies with the Recognition of Customary Marriages Act 120 of 1998.[210]

3. Civil Unions

58. The Civil Union Act 17 of 2006 altogether excludes minors from entering into a civil union. The Act defines a civil union as 'the voluntary union of two persons who are both *18 years of age or older*, which is solemnised and registered ... in accordance with the procedures prescribed in this Act ... ' (emphasis added).[211] The phrase '18 years of age or older' suggests that civil unions are restricted to

---

204. Matrimonial Property Act 88 of 1984, s. 24(1).
205. *Ibid.*, s. 24(2). *See* further Part III, Ch. 4, §3 below.
206. Marriage Act 25 of 1961, s. 26(2) and (3).
207. Recognition of Customary Marriages Act 120 of 1998, s. 3(3)(a), (3)(b) and (4)(a) read with s. 25(1) and (4) of the Marriage Act 25 of 1961; Children's Act 38 of 2005, s. 18(3)(c)(i) and (5).
208. Marriage Act 25 of 1961, s. 24A read with s. 3(5) of the Recognition of Customary Marriages Act 120 of 1998; Matrimonial Property Act 88 of 1984, s. 24(1) read with s. 8(4)(a) of the Recognition of Customary Marriages Act.
209. *See* Heaton & Kruger, *Family Law*, 227–228 in this regard.
210. Recognition of Customary Marriages Act 120 of 1998, s. 3(4)(c).
211. Section 1.

adults. Unlike the Marriage Act 25 of 1961 and the Recognition of Customary Marriages Act 120 of 1998, which allow a minor to enter into a civil or customary marriage provided that he or she obtains the consent of certain persons or institutions, the Civil Union Act does not provide for any exception to the rule that a civil union is a union between adults. Thus, anyone who has not yet turned 18 is absolutely incapable of entering into a civil union.

§3. Minors' Responsibility for Delicts (Torts)

I. *Infantes*

59. In order to incur delictual liability a person must be accountable. Accountability is possible only if the person has the mental ability to distinguish right from wrong and to act in accordance with that distinction.[212] As an *infans* does not have this ability, he or she cannot incur delictual liability that is based on fault. However, he or she can incur liability for delicts that are not based on fault because mental ability is irrelevant in the case of such delicts. Thus, an *infans* can incur liability under the *actio de pauperie* if his or her domestic animal causes damage, and he or she can incur vicarious liability if his or her employee commits a delict in the course of his or her employment.

An *infans*' guardian is not responsible for damage the *infans* causes, unless the *infans* acted as the guardian's agent or instrument or the guardian negligently failed to prevent the *infans* from causing the damage.[213] In these instances the guardian's personal fault is at issue, rendering the *infans*' mental inability irrelevant. If the guardian should have foreseen the damage and could have prevented it, he or she can incur delictual liability even if he or she was not present when the damage was caused.[214]

II. Minors

60. In South African law, a rebuttable presumption operates that minors between the ages of 7 years and puberty are not accountable for their delicts, and that minors over the age of puberty are accountable for their delicts.[215] Thus, a child below the age of puberty cannot be held liable for his or her delict unless it is proved that he or she had the mental ability to distinguish right from wrong and to act in accordance with that distinction when the delict was committed, while a child over the age of puberty is liable for his or her delict unless it is proved that he or she did not have the mental ability to distinguish right from wrong and to act in accordance with that distinction.

212. *Weber v. Santam Versekeringsmaatskappy Bpk* 1983 (1) SA 381 (A).
213. *See*, e.g. *Wessels v. Ten Oven* 1938 TPD 26; *De Beer v. Sergeant* 1976 (1) SA 246 (T); *Maylett v. Du Toit* 1989 (1) SA 90 (T); *Godfrey v. Campbell* 1997 (1) SA 570 (C).
214. *De Beer v. Sergeant* 1976 (1) SA 246 (T).
215. *Weber v. Santam Versekeringsmaatskappy Bpk* 1983 (1) SA 381 (A).

A minor's guardian is liable for a delict the minor commits if the minor is the guardian's agent or instrument in committing the delict, or if the guardian negligently fails to prevent the minor from causing harm. If the guardian employs the minor, he or she can also incur vicarious liability for delicts the minor commits in the course of his or her employment.

§4. Minors' Responsibility for Crimes

I. *Infantes*

61. An *infans* can never be criminally liable.[216]

II. Minors

62. In terms of the Child Justice Act 75 of 2008, a minor below the age of 10 years cannot be held criminally accountable for his or her actions.[217]

A child between 10 and 14 years of age is presumed to be criminally unaccountable.[218] Such a child has criminal capacity only if the State proves beyond reasonable doubt that when the alleged crime was committed, the child had the capacity to understand the difference between right and wrong and to act in accordance with that understanding.[219] To determine whether the child had such capacity, a probation officer must assess the child and prepare an assessment report. The report and all other evidence are considered by an inquiry magistrate or a Child Justice Court.[220] The inquiry magistrate or Child Justice Court may further order an evaluation of the child's criminal capacity by a suitably qualified person.[221]

Children over the age of 14 are criminally accountable in the same way as adults, but they are usually punished more leniently because youth is a mitigating (extenuating) circumstance in sentencing.[222]

63. Any minor who is charged with a crime has a constitutional right not to be detained except as a measure of last resort. If the minor is detained, he or she has the constitutional rights relating to freedom and security of the person and the rights of arrested, detained and accused persons that are afforded all detainees. In addition, a minor may only be detained for the shortest possible period and has the right to be kept separately from detained adults and to be treated in a manner and kept in

216. Child Justice Act 75 of 2008, s. 7(1) and (3).
217. *Ibid.*
218. Section 7(2) and (3).
219. Section 11(1).
220. Sections 11(2), 34–35 and 40. A 'Child Justice Court' is any court provided for in the Criminal Procedure Act 51 of 1977 which deals with the bail application, plea, trial or sentencing of a child: Child Justice Act 75 of 2008, s. 1.
221. Child Justice Act 75 of 2008, s. 11(3).
222. *See*, e.g., *S. v. Dlamini* 1992 (1) SA 18 (A); *S. v. Malgas* 2001 (2) SA 1222 (SCA).

conditions that take account of his or her age.[223] Furthermore, the Child Justice Act 75 of 2008 provides various options for diverting children away from the formal, mainstream criminal justice system.

64. Criminal trials against minors and proceedings in the Children's Court are held *in camera*.[224] In other words, unless the presiding officer grants a specific person permission to be present, the proceedings are closed to anyone whose presence is not necessary in connection with the proceedings.

§5. CRIMES AGAINST CHILDREN

65. As a rule, any crime that can be committed against an adult can also be committed against a child. However, there are certain crimes of which only a minor can be the victim. For example, only a newborn child can be the victim of the common-law crime of infanticide (killing of a newborn child), and only a young child can be the victim of the common-law crime of exposure of an infant (unlawful and intentional abandonment of a young child in a place or in circumstances where he or she is likely to die from exposure). Several statutory offences are also restricted to child victims. They include sexual exploitation or sexual grooming of a child;[225] failing to inform the police that a sexual offence has been committed against a child;[226] abuse, deliberate neglect or abandonment of a child;[227] failing to provide a child with adequate food, clothing, accommodation and medical treatment while being able to do so;[228] having contact with a child in contravention of a written police notice;[229] and contravening an order the High Court, a Regional Court or a Children's Court has issued in terms of the Children's Act 38 of 2005.[230]

223. Constitution, s. 28(1)(g).
224. Children's Act 38 of 2005, s. 56; Child Justice Act 75 of 2008, s. 63(5).
225. Criminal Law (Sexual Offences and Related Matters) Amendment Act 32 of 2007, ss 17 and 18. *See also* s. 141(1)(b) of the Children's Act 38 of 2005, which prohibits using, procuring, offering or employing a child for purposes of commercial sexual exploitation.
226. Criminal Law (Sexual Offences and Related Matters) Amendment Act 32 of 2007, s. 54(1)(a) and (b).
227. Children's Act 38 of 2005, s. 305(3)(a) and (b). These offences can only be committed by a parent, guardian, or another person who has parental responsibilities and rights in respect of a child, or by a caregiver or person who has no parental responsibilities and rights in respect of a child but voluntarily cares for the child.
228. Children's Act 38 of 2005, s. 305(4). The offence is limited to persons who are legally liable to maintain the child.
229. Children's Act 38 of 2005, s. 153(1)(b) read with s. 305(1)(p)(ii).
230. *Ibid.*, s. 305(1)(q).

§6. Minors' Capacity to Engage in Legal Proceedings

I. *Infantes*

66. Because an *infans* does not have capacity to litigate, he or she cannot be a party to a lawsuit even with the assistance of his or her guardian. The guardian must always litigate on the *infans*' behalf.[231]

II. Minors

67. Generally speaking, a minor has limited capacity to be a party to civil proceedings. He or she must sue or be sued in his or her own name with his or her guardian's assistance. Alternatively, the guardian may sue or be sued on the minor's behalf.[232] If the minor does not have a guardian, if the guardian refuses to act, if the minor litigates against the guardian, or if there is a clash of interests between the guardian and the minor, a *curator ad litem* is usually appointed to assist the minor.[233] Using its powers as upper guardian of all minors, the High Court may itself assist a minor in litigation.[234]

In criminal proceedings the guardian's assistance is not needed. There are also some exceptional cases where a minor may conduct civil litigation without assistance. They include an application to court for consent to marry without parental consent,[235] and an application for a domestic violence protection order.[236] Furthermore, the court may grant the minor *venia agendi* (permission to conduct litigation in his or her own name without any assistance) for purposes of particular civil proceedings.[237]

68. There is some authority for the view that civil proceedings in which a minor did not have the requisite assistance are invalid.[238] However, the view that a judgment in favour of an unassisted minor is valid, while a judgment against him or her is invalid, also enjoys support.[239] The latter view echoes the rules that apply in respect of a minor's unassisted contract, namely that a contract that confers rights

231. Voet, *Commentarius ad Pandectas*, 2.4.4.

232. *See*, e.g., *Wolman v. Wolman* 1963 (2) SA 452 (A); *President Insurance Co Ltd v. Yu Kwam* 1963 (3) SA 766 (A).

233. *See*, e.g., *Van Rij v. Employers' Liability Assurance Corporation Ltd* 1964 (4) SA 731 (T); *Ex parte Visser: In re Khoza* 2001 (3) SA 524 (T); *Ex parte Oppel* 2002 (5) SA 125 (C).

234. *Vista University, Bloemfontein Campus v. Student Representative Council, Vista University* 1998 (4) SA 102 (O). *See* Part II, Ch. 6, §5 below on the High Court's powers as upper guardian.

235. *Lalla v. Lalla* 1973 (2) SA 561 (A).

236. Domestic Violence Act 116 of 1998, s. 4(4).

237. *See*, e.g., *Ex parte Dreyer* (1908) 18 CTR 205; *Mahomed Hassan v. Minister of Justice* 1911 TPD 1163; *Ex parte Hartenberg* 1946 (1) PH M10 (C); *Ex parte Goldman* 1960 (1) SA 89 (D).

238. *See*, e.g., *Swart v. Muller* (1909) 19 CTR 475; *Lasersohn v. Olivier* 1962 (1) SA 566 (T); *O'Linsky v. Prinsloo* 1976 (4) SA 843 (O).

239. *See*, e.g., Voet, *Commentarius ad Pandectas*, 5.1.11; A. Cockrell, *Capacity to Litigate*, in *Boberg's Law of Persons and the Family* 906 (B. van Heerden, A. Cockrell & R. Keightley eds., Juta & Co, Ltd 2d ed. 1999); Boezaart, *Law of Persons*, 92; Kruger & Skelton (eds), *The Law of Persons in South Africa*, 141.

on an unassisted minor without imposing duties on him or her is valid, while one which imposes duties on him or her may be set aside.

Chapter 4. Names

§1. Composition of a Name

69. The registration of a person under a particular name or surname, and changes to a person's name and/or surname are governed by the Births and Deaths Registration Act 51 of 1992.

South Africans have one or more forenames (first names) followed by a surname. No birth may be registered unless a forename and a surname have been assigned to the child.[240] Thus, a child may not be registered as, for example, AB Khumalo or Malcolm X. There are no limitations on the forename(s) or the number of forenames a person may be given.

§2. Surname

I. Acquisition of the Surname

70. A child who is born of parents who are married to each other at the time of his or her conception or birth or at any intervening time acquires the surname of either parent or a double-barrel surname consisting of both parents' surnames.[241] A civil union has the same consequences as a civil marriage.[242] Thus, a child who is born of persons who are civil union partners at the time of his or her conception or birth or at any intervening time also acquires the surname of either parent or a double-barrel surname consisting of both parents' surnames. This rule applies regardless of whether the civil union partners are of the same or the opposite sex.

A child born of unmarried parents acquires his or her mother's surname unless the child's parents agree that the child should bear his or her father's surname.[243] The Act does not make provision for the child to be registered under a double-barrel surname consisting of both parents' surnames. If the parents marry each other after the child's birth has been registered, the population register will, on application to the Director-General of Home Affairs, be altered and the child's birth will be registered as if the child's parents were legally married to each other at the time of his or her birth.[244] If this happens, the child's surname can be changed to the father's surname or a double-barrel surname.

An adopted child acquires his or her adoptive parent's surname, unless the court which makes the adoption order orders otherwise.[245] If the child is adopted by a

240. Section 9(6).
241. Section 9(2) read with s. 10 and the definition of 'child born out of wedlock' in s. 1.
242. Civil Union Act 17 of 2006, s. 13(2)(a). *See also* the definition of 'marriage' in s. 1 of the Births and Deaths Registration Act 51 of 1992, which includes a civil union concluded in terms of the Civil Union Act.
243. Section 10.
244. The application may be brought by either parent or by the child's guardian if the child is a minor, or by the child himself or herself if he or she already is a major: s. 11(1).
245. Children's Act 38 of 2005, s. 242(2)(b).

married couple or by civil union partners, he or she can acquire either parent's surname or a double-barrel surname consisting of both parents' surnames.[246]

71. Most women still assume their husband's surname when they marry. However, this is merely a matter of custom. Legally, a wife in a civil or customary marriage may retain her maiden name, assume her husband's surname or create a double-barrel surname consisting of both spouses' surnames.[247] In a marriage, this rule is restricted to wives, and in a heterosexual civil union, it is restricted to the female civil union partner.[248] However, in a same-sex civil union it seems to apply to both civil union partners.[249]

Many women use their husband's surname or a double-barrel surname in their private lives while retaining their maiden name for career purposes. Others use their husband's surname in their private lives and a double-barrel surname for career purposes. If a wife chooses to acquire her husband's surname or a double-barrel surname, she may at any time resume any surname she bore at any prior time or add her 'married' surname to any surname she bore at any prior time. A divorced or widowed woman may resume a surname she bore at any previous time.[250] These rules also apply to civil union partners.[251]

II. Change of the Surname

72. As a rule, no one may assume, describe himself or herself by, or pass under a surname other than that under which he or she has been included in the population register.[252] This rule is subject to the exceptions regarding married, divorced and widowed women and civil union partners discussed immediately above. Any person other than a married, divorced or widowed woman, a civil union partner or a former civil union partner who wants to assume a different surname must apply to the Director-General of Home Affairs for authorization to do so. If the Director-General is satisfied that there is a good and sufficient reason for the change of surname, he or she may authorize the change.[253] In the case of a minor, an application for a change of the child's surname on the ground of a good and sufficient reason must be made by either of the child's parents.[254]

73. On application by the child's mother, the surname of a child who was born of parents who were married to each other or were each other's civil union partners

246. Births and Deaths Registration Act 51 of 1992, s. 9(2) read with s. 242(2)(b) of the Children's Act 38 of 2005.
247. Section 26(1).
248. A husband or male civil union partner who wants to assume the surname of his wife or civil union partner must apply to the Director-General of Home Affairs for permission to do so: s. 26. This sex-based distinction may well be unconstitutional: Heaton & Kruger, *Family Law*, 59.
249. *See* further Part II, Ch. 1, §4 below.
250. Section 26(1).
251. Section 26(1) read with s. 13(2) of the Civil Union Act 17 of 2006.
252. Section 26(1).
253. Section 26.
254. Section 25(2).

may be changed to the mother's surname if the marriage or civil union is dissolved by the father's death. The mother may also make such an application, if the marriage or civil union is dissolved by divorce, but then she needs the written consent of the child's father, unless the court dispenses with his consent or sole guardianship has been awarded to her. If the mother remarries or enters into a new civil union after the divorce, she may apply to have the child's surname changed to the surname she herself bears. She needs the written consent of the child's father and of her new husband or civil union partner, unless the court dispenses with the need for consent. If sole guardianship has been awarded to her, she does not need the father's consent but she still needs the consent of her new husband or civil union partner. A widow who remarries or enters into a new civil union may also apply to have her child's surname changed to the surname she chooses to be known under. She needs the written consent of her new husband or civil union partner, unless the court dispenses with the need for consent.[255]

If the mother of a child who was born of unmarried parents marries or enters into a civil union with someone other than the child's father, she may apply to have the child's surname changed to correspond to hers. She needs the written consent of her husband or civil union partner to apply for the change. If the child bears his or her father's surname, she also needs the father's written consent, unless the court grants exemption from the consent requirement or the mother has sole guardianship.[256]

If a minor is in the care of a legal guardian, the legal guardian may apply for alteration of the child's surname to his or her surname.[257]

§3. Forename/First Name

74. An adult person or a parent on behalf of his or her child may apply to the Director-General for alteration of his or her forename.[258] The Births and Deaths Registration Act 51 of 1992 does not stipulate the grounds on which such an application will be allowed, but in terms of section 28(2) of the Constitution a child's best interests are of paramount importance in every matter concerning the child. If the child's parents have bestowed a pejorative or very embarrassing name on the child, the Director-General would, presumably, grant the application in the best interests of the child.

255. Section 25(1) and (1A).
256. *Ibid.*
257. Section 25(1)(d).
258. Section 24(1).

Chapter 5. Nationality

75. Although nationality (citizenship)[259] is a fundamental right that is recognized and protected by the Constitution, it is of relatively little importance within the sphere of Private Law. As a rule, everybody who resides in South Africa is subject to the local rules of Private Law, regardless of his or her nationality.[260] However, certain rights, privileges and benefits are reserved for South African citizens. Among those are the rights to vote, form a political party, be a Member of Parliament, be president or deputy president of the country, and be a judge in the Constitutional Court.[261] To this extent, the legal capacity of non-South African citizens is limited.

76. Citizenship can be acquired by birth, descent or naturalization. Entering into a marriage or a civil union does not affect citizenship. Thus, a married person or civil union partner acquires and loses South African citizenship as if he or she were single, and no one acquires or loses South African citizenship simply because he or she marries or enters into a civil union.[262]

77. In terms of the Constitution, every child has the right to nationality as from the date of his or her birth.[263] The aim of this provision is to guard against statelessness rather than to entitle every child who is born in South Africa to South African citizenship.[264] Nevertheless, the South African Citizenship Act 88 of 1995 confers South African citizenship by birth on anyone who was born in or outside South Africa on or after 6 October 1995 if one of his or her parents was a South African citizen at the time of his or her birth.[265]

78. Citizenship by descent is conferred if a person who is born outside South Africa is adopted by a South African citizen and his or her birth is registered in terms of the Births and Deaths Registration Act.[266]

---

259. Strictly speaking there is a difference between nationality and citizenship, but these terms are often used interchangeably. On the difference between the terms, *see* R. Keightley, *Nationality*, in *Boberg's Law of Persons and the Family* 79 (B. van Heerden, A. Cockrell & R. Keightley eds., Juta & Co, Ltd 2d ed. 1999). The terms are used interchangeably in the present chapter.
260. Naturally, the operation of the rules of South African Private International Law must be borne in mind. On those rules, *see* the relevant monograph in this series.
261. Constitution, ss 19(1)(a), 19(3), 46(1)(b), 86(1), 91(3)(a), 106(1) and 174(1); Electoral Act 73 of 1998, s. 6(1).
262. South African Citizenship Act 88 of 1995, s. 14 read with s. 13(2) of the Civil Union Act 17 of 2006; *see also* the definitions of 'marriage', 'husband' and 'wife' in s. 1 of the South African Citizenship Act.
263. Section 28(1)(a).
264. Keightley, *Nationality*, 83; Keightley, *The Child's Right to a Nationality and the Acquisition of Citizenship in South African Law*, 14 S. Afr. J. Hum. Rights 411 et seq. (1998).
265. Section 2(1)(b). The Act came into operation on 6 Oct. 1995.
266. Section 3.

79. An alien may, on application to the Minister of Home Affairs and satisfaction of specific requirements, acquire citizenship by naturalization if he or she is granted a certificate of naturalization.[267] The requirements the person must meet are that he or she must:

(1) be an adult;
(2) have lawful permanent residence in South Africa;
(3) have been ordinarily resident in South Africa for a continuous period of at least five years immediately before the date of his or her application for citizenship;
(4) be of good character;
(5) intend to continue to reside in South Africa or to enter or continue in the service of the Government of South Africa, an international organization of which the Government is a member, or a person or association of persons resident or established in South Africa;
(6) be able to communicate in any one of the official languages of South Africa to the satisfaction of the Minister;
(7) have an adequate knowledge of the responsibilities and privileges of South African citizenship; and
(8) be a citizen of a country that allows dual citizenship; if the foreign country does not allow dual citizenship, the person must renounce his or her foreign citizenship and furnish the Minister with proof of such renunciation.[268]

267. Sections 4(1)(b), 4(2) and 5.
268. Section 5(1).

Chapter 6. Domicile and Residence

§1. Domicile

80. In terms of the rules of South African Private International Law, domicile, rather than nationality or residence, is the most important connecting factor in respect of matters of status, including capacity to act and capacity to inherit. The personal consequences of marriage and the proprietary consequences of marriage in the absence of an antenuptial contract are other examples of Private-Law matters that are determined according to the *lex domicilii*.[269]

Domicile is unrelated to a person's nationality and the country where he or she resides. A person's domicile is the place where he or she is legally deemed to be constantly present for the purpose of exercising his or her rights and fulfilling his or her obligations, even in his or her factual absence.[270] South African law distinguishes between domicile of origin, domicile of choice and domicile by operation of law (assigned domicile).

81. The fundamental rules of domicile are that no one can be without a domicile,[271] and that no one loses his or her existing domicile until he or she has acquired another domicile.[272] Any change of domicile must be proved on a balance of probabilities.[273]

Whether someone can simultaneously have more than one domicile has not been finally decided. The common-law authors are of the view that it is possible,[274] but aside remarks in judgments suggest the opposite.[275] Most modern South African authors also favour limiting a person to one domicile at a time.[276]

---

269. *See*, e.g., C. Forsyth, *Private International Law: The Roman-Dutch Law Including the Jurisdiction of the High Courts* 292 et seq. (Juta 5th ed. 2012), *See* further the monograph on South African Private International Law.
270. *See*, e.g., Heaton, *Law of Persons*, 41.
271. *See*, e.g., Barratt (ed.), *Law of Persons and the Family*, 127; Boezaart, *Law of Persons*, 33; B. Clark, *Domicile*, in *Boberg's Law of Persons and the Family* 104 (B. van Heerden, A. Cockrell & R. Keightley Juta & Co, Ltd 2d ed. 1999); Forsyth, *Private International Law*, 132; Heaton, *Law of Persons*, 41.
272. Domicile Act 3 of 1992, s. 3(1).
273. *Ibid*., s. 5.
274. *See*, e.g., Voet, *Commentarius ad Pandectas*, 5.1.92; Van Leeuwen, *Rooms-Hollands-Regt*, 5.6.1.
275. *See*, e.g., *Leviny v. Leviny* (1908) 25 SC 173; *Ex parte Donelly* 1915 WLD 29; *Webber v. Webber* 1915 AD 239; *Sukovs v. Van der Walt* [1998] 3 All SA 664 (O).
276. *See*, e.g., Barratt (ed.), *Law of Persons and the Family*, 127; Boezaart, *Law of Persons*, 33; Clark, *Domicile*, 104; Forsyth, *Private International Law*, 133; E. Kahn, *The South African Law of Domicile of Natural Persons* 14–17 (Juta 1972). But contrast E. Spiro, *Domicile in South African Law* Acta Juridica 66–69 (1962).

§2. Domicile of Origin

82. A person's domicile of origin is the domicile the law assigns to him or her at birth. Prior to the coming into operation of the Domicile Act 3 of 1992, a person's domicile of origin revived whenever he or she abandoned his or her domicile of choice without assuming a new domicile. In terms of the Act, a person's existing domicile continues to operate until he or she has acquired another domicile, whether by choice or operation of law.[277]

A person's domicile of origin never revives once he or she has lost it.[278] However, a person's domicile of choice or assigned domicile can be at the place of his or her domicile of origin, provided that the requirements for acquiring a domicile of choice or an assigned domicile at that place are met. For example: A child who is born in South Africa and lives with his or her parents in that country acquires a domicile of origin in South Africa. If the child subsequently emigrates with his or her parents to, say, Australia, he or she acquires an assigned domicile in Australia. If, as an adult, he or she left Australia with the intention of never returning to that country and he or she lawfully returned to South Africa with the intention of indefinitely living there, he or she would once again be domiciled in South Africa, but his or her South African domicile would then be a domicile of choice. It would not be his or her domicile of origin that revived because he or she had abandoned his or her Australian domicile.

§3. Domicile of Choice

83. Domicile of choice is the domicile someone who has capacity to act chooses for himself or herself by exercising his or her own free will. Every adult has the capacity to acquire a domicile of choice, unless he or she lacks the mental capacity to make a rational choice. This rule applies regardless of the person's sex or marital status.[279]

84. A person acquires a domicile of choice only if he or she is lawfully present at a particular place (*factum* requirement) and has the intention to settle there for an indefinite period (*animus* requirement).[280] Mere residence is not enough. The *factum* and *animus* requirements must at some time or another exist simultaneously but they need not come into being simultaneously.[281]

To establish whether a person's residence meets the *factum* requirement the situation is viewed objectively.[282] No specific period of residence is required but the

---

277. Section 3(1).
278. Section 3(2).
279. Section 1(1).
280. *Ibid.* While a person's application for refugee status or an appeal against or a review of refusal of his or her application is being considered, he or she is lawfully present in South Africa for purposes of the *factum* requirement: *Alam v. Minister of Home Affairs* 2012 (5) SA 626 (ECP).
281. *Grindal v. Grindal* 1997 (4) SA 137 (C).
282. *Chinatex Oriental Trading Co v. Erskine* 1998 (4) SA 1087 (C).

person must not simply be visiting the place.[283] As the Domicile Act 3 of 1992 recognizes only lawful residence for purposes of acquiring a domicile of choice,[284] an illegal alien (prohibited immigrant) and a deported person cannot acquire or retain a domicile of choice in South Africa.[285]

To establish whether a person complies with the *animus* requirement, a subjective test is used.[286] To satisfy the *animus* requirement the person must be able to carry out his or her intention of settling at the particular place.[287] Military staff, diplomats, public servants, employees of foreign governments or businesses, and prisoners were initially considered incapable of acquiring a domicile of choice at the place where they were stationed, posted or imprisoned, because their employers or the State determine where they are to reside and they, therefore, cannot give effect to their intention of settling at a particular place. The Act does not expressly deal with the acquisition of a domicile of choice by someone who is not free to decide where he or she wants to reside. It seems that since no provision expressly excludes a person whose presence at a particular place is not by choice from acquiring a domicile of choice there, such a person is competent to establish a domicile of choice in terms of the Act.[288]

§4. Domicile by Operation of Law (Assigned Domicile)

85. Any person who does not have the capacity to acquire a domicile of choice is domiciled at the place with which he or she is most closely connected.[289] This category of persons includes minors and people who do not have the mental capacity to make a rational choice.

In respect of a minor, the Domicile Act 3 of 1992 rebuttably presumes that the minor's parental home is his or her domicile if he or she normally lives with one or both of his or her parents. This is the position regardless of whether the child's parents are, or were ever, married to each other or are, or were ever, each other's civil union partners.[290]

---

283. *Ibid.*
284. Section 1(2).
285. *Ex parte Macleod* 1946 CPD 312; *Smith v. Smith* 1962 (3) SA 930 (FC); *Drakensbergpers Bpk v. Sharpe* 1963 (4) SA 615 (N). But *see also Van Rensburg v. Ballinger* 1950 (4) SA 427 (T), where the court held that a prohibited immigrant whom the authorities openly permitted to reside in South Africa could acquire a domicile of choice in the country. Even though the presence of a person who has applied for refugee status is precarious because his or her application might be dismissed, he or she can meet the *animus* requirement. However, the precarious presence is a factor which is taken into account to determine whether the person has in fact met the *animus* requirement: *Alam v. Minister of Home Affairs* 2012 (5) SA 626 (ECP).
286. *Chinatex Oriental Trading Co v. Erskine* 1998 (4) SA 1087 (C).
287. *Ex parte Quintrell* 1922 TPD 14.
288. Boezaart, *Law of Persons*, 45, 46; Heaton, *Law of Persons*, 45; Kruger & Skelton (eds), *The Law of Persons in South Africa*, 76; South African Law Commission, *Report on Domicile: Project 60* para. 3.76 (Government Printer 1990).
289. Sections 1(1) and 2.
290. Section 2(2) and (3) of the Domicile Act 3 of 1992; s. 2(3) read with s. 13(2) of the Civil Union Act 17 of 2006.

When a minor attains majority or a mentally ill person regains his or her capacity to make a rational choice, he or she retains his or her assigned domicile until he or she establishes a domicile of choice.[291]

291. Section 3(1).

Chapter 7. Mentally Handicapped Persons

§1. Introduction

86. Regardless of whether or not he or she has been declared mentally ill, South African law precludes a person who is de facto mentally ill from participating in legal interaction. The capacity of a person who suffers from a mental or physical disability may also be limited, but this happens only if the court appoints a curator for the person and/or for his or her estate and/or person (body). Consumption of alcohol or drugs may also affect a person's mental abilities and lead to a limitation of his or her capacity. Because the effects of these three sets of circumstances (namely, mental illness; mental or physical disability accompanied by a court order appointing a curator; and consumption of alcohol or drugs) on a person's capacity differ, they are discussed under separate headings below in this chapter.

§2. Mental Illness

87. A person is precluded from participating in legal interaction if he or she is mentally ill to such a degree that he or she cannot understand the nature, purport and consequences of his or her acts.[292] At common law, mentally ill persons, as a class, were confined to persons so devoid of their senses that they could not understand the consequences of their acts and could not make rational decisions at all. In modern law a much wider meaning is ascribed to mental illness. For example, a person is considered mentally ill even if he or she understands the nature and consequences of his or her juristic acts but is motivated or influenced by delusions caused by a mental illness.[293]

Whether or not a person was mentally ill when he or she concluded a particular legal transaction is a question of fact that must be determined on a preponderance of probabilities.[294] Declaring a person mentally ill (certification in terms of the Mental Health Care Act 17 of 2002) and/or the appointment of a curator or administrator for the person do not, as such, determine the matter or affect the person's capacity. On the one hand, someone who has not been certified does not have capacity to act, litigate or incur delictual or criminal liability if he or she is in fact mentally ill when performing the particular juristic act. On the other hand, a person who has been certified and/or for whom a curator or administrator has been appointed has capacity to act, litigate and incur delictual or criminal liability if he or she is in fact not mentally ill, that is, if he or she has a *lucidum intervallum* (lucid interval) when the juristic act is performed.[295] However, certification is important as far as onus of proof is concerned. In the case of an uncertified person, the onus of proof

292. *See*, e.g., *Pheasant v. Warne* 1922 AD 481; *Lange v. Lange* 1945 AD 332; *Theron v. AA Life Assurance Association Ltd* 1995 (4) SA 361 (A); *Eerste Nasionale Bank van Suidelike Afrika Bpk v. Saayman* 1997 (4) SA 302 (SCA).

293. *Lange v. Lange* 1945 AD 332.

294. *Ibid.*

295. *Prinsloo's Curators Bonis v. Crafford and Prinsloo* 1905 TS 669.

is on the party alleging that the person was mentally ill when the juristic act was performed,[296] while in the case of a certified person the onus is on the party alleging that the person was sane when the juristic act was performed.[297]

88. A mentally ill person has no capacity to act, litigate or incur delictual or criminal liability. Any transaction a mentally ill person enters into is void and cannot be ratified.[298] This is the position even if the person with whom the mentally ill person concluded the transaction was unaware of the mental illness.[299] However, a bona fide third party may have a remedy based on unjustified enrichment or *negotiorum gestio*, because these remedies are not based on contract, with the result that the mentally ill party's capacity to act is irrelevant.

A marriage or civil union is not automatically dissolved by the mental illness of one of the spouses or civil union partners,[300] but mental illness for which there is no reasonable prospect of a cure is a ground for divorce.[301] A parent's mental illness does not automatically terminate his or her parental responsibilities and rights,[302] but the court may make an appropriate order in respect of (elements of) the mentally ill parent's parental responsibilities and rights if this is in the best interests of his or her children.[303]

89. The High Court may appoint a *curator bonis* to look after a mentally ill person's property and to supplement his or her lack of capacity to act.[304] In legal proceedings a mentally ill person must be represented by a *curator ad litem*.[305] If necessary, a *curator personae* is appointed to care for or take decisions in respect of the person's person.[306] The High Court also has the power to recommend the appointment of an administrator to administer the property and carry on the business or undertaking of a mentally ill person.[307] Alternatively, the Master of the High Court may, on application by any adult, appoint an administrator in respect of the property of a mentally ill person.[308]

Generally, acts that are of a very personal nature cannot be performed by a curator. Thus, for example, a curator cannot institute an action for divorce, make a will, exercise parental responsibilities and rights, or consent to marriage on behalf of a

296. *Pheasant v. Warne* 1922 AD 481; *Vermaak v. Vermaak* 1929 OPD 13; *De Villiers v. Espach* 1958 (3) SA 91 (T).
297. *Prinsloo's Curators Bonis v. Crafford and Prinsloo* 1905 TS 669; *Pheasant v. Warne* 1922 AD 481; *Vermaak v. Vermaak* 1929 OPD 13; *Levin v. Mechanich* 1931 EDL 32.
298. *See*, e.g., *Pheasant v. Warne* 1922 AD 481; *Lange v. Lange* 1945 AD 332.
299. *Molyneux v. Natal Land and Colonization Co Ltd* 1905 AC 555 (PC) 561, (1905) 26 NLR 423.
300. *Barnes v. Hayward* 1944 CPD 203.
301. Divorce Act 70 of 1979, s. 5(1).
302. *Ex parte Human* 1948 (1) SA 1022 (O); *Ex parte Powrie* 1963 (1) SA 299 (W).
303. *See*, e.g., s. 28 of the Children's Act 38 of 2005.
304. *Minister of the Interior v. Cowley* 1955 (1) SA 307 (N).
305. *De Villiers v. Espach* 1958 (3) SA 91 (T).
306. *See*, e.g., *Ex parte Dixie* 1950 (4) SA 748 (W); *Clarke v. Hurst* 1992 (4) SA 630 (D).
307. Mental Health Care Act 17 of 2002, ss 61(1), 61(3), 63 and 65.
308. *Ibid.*, ss 59(1) and 60(1).

mentally ill person.[309] However, because the powers and duties of a *curator personae* relate to the mentally ill person's body, he or she may take decisions that relate to very personal issues, such as termination of a mentally ill woman's pregnancy and a mentally ill person's sterilization.[310]

90. In terms of the Mental Health Care Act 17 of 2002, mentally ill persons who have been certified enjoy special statutory rights, including the right to representation; confidentiality; having their person, human dignity and privacy respected; and being provided with care, treatment and rehabilitation services that improve their mental capacity to develop to their full potential and facilitate their integration into community life.[311] Furthermore, every person, body, organization or health establishment which provides care, treatment and rehabilitation services to a mentally ill person must take steps to ensure that he or she is protected from exploitation, abuse, degrading treatment and forced labour.[312] Care, treatment and rehabilitation services may not be used as punishment or for the convenience of other people; must be proportionate to the person's mental health status; and must be as un-intrusive as possible.[313] Except in urgent cases, the mentally ill person must be appropriately informed of his or her rights prior to the administration of care, treatment and rehabilitation services.[314] The Act also prohibits unfair discrimination on the ground of a person's mental health status; and provides that any determination concerning a person's mental health status must be based solely on factors that are relevant to the person's mental health status and not socio-political or economic status, cultural or religious background, or affinity.[315] A determination of a person's mental health status may furthermore be made only for purposes that are directly relevant to his or her mental health status.[316] Whenever these rights are exercised or duties performed regard must be had to the best interests of the mentally ill person.[317]

It has been judicially stated that a mentally ill person necessarily suffers from a mental incapacity or disability.[318] In accordance with this view, all mentally ill persons qualify for the protection that is afforded to disabled persons in terms of labour legislation and the anti-discrimination provisions in the Constitution and the Promotion of Equality and Prevention of Unfair Discrimination Act 4 of 2000.

309. *Ex parte AB* 1910 TPD 1332; *Lange v. Lange* 1945 AD 332; *Estate Watkins-Pitchford v. Commissioner for Inland Revenue* 1955 (2) SA 437 (A); *Spangenberg v. De Waal* [2008] 1 All SA 162 (T).
310. Choice on Termination of Pregnancy Act 92 of 1996, s. 5(4) read with s. 2(1)(b); Sterilisation Act 44 of 1998, ss 2(3)(b), and 3(1) and (2).
311. Sections 8(1), 8(2), 13 and 15.
312. Section 11.
313. Sections 8(3) and 11(1)(c).
314. Section 17. The urgent cases are listed in s. 9(1)(c).
315. Sections 10(1) and 12(1).
316. Section 12(2).
317. Section 7(2).
318. *Mitchell v. Mitchell* 1930 AD 217; *De Villiers v. Espach* 1958 (3) SA 91 (T).

§3. MENTAL AND PHYSICAL DISABILITY

91. If a person suffers from a mental or physical disability or incapacity which renders him or her incapable of managing his or her own affairs, the High Court may appoint a curator to administer the person's estate (*curator bonis*), litigate on his or her behalf (*curator ad litem*) and/or take care of his or her person (*curator personae*).[319] Although the court is not compelled to appoint a curator for someone who consents to the appointment, the person's consent is an important consideration.[320] Naturally, for any weight to be attached to the person's consent, he or she must be able to understand the proceedings.[321] The court does not regard it as proper that the disabled or incapacitated person personally apply to be placed under curatorship, because if the person is incapable of managing his or her own affairs, he or she, strictly, has no capacity to litigate. A family member or someone else who has an interest in the person's person or property usually makes the application.

92. The powers of a curator who is appointed for a mentally or physically disabled or incapacitated person are governed by the same rules and principles that apply to the curator of a mentally ill person. The *curator personae* of a pregnant woman who is in a state of continuous unconsciousness without a reasonable prospect that she will regain consciousness in time to request and consent to the termination of her pregnancy, may consent to the termination.[322]

93. A mentally or physically disabled or incapacitated person for whom a curator has been appointed has the capacity to conduct his or her own affairs whenever he or she is in fact able to do so. In other words, the appointment of the curator does not mean that the person is deprived of capacity to act and litigate or that he or she has lost his or her capacity to be held delictually or criminally liable. Thus, for example, the person may independently marry, make a will, enter into a contract and litigate if, at the moment of entering into the legal transaction, he or she is mentally able to do so.[323] However, the completion of prescription of a claim by or against someone who has been placed under curatorship is delayed until a year after the curatorship has ended.[324]

---

319. *See*, e.g., *Mitchell v. Mitchell* 1930 AD 217; *Ex parte Tomich* 1957 (4) SA 667 (N); *Ex parte Jacobs* 1965 (3) SA 270 (C); *Ex parte Powrie* 1963 (1) SA 299 (W).
320. *See*, e.g., *Mitchell v. Mitchell* 1930 AD 217; *Nkosi v. Minister of Justice* 1964 (4) SA 365 (W); *Ex parte Van der Linde* 1970 (2) SA 718 (O); *Ex parte Wilson: In re Morison* 1991 (4) SA 774 (T).
321. *Ex parte Van Dyk* 1939 CPD 202; *Ex parte Bell* 1953 (2) SA 702 (O).
322. The requirements that apply to termination of the pregnancy of a mentally disabled woman apply to termination of the pregnancy of an unconscious woman too: Choice on Termination of Pregnancy Act 92 of 1996, s. 5(4).
323. *See*, e.g., *Pienaar v. Pienaar's Curator* 1930 OPD 171; *Ex parte De Bruin* 1946 OPD 110; *Spies v. Smith* 1957 (1) SA 539 (A); *De Villiers v. Espach* 1958 (3) SA 91 (T).
324. Prescription Act 68 of 1969, s. 13(1).

94. Various Acts, including the Labour Relations Act 66 of 1995, Employment Equity Act 55 of 1998 and Promotion of Equality and Prevention of Unfair Discrimination Act 4 of 2000, confer special protection on the mentally and physically disabled.

§4. Intoxication with Alcohol or Drugs

95. Consuming alcohol or drugs may affect a person's mental abilities without rendering him or her mentally ill or disabled. If the effect of the consumption is such that the person is deprived of his or her powers of reasoning, his or her legal status may be affected.[325] The effect is usually only temporary.

The mere fact that the consumption of alcohol or drugs renders the person reckless, more easily persuadable, or more willing to enter into a particular transaction does not result in the transaction being invalid.[326] However, if the transaction is concluded when the consumption of alcohol or drugs has deprived the person of his or her powers of reasoning, the transaction is void and cannot be ratified. The onus of proof is on the party who alleges that the degree of intoxication by alcohol or drugs was such as to deprive the person of his or her powers of reasoning.[327] As unjustified enrichment and *negotiorum gestio* are not based on the existence of a valid agreement, intoxication does not affect a person's capacity to incur liability on these grounds.

If the consumption of alcohol or drugs diminishes a person's ability to appreciate the consequences of his or her actions, it may also affect his or her capacity to be held criminally or delictually accountable.

325. *See*, e.g., *Dennis v. Kupfel* (1896) 11 EDC 63; *Donovan v. Rowbotham* (1905) 19 EDC 38; *Goodman v. Pritchard* (1907) 28 NLR 227; *Van Metzinger v. Badenhorst* 1953 (3) SA 291 (T).
326. *Van Metzinger v. Badenhorst* 1953 (3) SA 291 (T).
327. *Goodman v. Pritchard* (1907) 28 NLR 227; *Van Metzinger v. Badenhorst* 1953 (3) SA 291 (T).

Chapter 8. Prodigals

96. A prodigal is someone who is not mentally ill or disabled but squanders his or her assets in an irresponsible and reckless way due to some defect in his or her power of judgement or character. To protect the prodigal and his or her family, his or her status may be restricted by an order of court.[328]

Any interested party, including the prodigal personally, may apply to the High Court for such an order. The order declares the spendthrift person to be a prodigal, appoints a *curator bonis* to administer the prodigal's estate, and interdicts (prohibits) the prodigal from administering his or her estate.[329] Prodigality, as such, does not affect a person's status. It is only once the person has been declared a prodigal and prohibited from administering his or her estate that his or her capacity is restricted.[330]

97. Once an order restricting a prodigal from administering his or her estate has been made, his or her capacity becomes analogous to that of a minor. The prodigal needs the consent of his or her curator to litigate and to enter into juristic acts by which he or she acquires obligations.[331] However, he or she may sue unassisted for a divorce and for an order to have the curatorship set aside or his or her curator dismissed.[332] Whether the prodigal may make a will is unclear. What is clear is that the prodigal's curator may not make a will on behalf of the prodigal or assist the prodigal in making a will.[333] Legislation bars an interdicted prodigal from occupying certain offices, such as being a trustee of an insolvent estate[334] or a director of a company.[335]

98. If an interdicted prodigal enters into a legal transaction in disregard of the court order restraining him or her from administering his or her estate, the transaction is voidable at the instance of his or her curator.[336] The other party cannot

---

328. *See*, e.g., *Ex parte McLinden* 1945 OPD 96; *Yared v. Yared* 1952 (4) SA 182 (T); *Traub v. Traub* 1955 (2) SA 671 (C); *Delius v. Delius* 1960 (1) SA 270 (N).
329. *See*, e.g., *In re Miller: Ex parte Keldie* (1892) 9 SC 414 (daughter); *Cillie v. Cillie* 1938 CPD 513 (former spouse); *Ex parte McLinden* 1945 OPD 96 (prodigal and his wife jointly); *Delius v. Delius* 1960 (1) SA 270 (N) (spouse).
330. *See*, e.g., *Cillie v. Cillie* 1938 CPD 513; *Ex parte McLinden* 1945 OPD 96; *Ex parte Wilding* 1953 (1) SA 633 (C); *Delius v. Delius* 1960 (1) SA 270 (N). It is doubted whether restricting a prodigal from administering his or her estate is constitutionally tenable: *see* Barratt (ed.), *Law of Persons and the Family*, 109; Heaton, *Law of Persons*, 137–138; J. Heaton, *Mental and Physical Disability; Prodigality*, in *Boberg's Law of Persons and the Family* 159–160 (B. van Heerden, A. Cockrell & R. Keightley eds., Juta & Co, Ltd 2d ed. 1999).
331. *Phil Morkel Bpk v. Niemand* 1970 (3) SA 455 (C).
332. *Ribbens v. Ribbens* 1965 (1) PH F5 (T).
333. *See*, e.g., Barratt (ed.), *Law of Persons and the Family*, 107–108; Boezaart, *Law of Persons*, 142; Heaton, *Law of Persons*, 136; Kruger & Skelton (eds), *The Law of Persons in South Africa*, 157; Spiro, *Parent and Child*, 112.
334. Insolvency Act 24 of 1936, s. 55(c).
335. Companies Act 71 of 2008, s. 69(7)(b).
336. *Phil Morkel Bpk v. Niemand* 1970 (3) SA 455 (C).

insist on the transaction being upheld, but he or she may hold the prodigal liable on the basis of unjustified enrichment, because such liability is not based on the prodigal's capacity to act.

99. An interdicted prodigal does not automatically regain full capacity when he or she abandons his or her prodigal tendencies. A court order discharging him or her from curatorship is required.

Chapter 9. Insolvents

100. The capacity of an insolvent (bankrupt) person whose estate has been sequestrated is limited in various respects. The limitations arise only once the insolvent's estate has been sequestrated, and come to an end once ten years have elapsed since the sequestration or when the insolvent is rehabilitated by an order of the High Court.[337]

The sequestration divests the insolvent of his or her estate.[338] If the insolvent is married in community of property, the joint estate and the separate estates of both spouses are sequestrated and both spouses are divested of the joint estate and their separate estates.[339] Subject to certain exceptions, all property the insolvent acquires during insolvency vests in the insolvent estate, which is administered by a trustee.[340]

101. Although sequestration curtails the insolvent's powers to control and administer his or her estate, it does not deprive him or her entirely of capacity to act. An insolvent may still enter into any contract which does not purport to dispose of property of the insolvent estate. If a contract adversely affects the insolvent estate or is likely to do so, the insolvent needs the trustee's written consent to enter into the contract. The insolvent also needs the trustee's consent to carry on, be employed in or have an interest in the business of a trader who is a general dealer or manufacturer. If the insolvent acts in breach of these limitations, the contract is valid if the property the transaction relates to was acquired after sequestration, the disposition was for valuable consideration, and the person with whom the insolvent transacted was unaware, and had no reason to suspect, that the estate was under sequestration.[341] Other contracts in breach of the limitations are voidable at the instance of the trustee.[342]

102. Sequestration stays all civil proceedings by or against the insolvent until a trustee is appointed to act on behalf of the insolvent estate,[343] but, for the rest, the sequestration does not affect the insolvent's capacity to litigate.[344]

---

337. Insolvency Act 24 of 1936, ss 129(1) and 127A(1), respectively.
338. Section 20(1)(a).
339. *See*, e.g., *De Wet v. Jurgens* 1970 (3) SA 38 (A); *Badenhorst v. Bekker* 1994 (2) SA 155 (N); *Du Plessis v. Pienaar* 2003 (1) SA 671 (SCA); *Voget v. Kleynhans* 2003 (2) SA 148 (C).
340. Section 20(1)(a) and (2)(b). *See* ss 23 and 82(6) of the Insolvency Act 24 of 1936 and s. 63 of the Long-Term Insurance Act 52 of 1998 for the exceptions.
341. Sections 23(2), 23(3) and 24(1).
342. *WL Carroll & Co v. Ray Hall Motors (Pty) Ltd* 1972 (4) SA 728 (T).
343. Section 20(1)(b).
344. *See*, e.g., *Ecker v. Dean* 1938 AD 102; *Nieuwoudt v. The Master* 1988 (4) SA 513 (A); *Grevler v. Landsdown* 1991 (3) SA 175 (T); *Voget v. Kleynhans* 2003 (2) SA 148 (C). *See also* s. 23 of the Insolvency Act 24 of 1936 which lists specific instances in which the insolvent may litigate in his or her own name and without the trustee's consent or co-operation.

103. Sequestration limits an insolvent's legal capacity by disqualifying him or her from holding certain offices, such as being a member of the National Assembly or a provincial legislature,[345] a director of a company,[346] or a trustee.[347]

345. Constitution, ss 47(1)(c) and 106(1)(c).
346. Companies Act 71 of 2008, s. 69(8)(b)(i).
347. Insolvency Act 24 of 1936, ss 55(a) and 58(a).

Part II. Family Law

Chapter 1. Marriage

§1. The Nature of Marriage and a Civil Union

104. Three types of marriages are fully recognized in South Africa. Each type has its own characteristics. The first type of marriage that is fully recognized is a civil marriage. Civil marriage is open to persons of all races and religions. A civil marriage is defined as the legally recognized life-long voluntary union between one man and one woman to the exclusion of all others.[348] This type of marriage is governed by the common law and the Marriage Act 25 of 1961 and must be solemnized by a marriage officer.

The second type of marriage that is fully recognized is a customary marriage. A customary marriage is a marriage that is concluded in terms of the customs and usages that are 'traditionally observed among the indigenous African peoples of South Africa and which form part of the culture of those peoples'.[349] Polygyny is permitted in customary marriages (in other words, a husband may take more than one wife), and these marriages are not solemnized by a marriage officer.

The last type of marriage that is fully recognized is a marriage concluded in terms of the Civil Union Act 17 of 2006. A marriage under the Civil Union Act is the monogamous, voluntary union of two persons of the same or the opposite sex, which is solemnized and registered in terms of the Act.[350] The parties to a civil union may call their union either a marriage or a civil partnership.[351] The consequences of the union are exactly the same regardless of whether the parties choose 'marriage' or 'civil partnership' as the appellation of their civil union.[352] In the remainder of this monograph, the term 'civil union', instead of 'marriage or civil partnership in terms of the Civil Union Act', is used when discussing relationships concluded in terms of this Act.

105. Monogamous marriages that are solemnized according to religious rites by a marriage officer who has been appointed in terms of the Marriage Act 25 of 1961 have dual validity because they qualify as both civil and religious marriages. The

348. *Seedat's Executors v. The Master (Natal)* 1917 AD 302.
349. Recognition of Customary Marriages Act 120 of 1998, s. 1.
350. Civil Union Act 17 of 2006, s. 1; *see also* ss 6 and 8(6).
351. *Ibid.*, ss. 1, 2(a) and 11.
352. *Ibid.*, s. 13.

religious and civil marriages exist side by side, with the consequences of the civil marriage being governed by South African common law and the legislation relating to civil marriages, and the consequences of the religious marriage being governed by the particular system of religious law in terms of which the marriage was solemnized. Christian and Jewish marriages usually have dual validity.

Religious marriages that are de facto polygynous and/or are not concluded in terms of the Marriage Act are afforded only limited recognition in terms of South African law. Many Muslim and Hindu religious officials do not apply to be appointed as marriage officers in terms of the Act, with the result that the marriages they solemnize are solely religious marriages that do not enjoy full legal recognition in South African law. Moves are afoot to address the absence of legal recognition of Muslim and Hindu marriages,[353] and the courts and legislature have already extended piecemeal recognition to these marriages for specific, limited purposes, including protection from domestic violence, testate and intestate succession by and maintenance for a surviving spouse, and enforcement of the spousal duty of support.[354] The aforementioned protection applies regardless of whether the marriage is de facto monogamous or polygynous. Furthermore, by virtue of judicial pronouncements, spouses in a de facto monogamous Muslim marriage may also claim maintenance pending divorce and enforce the contractual obligations that flow from the marriage as against each other, and the surviving spouse in a de facto monogamous Muslim marriage may institute the dependant's action for loss of support.[355]

353. The Draft Muslim Marriages Bill, 2010 was published for public comment in Jan. 2011: Gen. N. 37 in *G.G.* 33946 of 21 Jan. 2011. It seeks to afford full legal recognition to certain Muslim marriages. As the legislation is only in draft form, a detailed analysis of its provisions is out of place for present purposes. Hindu marriages will, it is hoped, also receive legislative attention in the future. The South African Law Reform Commission has initiated a project on these marriages (South African Law Reform Commission, 'Current Investigations', http://www.justice.gov.za/salrc/projects.htm, 31 Jan. 2019), which may result in draft legislation being published. *See also* General Introduction, §3 n. 66 above.

354. *See* the definition of 'domestic relationship' in s. 1 of the Domestic Violence Act 116 of 1998; *Daniels v. Campbell* 2004 (5) SA 331 (CC); *Khan v. Khan* 2005 (2) SA 272 (T); *Hassam v. Jacobs* [2008] 4 All SA 350 (C); *Hassam v. Jacobs* 2009 (5) SA 572 (CC); *Moosa v. Minister of Justice* 2018 (5) SA 13 (CC). In *Rose v. Rose* [2015] 2 All SA 352 (WCC), the Western Cape Division of the High Court, Cape Town incorrectly held that a wife in a Muslim marriage can claim post-divorce maintenance and a share of her husband's pension interest in terms of the Divorce Act 70 of 1979. The Muslim marriage at issue was concluded during the subsistence of a valid civil marriage. Because a civil marriage is monogamous, any other marriage that is concluded during its subsistence is void. Therefore, the Muslim marriage in *Rose* was void. Because the marriage was void, the Divorce Act could not have applied to it – after all, a marriage can only be dissolved by divorce if there is a marriage to begin with.

355. *Ryland v. Edros* 1997 (2) SA 690 (C); *Amod (Born Peer) v. Multilateral Motor Vehicle Accidents Fund (Commission for Gender Equality Intervening)* 1999 (4) SA 1319 (SCA); *AM v. RM* 2010 (2) SA 223 (ECP); *Hoosein v. Dangor* [2010] 2 All SA 55 (WCC); *TM v. ZJ* 2016 (1) SA 71 (KZD).

§2. THE CAPACITY TO ENTER INTO A MARRIAGE OR A CIVIL UNION

106. As the requirements for the capacity to enter into a civil marriage, a civil union and a customary marriage differ, each type of relationship is discussed separately.

I. Civil Marriage

A. *Engagement*

107. An engagement is a contract to marry on a specific or determinable future date. A valid engagement is not a prerequisite for the conclusion of a civil marriage.

If prospective spouses do enter into an engagement, they must, at the time of entering into the engagement, be in a position to conclude a civil marriage with each other. Thus, they may not be related within the prohibited degrees of relationship; neither of them may be below the age of puberty; they must be of the opposite sex; neither of them may be a party to an existing civil or customary marriage or civil union; they must have capacity to act; and so on.

A mentally ill person is absolutely incapable of getting engaged.[356] A minor who wants to get engaged must obtain his or her parents' consent. Both parents' consent is required unless the court orders otherwise, sole guardianship has been granted to one of the parents, or the child was born of unmarried parents and the child's father does not have guardianship of the child. If only one parent is alive, that parent's consent is required. If neither parent is alive or if neither parent has guardianship of the child, the consent of the child's legal guardian must be obtained.[357]

The parties to the engagement must reach agreement. A material mistake (such as a mistake regarding a party's identity or the impression that the promise to marry is merely a joke) renders the engagement void for lack of agreement. Material misrepresentation (such as misrepresentation regarding impotence, sterility, mental illness, or a serious physical or mental handicap),[358] duress, and undue influence render the engagement voidable.

108. An engagement is terminated by mutual agreement, the parties' marriage or either party's death. If one of the parties is a minor, withdrawal of parental consent also terminates the engagement because the marriage cannot go ahead without such consent.[359] Finally, an engagement may be lawfully terminated by one of the parties if he or she has a *justa causa* (sound reason) for doing so, such as one of the parties becoming mentally ill, sterile or impotent or committing a serious crime, or

---

356. *See* further Part I, Ch. 7, §2 above.

357. Children's Act 38 of 2005, s. 18(3)(c)(i) and (5) read with ss 19(1), 20 and 21(1); *see also* s. 5(1) of the Matrimonial Affairs Act 37 of 1953 and s. 6(3) of the Divorce Act 70 of 1979. If another person has been appointed as the minor's guardian, that person's consent is also required: Children's Act, s. 18(3)(c)(i) and (5).

358. *Thelemann v. Von Geyso* 1957 (3) SA 39 (W).

359. *Schoeman v. Rafferty* 1918 CPD 485; *Sipondo v. Nongauza* 1927 EDL 255.

the parties becoming involved in a serious argument concerning their future matrimonial property system.[360] In *Van Jaarsveld v. Bridges*,[361] the Supreme Court of Appeal stated in an aside comment that lack of desire by one of the parties to proceed with the marriage should also be a *justa causa* regardless of whose 'fault' it is that the marriage is no longer desired.

109. The contract of engagement can no longer be enforced by compelling an unwilling party to proceed with the marriage. Nor can the jilted party claim contractual damages for future loss based on breach of promise.[362] In other words, the jilted party cannot claim the benefits he or she would have received by virtue of the matrimonial property system which would have operated between the parties. For example, the jilted party cannot claim the portion of the other party's estate he or she would have received as a result of the marriage. Nor can he or she claim the maintenance he or she would have received during the subsistence of the marriage.

110. However, if breach of promise occurs in a manner that injures the honour, dignity or reputation of the jilted party, and the other party acted with the intention of injuring the jilted party's honour, dignity or reputation, the jilted party can claim satisfaction with the *actio iniuriarum*. It is irrelevant whether or not the termination had a *justa causa*.[363] The amount that is awarded is within the court's discretion. The court takes into account factors such as the way in which the breach of promise occurred, the motives for choosing that method of termination, the parties' social status, and their previous life experience.[364] The courts are hesitant to award satisfaction if one of the parties realized that he or she no longer loved the other like a prospective spouse should and then in a fair and open manner terminated the engagement.[365]

The party who commits breach of promise also forfeits the engagement ring and the gifts he or she gave to the jilted party. He or she must further return the engagement gifts the jilted party gave to him or her.[366]

360. *Hart v. Yates* (1896) 3 Off Rep 201.
361. 2010 (4) SA 558 (SCA).
362. *Cloete v. Maritz* 2013 (5) SA 448 (WCC). Although the judgment in *Cloete* is not binding throughout the country, it will in all probability be followed since it is based on guidelines the Supreme Court of Appeal provided in *Van Jaarsveld v. Bridges* 2010 (4) SA 558 (SCA).
363. *See*, e.g., *Van Jaarsveld v. Bridges* 2010 (4) SA 558 (SCA).
364. *See*, e.g., *Smit v. Jacobs* 1918 OPD 30; *Davel v. Swanepoel* 1954 (1) SA 383 (A); *Guggenheim v. Rosenbaum* 1961 (4) SA 21 (W).
365. *Mocke v. Fourie* (1893) 3 CTR 313; *Radloff v. Ralph* 1917 EDL 168; *Guggenheim v. Rosenbaum* 1961 (4) SA 21 (W); *Bull v. Taylor* 1965 (4) SA 29 (A).
366. On return of engagement gifts, *see*, e.g., Barratt (ed.), *Law of Persons and the Family*, 234; Heaton & Kruger, *Family Law*, 9–10; C. Himonga, *Marriage*, in *Wille's Principles of South African Law* 236 (F. du Bois ed., Juta & Co 9th ed. 2007); F.P. van den Heever, *Breach of Promise and Seduction in South African Law* 41 (Juta & Co, Ltd 1954); D. Visser, *Unjustified Enrichment* 543–546 (Juta 2008).

B. Different Sex

111. Persons of the same sex cannot enter into a civil marriage. A civil marriage in contravention of this rule is void.[367]

C. Consanguinity and Affinity

112. Various people who are related to each other by consanguinity (blood) or affinity (marriage)[368] are prohibited from entering into a civil marriage with each other. If they do marry, their civil marriage is void.[369]

Blood relations in the direct line (ascendants and descendants) are forbidden from marrying each other. Thus, for example, a father may not enter into a civil marriage with his daughter and a grandmother may not enter into a civil marriage with her grandson. The same applies to persons who are related to one another by affinity in the direct line.[370] Thus, for example, a man may not enter into a civil marriage with his former stepdaughter or his former mother-in-law.

Collateral blood relations may marry each other only if both of them are removed from their common ancestor by at least two degrees.[371] Therefore, a brother and sister or uncle and niece may not enter into a civil marriage with each other, but cousins may. Collateral relations by affinity may enter into a civil marriage with each other.[372] Thus, for example, once her existing civil marriage has been dissolved, a wife may enter into a civil marriage with her ex-husband's brother.

An adoptive parent may not marry his or her adopted child,[373] but a legal guardian may marry his or her minor ward. However, to guard against abuse of the minor and to protect the child's best interests, the legal guardian cannot consent to the civil marriage between himself or herself and the minor. The High Court must be approached to grant consent in its capacity as upper guardian of all minors.

D. Marriageable Age

113. As indicated above, minors below the age of puberty may not enter into a civil marriage. A civil marriage in contravention of this rule is void.[374]

A minor who has attained the minimum marriageable age needs consent to marry since he or she has limited capacity to act. Usually the consent of all the guardians of the minor is required. Sometimes the consent of the Minister of Home Affairs is

367. *W v. W* 1976 (2) SA 308 (W); *Simms v. Simms* 1981 (4) SA 186 (D).
368. For legal purposes, affinity is restricted to the relationship that comes into being between a married person and the blood relations of his or her spouse; it does not extend to the spouse's relations by affinity.
369. *M v. M* 1962 (2) SA 114 (GW).
370. Political Ordinance of 1580, Art. 8.
371. *Ibid.*, Arts 6 and 7.
372. Marriage Act 25 of 1961, s. 28.
373. Children's Act 38 of 2005, s. 242(2)(c) and (3).
374. *See* Part I, Ch. 3, §2 above.

also required. If the minor marries without the consent of his or her guardian, the marriage is voidable. If the Minister's consent was not obtained, the marriage is void, but the Minister may ratify the marriage.[375]

E. Prior Marriage or Civil Union

114. A civil marriage is void if either of the parties is already a party to a civil or customary marriage or a civil union.[376] The Recognition of Customary Marriages Act 120 of 1998 is the only law that provides for an exception to this rule, and this exception applies only if spouses who are married to each other at customary law enter into a civil marriage with one another. However, before the customary spouses may enter into the civil marriage, the husband's other customary marriages must first be dissolved.[377]

F. Failure to Consent

1. Duress

115. If a party to a civil marriage was forced to consent to the marriage by duress, the marriage is voidable.[378] Although there is no direct authority for the statement, undue influence should also render a civil marriage voidable.

2. Mistake

116. Only a material mistake excludes consent and renders the marriage void. A mistake concerning the identity of the other party (*error in personam*) and a mistake concerning the nature of the juristic act (*error in negotio*) are material. In practice, the only material mistake that occurs is one regarding the nature of the juristic act, such as if one of the parties thinks that the wedding ceremony is merely the registration of an engagement.[379]

Entering into a marriage of convenience does not amount to marrying while labouring under a material mistake. For example, if a man marries a friend's mistress in order to enable her to obtain permanent residence in South Africa, the marriage is valid.[380]

375. *Ibid.*
376. In respect of an existing civil marriage, *see*, e.g., *Seedat's Executors v. The Master (Natal)* 1917 AD 3; *Zulu v. Zulu* 2008 (4) SA 12 (D). In respect of an existing customary marriage, *see* s. 10(4) of the Recognition of Customary Marriages Act 120 of 1998, and in respect of an existing civil union, *see* s. 8(2) of the Civil Union Act 17 of 2006.
377. Recognition of Customary Marriages Act 120 of 1998, s. 10(1) read with s. 3(2).
378. *Smith v. Smith* 1948 (4) SA 61 (N).
379. *Benjamin v. Salkander* (1908) 25 SC 512; *Rubens v. Rubens* (1909) 26 SC 617; *Kanatopsky v. Kanatopsky* 1935 EDL 308.
380. *Martens v. Martens* 1952 (3) SA 771 (W).

3. Misrepresentation

117. If one of the parties persuades the other to enter into a civil marriage by making a material misrepresentation, the marriage is voidable. Thus, a husband can have the marriage set aside if he can prove that, at the time of the wedding, his wife concealed the fact that she was pregnant by another man (she concealed her pre-nuptial *stuprum*), and that he had been unaware of this state of affairs.[381] If the husband accepts the pregnancy, he loses his remedy.[382]

A civil marriage is also voidable if an impotent spouse knew of his or her impotence before the marriage and concealed the impotence.[383]

The case law on whether concealment of sterility renders a marriage voidable is not unanimous. In *Venter v. Venter*[384] it was held that the fraudulent concealment indeed renders the marriage of a sterile spouse voidable. However, in *Van Niekerk v. Van Niekerk*[385] it was held that if the procreation of children was an express or implicit aim of a couple's civil marriage, the mere fact of sterility renders the marriage voidable, regardless of whether or not it was fraudulently concealed. The approach in *Venter v. Venter* is generally preferred[386] and is also supported by the Constitutional Court's view in *National Coalition for Gay and Lesbian Equality v. Minister of Home Affairs*[387] that '[f]rom a legal and constitutional point of view procreative potential is not a defining characteristic of conjugal relationships'.

4. Mental Illness

118. As indicated above, a mentally ill person is absolutely incapable of marrying. Any marriage he or she enters into is void as a result of his or her incapacity to act. This is the position regardless of whether the person has been certified in terms of the Mental Health Care Act 17 of 2002.[388]

G. Failure to Comply with Necessary Formalities

119. The Marriage Act 25 of 1961 specifies the formalities that must be complied with before, during and after the wedding. Those requirements and the consequences of non-compliance with them are set out below in this chapter. As a rule,

381. *Stander v. Stander* 1929 AD 349.
382. *Kilian v. Kilian* 1908 EDC 377.
383. *See*, e.g., *Wells v. Dean-Willcocks* 1924 CPD 89; *Joshua v. Joshua* 1961 (1) SA 455 (GW); *B v. B* 1964 (1) SA 717 (T); *D v. D* 1964 (3) SA 598 (E).
384. 1949 (4) SA 123 (W).
385. 1959 (4) SA 658 (GW).
386. *See*, e.g., Erasmus, Van der Merwe & Van Wyk, *Lee and Honoré Family, Things and Succession*, para. 54 n. 2; Heaton & Kruger, *Family Law*, 37; J.E. Scholtens, *Sterility or Impotence?*, 78 S. Afr. Law J. 170 (1961). But contrast P.M.A. Hunt, *Error in the Contract of Marriage*, 80 S. Afr. Law J. 109 (1963).
387. 2000 (2) SA 1 (CC) para. 51.
388. *See* Part I, Ch. 7, §2 above.

failure to comply with the required formalities for a civil marriage renders the marriage void. However, the Marriage Act expressly provides for an exception to this rule if an error, omission or oversight regarding the question whether the parties are taking each other as man and wife, the declaration that a marriage has come into existence between the parties, or the giving of the right hand was committed in good faith or due to a physical disability. In such cases, the marriage is valid.[389] Further, in terms of a decision of a division of the High Court,[390] solemnization of a civil marriage in a garden, instead of in the places prescribed by the Marriage Act, does not render the marriage void.

H. Consequences

120. As is explained in more detail below in this chapter, non-compliance with some of the requirements for the validity of a civil marriage renders the marriage void, while non-compliance with others renders the marriage voidable.

II. Civil Union

A. Engagement

121. The rules regarding engagements preceding civil unions are the same as those relating to engagements preceding civil marriages.

B. Different Sex

122. The parties to a civil union may be of the same or of the opposite sex.[391]

C. Consanguinity and Affinity

123. In terms of the Civil Union Act 17 of 2006, a civil union may only be concluded by prospective civil union partners who would, apart from the fact that they may be of the same sex, not be prohibited from concluding a civil or a customary marriage.[392] Taken literally, this provision means that, regardless of their race, the parties to a civil union may not be within the prohibited degrees of relationship for purposes of concluding a civil or a customary marriage. Such a literal, a-contextual interpretation would lead to illogical and absurd results because, for example, African customary rules would have to be imposed on White, 'Coloured' or Asian people who have never had any connection to an African ethnic group. Thus, where

389. Marriage Act 25 of 1961, s. 30(3).
390. *Ex parte Dow* 1987 (3) SA 829 (D).
391. Civil Union Act 17 of 2006, ss 1 and 8(6).
392. *Ibid.*, s. 8(6).

there are differences between the prohibited degrees of relationship in respect of customary and civil marriages, the rules of customary law should be applied only to people who are subject to customary law.

D. Marriageable Age

124. The Civil Union Act 17 of 2006 precludes minors from entering into a civil union.[393] It is unclear whether a civil union in violation of this rule would be void (as is usually the position if a party lacks capacity to enter into a specific legal transaction) or whether the court would hold that the civil union is voidable (as is the position in respect of civil marriages by unassisted minors).[394]

E. Prior Marriage or Civil Union

125. A person who is a party to an existing civil or customary marriage may not enter into a civil union.[395] Nor may a party to an existing civil union enter into another civil union.[396] Violation of these rules renders the subsequent civil union void.

F. Failure to Consent

126. The principles according to which consent is dealt with in civil marriages apply equally to consent in respect of civil unions.

G. Failure to Comply with Necessary Formalities

127. The formalities that must be complied with before, during and after the civil union ceremony and the consequences of non-compliance with those formalities are governed by the Civil Union Act 17 of 2006. They are set out below in this chapter. No decision has yet been reported on non-compliance with the formalities for a civil union but, using the position in civil marriages as analogy, non-compliance would, as a rule, render the civil union void.

Like the Marriage Act 25 of 1961, the Civil Union Act expressly provides for an exception if an error, omission or oversight regarding the question whether the parties are taking each other as civil union partners, the declaration that a civil union

393. *See* Part I, Ch. 3, §2 above.
394. On the civil marriages of unassisted minors, *see* Part I, Ch. 3, §2 above.
395. Civil Union Act 17 of 2006, s. 8(3).
396. *Ibid.*, s. 8(1).

has come into existence between the parties, or the giving of the right hand was committed in good faith or owing to a physical disability. In such cases, the civil union is valid.[397]

H. Consequences

128. As is the position in respect of civil marriages, non-compliance with some of the requirements for the validity of a civil union renders the union void, while non-compliance with others renders the union voidable. The consequences of nullity and voidability are the same as those that operate in void and voidable civil marriages.

III. Customary Marriage

A. Pre-marital Negotiations

129. A customary marriage is preceded by various negotiations between the prospective spouses and their family groups. The negotiations concern, *inter alia*, the delivery of *lobolo* (bridewealth) for the bride.[398] Furthermore, a token of the agreement to enter into a customary marriage is sometimes given to the bride or her family. The token is often a ring, animals, clothing, household goods or money.[399]

130. Breach of the promise to enter into a customary marriage does not give rise to a claim for damages.[400] The rules regarding the return of any *lobolo* that was delivered in anticipation of the marriage differ between the various African groups.[401]

B. Different Sex

131. As a general rule, the parties to a customary marriage are of the opposite sex. However, in some groups a woman may validly marry another woman, or even more than one woman.[402] The Recognition of Customary Marriages Act 120 of 1998 affords recognition to all customary marriages which were validly concluded in terms of customary law prior to the coming into operation of the Act and which

397. *Ibid.*, s. 11(3).
398. On *lobolo*, *see* further below in this chapter.
399. *See*, e.g., N.J.J. Olivier et al., *Indigenous Law*, in *Law of South Africa* para. 90 (W.A. Joubert, founding ed., J.A. Faris planning ed., LexisNexis 2d ed. 2009).
400. *See*, e.g., R.-M. Jansen, *Family Law*, in *Introduction to Legal Pluralism in South Africa* 48 (C. Rautenbach & J.C. Bekker eds., LexisNexis 4th ed. 2014); Olivier et al., *Indigenous Law*, paras 90, 93–94.
401. On those rules, *see*, e.g., Jansen, *Family Law*, 48; Olivier et al., *Indigenous Law*, paras 91, 93–94.
402. *See*, e.g., B. Oomen, *Traditional Woman-to-Woman Marriages and the Recognition of Customary Marriages Act*, 63 J. Contemp. Roman-Dutch Law 274, 276–277 (2000).

still existed when the Act came into operation on 15 November 2000.[403] Thus, if a particular woman-to-woman customary marriage was valid in terms of the customary marriage law which operated when the Act came into operation, the marriage remains valid. The Act further recognizes any customary marriage which is concluded after the coming into operation of the Act, provided that the marriage is negotiated and entered into or celebrated in accordance with customary law.[404] Therefore, if the customary law of a particular group permits woman-to-woman customary marriages and women conclude such a customary marriage after the coming into operation of the Act, the marriage is valid.

C. Consanguinity and Affinity

132. A customary marriage that is concluded between parties who are within the forbidden degrees of relationship is void. The forbidden degrees of relationship in respect of a customary marriage are determined according to customary law.[405] The prohibited degrees of relationship differ between the various African groups. The KwaZulu Act on the Code of Zulu Law 16 of 1985 and the Natal Code of Zulu Law do not specify which relationships are prohibited, but they list certain family members who are not within the prohibited degrees of relationship for purposes of entering into a customary marriage in terms of Zulu law.[406] Outside KwaZulu-Natal, customary law is uncodified and can be difficult to establish, as is explained above.[407]

133. In the context of the forbidden degrees of relationship, the sororate and levirate customs should also be mentioned. The Recognition of Customary Marriages Act 120 of 1998 does not expressly deal with these customs. Thus, they are probably still permitted.[408] In terms of the sororate custom, a widower takes a 'seed raiser' to produce (more) children for his deceased wife's house. The 'seed raiser' is usually a member of the deceased wife's family – often one of her sisters. The levirate custom allows a deceased husband to be replaced by one of his paternal male relatives. Any child the deceased husband's widow has with this man is deemed to be her deceased husband's child.[409] The sororate and levirate customs are

---

403. Section 2(1). The date of commencement of the Act was proclaimed in Procl. R66 in *G.G.* 21700 of 1 Nov. 2000.
404. Section 2(2) read with s. 3(1).
405. Recognition of Customary Marriages Act 120 of 1998, s. 3(6).
406. KwaZulu Act on the Code of Zulu Law 16 of 1985, s. 37; Natal Code of Zulu Law, s. 37.
407. *See* General Introduction, §3 above. On the relevant rules, *see* e.g., T.W. Bennett, *Human Rights and African Customary Law under the South African Constitution* 207–208 (Cape Town, 1995); Jansen, *Family Law*, 55.
408. *See also* s. 2(2)(b) read with the definition of 'descendant' in s. 1 of the Reform of Customary Law of Succession and Regulation of Related Matters Act 11 of 2009 which recognizes a woman in a sororate customary marriage as a 'descendant' for purposes of intestate inheritance. On such a woman's right to inherit, *see* further Part IV, Ch. 1, §3 below.
409. On the levirate and sororate customs, *see*, e.g., KwaZulu Act on the Code of Zulu Law 16 of 1985, s. 56; Natal Code of Zulu Law, s. 56; Bennett, *Human Rights and African Customary Law*, 127–128; C. Himonga & T. Nhlapo (eds), *African Customary Law in South Africa. Post-Apartheid*

said to be a way in which an existing customary marriage is continued after the death of one of the spouses. Because an existing customary marriage is being continued, the requirements for a valid customary marriage do not again have to be met.[410] Thus, the parties may, conceivably, be within degrees of relationship that are forbidden for purposes of a new customary marriage.

D. Marriageable Age

134. The position as regards the validity of a customary marriage a minor concludes after the coming into operation of the Recognition of Customary Marriages Act 120 of 1998 is the same as that which operates in respect of a minor's civil marriage.[411]

E. Prior Marriage or Civil Union

135. If a person is a party to a civil marriage or a civil union, he or she may not enter into a customary marriage.[412] Nor may a party to a customary marriage enter into a civil marriage or a civil union. Any marriage or civil union concluded in contravention of these rules is void. The law permits only one exception, namely that customary spouses may enter into a civil marriage with each other provided that the husband's other customary marriages are dissolved first.[413]

136. A husband who is a party to a customary marriage may take further customary wives. However, a wife in a customary marriage may not take another husband. In other words, customary law allows polygyny but not polyandry.

The Recognition of Customary Marriages Act 120 of 1998 requires that a husband who wants to take another customary wife draw up a contract that specifies which matrimonial property system will operate in his polygynous customary marriage. He must seek court approval of this contract before he enters into the additional customary marriage.[414] Failure to obtain such a court-approved contract does not affect the validity of the marriage, since the requirement merely pertains to the spouses' matrimonial property system.[415]

---

and Living Law Perspectives 153–154 (Oxford University Press Southern Africa 2014); L.L. Mofokeng, *Legal Pluralism in South Africa: Aspects of African Customary, Muslim and Hindu Family Law* 38–40 (Van Schaik Publishers 2009); E. Curran & E. Bonthuys, *Customary Law and Domestic Violence in Rural South African Communities: Notes and Comments*, 21 S. Afr. J. Hum. Rights 628–629 (2005).

410. Bennett, *Human Rights and African Customary Law*, 198–199.

411. Recognition of Customary Marriages Act 120 of 1998, s. 3(3)(a), (3)(b) and (4)(a) read with s. 25(1) and (4) of the Marriage Act 25 of 1961; Children's Act 38 of 2005, s. 18(3)(c)(i) and (5).

412. Recognition of Customary Marriages Act 120 of 1998, s. 10(4); Civil Union Act 17 of 2006, s. 8(2).

413. Recognition of Customary Marriages Act 120 of 1998, s. 10(1) read with s. 3(2).

414. Section 7(6).

415. *MM v. MN* 2013 (4) SA 415 (CC). *See* further Part III, Ch. 4, §4 below.

F. Failure to Consent

137. The principles according to which it must be determined whether duress, mistake or mental illness affects the validity of a customary marriage are the same as those that apply to civil marriages and civil unions.

In Zulu Law, the bride must publicly declare to the official witness, who is appointed by the tribal chief, that the marriage is taking place of her own free will and with her consent.[416] In other customary systems the parties' consent can be given expressly or tacitly.[417]

If a husband in an existing customary marriage under Tsonga customary law wants to enter into another customary marriage, he must obtain his existing wife's consent, otherwise the subsequent customary marriage is void.[418]

G. Failure to Comply with Necessary Formalities

138. Although some sort of ceremony or rite often takes place to celebrate a customary marriage, the marriage is not solemnized by a marriage officer, and a ceremony or rite is not a prerequisite for the validity of the marriage. However, the bride must be handed over to her husband otherwise the customary marriage is void.[419]

H. Lobolo

139. Although the Recognition of Customary Marriages Act 120 of 1998 does not expressly state that delivery of *lobolo* is a requirement for the validity of a customary marriage, most African groups view *lobolo* as an essential element of a customary marriage and it therefore, generally, remains a requirement for a valid customary marriage.[420] *Lobolo* entails that the bridegroom or the head of his family gives property to the head of the bride's family in consideration of the customary marriage. Traditionally, *lobolo* consisted of livestock, but nowadays it often takes the form of money or household goods or a combination of livestock and other assets.

---

416. Code of Zulu Law 16 of 1985, ss 1, 38(1) and 42; Natal Code of Zulu Law, ss 1, 38(1) and 42.
417. *Ngcongolo v. Parkies* 1953 NAC (S) 103.
418. *MM v. MN* 2013 (4) SA 415 (CC). Although the decision specifically refers to Tsonga law, the court's statements on equality and dignity suggest that the same requirement will apply to other South African systems of customary law that may not require the first wife's consent.
419. *See*, e.g., *Mabena v. Letsoalo* 1998 (2) SA 1068 (T); *Fanti v. Boto* 2008 (5) SA 405 (C); *Ndlovu v. Mokoena* 2009 (5) SA 400 (GNP).
420. *Ibid.*

I. Consequences

140. As is the position in respect of civil marriages and civil unions, non-compliance with some of the requirements for the validity of a customary marriage renders the marriage void, while non-compliance with others renders the marriage voidable. The consequences of nullity and voidability of a customary marriage are the same as those that operate in void and voidable civil marriages and civil unions.

§3. FORMALITIES

141. Because the formalities in respect of a civil marriage, a civil union and a customary marriage differ, they are discussed separately.

I. Civil Marriage

142. The Marriage Act 25 of 1961 prescribes the formalities for a civil marriage. It requires that the marriage be solemnized by a marriage officer.[421] Failure to comply with this requirement results in nullity of the marriage.[422]

All magistrates, special justices of the peace and commissioners are ex officio marriage officers.[423] The Minister of Home Affairs may also appoint other persons, such as officers in the public, diplomatic or consular service, and ministers of religion or persons who hold a responsible position in a religious denomination or organization, as marriage officers.[424] A person who is a marriage officer by virtue of being a minister of religion or occupying a position of responsibility in a religious denomination or organization may refuse to solemnize a marriage that will not be in accordance with the rites, formularies, tenets, doctrine or discipline of his or her religious denomination or organization.[425]

If anyone erroneously, but in good faith, acted as a marriage officer, the Minister of Home Affairs may direct that he or she shall for all purposes be deemed to have been a marriage officer. The Minister may also issue such a directive if both spouses believed in good faith that the marriage officer had been duly appointed. In such event, the marriage is valid if all the other requirements for a valid civil marriage were met.[426]

Anyone who purports to solemnize a civil marriage without having the necessary authority to do so, and an authorized marriage officer who solemnizes a prohibited civil marriage, commits an offence.[427] This prohibition does not apply to a religious ceremony which does not purport to bring about a valid civil marriage.[428] Thus, for

421. Section 11(1).
422. *See*, e.g., *Moola v. Aulsebrook* 1983 (1) SA 687 (N); *Solomons v. Abrams* 1991 (4) SA 437 (W).
423. Section 2(1).
424. Sections 2(2) and 3(1).
425. Section 31.
426. Section 6(1)–(3).
427. Section 11(2).
428. Section 11(3).

example, anyone who is not a marriage officer and who solemnizes a marriage solely in terms of Muslim or Hindu religious rites does not commit an offence.

143. Before a civil marriage is solemnized, the bride and groom must furnish their identity documents or a prescribed affidavit to the marriage officer who is to solemnize the wedding.[429] Failure to comply with this requirement probably does not affect the validity of the marriage.[430]

144. The bride and groom and at least two witnesses must personally be present at the wedding.[431] If this requirement is not met, the marriage is void.[432]

The marriage may be solemnized at any time and on any day of the week.[433] It must be solemnized in a church or other building used for religious services, a public office, or a private dwelling house with open doors unless either of the parties cannot be present at any of these places due to serious or longstanding illness or serious bodily injury.[434] A division of the High Court has held that non-compliance with the requirement regarding the venue of the solemnization does not affect the validity of a civil marriage.[435]

145. The prescribed marriage formula must be used in solemnizing the marriage. The marriage officer must ask each party whether he or she declares that, as far as he or she is aware, there is no lawful impediment to the marriage and whether he or she takes the other party as his or her lawful wife or husband. The solemnization may not proceed unless both parties answer in the affirmative. If either party fails to answer in the affirmative, the marriage is void if the marriage officer nevertheless proceeds with the solemnization. If both parties do answer in the affirmative, the marriage officer instructs them to give each other the right hand, and then declares that the parties have been lawfully married.[436] It is at this moment that the civil marriage legally comes into existence. In the case of an error, omission or oversight with regard to the question put to each of the parties, the declaration that the marriage has been solemnized, or the requirement that the parties give each other the right hand, the marriage is nevertheless valid if the marriage officer and/or the spouses committed the error, oversight or omission in good faith or owing to a physical disability of one or both of the spouses, and the marriage was in every other respect valid and solemnized in accordance with the Marriage Act 25 of 1961.[437]

The blessing of a civil marriage according to religious rites is permitted, but is not a requirement for the validity of the marriage.[438]

---

429. Section 12.
430. Sinclair assisted by Heaton, *The Law of Marriage*, 383.
431. Section 29(4).
432. *Ibid.* The section specifically excludes capacity to marry in the absence of the parties' presence ('[n]o person shall ... be capable of contracting a valid marriage ... ').
433. Section 29(1).
434. Section 29(2).
435. *Ex parte Dow* 1987 (3) SA 829 (D).
436. Section 30(1).
437. Section 30(3).
438. Sections 30(2), 33 and 34.

146. After the solemnization of a civil marriage, the marriage register must be signed and the marriage registered.[439] Non-fulfilment of these requirements does not affect the validity of the marriage.[440]

II. Civil Union

147. The requirements for the solemnization of a civil union are prescribed by the Civil Union Act 17 of 2008. They resemble those that apply to a civil marriage.

A civil union must be solemnized by a marriage officer. As in the case of a civil marriage, failure to comply with the requirement of solemnization by a marriage officer results in nullity. All persons who are ex officio marriage officers in terms of the Marriage Act 25 of 1961 and all officers in the public, diplomatic or consular service who have been designated as marriage officers under the Marriage Act qualify as marriage officers for purposes of the Civil Union Act.[441] Thus, all secular marriage officers may solemnize civil marriages and civil unions, and their appointment as marriage officers for such marriages and unions is regulated by the same rules.

However, the position as regards the appointment of religious marriage officers for purposes of solemnizing civil unions differs from that which applies to civil marriages. A religious denomination or organization that wants to solemnize civil unions must apply to the Minister of Home Affairs for approval to do so.[442] If the Minister grants the approval, a minister of religion or a person holding a responsible position in the approved denomination or organization may apply to be designated as a marriage officer for purposes of solemnizing civil unions.[443] There is thus a dual process for the appointment of religious marriage officers for purposes of the solemnization of civil unions. If the request by the minister or person holding a responsible position is granted, he or she is a marriage officer for purposes of solemnizing civil unions for as long as he or she is a minister or occupies the responsible position.[444]

If any secular marriage officer (a marriage officer other than a religious marriage officer) informs the Minister of Home Affairs in writing that he or she objects on the ground of conscience, religion and belief to solemnizing same-sex civil unions, he or she will not be compelled to solemnize such civil unions.[445] This dispensation for secular marriage officers is set to disappear when the Civil Union Amendment Bill 11 of 2018 becomes law.

---

439. Section 29A. *See* further Part I, Ch. 2, §1 above on registration of the marriage.
440. *Ex parte Efron* 1940 CPD 199; *Ex parte Michaelson* 1941 (2) PH B57 (W).
441. Section 2(1) and (2) of the Marriage Act 25 of 1961 read with the definition of 'marriage officer' in s. 1 of the Civil Union Act 17 of 2006.
442. Section 5(1).
443. Section 5(4).
444. *Ibid.*
445. Section 6.

Anyone who purports to solemnize a civil union without having the necessary authority to do so and an authorized marriage officer who solemnizes a prohibited civil union commit an offence.[446]

148. As is the case in respect of a civil marriage, each of the prospective parties to a civil union must furnish the marriage officer with his or her identity document or the prescribed affidavit. If either party fails to do so, the marriage officer may not solemnize the civil union.[447] If the civil union is nevertheless solemnized, it is probably valid.

149. The parties to the civil union and at least two witnesses must be present at the civil union ceremony.[448] If this requirement is not met, the civil union is void.[449]

The civil union may be solemnized at any time and on any day of the week. It must be solemnized and registered in a public office or private dwelling, with open doors, or on the premises of such an office or dwelling, unless either of the parties cannot be present at any of these places due to serious or longstanding illness or serious bodily injury.[450]

150. Prior to the solemnization of the civil union, the marriage officer must ask the parties whether their civil union should be known as a marriage or a civil partnership.[451] The prospective civil union partners must further individually and in writing declare their willingness to enter into a civil union with one another and must sign the prescribed document signifying their willingness in the presence of two witnesses.[452] The marriage officer must solemnize the civil union using the term the parties chose, namely, 'marriage' or 'civil partnership'.[453]

151. In solemnizing the civil union, the marriage officer uses a formula that is slightly different from the one that is used for the solemnization of a civil marriage. The marriage officer asks each of the parties separately whether he or she declares that as far as he or she is aware there is no lawful impediment to the proposed marriage or civil partnership and that he or she takes the other party as his or her lawful spouse or civil partner. The solemnization may not proceed unless both parties answer in the affirmative. If either party fails to answer in the affirmative, the civil union is void if the marriage officer nevertheless proceeds with the solemnization. If both parties answer in the affirmative, the marriage officer instructs them to give

446. Section 14(1).
447. Section 7.
448. Section 10(2) and (3).
449. Section 10(3) expressly refers to competence to enter into a civil union ('[n]o person is competent to enter into a civil union through any other person acting as his or her representative').
450. Section 10(1) and (2).
451. Section 11(1).
452. Section 12(1).
453. Section 11(1).

each other the right hand, and then declares that they have been lawfully joined in a marriage or civil partnership.[454] It is at this moment that the civil union legally comes into existence.

In the case of an error, omission or oversight with regard to the question, declaration or giving of the right hand or if physical disability renders compliance with these provisions impossible, the civil union is nevertheless valid if it was in every other respect solemnized in accordance with the provisions of the Civil Union Act 17 of 2006.[455]

152. After the solemnization of the civil union, the marriage officer and two witnesses must sign the civil union register and the civil union must be registered.[456] Using the analogy of the civil marriage, it is submitted that non-fulfilment of these requirements does not affect the validity of the civil union.

III. Customary Marriage

153. As indicated above in this chapter, a customary marriage does not need to be solemnized by way of a prescribed ceremony. Once a customary marriage has come into existence it must be registered with the Department of Home Affairs, but non-registration does not affect the validity of the marriage.[457]

§4. Effects

154. The consequences of a civil marriage and a civil union correspond.[458] Therefore, the consequences of these two types of legal relationships are discussed together. A separate subheading is used for customary marriages because some of the personal effects of these marriages are governed by different rules to those that apply to civil marriages and civil unions.

I. Taking of Name

A. Civil Marriage and Civil Union

155. Spouses are not obliged to have a common family name but they may use the husband's surname as their common surname, if they like. Section 26(1) of the Births and Deaths Registration Act 51 of 1992 empowers wives to retain their maiden name, assume their husband's surname or create a double-barrel surname consisting of both spouses' surnames. Because the consequences of a civil union

454. Section 11(2).
455. Section 11(3).
456. Section 12(2) and (6).
457. Recognition of Customary Marriages Act 120 of 1998, s. 4.
458. Civil Union Act 17 of 2006, s. 13.

and a civil marriage correspond, the female civil union partner in a heterosexual civil union has the same options concerning her surname that a wife has in a civil marriage.

It seems that the provisions in the Civil Union Act 17 of 2006 which dictate that any reference to 'husband' or 'wife' in any Act other than the Marriage Act 25 of 1961 or the Recognition of Customary Marriages Act 120 of 1998 includes 'civil union partner' and that the legal consequences of a civil marriage apply 'with such changes as may be required by the context' to a civil union,[459] entail that both parties to a same-sex civil union may invoke the dispensation regarding surname.

156. A husband in a civil marriage needs the consent of the Director-General of Home Affairs to assume his wife's surname or to add it to his own.[460] This rule also applies to heterosexual civil unions. The rule is probably unconstitutional on the ground that it constitutes unjustifiable unfair sex and gender discrimination and unjustifiably violates inequality before the law and equal protection and benefit of the law.[461]

B. Customary Marriage

157. As in a civil marriage, a wife in a customary marriage may retain her maiden name, assume her husband's surname or create a double-barrel surname consisting of both spouses' surnames, while a husband may not assume his wife's surname or add it to his own without the consent of the Director-General of Home Affairs.[462] In a polygynous customary marriage all wives have the option of retaining their maiden name, assuming their husband's surname or creating a double-barrel surname.

II. The Duty of Consortium

A. Civil Marriage and Civil Union

158. A civil marriage and a civil union result in *consortium omnis vitae* between the spouses or civil union partners. *Consortium omnis vitae* includes various aspects of the common life of spouses or civil union partners, such as the duty to cohabit; to give each other companionship, comfort, love, affection and moral support; to have sexual intercourse; to care for and look after each other; and to support each other financially.[463] In the past, the husband in a civil marriage, being the head of

459. *Ibid.*, s. 13(1) and 13(2)(b).
460. Births and Deaths Registration Act 51 of 1992, s. 26(1).
461. The right to freedom from unfair discrimination and the right to equality before the law and equal protection and benefit of the law are contained in s. 9 of the Constitution. Section 36 of the Constitution contains the justification/limitation clause.
462. Births and Deaths Registration Act 51 of 1992, s. 26(1).
463. *See*, e.g., *Grobbelaar v. Havenga* 1964 (3) SA 522 (N); *Peter v. Minister of Law and Order* 1990 (4) SA 6 (E).

the family, had the decisive say in all matters concerning the common life of the spouses. He had the power to decide where the spouses were to live, what standard of living they were to adopt, where his wife could go, who she could associate with, what she could wear, whether she could take up paid employment, and so forth. A husband no longer has marital power over the person of his wife.[464] Now, she may independently decide what she wants to wear, who she wants to associate with, whether she wants to take up paid employment, and so forth, and the spouses are supposed to take decisions on their place of abode and standard of living together. The same applies to civil union partners.[465]

159. One of the most important elements of consortium is the right and duty to live together. During the subsistence of their marriage or civil union, both parties have the right to live in the common home, irrespective of the matrimonial property system that operates in the marriage or civil union and irrespective of who owns or rents the home. Thus, neither party may eject the other without providing him or her with suitable alternative accommodation or obtaining a court order authorizing ejectment.[466] A court that is approached for an order of ejectment takes all the circumstances of the case into account. The issues of whose fault it is that the parties' relationship has broken down and the interests of the children who live in the home play an important role.[467]

If, in the absence of a court order, one party threatens the other with ejectment, the threatened party can apply for an interdict to prohibit the ejectment. If one of them changes the locks and denies the other access to the home, the party who has been excluded from the home can seek a *mandament van spolie*, in terms of which the other party is ordered to provide him or her with access to the home.[468]

The right of a spouse or civil union partner to live in the common home does not operate as against third parties.[469] Thus, the right is of no use if, for example, the common home is repossessed or if the spouses or civil union partners are evicted due to non-payment of rent.

160. The duty of support and the right to occupy the common home can be enforced as between the spouses and, in the case of violation of consortium through acts of domestic violence, the victim can obtain a protection order in terms of the Domestic Violence Act 116 of 1998 against the perpetrator, sue him or her in delict and/or have him or her criminally charged.[470] For the rest, consortium is protected in an indirect manner by the threat of divorce. Spouses or civil union partners cannot enforce the right to enjoy each other's companionship, affection, and so on by

464. Matrimonial Property Act 88 of 1984, s. 11.
465. Civil Union Act 17 of 2006, s. 13.
466. *See*, e.g., *Badenhorst v. Badenhorst* 1964 (2) SA 676 (T); *Owen v. Owen* 1968 (1) SA 480 (E).
467. *See*, e.g., *Badenhorst v. Badenhorst* 1964 (2) SA 676 (T); *Du Plessis v. Du Plessis* 1976 (1) SA 284 (W); *Lovell v. Lovell* 1980 (4) SA 90 (T).
468. *See*, e.g., *Rosenbuch v. Rosenbuch* 1975 (1) SA 181 (W); *Oglodzinski v. Oglodzinski* 1976 (4) SA 273 (D); *Du Randt v. Du Randt* 1995 (1) SA 401 (O); *Mans v. Mans (Formerly Richens, Born Maddock)* [1999] 3 All SA 506 (C).
469. *Dique v. Van der Merwe* 2001 (2) SA 1006 (T).
470. Domestic Violence Act 116 of 1998, s. 7(1)(c) and (d).

means of a court order for restitution of conjugal rights.[471] Nor can one spouse or civil union partner obtain an interdict to prevent the other from infringing consortium, for example, by committing adultery.[472] If adultery or another type of infringement of consortium has already occurred, the wronged spouse or civil union partner cannot sue the offending spouse or civil union partner delictually (in tort) for the infringement.[473]

However, in terms of the common law, a third party who interferes with the consortium can be held liable in delict. In the past, a third party who had sexual intercourse with one of the spouses or civil union partners could be sued for adultery.[474] The action on the ground of adultery has been abolished,[475] and the actions on the ground of enticement and harbouring will probably go the same route. However, as the law stands, the latter actions can still be invoked by the wronged spouse or civil union partner. The action on the ground of enticement can be invoked if a third party intentionally persuades one of the spouses or civil union partners to leave the other,[476] while the action on the ground of harbouring can be invoked if a third party provides accommodation to a person with the intention of thereby breaking up the person's marriage or civil union and depriving his or her spouse or civil union partner of consortium.

B. Customary Marriage

161. A customary marriage also gives rise to *consortium omnis vitae*.[477] Like the consortium between spouses in a civil marriage and between civil union partners, the consortium between customary spouses encompasses the duty to cohabit; to provide each other with companionship, comfort, love, affection and moral support; to have sexual intercourse; to care for and look after each other; and to support each other financially. In a customary marriage, the spouses' life in common in a consortium also entails special rights, functions and obligations within the spouses' family groups, because a customary marriage binds together, not only the spouses, but also their families.[478]

The Recognition of Customary Marriages Act 120 of 1998 abolished the status of a customary wife as a perpetual minor and her husband's guardianship over her,[479] and granted her 'on the basis of equality with her husband … full status and capacity'.[480] Thus, as in a civil marriage or civil union, each wife in a customary

471. Divorce Act 70 of 1979, s. 14.
472. *See*, e.g., *Bruwer v. Joubert* 1966 (3) SA 334 (A); *Wassenaar v. Jameson* 1969 (2) SA 349 (W); *Osman v. Osman* 1983 (2) SA 706 (D).
473. *Ex parte AB* 1910 TPD 1332; *Currie v. Currie* 1942 NPD 362; *Asinovsky v. Asinovsky* 1943 CPD 131; *Lamprecht v. Lamprecht* 1948 (4) SA 416 (N).
474. *Bester v. Calitz* 1982 (3) SA 864 (O); *Wiese v. Moolman* 2009 (3) SA 122 (T).
475. *DE v. RH* 2015 (9) BCLR 1003 (CC).
476. *Woodiwiss v. Woodiwiss* 1958 (3) SA 609 (D).
477. Himonga, *Marriage*, 255.
478. *See*, e.g., Himonga & Nhlapo (eds), *African Customary Law in South Africa*, 92; Mofokeng, *Legal Pluralism in South Africa*, 37; Olivier et al., *Indigenous Law*, para. 119.
479. Sections 6 and 9 and the Schedule of the Act.
480. Section 6.

marriage may independently take decisions concerning her apparel, friends, associates, employment, and so forth, and the spouses are supposed to take decisions on their place of abode and standard of living together.

162. In the past, in a polygynous customary marriage, consortium operated within a system of ranking of wives which afforded a superior status to some wives as against each other, although the husband was not allowed to favour any wife.[481] Generally speaking, each marriage resulted in the establishment of a separate house with a specific rank. The rank of the house and the wife was determined by the ranking system adopted by the particular African group.[482]

Although the ranking of houses still operates today, it is unclear whether the differentiation in respect of the status of the wives in the various houses is still valid. The Recognition of Customary Marriages Act 120 of 1998 abolished the status of a customary wife as a perpetual minor and her husband's guardianship over her[483] and granted her 'on the basis of equality with her husband ... full status and capacity ... in addition to any rights that she may have at customary law'.[484] Because the Act confers the same status on a wife and a husband regardless of the number of wives a husband has, it is arguable that there can be no distinction between the ranks of the various wives as they all have the same status as their husband. Another view is that, although the Act creates equality between husband and wife, the phrase 'in addition to any rights that she may have at customary law' implies that the relative status of each wife in a polygynous customary marriage remains unaltered so that, for example, the chief wife retains the customary rights associated with her superior status.[485]

163. As in a civil marriage and a civil union, the duty of support (including the duty to be provided with accommodation) can be enforced as between the spouses, and a victim of domestic violence can obtain a protection order in terms of the Domestic Violence Act 116 of 1998, sue the perpetrator in delict and/or have the perpetrator criminally charged.[486]

If a third party interferes with the spousal consortium in a customary marriage, he or she can be held liable in delict just as he or she can be held liable if he or she

481. *See*, e.g., Olivier et al., *Indigenous Law*, para. 123.
482. On the establishment and ranking of houses, *see*, e.g., Himonga & Nhlapo (eds), *African Customary Law in South Africa*, 129; Mofokeng, *Legal Pluralism in South Africa*, 40–41; Olivier et al., *Indigenous Law*, paras 41–44.
483. Sections 6 and 9 and the Schedule of the Act.
484. Section 6.
485. L.P. Vorster, *Traditional Leadership in South Africa, Marriages and Succession*, 20 Obiter 90 (1999); J.G. Horn & A.M. Janse van Rensburg, *Practical Implications of the Recognition of Customary Marriages*, 27 J Juridical Sci. 61 (2002).
486. Domestic Violence Act 116 of 1998, s. 7(1)(c) and (d).

interferes with consortium in a civil marriage or a civil union. In the case of adultery, the liability can arise only in terms of customary law, because the common-law action on the ground of adultery has been abolished.[487] In some communities harbouring also constitutes a common-law as well as a customary delict.[488]

III. Sexual Intercourse

A. *Civil Marriage and Civil Union*

164. As was pointed out above in this chapter, sexual intercourse forms part of the duty of consortium. However, neither of the spouses or civil union partners may compel the other to engage in any form of sexual conduct. If he or she does so, he or she can be charged with rape, compelled rape, sexual assault, compelled sexual assault or compelled self-sexual assault.[489]

B. *Customary Marriage*

165. The position in respect of sexual intercourse in a customary marriage corresponds to that which applies in civil marriages and civil unions.

IV. Confidences in a Marriage or Civil Union

A. *Civil Marriage and Civil Union*

166. As a general rule, a spouse or civil union partner cannot be compelled to disclose communications his or her spouse or civil union partner made to him or her during the marriage or civil union. This privilege operates in civil and criminal proceedings.[490] However, in certain exceptional cases, a spouse or civil union partner may be compelled to testify against his or her spouse or civil union partner in a criminal trial. The exceptional cases include those where the accused is charged with a crime against the person of the spouse or civil union partner or a child of either of them, contravention of section 31(1) of the Maintenance Act 99 of 1998, bigamy, incest, abduction, certain offences in terms of the Criminal Law (Sexual Offences and Related Matters) Amendment Act 32 of 2007, and perjury.[491]

---

487. On the customary delict of adultery, *see*, e.g., Himonga & Nhlapo (eds), *African Customary Law in South Africa*, 200–203; N.J.J. Olivier, *Law of Delict*, in *Introduction to Legal Pluralism in South Africa* 163–165 (C. Rautenbach & J.C. Bekker eds., LexisNexis 4th ed. 2014); Olivier et al., *Indigenous Law*, paras 157–171.
488. On the customary delict of harbouring, *see*, e.g., Olivier et al., *Indigenous Law*, para. 188.
489. Criminal Law (Sexual Offences and Related Matters) Amendment Act 32 of 2007, s. 56(1).
490. Civil Proceedings Evidence Act 25 of 1965, ss 10(1) and 12; Criminal Procedure Act 51 of 1977, ss 195(1), 198(1) and 199.
491. Criminal Procedure Act 51 of 1977, s. 195(1).

167. Communications between spouses or civil union partners about a third party do not amount to publication for the purposes of an action for defamation.[492]

B. Customary Marriage

168. The position in respect of confidences in a customary marriage is the same as that which applies in civil marriages and civil unions.[493]

V. Contract

A. Civil Marriage and Civil Union

169. In the past, a wife in a civil marriage was subject to her husband's marital power unless the spouses concluded an antenuptial contract in which they excluded the marital power. As the marital power has been abolished, husbands and wives in civil marriages now have equal powers to enter into contracts with third parties and with each other. The same applies to civil union partners.[494]

If the marriage or civil union is out of community of property, the spouses or civil union partners are free to enter into contracts with each other or with third parties as they like. However, if the accrual system operates in a marriage or civil union out of community of property, this system may be terminated by the court on application by one of the spouses or civil union partners if the other's conduct (such as his or her contractual dealings) seriously prejudices or will probably seriously prejudice the applicant's right to share in the accrual at the dissolution of the marriage or civil union.[495] If the marriage or civil partnership is in community of property, the capacity to act of both of the spouses or civil union partners is limited because they require each other's consent to enter into certain transactions with third parties[496] and because they cannot enter into contracts with each other since they are co-owners of all their assets and co-debtors in respect of all their debts.[497]

B. Customary Marriage

170. In the past, a customary wife was a perpetual minor and was subject to her husband's guardianship.[498] The Recognition of Customary Marriages Act 120 of

492. *Whittington v. Bowles* 1934 EDL 142.
493. Civil Proceedings Evidence Act 25 of 1965, ss 10(1), 10A and 12; Criminal Procedure Act 51 of 1977, ss 195(1), 195(2), 198(1) and 199.
494. Civil Union Act 17 of 2006, s. 13(1).
495. Matrimonial Property Act 88 of 1984, s. 8. On this remedy, *see* further Part III, Ch. 4, §2 below.
496. Matrimonial Property Act 88 of 1984, s. 15.
497. *See* further Part III, Ch. 3, §2 below.
498. Black Administration Act 38 of 1927, s. 11(3); Code of Zulu Law 16 of 1985, s. 27; Natal Code of Zulu Law, s. 27.

1998 abolished these rules.[499] It further conferred 'full status and capacity, including the capacity to acquire assets and to dispose of them, to enter into contracts and to litigate' on her, but she enjoys these powers 'subject to the matrimonial property system governing the marriage'.[500] The latter qualification means that if the customary marriage is in community of property, the powers of the spouses are limited just like those of the parties to a civil marriage or civil union in community of property. In a polygynous customary marriage concluded before the coming into operation of the Recognition of Customary Marriages Act in which customary law governs the proprietary consequences, the powers of the spouses are also restricted: the husband and the wife of each house jointly exercise the rights relating to its house property and must do so in the best interests of the particular family unit, while the husband and all his wives jointly exercise the rights relating to all family property and must do so in the best interests of the whole family constituted by all the houses.[501] If a customary marriage is out of community of property, the spouses are free to enter into contracts with each other or with third parties as they like. However, if the accrual system operates in the marriage, the system may be terminated by the court on application by one of the spouses if the other's conduct seriously prejudices or will probably seriously prejudice the applicant's right to share in the accrual at the dissolution of the marriage.[502]

VI. Delict (Tort)

A. *Civil Marriage and Civil Union*

171. In terms of South African common law, spouses who are married in community of property cannot sue each other in delict.[503] Nowadays, a civil marriage or civil union does not exclude delictual actions between spouses or civil union partners even if the marriage or civil union is in community of property. However, if community of property operates in the marriage or civil union, one spouse or civil union partner may sue the other only for compensation in respect of bodily injuries caused either wholly or partly by the other spouse or civil union partner.[504] If the marriage or civil union is out of community of property, the spouses or civil union partners may sue each other for compensation arising from any delict.[505]

---

499. Recognition of Customary Marriages Act 120 of 1998, ss 6 and 9 and the Schedule.
500. *Ibid.*, s. 6.
501. *Ramuhovhi v. President of the Republic of South Africa* 2018 (2) SA 1 (CC).
502. Matrimonial Property Act 88 of 1984, s. 8. On this remedy, *see* further Part III, Ch. 4, §2 below.
503. *Tomlin v. London and Lancashire Insurance Co Ltd* 1962 (2) SA 30 (D).
504. Matrimonial Property Act 88 of 1984, s. 18 read with *Van der Merwe v. Road Accident Fund (Women's Legal Centre Trust as Amicus Curiae)* 2006 (4) SA 230 (CC).
505. In *C v. C* 1958 (3) SA 574 (SR) it was held that spouses who are married out of community of property cannot institute the *actio iniuriarum* against each other, but it is doubted whether this decision will be followed.

B. Customary Marriage

172. The same rules that apply to civil marriages and civil unions apply to customary marriages.

VII. Criminal Law

A. Civil Marriage and Civil Union

173. Spouses and civil union partners can be convicted of crimes they commit against each other. They can also be convicted of crimes they commit together or conspire to commit together.

B. Customary Marriage

174. The same rules that apply to civil marriages and civil unions apply to customary marriages.

VIII. Duty to Maintain (Duty of Support)

A. Civil Marriage and Civil Union

175. Spouses and civil union partners are obliged to maintain each other.[506] Maintenance includes the provision of accommodation, clothing, food, medical services and so forth.[507] The scope of the duty of support is determined by the social status of the parties, their means and income, and the cost of living.[508]

The duty can be enforced by means of legal action in the Maintenance Court in terms of the Maintenance Act 99 of 1998. The Act provides for civil and criminal sanctions for failure to comply with a maintenance order.[509] Because any order of the Maintenance Court has the effect of an order in a civil action,[510] enforcement of a maintenance order may also take place without resorting to the mechanisms provided for in the Maintenance Act. Thus, for example, the defaulter can be charged with contempt of court and committed to prison if found guilty.[511]

176. The duty of support terminates on dissolution of the marriage or civil union. If the spouses or civil union partners are not divorced but no longer share a

506. *See*, e.g., *Oberholzer v. Oberholzer* 1947 (3) SA 294 (O); *Reyneke v. Reyneke* 1990 (3) SA 927 (E).
507. *Ex parte Hugo* 1960 (1) SA 773 (T).
508. *See*, e.g., *Oberholzer v. Oberholzer* 1947 (3) SA 294 (O); *Young v. Coleman* 1956 (4) SA 213 (D).
509. Sections 16, 26–31 and 40.
510. Section 24(1).
511. *Bannatyne v. Bannatyne (Commission for Gender Equality as Amicus Curiae)* 2003 (2) SA 363 (CC).

joint household, the issue of who is at fault in respect of the breakdown of the relationship determines whether the duty continues. For example, if a husband has to support his wife and the separation is due to his fault (e.g., because his misconduct drove his wife away), his duty to maintain her continues.[512] The same applies if the parties agree to live apart.[513]

If the marriage or civil union is terminated by death, the surviving spouse or civil union partner may have a maintenance claim against the estate of his or her deceased spouse or civil union partner in terms of the Maintenance of Surviving Spouses Act 27 of 1990, and if the marriage or civil union is terminated by divorce, post-divorce maintenance can be sought in terms of the Divorce Act 70 of 1979.[514]

B. Customary Marriage

177. The same rules that apply to civil marriages and civil unions apply to customary marriages.

IX. Succession

A. Civil Marriage and Civil Union

178. When persons enter into a civil marriage or a civil union they acquire a right of intestate succession against one another.[515]

B. Customary Marriage

179. Like a civil marriage and a civil union, a customary marriage gives rise to rights of intestate succession.[516]

§5. Void and Voidable Marriages and Civil Unions

180. Unlike many foreign jurisdictions, South African law still distinguishes between void and voidable marriages. Although the Civil Union Act 17 of 2006 does not specify this, the same distinction probably applies to civil unions.

As the nature and consequences of a void and a voidable marriage are the same regardless of whether the marriage was a civil or a customary one, no distinction is

512. *Excell v. Douglas* 1924 CPD 472; *Pickles v. Pickles* 1947 (3) SA 175 (W); *Oelofse v. Grundling* 1952 (1) SA 338 (C).
513. *Excell v. Douglas* 1924 CPD 472.
514. On maintenance from a deceased spouse's estate, *see* Part III, Ch. 1, §5 below and on post-divorce maintenance, *see* Part II, Ch. 2, §3 below.
515. *See* Part IV, Ch. 1, §3 below.
516. *Ibid.*

made between these two types of marriages under this heading. Here, the term 'marriage' covers a civil marriage as well as a customary marriage, unless the context indicates otherwise.

181. A void marriage or civil union has no legal consequences. However, insofar as the status of children born of a void marriage or civil union is concerned, the nullity of the parental union is usually legally irrelevant. In most instances the children's parents would have lived together when the children were born and/or the children's father would have consented to being identified as their father or would have paid damages in terms of customary law and would have contributed to their upbringing and maintenance, with the result that both parents would have full parental responsibilities and rights, just as they would have had full parental responsibilities and rights if their marriage or civil union had been valid.[517]

As nullity of a void marriage or civil union is absolute, either of the parties or an interested third party may raise it. The nullity may be raised even after the parties' death. Although it is not essential to obtain a declaration that the marriage or civil union is void, such a declaratory order is usually sought for the purposes of legal certainty.[518]

182. The rule that a void marriage or civil union has none of the consequences of a valid marriage or civil union is subject to a common-law exception that applies to civil marriages. The exception is that a void civil marriage which amounts to a putative marriage has some of the consequences of a valid civil marriage for as long as at least one of the parties is bona fide. The consequences are that children who were born of the putative civil marriage are born of married parents[519] and that the patrimonial consequences of the putative marriage are determined by what benefits the bona fide party.[520]

A void civil marriage is a putative marriage, if one or both of the spouses entered into the marriage while being bona fide unaware that there was a defect which rendered the marriage void. The first requirement for the existence of a putative civil marriage is obviously that at least one of the spouses must have been unaware of the defect which rendered the marriage void. At common law, it was further required that the marriage must have been duly solemnized. It is unclear whether the latter requirement still forms part of South African law.[521]

183. A voidable marriage or civil union is one in which grounds are present, either when the marriage is entered into or before that time, on the basis of which the court can be requested to set the marriage aside. A voidable marriage or civil union remains in force and has all the normal legal consequences of a valid civil or

517. Children's Act 38 of 2005, ss 19(1), 20 and 21(1).
518. *Ex parte Oxton* 1948 (1) SA 1011 (C).
519. *See*, e.g., *Prinsloo v. Prinsloo* 1958 (3) SA 759 (T); *M v. M* 1962 (2) SA 114 (GW); *Ngubane v. Ngubane* 1983 (2) SA 770 (T).
520. *M v. M* 1962 (2) SA 114 (GW).
521. Due solemnization was required in, *inter alia*, *Ngubane v. Ngubane* 1983 (2) SA 770 (T) and *Solomons v. Abrams* 1991 (4) SA 437 (W), while it was not required in, *inter alia*, *Ramayee v. Vandiyar* 1977 (3) SA 77 (D) and *Moola v. Aulsebrook* 1983 (1) SA 687 (N).

customary marriage until it is set aside by a court order. Accordingly, a court order setting the marriage or civil union aside is essential. If a voidable marriage is not set aside, it remains in force until it is terminated by death or divorce.

When a voidable marriage is set aside, the effect of the decree of annulment is retroactive. Thus, all the consequences of the marriage are extinguished as from the date on which the marriage was solemnized. The status of the parties changes and they are in the same position as if they never married each other. However, the interests of third parties are protected because the validity of transactions concluded with third parties prior to the annulment of the marriage is not affected by the annulment. The status of a child who was conceived or born of a voidable marriage or civil union is also not affected. On the annulment of his or her parents' voidable marriage the child is treated like a child of divorcing parents.[522]

184. The grounds on which a civil marriage, a civil union and a customary marriage are void are considered above in this chapter. Briefly, the grounds on which a civil marriage is void are the following:

(1) The parties are of the same sex.
(2) The parties are related to each other within the prohibited degrees of relationship.
(3) One of the parties is below the age of puberty.
(4) A girl below 15 years of age or a male minor enters into a civil marriage without the written consent of the Minister of Home Affairs.
(5) One of the parties is already a party to a civil marriage, customary marriage or civil union with someone else.
(6) One of the parties is mentally ill at the time of entering into the marriage.
(7) The marriage is solemnized by someone who is not a competent marriage officer.
(8) No witnesses are present at the wedding ceremony.
(9) A party fails to answer in the affirmative when asked whether he or she takes the other party as his or her lawful spouse.

The grounds on which a civil union is void are the following:

(1) The parties are related to each other within the prohibited degrees of relationship.
(2) One of the parties is a minor.
(3) One of the parties is already a party to a civil marriage, customary marriage or civil union with someone else.
(4) One of the parties is mentally ill at the time of entering into the civil union.
(5) The civil union is solemnized by someone who is not a competent marriage officer.
(6) No witnesses are present at the civil union ceremony.

522. Children's Act 38 of 2005, s. 39.

(7) A party fails to answer in the affirmative when asked whether he or she takes the other party as his or her lawful spouse or civil union partner.

The grounds on which a customary marriage is void are the following:

(1) The parties are of the same sex, unless they belong to an ethnic group that permits woman-to-woman customary marriages.
(2) The parties are related to each other within the prohibited degrees of relationship.
(3) A girl below 15 years of age or a male minor enters into a customary marriage without the written consent of the Minister of Home Affairs.
(4) One of the parties is already a party to a civil marriage or a civil union with someone else or the wife is a party to an existing customary marriage.
(5) One of the parties is mentally ill at the time of entering into the marriage.
(6) The bride is not handed over to her husband.
(7) *Lobolo* is not paid or no agreement is reached about the payment of *lobolo*.
(8) Additional grounds, such as impotence, apply within certain ethnic groups.[523]

185. The grounds on which a civil marriage, a civil union and a customary marriage are voidable are considered above in this chapter. The grounds on which a civil or a customary marriage is voidable are the following:

(1) A minor marries without the consent of his or her parents or guardian or of the presiding officer of the Children's Court.
(2) The consent of the parties is obtained by duress, material mistake, undue influence or a serious misrepresentation, such as one relating to *stuprum*, impotence or sterility.

By analogy to the rules regarding civil marriages (and bearing in mind that a minor may not conclude a civil union), the only ground on which a civil union is voidable is that the consent of the parties was obtained by duress, material mistake, undue influence or a serious misrepresentation.

523. Impotence is one of the grounds of nullity that applies in Zulu law: KwaZulu Act on the Code of Zulu Law 16 of 1985, s. 77; Natal Code of Zulu Law, s. 77.

Chapter 2. Divorce

§1. Grounds

186. Irretrievable breakdown is a ground for divorce in civil marriages, civil unions and customary marriages.[524] In customary marriages it is the only ground for divorce. In civil marriages and civil unions two additional grounds for divorce are recognized, namely incurable mental illness and continuous unconsciousness.[525]

187. A marriage or civil union has broken down irretrievably if the relationship between the parties has reached such a state of disintegration that there is no reasonable prospect of the restoration of a normal marriage or civil union between them.[526] To determine whether the relationship has reached such a state of disintegration, the courts consider whether the consortium between the parties has been terminated or seriously disrupted.[527]

If one party alleges that the relationship has broken down irretrievably, while the other party denies this, or if the court is for any reason convinced that the parties might reconcile, it may postpone the proceedings to afford the parties an opportunity to attempt reconciliation.[528] If one of the parties is adamant that the marriage or civil union has broken down irretrievably, the possibility of reconciliation is very remote. In such event, the court does not usually order a postponement. Thus, in reality, a divorce can be obtained once one party has taken the unilateral decision to terminate the marriage or civil union.

188. A divorce will be granted on the ground of incurable mental illness if the plaintiff proves that the defendant has been admitted to an institution in terms of the Mental Health Care Act 17 of 2002 or is being detained as a state patient or mentally ill convicted prisoner at an institution; has not been unconditionally discharged for a continuous period of at least two years immediately prior to the institution of the divorce action; and there is no reasonable prospect that the defendant will be cured of his or her mental illness.[529] A divorce will be granted on the ground of continuous unconsciousness, if the plaintiff proves that the defendant is in a state of continuous unconsciousness caused by a physical disorder; the unconsciousness has lasted for a continuous period of at least six months immediately prior to the institution of the divorce action; and there is no reasonable prospect that the defendant will regain consciousness.[530]

---

524. Divorce Act 70 of 1979, ss 3(a) and 4; Civil Union Act 17 of 2006, s. 13; Recognition of Customary Marriages Act 120 of 1998, s. 8(1).
525. Divorce Act 70 of 1979, ss 3(b) and 5; Civil Union Act 17 of 2006, s. 13.
526. Divorce Act 70 of 1979, s. 4(1); Recognition of Customary Marriages Act 120 of 1998, s. 8(2).
527. *See*, e.g., *Schwartz v. Schwartz* 1984 (4) SA 467 (A); *Naidoo v. Naidoo* 1985 (1) SA 366 (T).
528. Divorce Act 70 of 1979, s. 4(3).
529. *Ibid.*, s. 5(1). The evidence of at least two psychiatrists is required to prove that there is no reasonable prospect of the defendant being cured.
530. Divorce Act 70 of 1979, s. 5(2). The evidence of at least two doctors is required to prove that there is no reasonable prospect that the defendant will regain consciousness.

If the defendant is mentally ill or unconscious, the plaintiff is not restricted to instituting a divorce action on the ground of the defendant's mental illness or unconsciousness. The plaintiff may seek a decree of divorce on the ground of the irretrievable breakdown of the marriage or civil union.[531]

If the plaintiff proceeds on the ground of the mental illness or unconsciousness of the defendant, the defendant enjoys special protection. Firstly, the court may appoint a legal practitioner to represent the defendant and it may order the plaintiff to bear the costs of the legal representation. Secondly, the court may require the plaintiff to furnish security for any patrimonial benefits to which the defendant may be entitled as a result of the divorce. Finally, the court may not order forfeiture of the patrimonial benefits of the marriage or civil union against the defendant.[532]

189. Generally speaking, a court has no discretion whether or not to grant a divorce if one of the grounds for divorce has been proven.[533] However, in the case of certain religious marriages that also qualify as civil marriages the court has the power to withhold a divorce order or to make any other order it considers just if, despite the granting of a divorce order, the parties or either of them will not be free to remarry unless the marriage is also dissolved in accordance with the prescripts of their religion or the religion of either of them, or unless a religious barrier to remarriage is removed. This power is subject to the proviso that the court may not withhold a divorce order, if the spouse within whose power it is to have the religious marriage dissolved or the religious barrier removed has taken all the necessary steps in this regard.[534]

The purpose of this provision is to relieve the desperate position in which, for example, a Jewish woman finds herself if her husband refuses to grant her a *get* (Jewish religious divorce).[535] In Jewish religious law, only the husband has the power to grant a *get*. As her secular divorce is meaningless under Jewish religious law, a wife who has not been granted a *get* cannot remarry in terms of this system of religious law.

§2. Procedure

190. The High Court or Regional Court may issue a divorce decree if the parties or either of them is domiciled in the court's area of jurisdiction on the date on which the action is instituted, or if either of them is ordinarily resident in the court's area of jurisdiction on that date and has been ordinarily resident in South Africa for at least one year immediately prior to that date.[536] These courts also have the power to

531. *Dickinson v. Dickinson* 1981 (3) SA 856 (W); *Krige v. Smit* 1981 (4) SA 409 (C); *Smit v. Smit* 1982 (4) SA 34 (O); *Ott v. Raubenheimer* 1985 (2) SA 851 (O).
532. Divorce Act 70 of 1979, ss. 5(3), 5(4) and 9(2). Forfeiture of benefits is discussed below in this chapter.
533. *Levy v. Levy* 1991 (3) SA 614 (A).
534. Divorce Act 70 of 1979, s. 5A.
535. *Raik v. Raik* 1993 (2) SA 617 (W).
536. Divorce Act 70 of 1979, s. 2(1) read with the definition of 'court' in s. 1(1); Recognition of Customary Marriages Act 120 of 1998, s. 8(1) read with the definition of 'court' in s. 1.

make an interim order regarding maintenance, a contribution towards the costs of the pending action, interim care of a child, and interim contact with a child while the divorce is pending.[537]

191. A divorce is instituted by way of action proceedings.[538] One of the spouses or civil union partners must personally institute the action; a curator does not have legal standing to institute divorce proceedings on behalf of a spouse or civil union partner.[539]

A divorce action deals with the divorce decree and all ancillary matters, such as maintenance; division of the parties' assets; guardianship and care of, and contact with children who were born of the marriage or civil union; and costs.

192. Although the adversarial (accusatorial) procedure remains the main procedural system in Family Law matters, there is growing support from legislative and judicial quarters for alternative dispute resolution, especially mediation.[540] The first official step in the direction of mediation in Family Law was contained in the Mediation in Certain Divorce Matters Act 24 of 1987. The title of the Act creates the impression that the Act is at least partly concerned with the provision of mediation services in divorce matters. Although the approach the Family Advocate adopts in terms of the Act is more conciliatory and closer to alternative dispute resolution than the traditional adversarial approach, it does not amount to true mediation. However, in respect of dissolution of customary marriages, the Recognition of Customary Marriages Act 120 of 1998 expressly recognizes the 'role, recognised in customary law, of any person, including any traditional leader, in the mediation, in accordance with customary law, of any dispute or matter arising prior to the dissolution of a customary marriage by a court'.[541] Thus, customary alternative dispute resolution may be used for, for example, mediating domestic disputes while a divorce is pending in a customary marriage, arriving at a settlement agreement, or getting the couple to attempt reconciliation.

§3. EFFECTS

193. Broadly speaking, the consequences of the dissolution of a civil marriage, a civil union and a customary marriage are the same. A major difference is that the court has the power to make a redistribution order in any customary marriage, while

537. Rule 43 of the Uniform Rules of Court; Rule 58 of the Rules of the Magistrates' Courts; *Baadjies v. Matubela* 2002 (3) SA 427 (W); *FN v. MN* [2014] JOL 32412 (GJ).
538. *Ex parte Inkley and Inkley* 1995 (3) SA 528 (C).
539. *Ex parte AB* 1910 TPD 1332; *Spangenberg v. De Waal* [2008] 1 All SA 162 (T).
540. *See*, apart from the Mediation in Certain Divorce Matters Act 24 of 1987, also s. 10(1A) of the Maintenance Act 99 of 1998; s. 5(1A) of the Domestic Violence Act 116 of 1998; s 8(3) of the Recognition of Customary Marriages Act 1998; ss 6(4), 21–22, 33–34, 49, 69–71 of the Children's Act 38 of 2005; *Van den Berg v. Le Roux* [2003] 3 All SA 599 (NC); *Townsend-Turner v. Morrow* 2004 (2) SA 32 (C); *MB v. NB* 2010 (3) SA 220 (GSJ); *FS v. JJ* 2011 (3) SA 126 (SCA).
541. Section 8(5).

the court's power to make a redistribution order is very limited in civil marriages and non-existent in civil unions, as is explained below in this chapter.

I. Settlement Agreements

194. Most divorcing parties regulate the division of their property, post-divorce maintenance, and parental responsibilities and rights in a settlement agreement. The court has the power to include the terms of the parties' settlement agreement in the divorce order.[542]

If the terms of the settlement agreement are not made an order of court, the agreement is merely a contract and cannot be enforced in the same way as an order of court. This means, *inter alia*, that if one of the parties fails to comply with the provisions of the deed of settlement, his or her property cannot immediately be attached in execution of the terms of the agreement and the party cannot be imprisoned for contempt of court.

195. A settlement agreement, or a term in a settlement agreement, which has been made an order of court can be amended, rescinded or suspended by the parties by mutual consent.[543] If either party refuses to agree to the amendment, rescission or suspension, the High Court or Regional Court may be approached if the dispute relates to parental responsibilities and rights and/or maintenance.[544] If the dispute relates only to maintenance, the Maintenance Court may be approached in terms of the Maintenance Act 99 of 1998. Being a contract, the settlement agreement may also be set aside on any of the grounds which operate in Contract Law.

If the terms of the deed of settlement have not been made an order of court, the parties can agree to vary or rescind the agreement. If either of them refuses to agree to the variation or rescission, the original agreement operates as it stands, unless the normal rules of Contract Law allow variation or rescission.

II. Property Division

A. General

196. The effect of divorce on the division of the property of the spouses or civil union partners depends on whether the marriage or civil union is in or out of community of property and, if it is out of community of property, whether the accrual system applies to it.[545] The division of the parties' assets further depends on whether or not the court orders forfeiture of patrimonial benefits and, in certain civil and all customary marriages, whether the court orders redistribution of assets.

542. Divorce Act 70 of 1979, s. 7(1); Civil Union Act 17 of 2006, s. 13; Recognition of Customary Marriages Act 120 of 1998, s. 8(4)(a); *Eke v. Parsons* 2016 (3) SA 37 (CC).
543. But *see DS v. RM* 2015 (3) SA 424 (WCC).
544. Divorce Act 70 of 1979, s. 8(1).
545. *See* Part III, Chs 3 and 4 below on the various matrimonial property systems.

197. If the court does not grant an order for forfeiture of benefits, the divorce order in respect of a marriage or civil union in community of property automatically operates as an order for division of the joint estate. If the spouses or civil union partners cannot reach agreement on how the estate is to be divided, the court may either order the division it deems just or appoint a liquidator (receiver) to divide the estate.[546] If a liquidator is not appointed, the division of the joint estate must be jointly administered by the spouses and neither spouse may alienate any of the assets of the former joint estate without the other's consent.[547]

B. Pension (Superannuation)

198. The pension interests of spouses or civil union partners are deemed to be part of their assets on divorce unless they married or entered into a civil union subject to complete separation of property on or after 1 November 1984.[548] The inclusion of the pension interest operates automatically. Thus, the court that makes the divorce order need not specifically declare that the pension interest is part of the joint estate of spouses who are married in community of property.[549] Logically, a spouse's pension interest should also automatically be included in his or her separate estate if he or she is married out of community of property, without the court having specifically to refer to the pension interest.[550]

If a spouse or civil union partner is a member of a pension fund other than a retirement annuity fund, his or her pension interest is the benefit to which he or she would have been entitled had he or she terminated his or her membership of the fund on the date of the divorce by resigning from his or her employment. If he or she is a member of a retirement annuity fund, his or her pension interest is equal to all the contributions he or she made to the fund up to the date of the divorce plus annual simple interest on those contributions calculated at the rate the Minister of Justice and Correctional Services prescribes in terms of the Prescribed Rate of Interest Act 55 of 1975.[551]

If the employment of the spouse or civil union partner ceased before the divorce and the spouse or civil union partner transferred his or her accrued pension benefit to an approved pension preservation fund or a provident preservation fund, his or her pension interest is equal to the benefits to which he or she would have been

546. *See*, e.g., *Dhanwanthi v. Shanduth* 1961 (2) SA 692 (N); *Van Onselen v. Kgengwenyane* 1997 (2) SA 423 (B).
547. *Gugu v. Zongwana* [2014] 1 All SA 203 (ECM).
548. Divorce Act 70 of 1979, s. 7(7)(a) and (c); Civil Union Act 17 of 2006, s. 13; Recognition of Customary Marriages Act 120 of 1998, s. 8(4)(a); Government Employees Pension Law, 1996, Procl. 21 in *G.G.* 17135 of 19 Apr. 1996, s. 1; Post and Telecommunication-related Matters Act 44 of 1958, ss 1, 10B and 10F.
549. *GN v. JN* 2017 (1) SA 342 (SCA).
550. *See also* Heaton & Kruger, *Family Law*, 134; J. Heaton *The Proprietary Consequences of Divorce* in *The Law of Divorce and Dissolution of Life Partnerships in South Africa* 74, 77 (J. Heaton ed., Juta 2014); J. Heaton *The Law of Persons and Family Law*, Annu. Surv. S. Afr. Law 424 (2015).
551. Definition of 'pension interest' in s. 1 of the Divorce Act 70 of 1979. The total amount of annual simple interest may not exceed the fund return on the portion of the pension interest to which the non-member spouse or civil union partner is entitled: Pension Funds Act 24 of 1956, s. 37D(5).

entitled in terms of the rules of the preservation fund had his or her membership of the fund terminated on the date of the divorce.[552]

A pension interest differs from a pension benefit. Only a pension interest is deemed to be an asset on divorce. A pension interest is an interest which has not yet accrued by the time of the divorce. In contradistinction, a pension benefit relates to a benefit which has already accrued. Because an accrued benefit became part of the estate of the member of the fund (or the joint estate if the marriage or civil union is in community of property) when it accrued to the member spouse or civil union partner it is unnecessary to deem the benefit to be part of his or her assets on divorce.[553] A resignation benefit which accrues to a spouse or civil union partner prior to divorce and which is not transferred to an approved preservation fund is a pension benefit – not a pension interest – even if the spouse or civil union partner elects to defer payment of the amount until his or her retirement age.[554]

If someone is getting divorced for a second or a further time, the amount of the pension interest that is deemed to be part of his or her estate for purposes of the latest divorce is reduced by any amount of the pension interest that was awarded to his or her former spouse(s) or civil union partner(s) in the first or further divorce.[555]

199. The court that grants a decree of divorce may order the fund of which a spouse or civil union partner is a member to pay any part of the member's pension interest to which his or her spouse or civil union partner is entitled, to the non-member spouse or civil union partner when the pension accrues to the member.[556] As a rule, the non-member's portion of the pension interest is deemed to accrue to the member on the date of the divorce.[557] However, if the pension fund falls under the Pension Funds Act 24 of 1956 and the divorce occurred before 13 September 2007, the portion is deemed to have accrued on 13 September 2007.[558] If the spouse is a member of the Government Employees Pension Fund and the divorce occurred before 14 December 2011, the portion is deemed to have accrued on 14 December 2011.[559] If the spouse is a member of the Post Office Retirement Fund and the divorce occurred before 27 January 2014, the portion is deemed to have accrued on 27 January 2014.[560]

552. Pension Funds Act 24 of 1956, s. 37D(6).
553. *De Kock v. Jacobson* 1999 (4) SA 346 (W); *Government Employees Pension Fund v. Naidoo* 2006 (6) SA 304 (SCA); *Elesang v. PPC Lime Ltd* 2007 (6) SA 328 (NC).
554. *Eskom Pension and Provident Fund v. Krugel* 2012 (6) SA 143 (SCA).
555. Divorce Act 70 of 1979, s. 7(7)(b); *see also* s. 37D(1)(d)(i) of the Pension Funds Act 24 of 1956; ss 21(1) and 24A(1) of the Government Employees Pension Law, 1996, Procl. 21 in *G.G.* 17135 of 19 Apr. 1996; ss 10B(1) and 10F(1) of the Post and Telecommunication-related Matters Act 44 of 1958.
556. Divorce Act 70 of 1979, s. 7(8)(a)(i).
557. Pension Funds Act 24 of 1956, s. 37D(4)(a); Government Employees Pension Law, 1996, Procl. 21 in *G.G.* 17135 of 19 Apr. 1996, s. 24A(2)(a); Post and Telecommunication-related Matters Act 44 of 1958, s. 10F(2)(a).
558. Pension Funds Act 24 of 1956, s. 37D(4)(d).
559. Government Employees Pension Law, 1996, Procl. 21 in *G.G.* 17135 of 19 Apr. 1996, s. 24A(2)(j).
560. Post and Telecommunication-related Matters Act 44 of 1958, s. 10F(2)(j). The different dates apply because the spouses of members of the Government Employees Pension Fund and the Post Office Retirement Fund initially could not share in the members' pension interests on divorce since the particular pension funds do not fall under the Pension Funds Act 24 of 1956. The differentiation

C. Forfeiture

200. The court that makes a divorce order has the power to make an order for total or partial forfeiture of the patrimonial benefits of the marriage or civil union if it is satisfied that, in the absence of the order, one party will be unduly benefited in relation to the other.[561] The party who seeks forfeiture must establish the nature and extent of the benefit that is to be forfeited.[562]

In deciding whether or not to order forfeiture, the court must take the duration of the marriage or civil union, the circumstances which led to the breakdown of the marriage or civil union, and any substantial misconduct on the part of either party into account.[563] Because the court is not empowered to consider 'any other factor' in making its decision, only these three factors may be considered. Consequently, factors such as fairness or the reason why particular assets were acquired are irrelevant, and forfeiture may not be used as an adjustive mechanism which allows deviation from the normal consequences of the matrimonial property system on the ground that the court considers deviation fair and just.[564]

201. Since a spouse or civil union partner does not benefit from an asset he or she brought into the marriage or civil union, he or she cannot be ordered to forfeit such asset.[565] Thus, in a marriage or civil union in community of property, the only benefits which can be forfeited are the assets brought into the marriage or civil union by, or acquired as a result of, the efforts of the other spouse or civil union partner.[566] These benefits include the right to occupy premises in terms of a tenancy, residential permit or statutory lease which was conferred on the spouse or civil union partner against whom the forfeiture order operates but in respect of which the other spouse or civil union partner paid the rent.[567]

Benefits which can be forfeited in the case of a marriage or civil union out of community of property include the right to share in the accrual of the estate of the other spouse or civil union partner,[568] benefits by virtue of a succession clause, and settlements conferred in the parties' antenuptial contract.[569] Whether benefits

---

between spouses of members of the various pension funds was successfully challenged on constitutional grounds: *Wiese v. Government Employees Pension Fund* 2012 (6) BCLR 599 (CC); *Ngewu v. Post Office Retirement Fund* 2013 (4) BCLR 421 (CC); *Minister of Communications v. Ngewu* 2014 (3) BCLR 364 (CC). As a result, the Government Employees Pension Law, 1996, Procl. 21 in *G.G.* 17135 of 19 Apr. 1996 and the Post and Telecommunication-related Matters Act were appropriately amended.

561. Divorce Act 70 of 1979, s. 9(1); Civil Union Act 17 of 2006, s. 13; Recognition of Customary Marriages Act 120 of 1998, s. 8(4)(a).
562. *Engelbrecht v. Engelbrecht* 1989 (1) SA 597 (C); *JW v. SW* 2011 (1) SA 545 (GNP).
563. Divorce Act 70 of 1979, s. 9(1).
564. *Wijker v. Wijker* 1993 (4) SA 720 (A); *Botha v. Botha* 2006 (4) SA 144 (SCA); *Tlou v. Ralebipi* [2016] 4 All SA 251 (GP).
565. *JW v. SW* 2011 (1) SA 545 (GNP).
566. *See*, e.g., *Ex parte De Beer* 1952 (3) SA 288 (T); *Steenberg v. Steenberg* 1963 (4) SA 870 (C); *Leeb v. Leeb* [1999] 2 All SA 588 (N).
567. *Persad v. Persad* 1989 (4) SA 685 (D); *Toho v. Diepmeadow City Council* 1993 (2) SA 679 (W); *Moremi v. Moremi* 2000 (1) SA 936 (W).
568. Matrimonial Property Act 88 of 1984, s. 9 read with s. 13 of the Civil Union Act 17 of 2006.
569. *Watt v. Watt* 1984 (2) SA 455 (W).

acquired during the subsistence of the marriage or civil union without having been conferred in the parties' antenuptial contract can be forfeited, is unclear. In some cases it has been held that patrimonial benefits are fixed by the terms of the parties' antenuptial contract and that donations which fall outside the terms of the antenuptial contract cannot be forfeited.[570] In other cases it has been held that benefits obtained during the subsistence of the marriage or civil union can also be forfeited.[571]

Only those benefits which exist at the time of the divorce can be forfeited. Thus, for example, if a spouse or civil union partner is ordered to forfeit a retirement annuity, it is only the value of the annuity as a pension interest at the date of the divorce that is forfeited. The forfeiture order does not entitle the party in whose favour the order operates to claim growth that accumulates after the divorce.[572]

D. Redistribution of Assets

202. As the law regarding redistribution of assets on divorce differs markedly depending on whether a civil marriage, a civil union or a customary marriage is being dissolved, the position in respect of each type of relationship is discussed under a separate heading.

1. Civil Marriages

203. One of the reasons for the introduction of the accrual system was that it was considered unfair that a spouse who married out of community of property could not share in the assets the other spouse acquired during the subsistence of the marriage. Because the accrual system was not imposed retroactively, the legislature inserted section 7(3)–(6) into the Divorce Act 70 of 1979 to assist spouses who married out of community of property prior to 1 November 1984 (the date on which the Matrimonial Property Act 88 of 1984, which introduced the accrual system, came into operation).

Section 7(3)–(6) empowers the court that makes a divorce order to order transfer of the assets or part of the assets of one spouse to the other if this is just. The court's power is subject to a number of restrictions, as is indicated below. Furthermore, the power was originally available only in respect of civil marriages of White, 'Coloured' and Asian persons, but when the Marriage and Matrimonial Property Law Amendment Act 3 of 1988 came into operation on 2 December 1988 it was extended to the dissolution of civil marriages of Black persons by divorce.[573]

570. *See*, e.g., *Dawson v. Dawson* (1892) 9 SC 446; *Kilroe v. Kilroe* 1928 WLD 112; *Watt v. Watt* 1984 (2) SA 455 (W).
571. *See*, e.g., *Kohn v. Kohn* 1914 WLD 9; *Martin v. Martin* 1925 EDL 264.
572. *Old Mutual Life Assurance Co (SA) Ltd v. Swemmer* 2004 (5) SA 373 (SCA).
573. The Constitutional Court also extended the power to the dissolution of marriages concluded without an antenuptial contract in terms of the now-repealed Transkei Marriage Act 21 of 1978: *Holomisa v. Holomisa* 2019 (2) BCLR 247 (CC).

204. The court's power to order transfer of assets is restricted to civil marriages which are subject to complete separation of property and were concluded prior to 1 November 1984, in the case of White, 'Coloured' or Asian persons, or prior to 2 December 1988, in the case of Black persons. It is further required that the parties must not have entered into a settlement agreement; that the spouse who seeks redistribution must have contributed directly or indirectly to the maintenance or increase of the other spouse's estate during the subsistence of the marriage; and that the contribution renders redistribution equitable and just.[574]

205. The required contribution can be made by the rendering of services, saving of expenses which would otherwise have been incurred, or in any other manner.[575] Performing domestic and childcare duties qualifies as a contribution.[576]

Whether a contribution has been made is a purely factual finding. The applicant must prove the contribution, but a monetary value need not be placed on it.[577] Nor need the applicant prove a causal link between his or her contribution and every asset in the respondent's estate.[578]

Once it has been proven that a contribution was made, the determination whether it would be equitable and just to order transfer of assets is left to the discretion of the court.[579]

206. In addition to the applicant's contribution, the court must take the following factors into consideration when it decides whether or not to order transfer and what the extent of the transfer should be:[580]

(1) The existing means and obligations of the parties, including any obligation which a husband who entered into a civil marriage while being married to another woman at customary law may have to his customary wife.[581]
(2) Any donation one spouse made to the other during the subsistence of the marriage, or which is still owed in terms of the spouses' antenuptial contract.
(3) Any order for forfeiture of patrimonial benefits.

---

574. Divorce Act 70 of 1979, s. 7(3) and (4).
575. *Ibid.*, s. 7(4).
576. *See*, e.g., *Beaumont v. Beaumont* 1987 (1) SA 967 (A); *Katz v. Katz* 1989 (3) SA 1 (A); *Bezuidenhout v. Bezuidenhout* 2005 (2) SA 187 (SCA); *Buttner v. Buttner* 2006 (3) SA 23 (SCA).
577. *Katz v. Katz* 1989 (3) SA 1 (A); *Raik v. Raik* 1993 (2) SA 617 (W); *Buttner v. Buttner* 2006 (3) SA 23 (SCA).
578. *Bezuidenhout v. Bezuidenhout* 2005 (2) SA 187 (SCA).
579. *Beaumont v. Beaumont* 1987 (1) SA 967 (A).
580. Divorce Act 70 of 1979, s. 7(5).
581. The latter obligation exists only in a civil marriage that was concluded before the Marriage and Matrimonial Property Law Amendment Act 3 of 1988 came into operation. Prior to the commencement of this Act, a man could enter into a civil marriage while being married to another woman in terms of customary law. The civil marriage did not affect the proprietary rights of the wife in the customary marriage: Black Administration Act 38 of 1927, s. 22(7). The latter section has since been repealed: Repeal of the Black Administration Act and Amendment of Certain Laws Act 28 of 2005, s. 1(4). However, the essence of s. 22(7) of the Black Administration Act has been re-cast in s. 7(1) of the Reform of Customary Law of Succession and Regulation of Related Matters Act 11 of 2009.

(4) Any other factor which, in the opinion of the court, should be taken into account.

One of the 'other' factors the courts have taken into account is misconduct, provided that there is 'conspicuous disparity' between the spouses' misconduct.[582] If both parties are blameworthy, misconduct is not taken into account unless there is an imbalance in the parties' misconduct that makes it inequitable to ignore their respective degrees of fault.[583] If only one party was at fault, his or her misconduct may be taken into account, especially if it was gross and prolonged.[584] A conservative approach has to be adopted to taking misconduct into account,[585] and the significance of misconduct should be assessed in view of prevailing social mores and attitudes.[586]

The court further takes the interrelationship between property division and post-divorce maintenance into account in order to determine how justice can best be achieved. If circumstances permit, the court applies the clean-break principle by making only an order for transfer of assets and no maintenance order.[587] In practice, the clean-break principle is increasingly being applied in our law – sometimes without proper consideration being given to whether it causes injustice and results in substantive gender inequality.

Other factors the courts have taken into account include exchange-rate variations between the date of valuation of the spouses' foreign properties and the date of the court order; a material unforeseen deviation from the value the spouses agreed upon in respect of certain assets; the need for finality in litigation; the need not to jeopardize the financial survival of the businesses which constitute a large part of the wealth of one of the spouses; the fiscal implications of compelling a spouse to sell particular assets in order to be able to pay an amount to his or her spouse; and the implications of selling property which serve as security for credit facilities granted to one of the spouses.[588]

207. All the assets which fall into a spouse's estate can be taken into account for purposes of ordering transfer of assets, including assets a spouse inherited or received as donations during the subsistence of the marriage.[589] The capitalized value of an interest in a retirement annuity from which a monthly income is derived can also be taken into account,[590] but it seems that the capitalized value of a living

582. *Beaumont v. Beaumont* 1987 (1) SA 967 (A) 994I; *see also Kritzinger v. Kritzinger* 1989 (1) SA 67 (A); *Kretschmer v. Kretschmer* 1989 (1) SA 566 (W); *Archer v. Archer* 1989 (2) SA 885 (E).
583. *Buttner v. Buttner* 2006 (3) SA 23 (SCA).
584. *Beaumont v. Beaumont* 1987 (1) SA 967 (A); *Archer v. Archer* 1989 (2) SA 885 (E); *Buttner v. Buttner* 2006 (3) SA 23 (SCA); *CC v. MVC* 2014 (2) SA 430 (GJ).
585. *See*, e.g., *Beaumont v. Beaumont* 1987 (1) SA 967 (A); *Buttner v. Buttner* 2006 (3) SA 23 (SCA); *RP v. PP* 2016 (4) SA 226 (KZP).
586. *RP v. PP* 2016 (4) SA 226 (KZP).
587. *Beaumont v. Beaumont* 1987 (1) SA 967 (A).
588. *Bezuidenhout v. Bezuidenhout* 2005 (2) SA 187 (SCA); *Kirkland v. Kirkland* 2006 (6) SA 144 (C).
589. *Van Zummeren v. Van Zummeren* [1997] 1 All SA 91 (E); *Jordaan v. Jordaan* 2001 (3) SA 288 (C); *Buttner v. Buttner* 2006 (3) SA 23 (SCA); *Kirkland v. Kirkland* 2006 (6) SA 144 (C).
590. *Kirkland v. Kirkland* 2006 (6) SA 144 (C).

annuity from which a monthly income is derived cannot.[591] The assets of an *inter vivos* discretionary trust that was created during the subsistence of the marriage may be taken into account if it is proved that one spouse transferred personal assets to the trust and dealt with them as if they were trust assets 'with the fraudulent or dishonest purpose' to avoid properly accounting for the value of his or her estate and 'thereby [to] evade payment of what was due to' the other spouse.[592] However, something fortuitous such as trust benefits which have not yet vested in a spouse may not be taken into account;[593] nor may a loan a spouse made to his or her child and which he or she does not intend ever recovering.[594]

The applicant need not have made a contribution to specific assets for those assets to be taken into account. The mere fact that the applicant made a contribution to the respondent's estate is sufficient.[595]

As far as this is practicable, it is the value of the spouses' estates at the date of the divorce that must be considered.[596] If using the date of the order is not practicable, the appropriate date must be determined 'with due consideration to the relevant facts of the matter and the course of its litigation, and not at litis contestatio'.[597]

208. When the judicial discretion to transfer assets was introduced into our law, some divisions of the High Court adopted the guideline that one-third of the total value of the spouses' assets should be allocated to the spouse who owns fewer assets.[598] This approach was in line with the starting point which operated in English law at that stage. This starting point, and all others, was rejected by the Supreme Court of Appeal, which held that the court should start 'with a clean slate' and then fill in 'the void by looking at all the relevant facts and working through all the relevant considerations, and finally exercising a discretion as to what would be just, completely unfettered by any starting point'.[599] However, in practice, the one-third/two-thirds division continued to be applied. Early this century the High Court in Cape Town held that equality should be the yardstick.[600] The Supreme Court of

591. In *ST v. CT* 2018 (5) SA 479 (SCA), the Supreme Court of Appeal held that the capitalized value of a living annuity is not an asset in a spouse's estate and can, accordingly, not be taken into account for purposes of calculating the accrual. Logically, the same should hold true in respect of taking the capitalized value into account for purposes of redistribution of assets.

592. *REM v. VM* 2017 (3) SA 371 (SCA) para. 20. *See also Badenhorst v. Badenhorst* 2006 (2) SA 255 (SCA) where it was held that the value of trust assets may be taken into account to determine the value of the estate of one of the spouses if the trust is merely the alter ego of the particular spouse. There must be evidence that the spouse controlled the trust and, but for the trust, would have acquired and owned the assets in his or her own name. Control must be de facto and not necessarily *de iure*. To determine whether a party has such control, the terms of the trust deed and the evidence of how the affairs of the trust were conducted during the marriage must be considered.

593. *Beira v. Beira* 1990 (3) SA 802 (W).

594. *Kirkland v. Kirkland* 2006 (6) SA 144 (C).

595. *Van Zummeren v. Van Zummeren* [1997] 1 All SA 91 (E); *Jordaan v. Jordaan* 2001 (3) SA 288 (C).

596. *Katz v. Katz* 1989 (3) SA 1 (A).

597. *RP v. PP* 2016 (4) SA 226 (KZP); the quoted phrase appears in para. 59.

598. *Beaumont v. Beaumont* 1985 (4) SA 171 (W); *Van Gysen v. Van Gysen* 1986 (1) SA 56 (C); *MacGregor v. MacGregor* 1986 (3) SA 644 (C).

599. *Beaumont v. Beaumont* 1987 (1) SA 967 (A) 998F–G.

600. *Childs v. Childs* 2003 (3) SA 138 (C); *Kirkland v. Kirkland* 2006 (6) SA 144 (C).

Appeal quickly rejected equal sharing as a starting point and reiterated that the court must start with a clean slate and not use guidelines or starting points.[601]

209. The court has a very wide discretion regarding the form of the transfer it orders.[602] It is not bound to order transfer of a specific asset or specific assets to the successful applicant. It may order that a sum of money be transferred in lieu of asset(s).[603]

Regardless of whether the court orders transfer of assets or a sum of money in lieu of assets, it may impose such conditions as it deems just for the satisfaction of its order. These conditions may include the furnishing of security, payment of interest, or payment by means of instalments.[604]

2. Civil Unions

210. Civil unions have only been permitted since 30 November 2006.[605] Because section 7(3) of the Divorce Act 70 of 1979 permits redistribution of assets only if the parties married prior to 1 November 1984 or 2 December 1988, redistribution is not available in any civil union.

3. Customary Marriages

211. In terms of the Recognition of Customary Marriages Act 120 of 1998, the court has the power to redistribute assets whenever it dissolves a customary marriage by divorce.[606] This is the position regardless of when the customary marriage was concluded and regardless of the matrimonial property system that operates in it.

In the case of dissolution of a polygynous customary marriage, the court must take all relevant factors, including a postnuptial alteration of the spouses' matrimonial property system, into consideration.[607] If the husband entered into another customary marriage after the coming into operation of the Recognition of Customary Marriages Act, the court must also take the court-approved antenuptial contract regarding the matrimonial property system of the polygynous marriage into account.[608]

601. *Bezuidenhout v. Bezuidenhout* 2005 (2) SA 187 (SCA).
602. *Beaumont v. Beaumont* 1987 (1) SA 967 (A); *Childs v. Childs* 2003 (3) SA 138 (C).
603. *Archer v. Archer* 1989 (2) SA 885 (E); *Bezuidenhout v. Bezuidenhout* 2005 (2) SA 187 (SCA).
604. Divorce Act 70 of 1979, s. 7(6).
605. Civil Union Act 17 of 2006, s. 16.
606. Section 8(4)(a) and (b) read with *Gumede v. President of the Republic of South Africa* 2009 (3) SA 152 (CC).
607. Postnuptial alteration of the matrimonial property system that operates in a customary marriage is governed by s. 7(4) and (5) of the Recognition of Customary Marriages Act 120 of 1998.
608. On such contract, *see* Part III, Ch. 4, §4 below.

212. Affording all spouses in customary marriages the remedy of seeking redistribution while limiting it to only a few spouses in civil marriages and completely denying it to civil union partners unjustifiably limits the constitutional rights to equality and dignity and is therefore unconstitutional.[609]

III. *Lobolo*

213. Customary marriages are accompanied by the payment of *lobolo.*[610] Sometimes *lobolo* is even paid in respect of a civil marriage between Black persons. *Lobolo* is not part of the spouses' matrimonial property. It is given to the head of the bride's family in consideration of the marriage and is regulated by the contract between the bridegroom and the head of the bride's family. For this reason, the *lobolo* contract is not automatically terminated by the spouses' divorce. Nor is the *lobolo* divided between the spouses on divorce.[611]

IV. Post-Divorce Maintenance

214. The duty of support between spouses or civil union partners comes to an end when their marriage or civil union is terminated. However, as indicated above in this chapter, one spouse or civil union partner may incur a duty to pay post-divorce maintenance to the other if the parties agree on payment of such maintenance in a settlement agreement. If they are unable to reach agreement, the party who seeks post-divorce maintenance may ask the court to make a maintenance order in his or her favour.[612] In such event, the court may make any maintenance order it finds just, taking into account the factors that are listed in section 7(2) of the Divorce Act 70 of 1979. The court considers each case on its merits in light of all its facts and circumstances.[613] However, it will not make a maintenance order unless the person who is seeking post-divorce maintenance proves that he or she needs it.[614]

The factors which the court must consider are the following:

(1) The parties' existing or prospective means.
(2) The parties' respective earning capacities.
(3) The financial needs and obligations of the parties.
(4) The age of each party.

---

609. *See also SB v. RB* [2015] 2 All SA 232 (ECLD, George). *See* further Barratt (ed.), *Law of Persons and the Family*, 359; Heaton & Kruger, *Family Law*, 142–143; Heaton *The Proprietary Consequences of Divorce*, 107.

610. *See* Part I, Ch. 1, §2 above.

611. On the rules regarding the return of *lobolo, see*, e.g., Jansen, *Family Law*, 114; Mofokeng, *Legal Pluralism in South Africa*, 94.

612. Divorce Act 70 of 1979, s. 7(2); Civil Union Act 17 of 2006, s. 13; Recognition of Customary Marriages Act 120 of 1998, s. 8(4)(a).

613. *See*, e.g., *Swart v. Swart* 1980 (4) SA 364 (O); *Grasso v. Grasso* 1987 (1) SA 48 (C); *Beaumont v. Beaumont* 1987 (1) SA 967 (A).

614. *EH v. SH* 2012 (4) SA 164 (SCA).

(5) The duration of the marriage or civil union.
(6) The standard of living the parties enjoyed during the marriage or civil union.
(7) The conduct of each party insofar as it may be relevant to the breakdown of the marriage or civil union. In particular, gross misconduct is considered.[615]
(8) Any order for transfer of assets by one party to the other.
(9) Any other factor which, in the court's opinion, should be taken into account.

In the case of a customary marriage, the court must also take into account any provision or arrangement that has been made in accordance with customary law, such as payment of *lobolo* and *isondlo* (delivery of an animal by a father to the person who raised his child).[616]

Some of the 'other' factors the courts have taken into account in respect of post-divorce maintenance are a party's post-divorce child-care responsibilities; the best interests of the parties' children; the inflation rate; the frankness with which each party conveyed his or her financial position and needs; and the patriarchal nature of the parties' marriage.[617]

The mere fact that the person who is seeking maintenance is living with another person in a life partnership does not disentitle him or her to post-divorce maintenance. However, if he or she is being fully maintained by his or her life partner, he or she does not need maintenance from his or her former spouse. For this reason, post-divorce maintenance will not be awarded.[618]

215. The courts no longer favour the view that if one of the parties is wealthy, the other party need not drop his or her standard of living or enter the labour market after the divorce.[619] Further, in keeping with international trends, South African courts have moved away from making permanent maintenance awards towards applying the clean-break principle. Spouses and civil union partners who are in paid employment are increasingly denied maintenance, because they are assumed to be able to meet their own maintenance needs even if they have a much lower earning capacity than their spouse or civil union partner. Employable spouses and civil union partners who are not engaged in paid employment at all and those who are engaged in only limited paid employment are expected to take up or to increase their participation in such employment after divorce, and are granted rehabilitative maintenance only.[620] Unfortunately, the clean-break principle is all too frequently applied in a way that ignores or underplays the long-term consequences of domestic and child-care responsibilities and career sacrifices, with the result that gender inequality is reinforced by the courts' reluctance to make awards for permanent maintenance or for long periods of rehabilitative maintenance.

---

615. *Beaumont v. Beaumont* 1987 (1) SA 967 (A); *Buttner v. Buttner* 2006 (3) SA 23 (SCA).
616. Recognition of Customary Marriages Act 120 of 1998, s. 8(4)(e).
617. *See*, e.g., *Vedovato v. Vedovato* 1980 (1) SA 772 (T); *Grasso v. Grasso* 1987 (1) SA 48 (C); *Buttner v. Buttner* 2006 (3) SA 23 (SCA); *Kooverjee v. Kooverjee* 2006 (6) SA 127 (C).
618. *EH v. SH* 2012 (4) SA 164 (SCA).
619. *Botha v. Botha* 2009 (3) SA 89 (W).
620. *See*, e.g., *V v. V* 1998 (4) SA 169 (C); *Joubert v. Joubert* [2004] 1 All SA 426 (C); *Pillay v. Pillay* 2004 (4) SA 81 (SE); *Kooverjee v. Kooverjee* 2006 (6) SA 127 (C); *MB v. NB* 2010 (3) SA 220 (GSJ); *AV v. CV* 2011 (6) SA 189 (KZP).

216. If a spouse or civil union partner does not obtain a maintenance order in his or her favour on divorce, he or she cannot later claim maintenance. Because a maintenance order cannot be obtained after divorce, spouses or civil union partners who do not need maintenance at the time of the divorce sometimes apply for token (nominal) maintenance. They claim a very small amount of maintenance with the objective that the amount can later be varied upward should this become necessary. Token awards are not made as a matter of course. The applicant must show that the factors which apply to all applications for post-divorce maintenance indicate that such an award is just.[621]

217. An order for post-divorce maintenance may be rescinded, suspended or varied if there is sufficient reason for doing so.[622]

Either party or both of them may waive the right to apply for rescission, variation or suspension,[623] but the courts do not lightly find that a waiver has occurred, and they have adopted widely divergent views on what constitutes a waiver.[624]

218. If the duty to pay maintenance arises from the terms of a settlement agreement that has been included in the divorce order, the duty comes to an end as stipulated in the agreement.[625] If the duty does not arise from the terms of a settlement agreement, the court may order payment of maintenance for any period of time until the party in whose favour the order operates remarries or enters into another civil union or until the party who is liable for maintenance dies.[626]

V. Children

219. As in any other matter regarding a child, the best interests of the child are the paramount concern in the case of divorce.[627] When it makes an order regarding a child in a divorce, the court must take the factors that are listed in the Children's Act 38 of 2005 in respect of the best interests of the child into account.[628] Furthermore, the court may not grant a decree of divorce until it is satisfied that the arrangements that have been made for the welfare of any minor or dependent child of the

621. *Buttner v. Buttner* 2006 (3) SA 23 (SCA).

622. Divorce Act 70 of 1979, s. 8(1); Maintenance Act 99 of 1989, s. 16(1)(b). But *see Botha v. Botha* 2005 (5) SA 228 (W) where the court, clearly incorrectly, held that s. 8 of the Divorce Act relates only to variation of orders made in respect of children. South African courts regularly rely on s. 8 when they vary a maintenance order made in favour of a former spouse: *see*, e.g., *Purnell v. Purnell* 1989 (2) SA 795 (W); *Rubenstein v. Rubenstein* 1992 (2) SA 709 (T); *Georghiades v. Janse van Rensburg* 2007 (3) SA 18 (C); *Welgemoed v. Mennell* 2007 (4) SA 446 (SE).

623. *Schutte v. Schutte* 1986 (1) SA 872 (A); *Polliack v. Polliack* 1988 (4) SA 161 (W); *Luttig v. Luttig* 1994 (1) SA 523 (O).

624. *See*, e.g., *Davis v. Davis* 1993 (1) SA 621 (C); *Girdwood v. Girdwood* 1995 (4) SA 698 (C); *Hoal v. Hoal* 2002 (3) SA 209 (N); *Georghiades v. Janse van Rensburg* 2007 (3) SA 18 (C).

625. *Hodges v. Coubrough* 1991 (3) SA 58 (D); *Odgers v. De Gersigny* 2007 (2) SA 305 (SCA).

626. Divorce Act 70 of 1979, s. 7(2); *Kruger v. Goss* 2010 (2) SA 507 (SCA).

627. Constitution, s. 28(2); Children's Act 38 of 2005, ss 6(2)(a) and 9.

628. Children's Act 38 of 2005, s. 7(1) read with s. 6(1) and (2). On the best interests of the child generally, *see* further Part II, Ch. 6, §1 below.

marriage or civil union are satisfactory or the best that can be achieved in the circumstances, and until it has considered the report and recommendations the Family Advocate has submitted in terms of the Mediation in Certain Divorce Matters Act 24 of 1987.[629]

220. In terms of the Mediation in Certain Divorce Matters Act 24 of 1987, a Family Advocate enquires into the welfare of the child if the court instructs him or her to do so, either of the parents requests an enquiry, or the Family Advocate is of the view that the child's interests demand an enquiry and requests the court to authorize an enquiry.[630] In the enquiry, the Family Advocate is assisted by a Family Counsellor, who is usually a social worker.[631]

The purpose of the enquiry is to enable the Family Advocate to furnish the court with a report and recommendations on any matter concerning the welfare of a minor or dependent child born of the marriage or civil union.[632] The Family Advocate does not act as the child's legal representative; he or she is an advisor to the court.[633]

The court is not obliged to accept the Family Advocate's report and/or recommendations. It may reject them completely or in part, or accept the Family Advocate's factual findings but make an order that differs from the Family Advocate's recommendations.[634]

A Family Advocate may be instructed to appear at the trial of a divorce action, and he or she may adduce evidence and cross-examine witnesses.[635]

221. Apart from considering the report and recommendations of the Family Advocate, the court may also cause any investigation it deems necessary to be carried out and may order any person to appear before it.[636] Thus, for example, the court may make an order that the child must be interviewed by a psychologist, that the psychologist's report must be submitted to the court, and/or that the psychologist must appear in court to give evidence. Either parent, or both of them, may be ordered to pay the costs of the investigation and appearance.[637]

The court may also appoint a legal representative for the child and order the child's parents, or either of them, to pay the costs of the legal representation.[638] The child also has a constitutional right to legal representation if absence of such representation would result in substantial injustice. In the latter event, the legal representation is provided by the State, at state expense.[639]

629. Divorce Act 70 of 1979, s. 6(1); Civil Union Act 17 of 2006, s. 13; Recognition of Customary Marriages Act 120 of 1998, s. 8(4)(a).
630. Section 4(1) and (2).
631. Section 3(1).
632. Section 4(1).
633. *Soller v. G* 2003 (5) SA 430 (W).
634. *Van den Berg v. Le Roux* [2003] 3 All SA 599 (NC).
635. Section 4(3).
636. Divorce Act 70 of 1979, s. 6(2).
637. *Ibid.*
638. *Ibid.*, s. 6(4).
639. Constitution, s. 28(2)(h).

222. The child has a right to participate in the matters regarding the divorce that affect him or her if he or she is of an age, maturity and stage of development to be able to participate. The child's views must receive due consideration.[640] It is very rare for the child to appear in court in person to present his or her views. The court usually relies on the Family Advocate to establish the child's views and to include them in his or her report.[641]

223. Once the court has considered the reports and recommendations, and is satisfied that the arrangements are satisfactory or the best that can be achieved, it may make any order it deems fit with regard to the guardianship or care of, and contact with, a minor child born of the parties, and the maintenance of a minor or dependent child born of the parties.[642]

Unlike the position in many foreign jurisdictions, the South African legislation regulating divorce does not empower the court to make an order in respect of a stepchild. The court's power is restricted to orders regarding children born of the divorcing parties. However, if the court that hears a divorce action is the High Court, it may use its power as upper guardian of all minors to make an order in respect of a stepchild of one of the parties.[643]

224. If the court makes no order regarding guardianship or care, both parents retain guardianship and care and may exercise these rights independently, subject to certain exceptions. The same applies if the court makes an order retaining both parents as guardians and care-giving parents.[644]

If the court deviates from the usual position and awards guardianship to one of the parents, that parent exercises guardianship alone, but the other parent's consent is still required for the child's marriage and adoption.[645] If the court awards sole guardianship to one of the parents, it means that, with the exception of the child's adoption, that parent becomes the child's only guardian to the exclusion of the other parent. Sole guardianship is not readily awarded. It may, for example, be awarded

640. Children's Act 38 of 2005, s. 10.
641. *See*, e.g., A. Palmer, *The Best Interests Criterion: An Overview of Its Application in Custody Decisions Relating to Divorce in the Period 1985–1995*, in *Children's Rights* 112 (R. Keightley ed., Juta & Co, Ltd 1996); J. Sloth-Nielsen, *Realising Children's Rights to Legal Representation and to be Heard in Judicial Proceedings: An Update*, 24 S. Afr. J. Hum. Rights 503 (2008).
642. Divorce Act 70 of 1979, s. 6(3).
643. On the court's powers as upper guardian, *see* Part II, Ch. 6, §5 below.
644. The position if more than one person has parental responsibilities and rights in respect of a child is discussed in Part II, Ch. 6, §4 below. In the context of the power of a parent or guardian to have care of his or her child, the terms 'care-giving parent' (or 'care-giving person') and 'non-care-giving parent' are used in preference to 'caregiver' and 'non-caregiver' because the definition of 'care-giver' in s. 1(1) of the Children's Act 38 of 2005 attaches a particular meaning to the term which excludes a parent and guardian.
645. Section 233(1)(a) of the Children's Act 38 of 2005 expressly requires both parents' consent to the adoption of their child. As regards consent to marry, s. 6(3) of the Divorce Act 70 of 1979 and s. 5(1) of the Matrimonial Affairs Act 37 of 1953 distinguish between guardianship and sole guardianship and refer to 'the power to consent to the marriage of the child' only in the context of sole guardianship. This distinction suggests that a parent of a child born of married parents only has the sole power to consent to the minor's marriage if he or she has been awarded sole guardianship.

where the other parent's whereabouts are unknown or where he or she has shown no interest in the child or in performing his or her duties as guardian.

225. Insofar as care is concerned, the maternal preference no longer applies. In terms of this preference, mothers are preferred on the stereotypical assumption that they are better at providing care than fathers are. The modern view is that in considering the child's best interests the court may have regard to maternity, but may not afford undue weight to it or turn it into the only consideration.[646] *Inter alia* because of the constitutional gender equality provisions[647] and an increased emphasis on the child's right to have a continuing relationship with both parents,[648] joint legal care has more or less become the norm, and joint physical care is sometimes awarded. Joint legal care is limited to joint decision-making about important issues, while joint physical care entails that the child spends substantial amounts of time, such as part of each week, or alternate weeks, with each parent.

The court may impose limitations on a parent's right of care,[649] such as that he or she may not remove the child from the court's area of jurisdiction without the other parent's consent.[650] Such limitation entails that, over and above requiring the other parent's consent for the child's departure or removal from South Africa,[651] the care-giving parent may not freely relocate with the child within South Africa; nor may he or she take the child on holiday to another area of jurisdiction without the other parent's permission. Such an order is sometimes made when it is feared that the care-giving parent will run away with the child. Awarding contact to the non-care-giving parent does not mean that the care-giving parent may not remove the child from the court's area of jurisdiction.[652]

The court may award split or divided care to divorcing parents. This type of care entails that one parent has care of some children and the other parent has care of the other children. Such an order is not granted lightly, because the courts are loath to separate siblings. Split or divided care is normally awarded only if the care-giving parent neglects some of the children, or if the change will bring about a substantial improvement in a particular child's position.[653] Sometimes split or divided care refers to giving care first to one parent and then to the other parent. For example, a child's mother may have care while the child is young, with his or her father gaining care when he or she reaches a specified age.

The court also has the power to award sole care to either parent. This may happen, for example, if one of the parents has abused the child. In exceptional cases the court may deprive both parents of care and award it to a third party.[654]

646. *Madiehe (born Ratlhogo) v. Madiehe* [1997] 2 All SA 153 (B); *Van Pletzen v. Van Pletzen* 1998 (4) SA 95 (O); *Ex parte Critchfield* 1999 (3) SA 132 (W); *K v. M* [2007] 4 All SA 883 (E).
647. *See inter alia* s. 9 of the Constitution.
648. *Krugel v. Krugel* 2003 (6) SA 220 (T).
649. *Soller v. G* 2003 (5) SA 430 (W).
650. *See*, e.g., *Di Bona v. Di Bona* 1993 (2) SA 682 (C).
651. Children's Act 38 of 2005, s. 18(3)(c)(iii).
652. *See*, e.g., *Theron v. Theron* 1939 WLD 355; *Stock v. Stock* 1981 (3) SA 1280 (A).
653. *Van der Linde v. Van der Linde* 1996 (3) SA 509 (O).
654. *Edge v. Murray* 1962 (3) SA 603 (W).

Homosexuality is not a ground for denying a parent care or contact.[655]

226. Parents who are getting divorced may agree on how contact should occur. Their agreement may be in general terms, such as that the non-care-giving parent will have reasonable contact, or it may be very specific as to the frequency of contact, the times during which and the places where contact may be exercised, and so forth. If the parties do not enter into an agreement or if the court does not make an order in accordance with the terms of their agreement, the court may make whatever order it deems fit regarding contact.

The court may structure contact or make an order in general terms. If reasonable contact is awarded, the non-care-giving parent may have contact with the child at reasonable times, places and intervals. If the parents cannot agree on what is reasonable, the care-giving parent has the final say, but he or she may not impose unreasonable restrictions or conditions that negate contact.[656] If the parents are unable to agree on what constitutes reasonable contact, either of them may approach the court for an order structuring contact as it sees fit.[657]

The court may impose any conditions and/or restrictions on contact that it deems in the best interests of the child. For example, if siblings are not in the same parent's care, the court may order that contact be exercised in such a way that the children spend their weekends together.[658]

If the relationship between the child and one of his or her parents is very poor, the court may order phased-in contact in terms of which contact initially occurs only occasionally, and becomes more regular as the relationship improves. The court may also postpone contact until a parent has, for example, successfully undergone treatment for alcoholism, drug-dependency or abusive behaviour. A parent's contact may also be suspended pending a psychological or psychiatric evaluation to determine whether contact is in the child's best interests and/or pending psychological or psychiatric treatment or therapy.[659]

The court may also order contact under supervision of a specified person, such as the care-giving parent or his or her representative, a social worker, psychologist, psychiatrist, or an independent person nominated by the Family Advocate.[660] Such an order is usually made if contact entails a clear risk to the child (such as abuse or abduction) or if a long period of time has elapsed since the child last had contact with the parent.

The court may prohibit personal contact but allow communication by means of telephone calls, letters, video calls, electronic mail, mobile phone text messages, and so forth.

The court will deny a parent contact only if this is in the child's best interests.[661] The mere fact that the child is opposed to contact does not mean that contact must

---

655. *V v. V* 1998 (4) SA 169 (C); *Van Rooyen v. Van Rooyen* [2001] 2 All SA 37 (T).
656. *See*, e.g., *Vucinovich v. Vucinovich* 1944 TPD 143; *Marais v. Marais* 1960 (1) SA 844 (C); *Du Preez v. Du Preez* 1969 (3) SA 529 (D).
657. *Marais v. Marais* 1960 (1) SA 844 (C); *Bongers v. Bongers* 1965 (2) SA 82 (O).
658. *Van Rooyen v. Van Rooyen* [2001] 2 All SA 37 (T).
659. *R. v. H* 2005 (6) SA 535 (C).
660. *See*, e.g., *Clutton v. Clutton* 1929 EDL 174; *Sonderup v. Tondelli* 2001 (1) SA 1171 (CC).
661. *See*, e.g., *Van den Berg v. Van den Berg* 1959 (4) SA 259 (W); *Dawn v. Dawn* 1968 (1) PH B3 (D).

be denied. The child's views and the reasons for his or her opposition to contact must be considered with due regard to his or her age, maturity and stage of development.[662]

227. After their divorce, both parents remain obliged to support their children in accordance with their respective means.[663] Normally, the parent with whom the children do not live is ordered to pay a specified monthly amount of maintenance to the parent with whom the children reside.

If a child has already attained majority but is still dependent on his or her parents for maintenance, he or she must personally claim maintenance, because an adult child's parent does not have legal standing to claim maintenance on his or her behalf.[664]

228. An order regarding guardianship, care, contact or maintenance may be rescinded, varied or suspended if there is sufficient reason for doing so.[665] If the Family Advocate instituted an enquiry in terms of the Mediation in Certain Divorce Matters Act 24 of 1987 with regard to the application for rescission, variation or suspension, the court must consider the Family Advocate's report and recommendations before making an order.[666]

VI. Costs

229. The court is not bound to make an order for costs in favour of the successful party in a divorce. It may make any costs order it considers just in view of the parties' means and their conduct insofar as it may be relevant.[667]

VII. Remarriage

230. Once a divorce order has been granted, both parties may enter into another marriage or civil union.

662. Children's Act 38 of 2005, s. 10.
663. Maintenance Act 99 of 1998, s. 15(3)(a)(i) and (ii); Children's Act 38 of 2005, s. 21(2).
664. *Smit v. Smit* 1980 (3) SA 1010 (O); *Butcher v. Butcher* 2009 (2) SA 421 (C).
665. Divorce Act 70 of 1979, s. 8(1); Maintenance Act 99 of 1998, s. 16(1)(b).
666. Divorce Act 70 of 1979, s. 8(1); Maintenance Act 99 of 1998, s. 10(1A).
667. Divorce Act 70 of 1979, s. 10.

Chapter 3. Cohabitation Without Marriage or a Civil Union

§1. Introduction

231. Various terms are used to signify the relationship of adults who live together in an intimate relationship without having entered into a marriage or civil union with each other. The most common terms are 'life partnership', 'domestic partnership' and 'cohabitation'. In this monograph, the term 'life partnership' is used because it has acquired a recognized meaning in South African law and is commonly employed by the courts.[668] However, the South African Law Reform Commission prefers the term 'domestic partnership' and has used it in its report and draft legislation on these relationships.[669]

Although a life partnership does not automatically confer the consequences of a legally recognized marriage or civil union on the parties to the relationship, some Acts afford specific spousal benefits to the parties, and court decisions have extended additional benefits to same-sex life partners. As is explained below in this chapter, life partners can also acquire protection for their life partnership by employing ordinary legal rules and remedies that are available to all legal subjects, such as contracts and wills.

Since self-regulation and piecemeal extension of rights and duties are unsatisfactory means to regulate life partnerships, regulation of these relationships by means of legislation was recommended and the draft Domestic Partnerships Bill, 2008 was published for public comment as long ago as 2008.[670] Unfortunately, it has made no further progress down the path to becoming law.

§2. Definition

232. For present purposes, a life partnership is defined as a same-sex or heterosexual relationship which is analogous to, or has many of the characteristics of, a marriage or civil union.

Determining whether a life partnership has come into existence can be a complicated matter. In the case of contractual benefits, such as employment-related benefits, the particular contract sometimes stipulates the requirements that must be met. Legislation also sometimes mentions specific requirements.[671] In cases that have come before the courts an inconsistent range of factors has been used to determine whether parties qualify as life partners. In most of the cases, the issue of whether

668. The Constitutional Court first used the term in *National Coalition for Gay and Lesbian Equality v. Minister of Home Affairs* 2000 (2) SA 1 (CC).
669. South African Law Reform Commission, *Project 118 Report on Domestic Partnerships*, (Government Printer 2006) and the draft Bill attached to the report.
670. Gen.N. 36 in *G.G.* 30663 of 14 Jan. 2008.
671. *See*, e.g., the definition of 'spouse' in s. 1 of Estate Duty Act 45 of 1955 and s. 1 of the Income Tax Act 58 of 1962.

the life partners had undertaken a duty of support was considered to be determinative – especially if the specific benefit in issue had financial implications.[672] However, in cases relating to the acquisition of parental responsibilities and rights the existence of a duty of support between the life partners was not considered determinative.[673] In some cases, permanency was considered important,[674] while in others the issue of whether the life partners had a *consortium omnis vitae* or 'life relationship similar … to marriage' was considered particularly relevant.[675] In view of the different factors that have been considered important, determining whether a particular couple qualifies as life partners is somewhat of a guessing game at present.

§3. Effects

233. It has already been pointed out that life partners do not automatically enjoy all the benefits the law affords to spouses and civil union partners. However, some Acts confer specific spousal benefits on life partners. Thus, *inter alia*, property accruing to a surviving life partner from his or her deceased life partner's estate is exempt from estate duty; donations between life partners are exempt from donations tax; a permanent life partner is treated like a spouse for purposes of the Pension Funds Act 24 of 1956; life partners can obtain domestic violence protection orders; life partners are in the same position as spouses in respect of surrogacy; and life partners may jointly adopt children.[676] Further, medical aid schemes generally allow their members to register their life partners as their dependants, and some employers confer housing and other benefits on life partners as if they are spouses.

234. Court decisions have extended additional spousal benefits to same-sex life partners: for example, a same-sex life partner of a permanent South African resident qualifies for the exemptions that apply to a spouse of a permanent South African resident; the phrase 'a member of the policy holder's family' in an insurance policy includes the policyholder's long-standing same-sex life partner; a judge's same-sex life partner enjoys the same benefits as a judge's spouse; and a surviving

672. *See*, e.g., *Satchwell v. President of the Republic of South Africa* 2002 (6) SA 1 (CC); *Satchwell v. President of the Republic of South Africa* 2003 (4) SA 266 (CC); *Gory v. Kolver (Starke Intervening)* 2007 (4) SA 97 (CC).

673. *Du Toit v. Minister for Welfare and Population Development* 2003 (2) SA 198 (CC); *J v. Director General, Department of Home Affairs* 2003 (5) BCLR 463 (CC).

674. *See*, e.g., *Du Toit v. Minister for Welfare and Population Development* 2003 (2) SA 198 (CC); *J v. Director General, Department of Home Affairs* 2003 (5) BCLR 463 (CC); *Gory v. Kolver (Starke Intervening)* 2007 (4) SA 97 (CC).

675. *National Coalition for Gay and Lesbian Equality v. Minister of Home Affairs* 2000 (2) SA 1 (CC).

676. Estate Duty Act 45 of 1955, s. 4(q) read with the definition of 'spouse' in s. 1; Pension Funds Act 24 of 1956, s. 1; Income Tax Act 58 of 1962, s. 56(1)(b) read with the definition of 'spouse' in s. 1; Domestic Violence Act 116 of 1998, s. 4(1) read with the definitions of 'complainant' and 'domestic relationship' in s. 1; Children's Act 38 of 2005, ss 231(1)(a)(ii), 293, 297 and 299.

same-sex life partner may inherit as intestate heir from his or her same-sex life partner's estate.[677] Heterosexual life partners, however, have not been afforded judicial protection.[678] Whether the differentiation between same-sex and heterosexual life partners will withstand constitutional scrutiny in future is doubted.[679]

Same-sex and heterosexual life partners can claim damages for loss of support resulting from the death of a life partner who had undertaken to maintain them.[680] However, it should be noted that the action for loss of support is not a spousal benefit; it is a sui generis remedy that is not based on the existence of a valid marriage.[681]

235. Life partners can acquire some protection for their life partnership by nominating each other as beneficiaries in life insurance and other policies; drawing up wills in which they nominate each other as beneficiaries; appointing each other as agents to buy assets or incur expenses in their joint name;[682] jointly entering into contracts to purchase, lease or rent property or accommodation; and so forth. If life partners jointly enter into a contract with a third party, the terms of the contract determine each life partner's rights and duties. Usually, the life partners are joint

---

677. *National Coalition for Gay and Lesbian Equality v. Minister of Home Affairs* 2000 (2) SA 1 (CC); *Farr v. Mutual & Federal Insurance Co Ltd* 2000 (3) SA 684 (C); *Satchwell v. President of the Republic of South Africa* 2002 (6) SA 1 (CC); *Satchwell v. President of the Republic of South Africa* 2003 (4) SA 266 (CC); *Gory v. Kolver (Starke Intervening)* 2007 (4) SA 97 (CC); *Laubscher v. Duplan* 2017 (2) SA 264 (CC).

678. In *Volks v. Robinson* 2005 (5) BCLR 446 (CC) the majority of the Constitutional Court held that the law may distinguish between married and unmarried people and accord benefits to spouses which it denies to unmarried people, because unmarried people's choice not to marry justifies withholding those benefits from them.

679. In the past, the sympathetic judicial approach towards same-sex life partners was based on the view that, because same-sex life partners could not marry, the absence of a marriage between them did not justify excluding them from the specific spousal benefits the cases dealt with. Nowadays, same-sex life partners can enter into a civil partnership or a marriage in terms of the Civil Union Act 17 of 2006. Therefore, it might be argued that the law should withhold protection from them if they fail to enter into a civil union, like it withholds protection from heterosexual life partners who do so. Then again, the majority judgment in *Volks* – which is the foundation for withholding protection from heterosexual life partners (*see* the previous footnote) – has been stridently criticised, and the Constitutional Court seems to accept that the judgment should be reconsidered. In his minority concurring judgment in *Laubscher v. Duplan*, Froneman J concluded that '*Volks* cannot stand', because 'the criticisms [of the judgment] appear to be valid' and *Volks* reflects views that are 'not inclusive enough in the present social context' (paras [60], [84]). As the principles decided in *Volks* did not fall within the scope of the facts of *Laubscher*, the court did not have to reconsider *Volks*. The majority of the court nevertheless stated that '[t]he reasons put forward in … [Froneman J's judgment] as to why the judgment of *Volks* cannot stand are stimulating and persuasive' (para. [53]). Therefore, one should be hesitant to support extension of the choice argument relied on in *Volks*. *See also* Heaton, *Law of Persons*, 10; J. Heaton, *Parental Responsibilities and Rights*, in *Commentary on the Children's Act* 3–54 (C.J. Davel & A.M. Skelton eds., loose-leaf Juta & Co, Ltd 2007).

680. *See*, e.g., *Du Plessis v. Road Accident Fund* 2004 (1) SA 359 (SCA); *Paixão v. Road Accident Fund* 2012 (6) SA 377 (SCA); *Engela v. Road Accident Fund* 2016 (1) SA 214 (GJ).

681. *See*, e.g., *Santam Bpk v. Henery* 1999 (3) SA 421 (SCA); *Amod (born Peer) v. Multilateral Motor Vehicle Accidents Fund (Commission for Gender Equality Intervening)* 1999 (4) SA 1319 (SCA); *Paixão v. Road Accident Fund* 2012 (6) SA 377 (SCA).

682. *Thompson v. Model Steam Laundry Ltd* 1926 TPD 674.

owners of the assets acquired and joint debtors in respect of the duties incurred.[683] If they are joint owners of an asset, neither of them may exclude the other from using or controlling the asset. However, unless they have entered into a partnership agreement, either of them may alienate his or her share of the jointly owned property without the other's consent. If the life partnership breaks down and the life partners cannot agree on how jointly owned property is to be divided, either of them may approach the court under the *actio communi dividundo*. If the *actio communi dividundo* is granted, the court either orders whatever division it deems just, or appoints a receiver (liquidator) to divide the assets.

Life partners may also expressly or tacitly enter into a contract of universal partnership with each other. A tacit universal partnership exists if the facts indicate that it is more probable than not that the partnership agreement was concluded.[684]

In addition to the general requirements for entering into a contract, such as reaching agreement, the parties must also meet the specific requirements for the formation of a universal partnership, namely:[685]

(1) Each party must bring money, labour or skill into the partnership or undertake to bring something into it. The rendering of domestic and child-care services qualifies as a contribution.[686]
(2) The venture must be carried on for the parties' joint benefit. This requirement is satisfied, *inter alia*, if the parties intended to share everything and one of them shared in the benefits of the other's financial contribution while the latter party shared in the benefits of the former's domestic and child-care contributions.[687]
(3) The objective must be to make a profit, but the profit need not be commercial.[688]

If a universal partnership comes into existence between life partners, they jointly own the partnership property in undivided shares. The proportion in which they own the property is determined by the partnership agreement. If they failed to make an express arrangement in this regard, each life partner's contribution to the partnership determines his or her share of the property.[689]

683. If the life partners are jointly liable, each of them may be sued only for his or her share of the debt. Some contracts impose joint and several liability on debtors, in which case each life partner may be sued for the full debt.
684. *See*, e.g., *Mühlmann v. Mühlmann* 1984 (3) SA 102 (A); *Sepheri v. Scanlan* 2008 (1) SA 322 (C); *Ponelat v. Schrepfer* 2012 (1) SA 206 (SCA); *Butters v. Mncora* 2012 (4) SA 1 (SCA).
685. *See*, e.g., *Rhodesia Railways v. Commissioner of Taxes* 1925 AD 438; *Pezzutto v. Dreyer* 1992 (3) SA 379 (A); *Zulu v. Zulu* 2008 (4) SA 12 (D); *Ponelat v. Schrepfer* 2012 (1) SA 206 (A); *RD v. TD* 2014 (4) SA 200 (GP); *Booysen v. Stander* 2018 (6) SA 528 (WCC).
686. *Isaacs v. Isaacs* 1949 (1) SA 952 (C); *Butters v. Mncora* 2012 (4) SA 1 (SCA).
687. *Butters v. Mncora* 2012 (4) SA 1 (SCA).
688. *Ally v. Dinath* 1984 (2) SA 451 (T); *Ponelat v. Schrepfer* 2012 (1) SA 206 (A); *Butters v. Mncora* 2012 (4) SA 1 (SCA).
689. *Isaacs v. Isaacs* 1949 (1) SA 952 (C); *Mühlmann v. Mühlmann* 1981 (4) SA 632 (T) (confirmed on appeal: 1984 (3) SA 102 (A)).

During the subsistence of the universal partnership, the normal rules of the law of partnership apply. Thus, for example, one of the partners may not alienate partnership property without the other's consent, use it as security for a personal debt, or entirely exclude the other partner from controlling any or all of it.

Termination of a universal partnership is also governed by the terms of the partners' agreement. If their agreement does not deal with termination, the ordinary rules of the law of partnership apply. Thus, for example, a universal partnership comes to an end when one of the partners dies. As the law of partnership provides that a former partner may not remain in exclusive possession and occupation of partnership property after the termination of the partnership unless the partners have agreed that this may be done or unless the deceased partner bequeathed the property to the surviving partner, a surviving life partner may be ordered to vacate immovable property owned by the universal partnership.[690]

Entering into a life partnership contract (cohabitation or domestic partnership contract) provides another contractual option for regulating the consequences of a life partnership. The contract need not be in writing and need not even be concluded expressly. However, proving a tacit contract can be very difficult. The party who relies on the existence of the contract or the particular term must prove that the parties' conduct was such that it justifies an inference that they intended to, and did, contract on the terms alleged.[691]

A life partnership contract may contain any provision which is not contrary to the law or public policy. Thus, the life partners may, *inter alia*, undertake to maintain each other while the relationship lasts, agree on post-separation maintenance, deal with ownership of property, agree on liability for debts in respect of household necessaries, and agree on occupation of the common home during the subsistence of the life partnership and after its termination. If life partners agree on a duty of support, this contractual duty can be enforced in terms of the Maintenance Act 99 of 1998[692] and enables a surviving life partner to institute the dependant's action for loss of support if the deceased life partner is killed by a third party.[693]

As a rule, a contract binds only the parties to it. However, if life partners agree that one of them will support the other, this agreement is protected by way of the common-law action for damages for loss of support if a third party kills the life partner who incurred the contractual duty of support.[694]

236. Finally, if one life partner has been enriched at the other's expense, the impoverished life partner can, in certain circumstances, institute an enrichment claim against the enriched life partner. However, as South African law does not yet recognize a general enrichment claim,[695] enrichment liability is usually of limited use to life partners.

690. *Botha v. Deetlefs* 2008 (3) SA 419 (N).
691. *McDonald v. Young* 2012 (3) SA 1 (SCA).
692. Section 2(1).
693. *See*, e.g., *Paixão v. Road Accident Fund* 2012 (6) SA 377 (SCA)); *Engela v. Road Accident Fund* 2016 (1) SA 214 (GJ).
694. *Du Plessis v. Road Accident Fund* 2004 (1) SA 359 (SCA); *Paixão v. Road Accident Fund* 2012 (6) SA 377 (SCA).
695. *Nortjé v. Pool* 1966 (3) SA 96 (A).

Chapter 4. Filiation

§1. Children Born of Married Parents

I. The Status of Legitimacy

237. Until fairly recently, South African law categorized children as either legitimate or illegitimate (children born out of wedlock, extra-marital children). The Children's Act 38 of 2005 moved the descriptive focus to the child's parents. Thus, it refers to a married or an unmarried father, a married or an unmarried mother, a married or an unmarried person, and married parents,[696] and not to the child's legitimacy or illegitimacy. Therefore, 'child born of married parents' and 'child born of unmarried parents' are the more up-to-date descriptions for children.

Originally, 'illegitimate' children suffered from a number of legal disabilities, and the rules regarding their parents' responsibilities and rights differed markedly from those that applied to the responsibilities and rights of parents of 'legitimate' children. On 1 July 2007, when the first batch of sections of the Children's Act came into operation,[697] the rules regarding the acquisition of parental responsibilities and rights in respect of children born of unmarried parents changed radically. Although the Act does not completely eliminate the relevance of the marital status of a child's parents insofar as parental responsibilities and rights are concerned, many unmarried parents now have exactly the same parental responsibilities and rights as married parents.[698] The status of 'legitimacy' has therefore lost much of its legal relevance. A remaining fundamental distinction between married and unmarried parents is that all married parents automatically have full parental responsibilities and rights in respect of their children, which they exercise jointly unless a court issues a different order, while only some unmarried parents jointly have full parental responsibilities and rights.

II. Acquiring the Legal Status of a Child Born of Married Parents

A. Marriage or Civil Union of the Child's Parents

238. A child is born of married parents if his or her parents are legally married to each other or are the parties to a valid civil union with each other at the time of his or her conception or birth or at any intervening time.[699] Thus, even if a child's parents were married for only a short time while he or she was still in his or her mother's womb, he or she qualifies as a child born of married parents. For purposes

696. *See*, e.g., ss 19–21, 38, 40 and 233.
697. Proclamation 13 in *G.G.* 30030 of 29 Jun. 2007. The remaining sections came into operation on 1 Apr. 2010: Procl. R12 in *G.G.* 33076 of 1 Apr. 2010.
698. *See* Part II, Ch. 6, §3 below.
699. Civil Union Act 17 of 2006, s. 13; Grotius, *Inleidinge tot de Hollandsche Rechts-geleerdheid*, 1.12.2, 1.12.3; D.G. van der Keessel, *Theses Selectae Juris Hollandici et Zelandici* 169 (F Muller, 1860); Van Leeuwen, *Rooms-Hollands-Regt*, 1.7.2; Voet, *Commentarius ad Pandectas*, 1.6.6.

of determining whether a child is born of married parents, marriage is defined in broad terms that include civil, customary and, even, religious marriages.[700]

If the unmarried parents of a child marry each other or enter into a civil union with each other after the child's birth, the child becomes a child born of married parents from the date of his or her birth. This is the position even if the child's parents could not legally have married each other or entered into a civil union with each other at the time of the child's conception or birth, for example, because one of them was still married to another person.[701]

If the child's mother marries a man who is not the child's father or enters into a civil union with such a man, the child remains a child born of unmarried parents and his or her mother's husband does not acquire parental responsibilities and rights as a result of the marriage or civil union.

B. Status of a Child of a Void Marriage

239. As a void marriage or civil union has no legal consequences, a child born from such a relationship is born of unmarried parents. However, as indicated above, the nullity of the parental marriage or civil union is usually legally irrelevant insofar as the acquisition of parental responsibilities and rights is concerned. Further, the rule that a void civil marriage has none of the consequences of a valid marriage is subject to the rule that children born of a putative marriage are born of married parents.[702]

C. Status of a Child of a Voidable Marriage

240. A child who is conceived or born of a voidable marriage or civil union is a child born of married parents. When the marriage or civil union is annulled, the child is treated like a child of divorcing parents.[703]

III. Disputes as to Birth of Married Parents

241. If a child is born of a married woman or a woman who is a party to a heterosexual civil union, it is rebuttably presumed that the woman's husband or male civil union partner, and not some third party, is the child's father. This presumption is expressed in the maxim *pater est quem nuptiae demonstrant* (the marriage indicates who the father is).[704] The presumption applies to children conceived before

700. *See* the definition of 'marriage' in s. 1(1) of the Children's Act 38 of 2005.
701. Children's Act 38 of 2005, s. 38(1) and (2).
702. *See* Part II, Ch. 1, §5 above.
703. Children's Act 38 of 2005, s. 39.
704. Grotius, *Inleidinge tot de Hollandsche Rechts-geleerdheid*, 1.12.3; Voet, *Commentarius ad Pandectas*, 1.6.6.

the marriage or heterosexual civil union and born during its existence, and to children conceived during the marriage or civil union and born after its dissolution. If a woman remarries or enters into a new heterosexual civil union shortly after the dissolution of her previous marriage or civil union and gives birth to a child during the early stages of the new marriage or civil union, her new husband or civil union partner is rebuttably presumed to be the father of the child.[705]

In terms of section 13(1) of the Civil Union Act 17 of 2006, the legal consequences of a civil marriage apply to a civil union 'with such changes as may be required by the context'. It is unclear whether this means that an adapted version of the *pater est quem nuptiae demonstrant* presumption applies to same-sex civil unions. The presumption specifically refers to a father, while there are two male or two female parties in a same-sex civil union. Furthermore, in the case of a same-sex civil union procreation involves artificial fertilization, and in the case of a male couple it involves surrogate motherhood too (unless the child is conceived through an adulterous relationship with a third party of the opposite sex). As the rules regarding artificial fertilization and surrogate motherhood usually determine who the child's parents are in the case of a same-sex civil union, application of an adapted version of the *pater est quem nuptiae demonstrant* presumption to same-sex civil unions is probably not viable.[706]

242. If a dispute arises as to whether a child was born of married or unmarried parents, the party who alleges that the child was not born of the spouses or civil union partners must rebut the *pater est quem nuptiae demonstrant* presumption. Any interested person, including the child, the child's mother, or her husband or civil union partner, may rebut the presumption.[707] Thus, for example, the child may rebut the presumption in order to enable him or her to inherit from his or her unmarried father, or the mother's husband may rebut the presumption in order to escape the parental duty of support.

The presumption can be rebutted by evidence which shows, on a balance of probabilities, that the man who is presumed to be the child's father is not really the child's father.[708] Such evidence includes sterility; impotence or absence during the period when the child could have been conceived; and scientific tests (such as DNA tests)[709] which exclude the presumed father from paternity.[710] Evidence that the

---

705. Voet, *Commentarius ad Pandectas*, 1.6.9. Although Voet only refers to cases where the previous husband had died there is no reason to limit the rule to dissolution of the marriage by death.

706. *See also* Heaton, *Law of Persons*, 56; Heaton & Kruger, *Family Law*, 211; H. de Ru, *A Historical Perspective on the Recognition of Same-sex Unions in South Africa*, 19 Fundamina 247 (2013).

707. Civil Proceedings Evidence Act 25 of 1965, s. 3.

708. *Van Lutterveld v. Engels* 1959 (2) SA 699 (A).

709. The court's power to compel a child or an alleged or presumed parent to submit to scientific tests is a controversial matter. One parent cannot compel the other to submit to such tests. However, either of them may approach the court for an order compelling the other to submit himself or herself and the child to such tests, but it is by no means certain that the court will grant the order. Although the Supreme Court of Appeal held that the High Court as upper guardian of all minors has the power to dispense with a parent's consent to tests on the child, it also stated that it may sometimes be in the child's best interests not to establish the truth regarding his or her biological parentage: *YM v. LB* 2010 (6) SA 338 (SCA). Furthermore, it is still unclear whether the court has the power to order tests on an unwilling parent: Boezaart, *Law of Persons*, 106–110; Heaton, *Law*

child's mother had sex with another man during the period when the child could have been conceived is insufficient to disprove paternity.[711] The same applies to evidence that the physical features of the child do not resemble those of the presumed father, although physical appearance may be considered in conjunction with other factors which disprove paternity.[712] Evidence that contraception was used is also insufficient to disprove paternity.[713]

243. In the past, our courts were hesitant to declare a child who was born of a married woman to be born of unmarried parents.[714] Now that it has become easier for unmarried fathers to obtain parental responsibilities and rights and the difference between the legal position of children born of married parents and those born of unmarried parents is relatively small, this hesitancy ought to grow weaker.

IV. Effects of Birth of Married Parents

244. If a child is born of married parents, both parents automatically have full parental responsibilities and rights in respect of the child from the time of his or her birth.[715] Thus, both parents are the child's guardians and both of them have the responsibility and right to care for the child, to maintain contact with the child and to contribute to the child's maintenance, unless a court makes a different order.[716]

§2. Children Born of Unmarried Parents

I. Acquiring the Legal Status of a Child Born of Unmarried Parents

245. A child is born of unmarried parents if his or her parents are not the parties to a marriage or civil union with each other at the time of his or her conception or birth or at any intervening time.

---

of Persons, 62–64; W. Banoobhai & S. Hoctor, *The Court's Power to Compel DNA Testing in Paternity Disputes – LB v. YD 2009 5 SA 463 (T)*, 30 Obiter 791 et seq. (2009). The latter issue is particularly difficult because ordering a scientific test on an unwilling adult brings several constitutional rights into conflict – the paramountcy of the best interests of the child and the unwilling parent's rights to privacy, bodily integrity and dignity being among them (Constitution, ss 10, 12(2), 14 and 28(2)).

710. *See*, e.g., *Fitzgerald v. Green* 1911 EDL 432; *Williams v. Williams* 1925 TPD 538; *R. v. Isaacs* 1954 (1) SA 266 (N); *Van Lutterveld v. Engels* 1959 (2) SA 699 (A).
711. *S. v. Jeggels* 1962 (3) SA 704 (C); *Gin v. S.* 1966 (2) PH H335 (E); *A v. C* 1986 (4) SA 227 (C).
712. *Seetal v. Pravitha* 1983 (3) SA 827 (D); *M v. R* 1989 (1) SA 416 (O).
713. *R. v. Swanepoel* 1954 (4) SA 31 (O); *S. v. Jeggels* 1962 (3) SA 704 (C).
714. *See*, e.g., *F v. L* 1987 (4) SA 525 (W); *B v. E* 1992 (3) SA 438 (T).
715. Children's Act 38 of 2005, ss 19 and 20.
716. *Ibid.*, s. 18(2).

II. Disputes as to Paternity of a Child of Unmarried Parents

246. If a child is born of a woman who is not a party to a marriage or a civil union, the man who is proved to have had sex with the mother at any time when the child could have been conceived is presumed to be the child's father. The presumption is rebuttable by evidence to the contrary which raises a reasonable doubt.[717]

247. As in the case of the *pater est quem nuptiae demonstrant* presumption, any interested person may rebut the presumption,[718] and evidence of the alleged father's sterility, impotence or absence during the period when the child could have been conceived and scientific tests may be used to rebut the presumption.[719]

III. Effects of Birth of Unmarried Parents

A. *Parental Responsibilities and Rights*

248. Being born of unmarried parents no longer results in the child's father being recognized solely for purposes of providing maintenance and determining the prohibited degrees of relationship. Some unmarried parents now have exactly the same parental responsibilities and rights as married parents. This is the case if unmarried parents are each other's permanent life partners when the child is born.[720] Both unmarried parents also have full parental responsibilities and rights if, regardless of whether they ever lived together, the father consents or successfully applies to be identified as the child's father or pays damages in terms of customary law; contributes or has attempted to contribute to the child's upbringing; and contributes or has attempted to contribute to the child's maintenance.[721]

Unmarried parents whose child was born before 1 July 2007 and who meet the abovementioned requirements obtained joint full parental responsibilities and rights as from that date. If their child was born after that date, they acquire joint full parental responsibilities and rights from the moment of the child's birth just like married parents do.[722]

---

717. *Ibid.*, s. 36.
718. Civil Proceedings Evidence Act 25 of 1965, s. 3.
719. *See*, e.g., *Fitzgerald v. Green* 1911 EDL 432; *Williams v. Williams* 1925 TPD 538; *R. v. Isaacs* 1954 (1) SA 266 (N); *Van Lutterveld v. Engels* 1959 (2) SA 699 (A).
720. Children's Act 38 of 2005, s. 21(1)(a). If the parents cannot agree on whether they lived in a permanent life partnership when the child was born, the dispute must be referred for mediation by a Family Advocate, social worker, social service professional or other suitably qualified person: s. 21(3)(a).
721. Children's Act 38 of 2005, s. 21(1)(b). The question whether the requirements in s. 21(1)(b) apply conjunctively or are independent has not yet been settled: *see KLVC v. SDI* [2015] 1 All SA 532 (SCA), where the Supreme Court of Appeal left the question unanswered.
722. Children's Act 38 of 2005, s. 21(4). 1 Jul. 2007 is the date on which many of the sections of the Children's Act regarding parental responsibilities and rights came into operation: Procl. 13 in *G.G.* 30030 of 29 Jun. 2007.

249. If unmarried parents do not meet the abovementioned requirements, only the child's mother acquires parental responsibilities and rights on the child's birth, although the father is obliged to contribute to the child's maintenance.[723]

The father can obtain partial or full parental responsibilities and rights by entering into a parental responsibilities and rights agreement with the child's mother or by obtaining a court order to such effect. In terms of the Children's Act 38 of 2005, the father can acquire parental responsibilities and rights by entering into a parental responsibilities and rights agreement with a person who has parental responsibilities and rights in respect of his child.[724] The agreement vests the father with the responsibilities and rights that are set out in the agreement, provided that it is registered with a Family Advocate or is made an order of court on the parties' application.[725] The Family Advocate or court must be satisfied that the agreement is in the child's best interests.[726]

The Act also empowers anyone who has an interest in a child's care, well-being or development to approach the court for an order assigning contact or care to him or her.[727] The court must take the following factors into account when it considers the application:[728]

(1) The best interests of the child.
(2) The relationship between the applicant and the child, and between any other relevant person and the child.
(3) The degree of commitment the applicant has shown towards the child.
(4) The extent to which the applicant has contributed to expenses in connection with the child's birth and maintenance.
(5) Any other fact that should, in the opinion of the court, be taken into account.

If the court assigns care or contact to the unmarried father, the order does not affect the parental responsibilities and rights any other person has in respect of the child.[729] Thus, for example, an unmarried mother does not lose her parental responsibilities and rights or any element of those responsibilities and rights simply because the court assigns contact or care to the child's father. However, an application for assignment of contact and care may be combined with an application for termination, extension, suspension or circumscription of parental responsibilities and rights.[730] Thus, the unmarried father could ask the court to suspend particular aspects of the responsibility and right of care the mother enjoys and to assign them to him.

---

723. Children's Act 38 of 2005, ss 19, 21(1) and 21(2); Maintenance Act 99 of 1998, s. 15(3)(a)(iii). If the mother is still a minor, she cannot be her child's guardian. In such event, her guardian is the child's guardian unless the child's father has obtained guardianship of the child: s. 19(2).
724. Section 22(1).
725. Section 22(1), (2) and (4).
726. Sections 22(5) and 29(3). Section 7(1) of the Act contains a list of factors that must be taken into account in respect of the best interests of the child: *see* Part II, Ch. 6, §1 below.
727. Section 23(1).
728. Section 23(2).
729. Section 23(4).
730. Section 28(2).

A person who has an interest in the child's care, well-being or development may also approach the High Court for an order assigning guardianship to him or her.[731] The court must take the following factors into account when it considers the application:[732]

(1) The best interests of the child.
(2) The relationship between the applicant and the child, and between any other relevant person and the child.
(3) Any other fact that should, in the opinion of the court, be taken into account.

Furthermore, if the child already has a guardian, the applicant must give reasons why the existing guardian is not suitable to have guardianship.[733]

An unmarried father may further approach the High Court in its capacity as upper guardian of all minors for an order conferring any or all parental responsibilities and rights on him.

250. An unmarried father can acquire parental responsibilities and rights in respect of his child after the death of the child's mother if she has sole guardianship or sole care of the child and appoints him as her successor as guardian or to be vested with care in her will.[734] Before she makes the appointment, she must give due consideration to any views and wishes expressed by the child, bearing in mind his or her age, maturity and stage of development.[735]

B. Surname

251. A child born of unmarried parents usually bears his or her mother's surname. However, the child's birth may be registered under the surname of his or her father if the child's parents jointly request that the father's surname be used. If the child is to be registered under his or her father's surname, the father must acknowledge paternity in writing in the presence of the person to whom the notice of birth is given and enter his particulars on the notice of birth.[736]

C. Maintenance

252. Both parents have a duty to support their child regardless of whether the child is born of married or unmarried parents and regardless of whether either of them has guardianship or care of, or contact with the child. The duty is apportioned

---

731. Section 24(1).
732. Section 24(2).
733. Section 24(3).
734. Children's Act 38 of 2005, s. 27(1) and (2); Administration of Estates Act 66 of 1965, s. 72(1)(a)(ii).
735. Children's Act 38 of 2005, s. 31(1)(a) and (b)(iii); *see also* s. 10.
736. Births and Deaths Registration Act 51 of 1992, s. 10(1). *See* further Part I, Ch. 4, §2 above.

between the child's parents according to their respective means. If a parent dies, his or her estate is responsible for his or her child's maintenance. If neither of the child's parents or their estates can support the child, the duty of support passes to the child's grandparents.[737]

D. Inheritance

253. Birth of unmarried parents is irrelevant when determining a person's relationship to a deceased for purposes of the Law of Succession. This rule applies to testate and intestate succession.[738]

737. On the duty to support a child, *see* further Part II, Ch. 6, §2 below.
738. Wills Act 7 of 1953, s. 2D(1)(b); Intestate Succession Act 81 of 1987, s. 1(2). On a child's position as heir or beneficiary, *see* further Part IV, Ch. 1, §2 and §3 and Part IV, Ch. 2, §3 below.

Chapter 5. Adoption and Foster Care

§1. Adoption

I. Introduction

254. In South Africa, adoption can take place in two ways. The first method is a formal legal process by means of which existing parental responsibilities and rights are terminated by the Children's Court and parental responsibilities and rights are vested in the adoptive parent so that he or she becomes the adopted child's parent for all purposes.[739] This type of adoption is fully recognized and is governed by the Children's Act 38 of 2005.

The second type of adoption is customary adoption. It is not governed by legislation and does not occur by way of a formal legal process. It takes the form of a private, family arrangement.[740] Customary adoption does not yet enjoy full legal recognition in South Africa. However, it is increasingly argued that a child who has been adopted in terms of customary law should enjoy the same rights as a child who has been adopted in terms of the Children's Act. Two divisions of the High Court have recognized customary adoption for purposes of children's claims for compensation for loss of support resulting from the death of the parents who had adopted them in terms of customary law,[741] and one division has held that a child's right to claim maintenance from the person who adopted him or her in terms of customary law can be enforced in terms of the Maintenance Act 99 of 1998.[742] Because customary adoption is not yet fully recognized, the discussion below focuses on adoption in terms of the Children's Act.

II. Who May Adopt?

255. Spouses in a civil, customary or religious marriage; civil union partners; partners in a permanent life partnership;[743] and other persons sharing a common household and forming a permanent family unit (such as a husband and all his customary wives) may jointly adopt a child.[744] A widower, widow, or divorced or unmarried person may adopt a child on his or her own. The same applies to a person who is the child's foster parent; the spouse of the child's parent in a civil, customary or religious marriage; the civil union partner of the child's parent; or the

739. Children's Act 38 of 2005, s. 242(3) read with s. 239(1)(a). The Children's Court is the only court that may grant an adoption order: *Minister of Welfare and Population Development v. Fitzpatrick* 2000 (3) SA 422 (CC); *Ex parte Leask* [2007] 4 All SA 1018 (D).

740. *Metiso v. Padongelukfonds* 2001 (3) SA 1142 (T).

741. *Kewana v. Santam Insurance Co Ltd* 1993 (4) SA 771 (Tk); *Metiso v. Padongelukfonds* 2001 (3) SA 1142 (T).

742. *Maneli v. Maneli* 2010 (7) BCLR 703 (GSJ).

743. On life partnerships, *see* Part II, Ch. 3 above.

744. Children's Act 38 of 2005, s. 231(1)(a) read with the definition of 'marriage' in s. 1(1) and read with s. 13(2) of the Civil Union Act 17 of 2006.

permanent life partner of the child's parent.[745] If the child was born of unmarried parents, the child's biological father may adopt the child on his own.[746]

256. Only adults qualify as possible adoptive parents. In addition, a prospective adoptive parent must be fit and proper to be entrusted with full parental responsibilities and rights and be willing and able to undertake, exercise and maintain those responsibilities and rights. An adoption social worker must assess the prospective adoptive parent to determine whether he or she is indeed fit and proper to be entrusted with full parental responsibilities and rights and willing and able to undertake, exercise and maintain those responsibilities and rights.[747] The assessment must accompany the adoption application.[748]

257. Inter-racial, intercultural and interfaith adoptions are permitted, but differences between the racial, cultural and religious background of the child and the prospective adoptive parent need not be ignored. In his or her assessment of the prospective adoptive parent, the adoption social worker may take cultural and community differences between the child and the prospective adoptive parent into consideration.[749] Race and religion are not expressly mentioned, but they may be considered as factors relating to cultural and community differences.

258. An applicant for adoption may not be disqualified because of his or her financial status.[750] If the adoption application is successful, the adoptive parent may apply for social assistance.[751] There is no specific category of social assistance for adoptive parents, but an adoptive parent could apply for a child support grant or a care-dependency grant in terms of the Social Assistance Act 13 of 2004.

III. Consent to Adoption

A. The Guardians

259. An adoption can occur without consent if the child who is to be adopted is an orphan who does not have a guardian or caregiver who is willing and able to adopt him or her and the Children's Court is provided with certified copies of the death certificate of the parent or guardian or such other documentation as it may require.[752] In all other circumstances, the general rule is that the consent of all the guardians of the child is required.[753] This rule applies equally to children born of

745. Section 231(1)(b), (c) and (e).
746. Section 31(1)(d).
747. Section 231(2).
748. Section 239(1)(c).
749. Section 231(3).
750. Section 231(4).
751. Section 231(5).
752. Section 236(2).
753. Sections 18(3)(c), 233(1)(a) and (b).

married and unmarried parents.[754] Thus, if unmarried parents have joint guardianship, both of them must consent to their child's adoption. If a parent is a minor, he or she must be assisted by his or her guardian when he or she consents to the adoption.[755] If persons other than the child's parents are the child's guardians, their consent is required.[756]

However, the consent of a parent or guardian is not required if:[757]

(1) he or she is incompetent to give consent due to mental illness;
(2) he or she has abandoned the child, his or her whereabouts cannot be established, or his or her identity is unknown;
(3) he or she has abused or deliberately neglected the child, or has allowed the child to be abused or deliberately neglected;
(4) he or she has consistently failed to fulfil his or her parental responsibilities towards the child during the past twelve months;
(5) a court has divested him or her of the right to consent to the child's adoption; or
(6) he or she failed to respond to a notice of the proposed adoption within thirty days of service of the notice.

Furthermore, the consent of the unmarried biological father of the child is not required if:[758]

(1) he failed to acknowledge paternity by giving a written acknowledgement to the child's mother or the Clerk of the Children's Court before the child reached the age of six months, voluntarily paying maintenance for the child, paying damages in terms of customary law, or causing his particulars to be entered in the child's birth registration in terms of the Births and Deaths Registration Act 51 of 1992;
(2) the child was conceived as a result of incest; or
(3) following an allegation by the child's mother, the Children's Court found on a balance of probabilities that the child was conceived as a result of rape.

If a person who has consented to the child's adoption wants the Children's Court to grant an exemption in respect of another person's consent, he or she must submit a statement to that effect to the Clerk of the Children's Court so that the issue of whether there is a ground for exemption can be investigated.[759]

260. Before a parent or guardian consents to the adoption, he or she must be counselled by the adoption social worker who is facilitating the adoption.[760] The

754. Section 233(1)(a).
755. *Ibid.*
756. Sections 18(3)(c) and 233(1)(b).
757. Sections 233(2) and 236(1).
758. Sections 233(2) and 236(3) read with s. 236(4).
759. Section 237(2).
760. Section 233(4).

parent or guardian may withdraw his or her consent within sixty days after having given it and no adoption order may be made until this period has expired.[761]

B. The Child

261. If the child who is to be adopted is older than 10 years, his or her consent to the adoption is required. The same applies if the child is younger than 10 years but is of an age, maturity and stage of development to understand the implications of consenting to the adoption.[762] Before giving his or her consent, the child must be counselled by the adoption social worker who is facilitating the adoption.[763] The child may withdraw his or her consent within sixty days after having given it and no adoption order may be made until this period has expired.[764]

C. Dispensing with Consent

262. If a person, including the prospective adopted child, withholds consent to an adoption, his or her consent can be dispensed with and the adoption order granted if the Children's Court finds that the withholding of consent is unreasonable and the adoption is in the best interests of the child. In determining whether consent is being withheld unreasonably, the court must take all relevant factors into account, including the nature of the relationship between the child and the person who has been withholding consent during the past two years; any findings a court has made in this regard; and the prospects of a sound relationship developing between the child and the person in the immediate future.[765]

IV. Who May Be Adopted?

263. An adult cannot be adopted; only a minor can.[766] Furthermore, a minor can be adopted only if an adoption social worker has determined that the minor is adoptable.[767] A child is adoptable in any of the following circumstances:[768]

(1) He or she is an orphan and has no guardian or caregiver who is willing to adopt him or her.
(2) The whereabouts of his or her parent or guardian cannot be established.
(3) He or she has been abandoned.

761. Section 233(8).
762. Section 233(1)(c).
763. Section 233(4).
764. Section 233(8).
765. Section 241(1) and (2).
766. Section 230(1) read with the definition of 'child' in s. 1(1).
767. Section 230(1)(b) and (2).
768. Section 230(3).

(4) His or her parent or guardian has abused or deliberately neglected him or her, or has allowed him or her to be abused or deliberately neglected.
(5) He or she is in need of a permanent alternative placement.
(6) He or she is the stepchild of the prospective adoptive parent.
(7) His or her parent or guardian has consented to the adoption (unless consent is not required).[769]

The Director-General of Social Development keeps and maintains a register on adoptable children and suitable prospective adoptive parents. This register is called the Register on Adoptable Children and Prospective Adoptive Parents.[770]

264. A very young child who has been orphaned or abandoned must be made available for adoption as soon as possible unless this is not in his or her best interests.[771] In order to achieve the early adoption of the child, he or she may be placed in temporary safe care pending an application for, and the finalization of, his or her adoption.[772] Furthermore, the Director-General of Social Development, a provincial head of the Department of Social Development, or a designated child protection organization may apply to the High Court, a Regional Court, or a Children's Court for an order terminating or transferring any or all of the parental responsibilities and rights of the child's parent or guardian. The application may be brought without the consent of the child's parent or caregiver if the child is 3 years or younger and has been in alternative care for more than six months.[773]

V. Factors to Be Taken into Consideration

265. A prospective adoptive parent must apply to the Children's Court for an adoption order.[774] The application must be accompanied by an assessment of the applicant by the adoption social worker who is facilitating the adoption and by a report by the adoption social worker on the child's adoptability, the child's medical information and the issue of whether the adoption is in the child's best interests.[775] The application must also be accompanied by a letter by the provincial head of the Department of Social Development recommending the child's adoption.[776]

---

769. *See* above in this discussion on the circumstances in which consent is not required.
770. Section 232(1) read with the definition of 'RACAP' in s. 1(1).
771. Section 157(3).
772. Section 156(1)(e)(iii).
773. Section 135(1)(a) and (2).
774. Section 239(1)(a).
775. Section 239(1)(b) and (c) read with s. 231(2)(d).
776. Section 239(1)(d). In exceptional circumstances the court may condone non-compliance with this requirement: *In re XN* 2013 (6) SA 153 (GSJ); *JGB v. Presiding Officer, Children's Court, Wynberg* [2016] 3 All SA 167 (WCC).

The court that considers the adoption application must take all relevant factors into account. Such factors include differences in the cultural and religious background of the child, the child's parent(s) and the prospective adoptive parent; reasonable preferences the child's parent stated in his or her consent; and the adoption social worker's report.[777] Race is not expressly mentioned as a relevant factor.

266. The Children's Court may make an adoption order only if all of the following requirements are met:[778]

(1) The adoption is in the best interests of the child.[779]
(2) The prospective adoptive parent has been properly assessed by an adoption social worker and has been found to be fit and proper to have full parental responsibilities and rights and to be willing and able to undertake, exercise and maintain those responsibilities and rights.
(3) The required consent has been given and not withdrawn, or consent has been dispensed with.
(4) The child's foster parent or the child's unmarried biological father who is not the child's guardian has been given an opportunity to apply to adopt the child.[780]

VI. Effect of Adoption Order

267. Unless the Children's Court includes different terms in its order, an adoption order terminates all parental responsibilities and rights any person had in respect of the child immediately before the adoption as well as all rights and responsibilities the child had as against that person and that person's family members. The family members of the person also lose all claims to have contact with the child.[781] An exception applies if the child is adopted by his or her step-parent or by the life partner of the child's parent. In such event, the adoption does not terminate the parental responsibilities and rights of the child's parent.[782]

An adoptive parent acquires full parental responsibilities and rights in respect of the adopted child, and the adopted child and adoptive parent are for all purposes regarded as each other's child and parent.[783] However, the adoption does not permit any marriage, civil union or sexual intercourse which would have been prohibited had the child not been adopted.[784] Thus, the prohibited degrees of relationship for purposes of entering into a marriage or civil union and for committing the crime of

777. Section 240(1).
778. Section 240(2).
779. *See also* s. 230(1)(a).
780. *See also* s. 231(7)(a) and (8).
781. Section 242(1).
782. Section 242(2)(e).
783. Section 242(2)(a) and (3).
784. Section 242(2)(c).

incest remain intact. Because the adopted child and adoptive parent are regarded as each other's child and parent for all purposes, the adoption creates additional prohibited degrees of relationship.

Unless the adoption order provides otherwise, the adopted child acquires the adoptive parent's surname.[785]

The adoption order does not affect any property rights the child acquired before the adoption.[786]

VII. Access to Information, and Contact

268. In the past, most adoptions were closed. Thus, the adopted child and his or her adoptive parent did not know the identity of the biological parents of the child and the biological parents did not know the identity of their child's adoptive parent. Nowadays there is much more openness in adoptions.

If the child's biological parent or guardian and his or her prospective adoptive parent enter into a post-adoption agreement, the adoption may be an open one. A post-adoption agreement offers the parent or guardian a means of retaining a link and/or a relationship with the child after the adoption, provided that the agreement is confirmed by the Children's Court when it makes the adoption order.[787] The court will not confirm an agreement that is not in the best interests of the child.[788]

A post-adoption agreement only provides for communication, contact and the sharing of information. In terms of the agreement, the child's parent or guardian and any other person stipulated in the agreement (e.g., a biological grandparent or sibling of the child) acquires the right to communicate and have contact with the child after the adoption, and/or to be provided with information regarding the child. Such information may include medical information.[789]

The adoption social worker who facilitates the adoption must assist the parties in preparing the agreement and counsel them on its implications.[790] If the child is of an age, maturity and stage of development to understand the implications of a post-adoption agreement, the agreement may not be entered into without the child's consent.[791]

269. Another way in which an adoption can be open, or partially open, is if the Children's Court that makes the adoption order includes terms which deviate from the normal rule that all existing parental responsibilities and rights are terminated

785. Section 242(2)(b).
786. Section 242(2)(d).
787. Sections 234(4) and 242(1).
788. Section 234(4).
789. Sections 234(1) and 248(4).
790. Section 234(3).
791. Section 234(2).

and replaced by parental responsibilities and rights on the part of the adoptive parent.[792] The court may, for example, even in the absence of a post-adoption agreement, order that the adopted child is to have contact with his or her siblings, grandparents, or any other stipulated person.

270. Finally, the right to know is recognized in the context of adoption. Firstly, the adopted child has a right to know the identity of his or her biological parents but, unless a court orders disclosure in the child's best interests while he or she is still a minor, the child may only gain access to the information in the adoption register once he or she has attained majority.[793] The same applies to the right of the adoptive parents to obtain the information in the adoption register.[794]

Regardless of the age of the child, he or she and his or her adoptive parents are entitled to have access to any medical information regarding him or her or his or her biological parents if such information relates directly to his or her health.[795]

The biological parent and a person who had previously adopted the child may also have access to the information in the adoption register, but only once the adopted child has attained majority. Furthermore, access by the biological parent is dependent on written consent being given by the child and the adoptive parent.[796] However, when the biological parent gives his or her consent to the adoption of his or her child, he or she may limit the consent to the child's adoption by a specific person whose name is stated in the written consent.[797] In such event, the identity of the adoptive parent is known to the biological parent right from the start, but even then the biological parent is not entitled to have access to the information in the adoption register before the child has attained majority and the child and his or her adoptive parent have provided their written consent.[798]

VIII. Rescission

271. An adoption order may be rescinded on application by the adopted child's biological parent or guardian if rescission is in the best interests of the child and the consent of the child's parent or guardian to the adoption was required but not obtained. The child, the child's parent or guardian, or the adoptive parent may apply for rescission if rescission is in the best interests of the child and the adoptive parent did not qualify as such at the time when the adoption order was made.[799] The application must be brought within a reasonable time, which may not exceed two years from the date of the adoption.[800]

792. Section 242(1).
793. Section 248(1)(a) and (e).
794. Section 248(1)(b) and (e).
795. Section 248(3).
796. Section 248(1)(c).
797. Section 233(3).
798. Section 248(1)(c).
799. Section 243(3) read with s. 243(1).
800. Section 243(1) and (2).

If rescission is ordered, the effects of the adoption cease to apply as from the date of the rescission, and all responsibilities, rights and other matters terminated by the adoption order are restored. The court may simultaneously make a placement order in respect of the child or order that the child be kept in temporary safe care until an appropriate placement order can be made.[801]

IX. Inter-Country Adoption

272. Prior to the decision of the Constitutional Court in *Minister of Welfare and Population Development v. Fitzpatrick*,[802] foreigners were prohibited from adopting South African children. Now, South African law permits inter-country adoption and regulates it by means of the Children's Act 38 of 2005 and the Hague Convention on the Protection of Children and Co-operation in Respect of Inter-country Adoption.[803] In an attempt to prevent evasion of the rules on inter-country adoption, the Children's Act even provides that if a non-South African citizen who has an interest in the care, well-being and development of a child applies to the High Court for an order assigning guardianship of the child to him or her, the application must be regarded as an inter-country adoption.[804]

§2. Foster Care

I. Who May Foster?

273. A foster care placement must be made by means of an order of the Children's Court in terms of the Children's Act 38 of 2005.[805]

274. A family member of the child who is not the child's parent or guardian or a person who is not a family member of the child may be appointed as the child's foster parent.[806] Otherwise the child may be placed in a registered cluster foster care scheme.[807] In cluster foster schemes, foster families are grouped together for purposes of communal back-up and mutual support. Recognizing cluster foster care schemes enables organizations to operate these schemes.[808]

---

801. Section 244(1) and (2).
802. 2000 (3) SA 422 (CC).
803. Children's Act 38 of 2005, Ch. 16 and Sch. 1.
804. Section 25.
805. Children's Act 38 of 2005, s. 180(1).
806. A family member can be appointed as the child's foster parent regardless of whether or not he or she has a duty of support towards the child: *SS v. Presiding Officer, Children's Court, Krugersdorp* 2012 (6) SA 45 (GSJ); *NM v. Presiding Officer of Children's Court, Krugersdorp* 2012 (6) SA 45 (GSJ).
807. *See* the definitions of 'foster care' and 'foster parent' in s. 1(1) read with s. 180(1) and (3).
808. J. Gallinetti & J. Loffell, *Foster Care*, in *Commentary on the Children's Act* 12–16 (C.J. Davel & A.M. Skelton eds., loose-leaf Juta & Co, Ltd 2007). Cluster foster care schemes must be registered and must be managed as non-profit organizations in terms of the Non-profit Organizations Act 71

275. A prospective foster parent must be fit and proper to be entrusted with the foster care of the child; be willing and able to undertake, exercise and maintain the responsibilities of foster care; and have the capacity to provide an environment that is conducive to the child's growth and development.[809] A designated social worker must assess the prospective foster parent to determine whether he or she complies with these requirements.[810] If the child is to be placed in a cluster foster care scheme, the abovementioned requirements apply to any person employed at or involved in a non-profit organization managing a cluster foster care scheme.[811]

II. Who May Be Fostered?

276. Only a minor may be placed in foster care.[812] The Children's Court must make a finding that the child is in need of care and protection before he or she can be placed in foster care.[813] A child is in need of care and protection if he or she:[814]

(1) has been abandoned or orphaned and does not have the ability to support himself or herself and this inability is readily apparent;
(2) displays behaviour which cannot be controlled by his or her parent or caregiver;
(3) lives or works on the streets, or begs for a living;
(4) is addicted to a dependence-producing substance and is without support to obtain treatment for such dependency;
(5) has been exploited or lives in circumstances which expose him or her to exploitation;
(6) lives in or is exposed to circumstances which may seriously harm his or her physical, mental or social well-being;
(7) may be at risk if returned to the care of his or her parent, guardian or caregiver because there is reason to believe that the child will live in, or be exposed to, circumstances which may seriously harm his or her physical, mental or social well-being;
(8) is in a state of physical or mental neglect; or
(9) is being maltreated, abused, deliberately neglected or degraded by a parent, caregiver or family member, someone who has parental responsibilities and rights in respect of the child, or someone under whose control the child is.

---

of 1997: Children's Act 38 of 2005, s. 183(1). The management of the schemes is monitored by the provincial head of the Department of Social Development: Children's Act, s. 183(2).

809. Section 182(2)(a)–(c).
810. Section 182(2)(d).
811. Section 182(4).
812. Section 180(1) read with the definition of 'child' in s 1(1).
813. Sections 46(1)(a)(i) and 56(1)(e).
814. Section 150(1).

A child may also be in need of care and protection if he or she is a victim of child labour or is in a child-headed household, but in these circumstances a social worker must first investigate whether the child is indeed in need of care and protection.[815]

277. A foster parent or two foster parents sharing a common household may foster a maximum of six children, unless the children are siblings or blood relations or the Children's Court is of the view that exceeding that number is in the best interests of all the children.[816] More than six children may be placed in a registered cluster foster care scheme.[817]

III. Factors to Be Taken into Consideration

278. Before a child is placed in foster care, a designated social worker must prepare a report on the child and his or her circumstances. The Children's Court must take this report into consideration and also consider the best way of securing stability in the child's life.[818]

The report must deal with the cultural, religious and linguistic background of the child and the availability of a suitable person with a similar background who is willing and able to provide foster care to the child. A child may only be placed in the foster care of a person from a different cultural, religious and linguistic background if there is an existing bond between the person and the child, or a suitable and willing person with a similar background is not readily available to provide foster care to the child.[819]

In addition to the cultural, religious and linguistic background of the child and the foster parent, the report must deal with the conditions of the child's life. The social worker must *inter alia* assess the developmental, therapeutic and other needs of the child and give details of any family preservation services that have been considered or attempted. The report must also contain a permanency plan aimed at achieving stability in the child's life. The plan must take the child's age and developmental needs into account.[820]

IV. Effect of Foster Care Order

279. If a foster care order is made, the foster parent acquires many responsibilities and rights towards his or her foster child, and also becomes entitled to apply for a foster child grant.[821] The foster care placement may be subject to monitoring by the Children's Court and supervision by a social worker.[822]

---

815. Section 150(2). On child-headed households, *see* Part II, Ch. 8 below.
816. Section 185(1).
817. Section 185(2).
818. Sections 157(1) and 184(1).
819. Section 184(1) and (2).
820. Section 157(1)(a).
821. Social Assistance Act 13 of 2004, s. 8.
822. Children's Act 38 of 2005, ss 156(3)(a)(i), 156(3)(a)(iii) and 188(4).

A foster parent has all the parental responsibilities and rights in respect of his or her foster child that are set out in the foster care order; an order which amends the foster care order; an order assigning parental responsibilities and rights to the foster parent; or a foster care plan between the foster parent and the foster child's parent or guardian.[823] The foster parent may also acquire other responsibilities and rights in terms of the Children's Act 38 of 2005 or the regulations under the Act.[824] If the foster child has been abandoned, is an orphan, or family reunification is not in his or her best interests, the Children's Court may confer parental responsibilities and rights on the foster parent over and above those that are normally necessary for foster care to take place.[825]

A foster parent may not give or refuse any consent that is legally required in respect of his or her foster child without giving due consideration to any views and wishes expressed by the child's parent or guardian and by the child, bearing in mind the child's age, maturity and stage of development. Nor may the foster parent take any decision regarding contact between the child and a person who is a co-holder of parental responsibilities and rights together with the foster parent or regarding the assignment of guardianship or care in respect of the child to another person without giving due consideration to the views and wishes of the child and his or her parent or guardian. The same applies to a decision that is likely to significantly change, or to have an adverse effect on, the child's living conditions, education, health or personal relations with a parent or family member or, generally, on the child's well-being.[826]

280. The biological parent of a foster child, or anybody else who is legally liable for the child's maintenance, may be ordered to pay a single or a recurrent sum of money as a contribution towards the maintenance of the child or the treatment and the costs of special needs of the child.[827] Payment must be made to the person or institution specified by the Children's Court.[828] The court may order the liable party's employer to deduct the amount from his or her salary or remuneration and to pay it to the person or institution specified in the order.[829] The contribution order may be enforced by means of the mechanisms provided for in the Maintenance Act 99 of 1998 and the Reciprocal Enforcement of Maintenance Orders Act 80 of 1963.[830]

281. If the Children's Court that makes a foster care order is of the view that reunification between the foster child and his or her biological parent is possible and in the child's best interests, it must make the foster care placement subject to conditions providing for facilitation of such reunification by a designated social

823. Section 188(1)(a) and (c)–(e).
824. Section 188(1)(b) and (f).
825. Section 188(3).
826. Section 188(2) read with ss 18(3)(c) and 31(1)(b).
827. Section 161(1)(a)(i) read with the definition of 'respondent' in s. 1(1).
828. Section 164.
829. Section 165(1)(a).
830. Section 163.

worker.[831] If the child has not been reunited with his or her biological parents two months before the expiry of the foster care order, the social worker must submit a report to the Children's Court explaining why reunification did not occur and recommending any steps that may be taken to stabilize the foster child's life.[832] The Children's Court may order that the social worker must continue facilitating reunification or order termination of reunification services if there are no prospects of reunification.[833]

V. Duration of Foster Care

282. Because foster care is only available in respect of a minor, a foster care order or an extension of the order cannot operate beyond the foster child's eighteenth birthday.[834] However, the Children's Act 38 of 2005 allows the foster child to remain in foster care until the end of the year in which he or she turns 18.[835] The decision whether he or she wants to remain in foster care is entirely that of the foster child.[836]

The Act furthermore empowers the foster child or someone acting on behalf of the child to apply to the provincial head of the Department of Social Development for permission to remain in foster care until the end of the year in which he or she turns 21 if his or her foster parent is willing and able to continue to care for him or her and continuation of the foster care is necessary to enable the child to complete his or her education or training.[837] The decision whether or not to allow the foster child to remain in foster care is in the discretion of the provincial head.[838]

283. The initial placement of a child in foster care usually lapses after two years from the date on which the foster care order was made or after such shorter period as the order specified.[839] The Children's Court may extend the order for periods of up to two years at a time.[840]

However, if an abandoned or orphaned child is to be placed in foster care with a family member, the initial foster care placement may last for more than two years, last until the child becomes a major, or be extended for more than two years at a time if this will create stability in the child's life and be in the child's best interests. The same applies if there is no purpose in attempting reunification between the child and his or her biological parents.[841] If the placement lasts for more than two years,

831. Section 187(1); *see also* ss 156(3)(a)(ii) and 157(1)(b)(ii).
832. Section 187(2).
833. Section 187(3).
834. Section 159(3).
835. Section 176(1).
836. N. Zaal & C. Matthias, *Alternative Care*, in *Commentary on the Children's Act* 11–26 (C.J. Davel & A.M. Skelton eds., loose-leaf Juta & Co, Ltd 2007).
837. Section 176(2).
838. Zaal & Matthias, 11-26–11-27.
839. Section 159(1)(a).
840. Section 159(1)(b)
841. Section 186(2).

is extended by more than two years, or lasts until the child becomes a major, a social service professional must visit the foster child at least once every two years to monitor and evaluate the placement.[842]

If a child has been in foster care with a person other than a family member for more than two years, the foster care may be extended until the child becomes a major, and the court may order that no further social worker supervision and no further reports by a social worker are required if this will create stability in the child's life. However, a social service professional must still visit the foster child at least once every two years to monitor and evaluate the foster care placement.[843]

When deciding whether the period of foster care should be extended, the Children's Court must take the views of the child as well as those of his or her parent, his or her foster parent and any other person who has parental responsibilities and rights in respect of him or her into account.[844]

284. The Children's Court may terminate a foster care placement if this is in the best interests of the foster child. Before terminating the placement, the court must take all relevant factors into account. Those factors include the bond between the foster child and his or her biological parent if the biological parent is reclaiming care of the child; the bond between the foster child and his or her foster parent and between the child and the family of the foster parent; and the prospects of achieving permanency in the child's life by returning him or her to his or her biological parent, allowing him or her permanently to remain in foster care with the foster parent, placing him or her in any other alternative care, or having him or her adopted.[845]

842. Section 186(3).
843. Section 186(1) and (3).
844. Section 159(2).
845. Section 189(1) and (2).

Chapter 6. Parental Authority

§1. Introduction

285. Originally, the father of a child born of married parents had full parental authority (parental power) over his child, and the mother of a child born of unmarried parents had full parental authority over her child. The focus was on the parent's rights and interests, not on those of the child. Gradually, a greater awareness of and concern for the child's best interests developed. Nowadays, the focus is on the rights of the child, and the child's best interests are of paramount importance in every matter concerning the child.[846]

What is in a child's best interests is determined by the facts and context of each case. To assist bodies and persons who have to make decisions and engage in action regarding children, the Children's Act 38 of 2005 contains a checklist of factors regarding the best interests of the child which must be taken into account to the extent that they are relevant in each particular case.[847] These factors are the following:

(1) The nature of the personal relationship between the child and his or her parents, or any specific parent, and between the child and any other relevant person.
(2) The attitude of the parents, or any specific parent, towards the child and the exercise of parental responsibilities or rights in respect of the child.
(3) The capacity of the parents, any specific parent, or any other person, to provide for the child's needs, including his or her emotional and intellectual needs.
(4) The likely effect any change in the child's circumstances would have on the child, including the likely effect of the child's separation from either or both of his or her parents, a sibling, another child, or any other caregiver or person with whom the child has been living.
(5) The practical difficulty and expense of the child having contact with his or her parents, or a specific parent, and whether that difficulty or expense would substantially affect the child's right to maintain personal relations and direct contact with that parent on a regular basis.
(6) The child's need to remain in the care of his or her parent, family and extended family, and to maintain a connection with his or her family, extended family, culture or tradition.
(7) The child's age, maturity, stage of development, gender and background, and any other relevant characteristic of the child.
(8) The child's physical and emotional security and his or her intellectual, emotional, social and cultural development.
(9) Any disability the child has.
(10) Any chronic illness the child suffers from.

846. Constitution, s. 28(2); Children's Act 38 of 2005, ss 6(2)(a) and 9.
847. Section 7(1).

(11) The child's need to be brought up in a stable family environment or, if this cannot be achieved, in an environment resembling a family environment as closely as possible.
(12) The need to protect the child from any physical or psychological harm which may be caused by subjecting him or her to maltreatment, abuse, neglect, exploitation or degradation, exposing him or her to violence, exploitation or other harmful behaviour, or exposing him or her to maltreatment, abuse, degradation, ill-treatment, violence, or harmful behaviour towards another person.
(13) Any family violence involving the child or a family member of the child.
(14) Which action or decision would avoid or minimize further legal or administrative proceedings regarding the child.

The court must attach such weight to each of the relevant factors as it considers fit, and must ultimately reach a conclusion based on a value judgement about what is in the child's best interests in the particular case.[848] A child-centred approach, which requires 'a close and individualized examination of the precise real-life situation of the particular child involved', must be employed.[849]

286. The change in focus in the law of parent and child is reflected, *inter alia*, in the change in terminology from 'parental authority' to 'parental responsibilities and rights' in the Children's Act 38 of 2005. Other indications of the changed focus are that child participation is legally recognized and mandated by the Act; a delay in any action or decision regarding a child must be avoided as far as possible; an approach which is conducive to conciliation and problem-solving must be adopted; and a confrontational approach must be avoided.[850]

§2. The Contents of Parental Responsibilities and Rights

287. Parental responsibilities and rights include caring for the child, maintaining contact with the child, acting as the child's guardian, and contributing to the child's maintenance.[851]

I. Guardianship

288. Guardianship refers to administering and safeguarding a child's property and property interests, assisting or representing the child in administrative, contractual and other legal matters, and giving or refusing any consent that is legally

848. *See*, e.g., *K v. M* [2007] 4 All SA 883 (E); *P v. P* 2007 (5) SA 94 (SCA).
849. *S v. M (Centre for Child Law as Amicus Curiae)* 2008 (3) SA 232 (CC) para. 24.
850. Children's Act 38 of 2005, ss 6(4), 6(5), 10 and 31(1).
851. *See* the definition of 'parental responsibilities and rights' in s. 1(1) read with s. 18(2) of the Children's Act 38 of 2005.

required in respect of the child (such as consent to the child's marriage or adoption).[852] The administration of the child's estate includes acquiring and controlling assets and incurring and satisfying debts on the child's behalf. The parent must control the child's estate like a *bonus et diligens paterfamilias* (prudent and diligent person), otherwise the child can sue the parent for damages in delict (tort).[853] Provided that he or she acts openly and in good faith, the parent may assist the child in a juristic act in which the parent has an interest.[854]

289. Before a parent takes a decision regarding his or her child's marriage, adoption, departure or removal from South Africa, the child's application for a passport, or the alienation or encumbrance of any immovable property of the child, he or she must give due consideration to any views and wishes expressed by the child, bearing in mind the child's age, maturity and stage of development.[855]

II. Care

290. Care encompasses the following:[856]

(1) Within available means, providing the child with a suitable place to live, living conditions which are conducive to the child's health, well-being and development, and the necessary financial support.
(2) Safeguarding and promoting the child's well-being.
(3) Protecting the child from maltreatment, abuse, neglect, degradation, discrimination, exploitation and any other physical and moral harm or hazards.
(4) Respecting, protecting, promoting and securing the fulfilment of, and guarding against any infringement of the child's constitutional rights and the rights set out in the Children's Act 38 of 2005.
(5) Guiding and directing the child's education and upbringing in a manner that is appropriate to the child's age, maturity and stage of development.
(6) Guiding, advising and assisting the child in decisions he or she has to take, bearing in mind the child's age, maturity and stage of development.
(7) Guiding the child's behaviour in a humane manner.
(8) Maintaining a sound relationship with the child.
(9) Accommodating the child's special needs.
(10) Generally ensuring that the child's best interests are the paramount concern in all matters affecting the child.

From the above list it is clear that the person who has care may decide where the child is to reside, with whom the child may associate, which school the child is to

852. *See* the definition of 'guardianship' in s. 1(1) of the Children's Act 38 of 2005 read with s. 18(3).
853. Grotius, *Inleidinge tot de Hollandsche Rechts-geleerdheid*,1.8.7, 3.26.8; Voet, *Commentarius ad Pandectas*, 26.7.1, 27.8.12.
854. *Peffers v. Attorneys, Notaries & Conveyancers Fidelity Guarantee Fund Board of Control* 1965 (2) SA 53 (C).
855. Children's Act 38 of 2005, ss 10 and 31(1).
856. *See* the definition of 'care' in s. 1(1) of the Children's Act 38 of 2005.

attend, whether the child should undertake tertiary education, what religious education the child should receive, whether the child may attend specific social events, in which language the child is to be brought up, whether the child should receive medical treatment or undergo an operation, what the child may eat, what time the child is to go to bed, what toys the child may play with, what the child may read, what television programmes the child may watch, and so forth.[857]

The parent who has care also has the right to discipline the child which, at common law, included the right to impose moderate and reasonable corporal punishment.[858] However, in 2017 a division of the High Court ruled that corporal punishment by parents was unconstitutional.[859] The Constitutional Court is set to rule on an appeal against the judgment in 2019.[860]

291. The person who has care enjoys a broad discretion on how the responsibilities and rights encompassed by care are to be exercised, in which the court is loath to interfere unless the discretion is exercised in a manner that is not in the best interests of the child.[861]

292. Since the coming into operation of section 31(1) of the Children's Act 38 of 2005, the rights of the parent who has care have been subject to the requirement that he or she must give due consideration to any views and wishes expressed by the child before he or she takes a decision that affects contact between the child and a co-holder of parental responsibilities and rights or that is likely to significantly change or have an adverse effect on the child's living conditions, education, health or personal relations with a parent or family member or, generally, on the child's well-being. The same applies to taking a decision regarding the assignment of care to another person. The child's age, maturity and stage of development must be borne in mind when giving consideration to his or her views and wishes.[862] Furthermore, having regard to the child's age, maturity and stage of development, the child must be informed of any action or decision in a matter which significantly affects him or her, and, if he or she is of such an age, maturity and stage of development as to be able to participate, he or she has the right to participate in that matter in an appropriate way, with due consideration being given to his or her views.[863]

857. *See*, e.g., *Simleit v. Cunliffe* 1940 TPD 67; *Engar and Engar v. Desai* 1966 (1) SA 621 (T); *Allsop v. McCann* 2001 (2) SA 706 (C); *J v. J* 2008 (6) SA 30 (C).

858. *R. v. Janke & Janke* 1913 TPD 382; *Du Preez v. Conradie* 1990 (4) SA 46 (B).

859. *YG v. S* 2018 (11) SACR 64 (GJ).

860. A. Bolowana 'Constitutional Court Reserves Judgment on Corporal Punishment Matter', http://www.sabcnews.com/sabcnews/constitutional-court-reserves-judgement-on-corporal-punishment-matter/, 6 Feb. 2019.

861. *Martin v. Mason* 1949 (1) PH B9 (N).

862. Section 31(1)(a) and (b)(ii)–(iv).

863. Sections 6(5) and 10.

III. Contact

293. 'Contact' refers to maintaining a personal relationship with the child and communicating with him or her on a regular basis if he or she lives with someone else. Communication may take place in person or in another format (such as via telephone calls, telefaxes, letters, videos, video calls, electronic mail, mobile phone text messages, or electronic social networks).[864]

294. While a person exercises his or her right of contact in person, he or she temporarily has responsibilities and rights that are normally exercised by the person who has care, such as the right to determine where the child may stay, what the child may eat, what time the child is to go to bed, what toys the child may play with, what the child may read, and what television programmes the child may watch.

IV. Maintenance

295. The duty to support (maintain) a child extends to such maintenance as the child reasonably requires for his or her proper living and upbringing. It includes the provision of food, clothing, accommodation, medical care and a suitable education.[865]

296. Both parents are obliged to support their child regardless of whether the child is born of married or unmarried parents, regardless of whether either of them has guardianship or care of, or contact with the child, and regardless of whether the child was born of a first or a subsequent marriage or civil union.[866] The duty of support is apportioned between the parents according to their respective means[867] and lasts until the child dies, is adopted or becomes self-supporting.[868] If the child enters into a marriage or a civil union, the duty of support rests on the child's spouse or civil union partner first, but if the child's spouse or civil union partner is unable to support the child, the child can still claim maintenance from his or her parents, grandparents or siblings.[869] If a parent dies, his or her estate is responsible for his or her child's maintenance unless the deceased parent bequeathed assets to the child from which the child can meet his or her maintenance needs.[870]

If neither of the child's parents or their estates can support the child, the duty of support passes to the child's grandparents.[871] If neither the child's parents nor his or

864. *See* the definition of 'contact' in s. 1(1) of the Children's Act 38 of 2005.
865. Maintenance Act 99 of 1998, s. 15(2).
866. *Ibid.*, s. 15(3)(a)(iii) and (4).
867. *Ibid.*, s. 15(3)(a)(ii).
868. *See* s. 242(1) of the Children's Act 38 of 2005; *Gliksman v. Talekinsky* 1955 (4) SA 468 (W).
869. *Gliksman v. Talekinsky* 1955 (4) SA 468 (W).
870. *See*, e.g., *Carelse v. Estate De Vries* (1906) 23 SC 532; *Spies' Executors v. Beyers* 1908 TS 473; *Secretary for Inland Revenue v. Brey* 1980 (1) SA 472 (A); *Lambrakis v. Santam* 2000 (3) SA 1098 (W).
871. *See*, e.g., *Ex parte Jacobs* 1936 OPD 31; *Gliksman v. Talekinsky* 1955 (4) SA 468 (W); *Petersen v. Maintenance Officer, Simon's Town Maintenance Court* 2004 (2) SA 56 (C).

her grandparents can support him or her, the duty passes to his or her siblings regardless of whether they are full siblings or half-brothers and -sisters.[872]

297. The scope of the duty of support and the standard at which support must be provided depend on the circumstances of each case. Important considerations are the child's needs, age, state of health and intellectual ability; the financial resources and social standing of the person who is liable for maintenance; and the fact that the person in whose care the child is meets (at least part of) his or her duty of support by undertaking the responsibilities involved in exercising care.[873]

298. The duty to support a child can be enforced via the Maintenance Act 99 of 1998.[874] A warrant of execution can, *inter alia*, be issued against the maintenance debtor's property, or an order may be made for the attachment of his or her emoluments (salary, wage or allowance) or any present or future debt owing or accruing to him or her.[875] A maintenance defaulter may also be convicted of the crime of failing to provide a child with adequate food, clothing, accommodation and medical assistance while being able to do so. The latter crime is a statutory crime contained in the Children's Act 38 of 2005.[876] Because any order of the Maintenance Court has the effect of an order in a civil action,[877] enforcement of a maintenance order may take place without relying on the mechanisms provided for in the Maintenance Act. Thus, for example, the defaulter may be charged with contempt of court and committed to prison if found guilty.[878]

The Maintenance Act does not authorize attachment of a maintenance debtor's assets in respect of maintenance payments which are not yet due and in respect of which he or she is not yet in default. However, the High Court has held that section 28(2) of the Constitution compels it to protect the best interests of children of maintenance debtors who are likely to shirk their future maintenance responsibilities. Accordingly, it must afford effective relief to such children by employing remedies that fall outside the ambit of the Maintenance Act. Applying this view, the courts have ordered the retention of pension and provident fund withdrawal benefits, retirement annuities, and the proceeds of the sale of immovable property belonging to maintenance debtors for purposes of payment of future maintenance for their children.[879]

---

872. *Oosthuizen v. Stanley* 1938 AD 322; *Miller v. Miller* 1940 CPD 466; *Ex parte Pienaar* 1964 (1) SA 600 (T).
873. *See*, e.g., *Zimelka v. Zimelka* 1990 (4) SA 303 (W); *Mentz v. Simpson* 1990 (4) SA 455 (A); *Douglas v. Douglas* [1996] All SA 1 (A); *Bursey v. Bursey* 1999 (3) SA 33 (SCA).
874. Sections 16, 26–31 and 40.
875. Section 26(2)(a) read with ss 27–30.
876. Section 305(4).
877. Maintenance Act 99 of 1998, s. 24(1).
878. *Bannatyne v. Bannatyne (Commission for Gender Equality as Amicus Curiae)* 2003 (2) SA 363 (CC).
879. *Mngadi v. Beacon Sweets & Chocolates Provident Fund* 2004 (5) SA 388 (D); *Magewu v. Zozo* [2004] 3 All SA 235 (C); *Soller v. Maintenance Magistrate, Wynberg* 2006 (2) SA 66 (C); *Burger v. Burger* 2006 (4) SA 414 (D); *Gerber v. Gerber* [2007] ZAWCHC 65, 9 Nov. 2007, (unreported), http://www.saflii.org/za/cases/ZAWCHC/2007/65.html.

299. The duty of support is reciprocal. Therefore, a child is obliged to support his or her parents, grandparents and siblings. However, the duty to support parents, grandparents and siblings arises only if the parents, grandparents or adult siblings are indigent.[880] Furthermore, the child's duty arises only if the parent, grandparent or sibling does not have a spouse, civil union partner or child who can support him or her.[881] If a parent or grandparent has more than one child or grandchild, or a sibling has more than one sibling, the children, grandchildren or siblings must contribute according to their respective means.[882] The scope of the duty of support depends on the circumstances of each particular case, including the parties' social status and means.[883]

§3. Obtaining Parental Responsibilities and Rights

I. Birth

300. As a rule, a child's biological mother acquires full parental responsibilities and rights from the time of the child's birth. However, if the mother is an unmarried minor and neither she nor the child's biological father has guardianship in respect of the child, her guardian is the child's guardian, while she has all other parental responsibilities and rights in respect of the child.[884]

If the child was conceived as a result of artificial fertilization, the woman who gives birth to the child (birth mother) is for all purposes regarded as the child's mother, unless she is the child's surrogate mother in terms of a valid surrogate motherhood agreement.[885] In the case of surrogacy, the birth mother does not acquire parental responsibilities and rights even if her ovum was used for her artificial fertilization. Instead, the child is deemed to be the child of the commissioning parent(s) for all purposes as from the time of his or her birth.[886] If the surrogate motherhood agreement is invalid, the surrogate mother is for all purposes deemed to be the child's mother and the child has no relationship with the commissioning parent(s).[887]

880. *See*, e.g., *Oosthuizen v. Stanley* 1938 AD 322; *Smith v. Mutual & Federal Insurance Co Ltd* 1998 (4) SA 626 (C); *Tyali v. University of Transkei* [2002] 2 All SA 47 (Tk); *Fosi v. Road Accident Fund* 2008 (3) SA 560 (C).
881. *See*, e.g., *Barnes v. Union and South West Africa Insurance Co Ltd* 1977 (3) SA 502 (E); *Tyali v. University of Transkei* [2002] 2 All SA 47 (Tk).
882. *Oosthuizen v. Stanley* 1938 AD 322.
883. *Groves v. Baillie* 1942 WLD 34.
884. Children's Act 38 of 2005, s. 19(1) and (2).
885. *Ibid.*, s. 40(2) read with s. 297(1)(a).
886. *Ibid.*, ss 19(3) and 297(1).
887. *Ibid.*, s. 297(2).

II. Marriage or Civil Union

301. If a child is born of parents who are each other's spouses in a civil, customary or religious marriage or are each other's civil union partners, both parents have full parental responsibilities and rights in respect of the child from the time of his or her birth. The same applies if the parents marry each other or enter into a civil union with each other after the child's birth.[888]

III. Permanent Life Partnership

302. Both parents have full parental responsibilities and rights in respect of their child if they live together in a permanent life partnership when their child is born.[889]

IV. Acknowledging Paternity, Contributing to the Child's Upbringing, and Contributing to the Child's Maintenance

303. An unmarried biological father acquires full parental responsibilities and rights in respect of his child if, regardless of whether he has lived or is living with the child's mother, he consents or successfully applies to be identified as the child's father or pays damages in terms of customary law; contributes or has attempted to contribute to the child's upbringing; and contributes or has attempted to contribute to the child's maintenance. In these circumstances he has exactly the same parental responsibilities and rights as the child's mother.[890]

V. Parental Responsibilities and Rights Agreement

304. Any person who has an interest in the care, well-being and development of a child (such as an unmarried father or a grandparent) can acquire parental responsibilities and rights in respect of the child by entering into a parental responsibilities and rights agreement with the child's mother or another person who has parental responsibilities and rights in respect of the child.[891]

VI. Assignment by an Order of Court

305. A person who does not have parental responsibilities and rights can acquire them by means of a court order assigning all or some of them to him or her.[892]

---

888. *Ibid.*, ss 19 and 20.
889. *Ibid.*, s. 21(1)(a).
890. *Ibid.*, s. 21(1)(b).
891. *See* further Part II, Ch. 4, §2 above.
892. *Ibid.*

VII. Adoption

306. An adoptive parent has full parental responsibilities and rights in respect of his or her adopted child.[893]

VIII. Appointment in a Will

307. A person who has sole guardianship or sole care of a child may appoint a fit and proper person to act as his or her successor after his or her death. The appointment must be made in the will of the person who has sole guardianship or sole care.[894] Before making the appointment, the person must give due consideration to any views and wishes expressed by the child, bearing in mind the child's age, maturity and stage of development.[895]

§4. The Position if More than One Person Has Parental Responsibilities and Rights

308. If more than one person has parental responsibilities and rights in respect of a child, they may exercise those responsibilities and rights without each other's consent unless the Children's Act 38 of 2005, any other rule of law or a court order provides otherwise.[896] Thus, the starting point is that co-holders of parental responsibilities and rights may independently exercise their responsibilities and rights.

However, there are certain juristic acts for which the consent of all the guardians of a child is required, unless a court dispenses with the need for joint consent. These acts are the child's marriage; the child's adoption; the child's departure or removal from South Africa; the child's application for a passport; and the alienation or encumbrance of any immovable property of the child.[897]

In recent years, the courts have frequently been approached for orders authorizing one parent to emigrate with his or her child despite the other parent's objections. The child's best interests are the determining factor in deciding such cases.[898] To determine whether or not the proposed move is in the best interests of the child, the court evaluates the reasonableness of the parent's decision to move; the practical and other considerations on which the decision is based; and the extent to which the parent has engaged with and properly thought through the advantages and disadvantages of the proposed move for the child.[899] It must in particular take the factors regarding the best interests of the child that are listed in section 7(1) of the

893. *See* further Part II, Ch. 5, §1 above.
894. Children's Act 38 of 2005, s. 27(1) and (2).
895. *Ibid.*, ss 10, 31(1)(a) and 31(1)(b)(iii).
896. *Ibid.*, ss 18(4), 18(5) and 30(2).
897. *Ibid.*, s. 18(4) and (5) read with s. 18(3)(c).
898. *See*, e.g., *Jackson v. Jackson* 2002 (2) SA 303 (SCA); *F v. F* 2006 (3) SA 42 (SCA).
899. *F v. F* 2006 (3) SA 42 (SCA). Factors the courts have considered in this regard include the parent's desire to return home if he or she is a foreigner; the presence of family members in the foreign country; the stability of any relationship the parent may have with a new partner or spouse who

Children's Act into account.[900] Due consideration also has to be given to the views and wishes of the child if the child is of an age, maturity and stage of development to be able to participate.[901]

As a rule, a court will not lightly refuse the care-giving parent permission to emigrate with his or her child if the decision to emigrate is bona fide and reasonable, since it is usually not in the best interests of the child to thwart the care-giving parent in his or her endeavour to emigrate 'in pursuance of a decision reasonably and genuinely taken', because a frustrated and bitter parent cannot provide a child with a happy and secure environment.[902] Furthermore, courts must bear in mind that 'differential treatment of custodian parents and their non-custodian counterparts – who have no reciprocal legal obligation to maintain contact with the child and may relocate at will – may, and often does, indirectly constitute unfair gender discrimination' because it is still predominantly women who care for children.[903] However, each case must be decided on its facts and the court must not assume too readily that the care-giving parent's interests coincide or are compatible with the child's best interests.[904]

309. A further limitation on the exercising of common parental responsibilities and rights is that a person who holds parental responsibilities and rights must give due consideration to the views and wishes of all co-holders before taking any decision that is likely significantly to change, or to have a significant adverse effect on, a co-holder's exercise of parental responsibilities and rights.[905] Once the person has given such consideration to the co-holder's views and wishes, he or she may act independently.[906] Failing to give consideration to the co-holder's views and wishes does not render the decision invalid, but if a decision that is taken without giving due consideration to those views and wishes is not in the best interests of the child, it may be set aside by the court.[907]

310. In terms of the Children's Act 38 of 2005, a co-holder of parental responsibilities and rights may not surrender or transfer his or her parental responsibilities and rights. Co-holders may, however, agree that one of them will exercise any or all of the responsibilities and rights on behalf of the other co-holder(s). An agreement

---

resides or works in the foreign country; social benefits in the foreign country; the parent's employment opportunities and his or her financial and other prospects in the foreign country; educational opportunities for the child in the foreign country; the accommodation which is available in the foreign country; the child's ability to speak the particular foreign language; and safety concerns: *see*, e.g., *Van Rooyen v. Van Rooyen* 1999 (4) SA 435 (C); *Godbeer v. Godbeer* 2000 (3) SA 976 (W); *H v. R* 2001 (3) SA 623 (C)); *Latouf v. Latouf* [2001] 2 All SA 377 (T); *Jackson v. Jackson* 2002 (2) SA 303 (SCA); *F v. F* 2006 (3) SA 42 (SCA); *HG v. CG* 2010 (3) SA 352 (ECP); *JP v. JP* [2016] 1 All SA 794 (KZD).

900. Those factors are listed above in this chapter.
901. Children's Act 38 of 2005, ss 10 and 31(1).
902. *Jackson v. Jackson* 2002 (2) SA 303 (SCA) para. 2; *see also F v. F* 2006 (3) SA 42 (SCA).
903. *F v. F* 2006 (3) SA 42 (SCA) para. 12.
904. *F v. F* 2006 (3) SA 42 (SCA).
905. Section 31(2).
906. *J v. J* 2008 (6) SA 30 (C).
907. *Ibid.*

in terms of which a co-holder authorizes somebody to exercise parental responsibilities and rights on his or her behalf does not divest him or her of those responsibilities and rights.[908]

311. If co-holders of parental responsibilities and rights experience difficulties in exercising those responsibilities and rights, they must attempt to agree on a parenting plan before they approach the court for resolution of their difficulties.[909] If attempts to agree on a parenting plan fail, any of the co-holders may approach the High Court in its capacity as upper guardian of all minors for an order, and the court may compel an unwilling party to enter into a parenting plan.[910]

A parenting plan may regulate any matter in connection with parental responsibilities and rights.[911] It must be in writing, be signed by the parties, and be in the best interests of the child.[912] The co-holders of parental responsibilities and rights must seek the assistance of a Family Advocate, social worker or psychologist, or mediation through a social worker or other suitably qualified person when they prepare their parenting plan. Even if co-holders do not experience difficulties in exercising their responsibilities and rights, they may enter into a parenting plan, but then they need not seek the assistance of a Family Advocate, social worker or psychologist, or mediation by any person.[913]

A parenting plan may be registered with a Family Advocate or be made an order of court.[914] If it is registered with a Family Advocate, it may later be amended or terminated by the Family Advocate on application by the parties to the plan. If it is made an order of court, a further court order is required to amend or terminate it.[915]

§5. Judicial Interference with Parental Responsibilities and Rights

312. As the upper guardian of all minors, the High Court has a common-law power to interfere in the exercising of parental responsibilities and rights by any person or body if an order is required by the best interests of the child. For example, if the child's best interests demand this, the court may ratify acts a person performed whilst labouring under the mistaken belief that he or she was the child's guardian; appoint a parent and a third party as joint guardians; award contact to a

908. Section 30(3) and (4).
909. Section 33(2).
910. *M v. V (born N)* [2011] JOL 27045 (WCC).
911. Section 33(3).
912. Sections 33(4) and 34(1)(a).
913. Section 33(1) and (5).
914. Section 34(1)(b).
915. Section 34(4) and (5).

third party who does not have an inherent right to contact (such as a sibling, grandparent or step-parent); suspend a parent's guardianship and appoint a third party as the child's guardian; and review any type of order or ruling affecting the rights of the child.[916]

313. Various courts also have statutory powers to interfere in the exercising of parental responsibilities and rights. For example, section 5(1) of the Matrimonial Affairs Act 37 of 1953 empowers the High Court to make whatever order it deems fit in respect of guardianship or care of, or contact with, a child born of married parents who are divorced or are still married but live apart; and, in terms of section 25(4) of the Marriage Act 25 of 1961, the High Court has the power to consent to a minor's marriage if the minor's parent or guardian, or the presiding officer of the Children's Court withholds consent. In terms of section 6(3) of the Divorce Act 70 of 1979 read with section 13 of the Civil Union Act 17 of 2006, a division of the High Court or a Regional Court that grants a divorce has the power to make whatever order it deems fit with regard to the maintenance of a dependent child born of the marriage or civil union or with respect to the guardianship, care, and contact of a minor child born of the marriage or civil union. In terms of section 7(6) of the Domestic Violence Act 116 of 1998, a Magistrate's Court that issues a protection order against the perpetrator of domestic violence may refuse the perpetrator contact with a child or impose conditions in respect of contact if this is in the child's best interests.

Several provisions of the Children's Act 38 of 2005 also empower various courts to interfere in the exercise of a person's parental responsibilities and rights. Thus, for example, a court may dispense with a parent or guardian's consent to adoption; grant exemption from the requirement that all guardians must consent to the juristic acts for which joint consent is normally required; consent to an HIV-test on a child; dispense with consent to medical treatment or an operation on a child; order an abducting parent to return his or her child to the country from where the child was removed; assign guardianship, care or contact to a person; terminate, extend, suspend or circumscribe parental responsibilities and rights; and make a placement order in respect of a child who has been found to be in need of care and protection.[917]

314. In all instances where interference is at issue the court's decision must be based on the child's best interests, and the child must be allowed to participate in the matter, bearing in mind his or her age, maturity and stage of development.[918] Furthermore, a delay in any action or decision must be avoided, a confrontational approach must be avoided, and an approach which is conducive to conciliation and problem-solving must be adopted.[919]

916. *Yu Kwam v. President Insurance Co Ltd* 1963 (1) SA 66 (T); *Ex parte Kedar* 1993 (1) SA 242 (W); *Bethell v. Bland* 1996 (2) SA 194 (W); *P v. P* 2002 (6) SA 105 (N); *Soller v. Maintenance Magistrate, Wynberg* 2006 (2) SA 66 (C); *B v. B* 2008 (4) SA 535 (W).
917. Sections 18(4)–(5), 23–24, 28, 46, 129–130, 135(1), 156, 241, Ch. 17 and Sch. 2.
918. Children's Act 38 of 2005, ss 10 and 31(1).
919. *Ibid.*, s. 6(4) and (5).

§6. Termination of Parental Responsibilities and Rights

315. All parental responsibilities and rights or the aspects of parental responsibilities and rights a particular person has are terminated by the child's death or an order depriving the person of those responsibilities and rights. Most aspects of parental responsibilities and rights are also terminated by the parent's death and by the child's attainment of majority. However, the latter rule does not apply to maintenance, because a child who is unable to support himself or herself may claim maintenance from his or her parent's deceased estate, and an adult child may claim maintenance until he or she has become self-supporting.[920]

920. *See* Part II, Ch. 6, §IV above.

Chapter 7. Guardianship and Curatorship

§1. Appointment of a Legal Guardian or Curator

316. It was explained in the previous chapter that if a child is born of married parents, both parents are the child's guardians and they share care of the child, unless a court makes a different order. The same applies if unmarried parents live together at the time of the child's birth; or if the child's unmarried father consents or successfully applies to be identified as the child's father, pays damages in terms of customary law and contributes or attempts to contribute to the child's upbringing and maintenance. If an unmarried father obtains guardianship or care in terms of a court order or a court-confirmed parental responsibilities and rights agreement, the terms of the agreement or court order determine whether the parents share guardianship and/or care of their child.

If parents share guardianship and/or care and one of them dies, the other parent retains guardianship and/or care. If the deceased parent had sole guardianship or sole care, the other parent does not obtain guardianship or care as a result of the death unless he or she is a fit and proper person and was nominated as guardian or care-giving parent in the will of the parent who had sole guardianship or sole care.[921]

A parent may nominate somebody other than the surviving parent as the child's legal guardian or caregiver if the parent who makes the nomination has sole guardianship or sole care of the child, or if the other parent is prohibited by a court order from exercising guardianship or care.[922]

A parent may choose not to nominate a guardian for his or her child but rather to appoint only a *curator* or *curatrix bonis* (curator to the property) to administer the child's property for the duration of his or her minority.

Before a parent appoints someone as guardian or curator or to have care of his or her child after his or her death, he or she must give due consideration to any views and wishes expressed by the child, bearing in mind the child's age, maturity and stage of development.[923]

317. Only an adult may be a legal guardian or a curator,[924] and he or she may not be subject to curatorship[925] or have been declared incapable of holding the office of guardian or curator.[926] If the person was nominated in a will, he or she must not have been a witness to the will.[927]

---

921. Children's Act 38 of 2005, s. 27(1)–(3).
922. Matrimonial Affairs Act 37 of 1953, s. 5(3); Administration of Estates Act 66 of 1965, s. 72(1)(a); Children's Act 38 of 2005, s. 27(1).
923. Children's Act 38 of 2005, ss 10, 31(1)(a) and 31(1)(b)(iii).
924. *Dhanabakium v. Subramanian* 1943 AD 160.
925. Grotius, *Inleidinge tot de Hollandsche Rechts-geleerdheid*, 1.7.6; Voet, *Commentarius ad Pandectas*, 26.1.4.
926. Administration of Estates Act 66 of 1965, s. 85 read with s. 54(4).
927. Wills Act 7 of 1953, s. 4A.

318. A guardian who is nominated in a will is called a testamentary guardian or testamentary tutor, while a curator who is nominated in a will is called a curator nominate. A testamentary guardian or a curator nominate only acquires guardianship, care or the power to administer the child's property after the death of the child's parent, and only if he or she accepts the appointment as guardian or curator.[928] His or her appointment must be confirmed by the Master of the High Court.[929]

If a parent appoints more than one person as testamentary guardian or to be vested with care, any, several, or all of them may accept the appointment, unless the parent's will stipulates otherwise.[930]

319. If the testator's will expressly confers this power on him or her, a testamentary guardian or curator nominate may appoint another person to assist him or her or even to take his or her place. Someone who is appointed in this way is called an assumed tutor or an assumed curator. The appointment of an assumed tutor or assumed curator must be confirmed by the Master of the High Court.[931]

320. If a child has no legal guardian or tutor, the High Court[932] or the Master of the High Court[933] may appoint a guardian or curator for the child if his or her interests require this, for example, because he or she has inherited property. Such a guardian or curator is called a tutor dative or a curator dative. If a minor needs to be assisted in litigation and has no parent or legal guardian who can do so, if his or her parent or legal guardian refuses to assist him or her, if the minor litigates against his or her parent or legal guardian, or if there is a clash of interests between the parent or legal guardian and the child, the court usually appoints a *curator ad litem* to assist the minor in the litigation.[934]

§2. The Contents of Legal Guardianship and Curatorship

321. The rights, duties and powers of a legal guardian are determined by his or her letters of appointment. Generally, a legal guardian must administer and safeguard the property and property interests of the child, assist or represent the child in administrative, contractual and other legal matters, and give or refuse any consent which is required by law in respect of the child.[935] The legal guardian must use the

928. Children's Act 38 of 2005, s. 27(3).
929. Administration of Estates Act 66 of 1965, s. 71.
930. Children's Act 38 of 2005, s. 27(4).
931. Administration of Estates Act 66 of 1965, s. 71.
932. The High Court has the power to appoint a guardian for a minor in terms of its upper guardianship of all minors or in terms of s. 24 of the Children's Act 38 of 2005.
933. Administration of Estates Act 66 of 1965, s. 73.
934. *See*, e.g., *Van Rij v. Employers' Liability Assurance Corporation Ltd* 1964 (4) SA 731 (T); *Ex parte Visser: In re Khoza* 2001 (3) SA 524 (T); *Ex parte Oppel* 2002 (5) SA 125 (C). On a minor's capacity to litigate, *see* Part I, Ch. 3, §6 above.
935. Children's Act 38 of 2005, s. 18(3).

child's estate to provide for the child's maintenance.[936] If the estate is too small to provide adequate maintenance, the legal guardian must claim maintenance from the persons who are legally obliged to support the child.[937]

A legal guardian and a curator must act in good faith, with the necessary care and in the best interests of the child, and avoid conflicts between his or her interests and those of the child.[938] The Administration of Estates Act 66 of 1965 imposes several additional duties on legal guardians and curators, including the lodging of an inventory of the child's property and submission of an annual report on the administration of the child's property.[939]

§3. Termination of Legal Guardianship or Curatorship

322. Legal guardianship or curatorship comes to an end when the child dies or attains majority; the legal guardian or curator dies, resigns, or is disqualified or removed from office; the period of time or the purpose for which the legal guardian or curator was appointed expires or disappears; or the legal guardian or curator is discharged from office after having completed all his or her tasks.[940]

---

936. Administration of Estates Act 66 of 1965, ss 82(c)(iii) and 90(1).
937. *See*, e.g., Grotius, *Inleidinge tot de Hollandsche Rechts-geleerdheid*,1.9.9; Voet, *Commentarius ad Pandectas*, 26.7.1, 26.7.6, 27.2.1. On the duty to support a child, *see* Part II, Ch. 6, §2 above.
938. *Digesta* 26.7.39.2, 26.7.39.3, 26.7.39.7, 26.7.7; Grotius, *Inleidinge tot de Hollandsche Rechts-geleerdheid*,1.8.7; Van Leeuwen, *Rooms-Hollands-Regt*, 1.16.8, 1.16.12.
939. Administration of Estates Act 66 of 1965, ss 78(1)(a) and 83(1)(a).
940. *Ibid.*, s. 85 read with ss 54 and 56(1).

Chapter 8. Kinship and Relationships of Affinity

323. When persons enter into a civil or customary marriage or a civil union, the marriage or civil union has consequences not only for them, but also for their relations. The same applies to having or adopting children, because parenthood creates rights and duties not only between a child and his or her parents but also between the child and other relations of the parents.

The main areas where such kinship and relationship by affinity are relevant in South African Family and Succession Law are the prohibition on a marriage or civil union within certain degrees of relationship,[941] the right to inherit *ab intestato*,[942] and the reciprocal duty of support.[943] Insofar as affinity and the duty of support are concerned, the question arises whether a step-parent is obliged to support his or her stepchild even though he or she does not automatically have parental responsibilities and rights in respect of the child. In terms of the common law, a step-parent does not have a duty to maintain his or her stepchild, because the duty to support a child rests on blood relationship.[944] However, a division of the High Court has held a stepfather liable for his stepchildren's maintenance pending his divorce from the children's mother.[945] The court held, *inter alia*, that the child's constitutional right to parental care[946] extends to step-parents and covers a child's need for nutrition, shelter and health care services, thereby encompassing maintenance. Although this dictum was neither properly reasoned nor properly substantiated and the decision is not binding on other divisions of the High Court, the court's broad interpretation of parental care might find favour with other judges in future. Another division of the High Court has since held a stepfather liable for part of his stepson's school fees, but in this case the stepfather had, in the court's view, held the child out to be his 'ostensible son' and had incurred liability on that ground.[947] However, the court also stated that holding the stepfather liable for a contribution to his stepson's school fees would give due recognition to the child's right to family and parental care.

324. Informal kinship care occurs widely throughout South Africa. One of the main reasons for the widespread practice is the lack of employment opportunities in rural areas, which results in parents moving to urban centres in search of work and leaving their children behind to be cared for by grandparents and/or other members of the children's extended family. This phenomenon is particularly prevalent among Black South Africans and is partly a legacy of the homeland system and the *apartheid* policies of migrant labour and influx control. The HIV/AIDS pandemic has also resulted in many children being raised by members of their extended family or ending up in child-headed households.

---

941. *See* Part II, Ch. 1, §2 above.
942. *See* Part IV, Ch. 1, §2 and §3 below.
943. *See* Part II, Ch. 1, §4 and Ch. 6, §2 above.
944. *See*, e.g., *S. v. MacDonald* 1963 (2) SA 431 (C); *Mentz v. Simpson* 1990 (4) SA 455 (A).
945. *Heystek v. Heystek* [2002] 2 All SA 401 (T).
946. Constitution, s. 28(1)(b).
947. *MB v. NB* 2010 (3) SA 220 (GSJ). The quoted phrase appears at para. 20.

Although the number of children in child-headed households is quite small (around 58,000 in 2017),[948] these households are part of South African social circumstances to such a degree that they have received official recognition.[949] The Children's Act 38 of 2005 defines a child-headed household as one in which the parent, guardian or caregiver is terminally ill, has died or has abandoned the children; no adult family member is available to provide care; and a child over the age of 16 years has assumed the role of caregiver.[950] Once the provincial head of the Department of Social Development has recognized a household as a child-headed household, the child who is the head of the household may take all day-to-day decisions relating to the household and the children in it and may collect and administer any grant or assistance to which the children are entitled.[951] The child-headed household functions under the general supervision of an adult designated by a Children's Court, an organ of state, or a non-governmental organization. However, the adult may not take any decision regarding the household or the children without consulting the child who is the head of the household and the other children, taking into account the other children's age, maturity and stage of development.[952]

948. K. Hall & W. Sambu *Demography of South Africa's Children*, in *2017 South African Child Gauge* 103 (L. Jamieson, L. Berry & L. Lake eds., Children's Institute 2017); K. Hall & Z. Mokomane *The Shape of Children's Families and Households: A Demographic Overview* in *2018 South African Child Gauge* 36 (K. Hall et al., eds., Children's Institute, 2018).
949. Between 0.55% and 0.85% of all South African children lived in child-headed households between 2000 and 2007: H. Meintjies et al., *Orphans of the AIDS Epidemic? The Extent, Nature and Circumstances of Child-Headed Households in South-Africa*, 22 AIDS Care 42, 43, 45–47 (2010). In 2017, 0.3% of South African children lived in child-headed households: Hall & Sambu, *Demography of South Africa's Children*, 103; Hall & Mokomane, *The Shape of Children's Families and Households*, 35.
950. Section 137(1). Most children living in child-headed households have a living parent: Meintjies et al., *Orphans of the AIDS Epidemic?*, 43, 46–47.
951. Children's Act 38 of 2005, s. 137(1), (5)(a) and (7).
952. *Ibid.*, s. 137(2) and (6).

Part III. Matrimonial Property Law

Chapter 1. Rights and Obligations of Spouses and Civil Union Partners

§1. General Principles

325. The proprietary rights and obligations of spouses in civil and customary marriages and civil union partners depend on the matrimonial property system that operates in their marriage or civil union. As is explained in more detail below,[953] all civil marriages, all civil unions and all monogamous customary marriages are in community of property, unless the parties exclude this consequence in an antenuptial contract. Parties who exclude community of property in an antenuptial contract may select any variation of separation of property they see fit. The accrual system is the default system in marriages and civil unions out of community of property. Thus, this system applies to a marriage or civil union out of community of property unless it is excluded in the parties' antenuptial contract.[954]

In the case of a de facto polygynous customary marriage, the date of conclusion of the marriage determines the proprietary consequences of the marriage as well as the proprietary rights and obligations of the spouses. If the polygynous customary marriage was concluded before the coming into operation of the Recognition of Customary Marriages Act 120 of 1998 on 15 November 2000, customary law governs the proprietary consequences of the marriage and the proprietary rights and obligations of the spouses. Since 15 November 2000, any husband in an existing customary marriage (whether polygynous or monogamous) who wants to take another customary wife has had to draw up a contract that sets out the matrimonial property system that will operate in the polygynous marriage, and he has had to obtain court approval of this contract before entering into the additional customary marriage. The court-approved contract regulates the proprietary consequences and the proprietary rights and obligations of the spouses once the marriage is concluded.[955]

953. *See* Ch. 3, §1 below in this part.
954. *See* Ch. 3, §1 and Ch. 4, §2 below in this part.
955. *See* Ch. 4, §4 below in this part.

§2. The Household Expenses

326. Regardless of the matrimonial property system that operates in a civil or customary marriage or a civil union, both of the spouses or civil union partners have the power to buy household necessaries on credit. Either of them or both of them together can be sued for the debt in respect of the household necessaries.[956]

The capacity to buy household necessaries on credit is dependent on the existence of a valid marriage or civil union; the existence of a joint household between the spouses or civil union partners; and the commodities indeed being household necessaries. Household necessaries are everyday items which are needed for the running of the joint household. These items include food, clothing, medical and dental services, and food and veterinary services for the family's pets, provided that the particular items were necessary in the particular household at the time when they were acquired on credit.[957]

327. In marriages and civil unions in community of property, the expenses relating to household necessaries are paid from the joint estate, and neither of the spouses or civil union partners has a right of recourse against the other if he or she pays a disproportionate share of the expenses relating to household necessaries.

If the marriage or civil union is out of community of property, each spouse or civil union partner must contribute to expenses for household necessaries on a pro rata basis according to his or her means. In a civil marriage out of community of property that was concluded before the coming into operation of the Matrimonial Property Act 88 of 1984 on 1 November 1984, a spouse who contributes more than his or her pro rata share has a right of recourse against the other spouse. In marriages and civil unions concluded out of community of property after 1 November 1984 there is no automatic right of recourse, but the spouses or civil union partners may agree on a right of recourse.[958]

§3. The Matrimonial Home

328. Ownership of the matrimonial home is determined by the normal rules that apply to the matrimonial property system that operates in the parties' civil or customary marriage or civil union. Thus, if the marriage or civil union is in community of property, the common home falls into the joint estate, unless it has been excluded in the parties' antenuptial contract or one of them inherited it or received it by way of a donation and the testator or donor excluded it from the joint estate.[959] If the marriage or civil union is out of community of property, the matrimonial home is

956. Matrimonial Property Act 88 of 1984, ss 17(5) and 23.

957. *See*, e.g., *Reloomel v. Ramsay* 1920 TPD 371; *Bing and Lauer v. Van den Heever* 1922 TPD 279; *Voortrekkerwinkels (Ko-operatief) Bpk v. Pretorius* 1951 (1) SA 730 (T). On the two approaches the courts have used to determine whether a particular item is a household necessary for a particular household, *see*, e.g., Sinclair assisted by Heaton, *The Law of Marriage*, 447–452.

958. Matrimonial Property Act 88 of 1984, s. 23(1)–(4).

959. *See* Ch. 3, §2 below in this part.

owned by the spouse or civil union partner who acquired it.[960] If the spouses or civil union partners acquired the home jointly, they are joint owners of the property in the proportion in which it has been registered in their names.

329. Regardless of which spouse or civil union partner owns the home and regardless of whether the marriage or civil union is in or out of community of property, both parties have the right to live in the home during the subsistence of the marriage or civil union.[961]

§4. TRANSACTIONS BETWEEN SPOUSES OR CIVIL UNION PARTNERS

330. If a civil or customary marriage or civil union is in community of property, the spouses or civil union partners cannot enter into contracts with each other since they are co-owners of the joint estate.[962] If the marriage or civil union is out of community of property, the spouses or civil union partners are free to enter into contracts with each other and with third parties as they like. The only exception to the latter rule is that spouses who are married subject to complete separation of property (i.e., spouses who are married out of community of property, out of community of profit and loss, and without the accrual system) may not enter into a *societas universorum bonorum* (i.e., a universal partnership relating to present and future assets, liabilities, profits and losses) with each other.[963]

In the case of a de facto polygynous customary marriage, the spouses' powers to enter into transactions with each other depend on whether the marriage came into existence before or after the coming into operation of the Recognition of Customary Marriages Act 120 of 1998. If the marriage existed before 15 November 2000, customary law governs the powers of the spouses to enter into transactions with each other.[964] In terms of customary law as interpreted by the Constitutional Court, the capacity of the spouses is limited in that the husband and the wife of each house must jointly exercise the rights relating to the house property, while the husband and all his wives must jointly exercise the rights relating to all family property.[965] If the polygynous customary marriage was concluded after the coming into operation of the Act, the terms of the court-approved contract that sets out the matrimonial property system regulate the proprietary consequences and thus also the powers of the spouses to enter into contracts with each other.[966]

960. *See* Ch. 4, §2 below in this part.
961. *See* Part II, Ch. 1, §4 above.
962. *See* Ch. 3, §2 below in this part.
963. *See*, e.g., *JW v. CW* 2012 (2) SA 529 (NCK); *RD v. TD* 2014 (4) SA 200 (GP).
964. Recognition of Customary Marriages Act 120 of 1998, ss. 6 and 7(1) read with *Gumede v. President of the Republic of South Africa* 2009 (3) SA 152 (CC).
965. *Ramuhovhi v. President of the Republic of South Africa* 2018 (2) SA 1 (CC).
966. Recognition of Customary Marriages Act 120 of 1998, s. 7(6). *See* further Ch. 4, §4 below in this part.

§5. Maintenance Between Spouses or Civil Union Partners

331. Spouses in civil and customary marriages and civil union partners are reciprocally obliged to support each other financially during the subsistence of the marriage or civil union.[967]

332. If a civil or customary marriage or a civil union is dissolved by divorce, the spouses or civil union partners can agree on payment of post-divorce maintenance, or the court may make any order it deems just in this regard.[968]

333. If a civil or customary marriage or a civil union is terminated by death, the survivor may claim maintenance from the estate of the deceased in terms of the Maintenance of Surviving Spouses Act 27 of 1990 if he or she is unable to provide for his or her reasonable maintenance needs from his or her own means and earnings.[969] The claim is restricted to the reasonable maintenance needs of the survivor until he or she dies, remarries, or enters into a new civil union.[970] The survivor may lodge a claim for maintenance regardless of the matrimonial property system that operated in the marriage or civil union and regardless of whether or not he or she is to inherit from the deceased. However, any property the survivor owns as a result of the matrimonial property system (such as half the joint estate or a share of the accrual of the deceased's estate) and property he or she will inherit from the deceased are taken into account when considering whether he or she has sufficient means to be able to provide his or her own maintenance.[971]

When determining the survivor's reasonable maintenance needs the following factors must be taken into account:

(1) The amount available in the deceased estate for distribution to heirs and legatees.
(2) The existing and expected means,[972] earning capacity, financial needs and obligations of the survivor.
(3) The duration of the marriage or civil union.
(4) The standard of living of the survivor during the subsistence of the marriage or civil union.
(5) The age of the survivor at the time of the deceased's death.
(6) Any other relevant factor.[973]

967. *See* Part II, Ch. 1, §4 above.
968. *See* Part II, Ch. 2, §3 above.
969. Section 2(1). Spouses in de facto monogamous and de facto polygynous Muslim marriages that are dissolved by death may also invoke the provisions of the Act: *Daniels v. Campbell* 2004 (5) SA 331 (CC); *Hassam v. Jacobs* [2008] 4 All SA 350 (C).
970. Section 2(1).
971. Section 1.
972. These means refer solely to the survivor's own means; voluntary payments made to the survivor by his or her children are not taken into account: *Oshry v. Feldman* 2010 (6) SA 19 (SCA).
973. Section 3.

The claim of the survivor must be proved and disposed of in terms of the Administration of Estates Act 66 of 1965.[974] Thus, the claim must be lodged with the executor of the deceased's estate. The claim has the same order of preference in respect of other claims against the deceased's estate as that of a dependent child of the deceased. If the claims of the survivor and a dependent child of the deceased compete with one another and there are insufficient resources from which they can be met, they are reduced proportionately.[975]

In addition to the usual powers the executor has under the Administration of Estates Act,[976] the Maintenance of Surviving Spouses Act expressly empowers the executor to enter into an agreement with the survivor and interested heirs and legatees in order to settle the survivor's maintenance claim either fully or partially. In terms of this agreement, a trust may be created; assets or a right in assets of the deceased's estate may be transferred to the survivor or to the trust; or an obligation may be imposed on an heir or legatee.[977] Thus, for example, the agreement may provide that the former matrimonial home and/or a lump sum of money will be transferred to the survivor; assets will be transferred to a trust of which the survivor will be the beneficiary; or the survivor will have a usufruct over the former matrimonial home, which will allow him or her to remain in the home. If the parties are unable to reach agreement on the maintenance claim and/or the way in which it is to be settled, the court may be approached for an order, including an order for payment of a lump sum of maintenance.[978]

It seems that a customary marriage is not always dissolved by death, since the sororate and levirate customs apparently still form part of customary law.[979] A surviving spouse who is a party to a marriage in which the sororate or levirate custom is applied, can probably not institute a claim in terms of the Maintenance of Surviving Spouses Act, since he or she remains a party to an existing customary marriage. However, in other customary marriages, the surviving spouse's claim for maintenance from the deceased spouse's estate is governed by the same rules that apply to civil marriages and civil unions. In the case of a de facto polygynous customary marriage, the fact of there being several customary wives would obviously be relevant in determining each wife's reasonable maintenance needs. If the maintenance claims of the surviving wives compete with one another and there are insufficient resources from which they can be met, the claims will, presumably, by analogy to the rule regarding competing claims of a single surviving spouse and a dependent child of the deceased spouse, all be reduced proportionately.

---

974. Section 2(3)(a).
975. Section 2(3)(b).
976. *See* Part IV, Ch. 4 below.
977. Section 2(3)(d).
978. *Oshry v. Feldman* 2010 (6) SA 19 (SCA).
979. *See* Part II, Ch. 1, §2 above.

Chapter 2. The Marriage or Civil Union Settlement

334. The prospective parties to a marriage or civil union may include donations to each other in their antenuptial contract. Such donations are called 'marriage settlements' or 'civil union settlements'.

Before the coming into operation of the Matrimonial Property Act 88 of 1984 on 1 November 1984 such settlements were common, because they were exempt from the prohibition on donations between spouses which used to operate in marriages out of community of property.[980] As the Act abolished this prohibition,[981] donations need no longer be included in the parties' antenuptial contract. However, if they are included in the parties' antenuptial contract, they enjoy some protection in the case of insolvency of the donor. If a donated asset is transferred, delivered or paid in good faith within three months of the date of the parties' marriage or civil union, the donation cannot be set aside as a disposition without value if the donor's estate is sequestrated more than two years after the registration of the antenuptial contract.[982]

335. In principle, a marriage or civil union settlement becomes irrevocable when the marriage or civil union takes place. However, the donor and donee can, by agreement, cancel or amend the donation during the subsistence of their marriage or civil union.

The settlement may be subject to a time clause or condition, but the clause or condition must not be void for vagueness, as is the case, for example, if a husband undertakes to give property to his wife at such time and in such quantities as may seem expedient to him.[983]

A marriage or civil union settlement is frequently accompanied by a reversion clause. The reversion clause stipulates an event upon which the donation will revert to the donor, for example, if the donee predeceases the donor.[984] A reversion clause is enforceable unless it violates the institution of marriage/civil union or its sanctity, for example, by encouraging divorce.[985]

980. The prohibition on donations between spouses did not apply to marriages in community of property because such spouses cannot make donations to each other as they own the joint estate in undivided half shares: *see* the next chapter below. If one spouse were to make a donation to the other from his or her half of the joint estate, the donated item would come out of the joint estate and fall back into it.

981. Section 22.

982. Insolvency Act 24 of 1936, s. 27.

983. *Towert v. Towert* 1956 (1) SA 429 (W); *Murray v. Murray* 1959 (3) SA 84 (W); *Kantor v. Kantor* 1962 (3) SA 207 (T).

984. *Wilson v. Wilson* 1946 EDL 33.

985. *Cumming v. Cumming* 1984 (4) SA 585 (T).

Chapter 3. The Legal Matrimonial Regime

§1. Introduction

336. The primary matrimonial property system in South Africa is universal community of property, that is, community of property and community of profit and loss. This system is commonly called, simply, 'community of property'.

Because community of property is the primary matrimonial property system, it is rebuttably presumed that when a couple enters into a civil marriage, a civil union or a monogamous customary marriage, their marriage or civil union is subject to community of property.[986] The same applies if spouses who are married at customary law subsequently enter into a civil marriage with each other,[987] and if a minor marries without consent and without an antenuptial contract and the marriage is not set aside due to the lack of consent.[988]

The presumption is rebutted by proving any of the following:

(1) The existence of a valid antenuptial contract in which the parties excluded community of property.[989]
(2) The existence of a valid postnuptial notarial contract in which the parties excluded community of property.[990]
(3) The *lex domicilii* of the husband or male civil union partner at the time of the marriage or civil union dictates that the marriage or civil union is out of community of property. This is so because South African law provides that the husband's *lex domicilii* at the time of the wedding dictates the matrimonial property system.[991] As there is no 'husband' in a same-sex civil union, this rule fails to cater for such unions.
(4) The spouses are Black persons who entered into a civil marriage which is governed by section 22(6) of the Black Administration Act 38 of 1927. In terms of this section, civil marriages Black persons entered into before the coming into operation of the Marriage and Matrimonial Property Law Amendment Act 3 of 1988 on 2 December 1988 are out of community of property, unless the spouses made a joint written declaration before a magistrate, commissioner or marriage officer, within one month prior to the marriage, that they wished to marry in community of property, profit and loss.[992]

---

986. *Edelstein v. Edelstein* 1952 (3) SA 1 (A) read with s. 13 of the Civil Union Act 17 of 2006 and s. 7(2) of the Recognition of Customary Marriages Act 120 of 1998.
987. Recognition of Customary Marriages Act 120 of 1998, s. 10(2).
988. Matrimonial Property Act 88 of 1984, s. 24(2). Whether this section applies to a customary marriage a minor concluded without consent is unclear: *see* Heaton & Kruger, *Family Law*, 227–228.
989. On antenuptial contracts, *see* Ch. 4, §1 below in this part.
990. On postnuptial alteration of the matrimonial property system, *see* below in this chapter.
991. *Frankel's Estate v. The Master* 1950 (1) SA 220 (A).
992. The Marriage and Matrimonial Property Law Amendment Act 3 of 1988 repealed s. 22(6) of the Black Administration Act 38 of 1927. Thus, all civil marriages that have been concluded since 2 Dec. 1988 are subject to the same rules, regardless of the race of the spouses.

§2. COMMUNITY OF PROPERTY

I. The Joint Estate

337. If community of property operates in a marriage or civil union, the estates of the spouses or civil union partners are merged into a single joint estate when they marry or enter into the civil union. The transfer of the parties' assets and liabilities to the joint estate takes place automatically by operation of law.[993]

The joint estate exists until the marriage or civil union is terminated, or until a court orders division of the joint estate in terms of section 20 of the Matrimonial Property Act 88 of 1984.[994] While the joint estate exists, each spouse or civil union partner owns an undivided and indivisible half-share of the joint estate.[995]

338. As a rule, the joint estate is comprised of all the assets and liabilities the spouses or civil union partners have at the time of entering into the marriage or civil union and all the assets and liabilities they acquire during the marriage or civil union. However, certain assets fall outside the joint estate. Those assets are the separate property of the spouse or civil union partner who acquires them.

The following assets are separate property:

(1) Assets excluded from the joint estate in the antenuptial contract of the spouses or civil union partners.[996]
(2) Assets a third party donates or bequeaths to one of the spouses or civil union partners subject to the condition that the asset must not become part of the joint estate.[997]
(3) Assets that are subject to a *fideicommissum* or usufruct.[998]
(4) *Jocalia* (engagement gifts).[999]
(5) Benefits due to a wife in terms of section 17 of the Friendly Societies Act 25 of 1956.[1000]
(6) Any amount a spouse or civil union partner recovers by way of non-patrimonial damages for a delict committed against him or her.[1001] This exclusion extends to disability payments the injured party receives in terms of an insurance policy.[1002]

---

993. *Ex parte Menzies* 1993 (3) SA 799 (C); *Corporate Liquidators (Pty) Ltd v. Wiggill* 2007 (2) SA 520 (T).
994. On s. 20, *see* further below in this chapter.
995. *See*, e.g., *Estate Sayle v. Commissioner for Inland Revenue* 1945 AD 388; *De Wet v. Jurgens* 1970 (3) SA 38 (A); *Ex parte Menzies* 1993 (3) SA 799 (C); *Mazibuko v. National Director of Public Prosecutions* 2009 (6) SA 479 (SCA).
996. *See*, e.g., *Blatchford v. Blatchford's Executors* (1861) 1 EDC 365; *Ex parte Lelie* 1945 WLD 167.
997. *Ex parte Lelie* 1945 WLD 167.
998. *See*, e.g., *Van der Merwe v. Van Wyk* 1921 EDL 298; *Barnett v. Rudman* 1934 AD 203; *Van Wyk v. Groch* 1968 (3) SA 240 (E).
999. *See*, e.g., *Barkhan v. Barkhan* 1960 (4) SA 288 (W); *Levin v. Levin* 1960 (4) SA 469 (W).
1000. This exclusion is probably unconstitutional as it applies only to wives: Heaton & Kruger, *Family Law*, 65.
1001. Matrimonial Property Act 88 of 1984, s. 18(a).
1002. *Van den Berg v. Van den Berg* 2003 (6) SA 229 (T).

(7) Damages received as a result of bodily injury inflicted on the recipient by his or her spouse or civil union partner.[1003]
(8) Costs awarded to one of the spouses or civil union partners in a matrimonial action between the spouses or civil union partners.[1004]
(9) Such part of the proceeds of the disposal of assets of the joint estate that have been forfeited to the State as the court excludes from the Criminal Assets Recovery Account in terms of the Prevention of Organised Crime Act 121 of 1998.[1005]

If an asset is the separate property of one of the spouses or civil union partners, it cannot be attached for a debt of the other spouse or civil union partner if the spouses or civil union partners are solvent.[1006] However, in the case of insolvency, all the property of both parties falls into the insolvent estate. Thus, the joint estate and the separate property of both of the spouses or civil union partners are available for settling debts on insolvency.[1007]

339. As is the case in respect of their assets, the general rule is that all the debts of both of the spouses or civil union partners fall into the joint estate.

The spouses or civil union partners are joint debtors in respect of debts that bind the joint estate. This rule *inter alia* implies that one of them cannot stand surety for the debts of the other, because those debts are joint debts. This is the position even if the party who stands surety has separate property.[1008]

340. In an antenuptial contract, one spouse or civil union partner may exclude liability for the debts the other spouse or civil union partner incurred before the marriage or civil union. In such event, those debts remain the separate debts of the antenuptial debtor.

A debt that arises as a result of a delict committed by one of the spouses or civil union partners is also a separate debt of the spouse or civil union partner who incurred it. The debt must be recovered from the separate property of that spouse or civil union partner. However, if there is no, or insufficient, separate property, the debt can be recovered from the joint estate. Insofar as the debt is recovered from the joint estate, an adjustment must be made in favour of the other spouse or civil union partner when the joint estate is terminated.[1009]

341. Whether a contractual debt incurred during the marriage or civil union is recoverable from the joint estate or from the separate property of the spouse or civil

1003. Matrimonial Property Act 88 of 1984, s. 18(b).
1004. *Comerma v. Comerma* 1938 TPD 220; *Wulfsohn v. Van der Gryp* 1961 (1) SA 596 (W).
1005. *Mazibuko v. National Director of Public Prosecutions* 2009 (6) SA 479 (SCA).
1006. *See*, e.g., Erasmus, Van der Merwe & Van Wyk, *Lee and Honoré Family, Things and Succession*, para. 84; Heaton & Kruger, *Family Law*, 67; Himonga, *Marriage*, 274.
1007. *De Wet v. Jurgens* 1970 (3) SA 38 (A); *Badenhorst v. Bekker* 1994 (2) SA 155 (N); *Du Plessis v. Pienaar* 2003 (1) SA 671 (SCA).
1008. *Nedbank Ltd v. Van Zyl* 1990 (2) SA 469 (A); *Du Plessis v. Pienaar* 2003 (1) SA 671 (SCA). In terms of South African law, a person cannot stand surety for his or her own debt.
1009. Matrimonial Property Act 88 of 1984, s. 19.

union partner who incurred the debt depends on whether or not the spouse or civil union partner had the capacity to bind the joint estate. This, in turn, depends on whether, if required, the other spouse or civil union partner's consent to the transaction was obtained.[1010] If the spouse or civil union partner who incurred the debt indeed had the capacity to bind the joint estate, the debt becomes a joint debt which can be recovered from the joint estate. If the debt is recoverable from the joint estate, both of the spouses or civil union partners can be sued jointly for the debt, or the spouse or civil union partner who incurred the debt can be sued for it.[1011] The debt is settled from the joint estate, regardless of whether both of the spouses or civil union partners are sued or only the original debtor is sued.

II. Administration of the Joint Estate

342. The Matrimonial Property Act 88 of 1984 governs administration of the joint estate.[1012] In terms of the Act, the parties to a marriage or civil union in community of property have equal powers to administer the joint estate and to incur debts that bind the joint estate.[1013] The starting point is that either of them may perform any juristic act with regard to the joint estate without the other's consent.[1014] However, the consent of the other spouse or civil union partner is required for entering into certain juristic acts. The acts for which the consent of both of the spouses or civil union partners is required are those that are considered to be of such importance that unilateral action could lead to serious friction.[1015] They include alienating or burdening immovable property which forms part of the joint estate, or conferring any other real right in it; entering into a suretyship; receiving credit under a credit agreement as defined in the National Credit Act 34 of 2005; purchasing immovable property under a contract of sale as defined in the Alienation of Land Act 68 of 1981; alienating, ceding or pledging shares, stock, debentures, debenture bonds, insurance policies, mortgage bonds, fixed deposits or similar assets or any investment in a financial institution by or on behalf of the other spouse or civil union partner; alienating or pledging joint assets held mainly as investments; withdrawing money credited to the name of the other spouse or civil union partner in any account in a banking institution or post office savings bank; instituting or defending legal proceedings that do not relate to the separate property, profession, trade or business of the litigating spouse or civil union partner or to the recovery of non-patrimonial damages for a delict committed against him or her; alienating or pledging furniture or other effects of the common household, such as curtains and household appliances, which form part of the joint estate; and donating any asset from the joint

1010. The consent requirement is discussed under the next heading below.
1011. Matrimonial Property Act 88 of 1984, s. 17(5).
1012. *See also* s. 7(3) of the Recognition of Customary Marriages Act 120 of 1998.
1013. Section 14.
1014. Section 15(1).
1015. South African Law Commission, *Report Pertaining to Matrimonial Property Law with Special Reference to the Matrimonial Affairs Act, 1953, the Status of the Married Woman, and the Law of Succession in so far as it Affects the Spouses RP26/1982* para. 19.2 (Government Printer, 1982).

estate to a third party if the donation will unreasonably prejudice the interest of the other spouse or civil union partner in the estate.[1016]

An exemption applies to some of the transactions for which consent is usually required, if they are performed by a spouse or civil union partner in the ordinary course of his or her profession, trade or business.[1017] Transactions on the stock exchange concerning listed securities and transactions concerning deposits at a banking institution in the name of the spouse or civil union partner who wishes to deal with the deposits are also exempted from the consent requirement.[1018] Further, the court has the power to dispense with consent if it is being unreasonably withheld, or if it cannot be obtained and the court is satisfied that a good reason exists for dispensing with consent.[1019]

343. A bona fide third party who concludes a transaction for which the consent of both of the spouses or civil union partners was required but not obtained is protected by the Matrimonial Property Act 88 of 1984. If the third party did not know and could not reasonably have known that consent was required or was not obtained, the transaction is deemed to have been entered into with the required consent.[1020] Thus, insofar as a bona fide third party is concerned, the transaction is valid and enforceable.[1021]

The Act does not prescribe how it must be established whether the third party could reasonably have known that consent was required or not given. It has been held that the use of the word 'reasonably' implies that an objective test must be used. Thus, the matter must be considered from the point of view of the reasonable person in the third party's position.[1022] However, it has also been held that the circumstances of the particular case may dictate that the third party must 'do more than rely upon a bold assurance by another party regarding his or her marital status' and that he or she must undertake 'an adequate inquiry'.[1023]

The Act is silent on the consequences if the third party knew that consent was necessary and was not obtained, but from the case law it appears that the transaction is void.[1024]

344. The spouse or civil union partner whose consent was required and not obtained is also protected by the Act. He or she can claim an adjustment in his or her favour when the joint estate is terminated, provided that his or her spouse or

1016. *See* ss 15(2), 15(3) and 17(1) for a full list of the transactions for which consent is required.
1017. Sections 15(6) and 17(1)(c).
1018. Section 15(7).
1019. Section 16(1).
1020. Section 15(9)(a).
1021. Spouses or civil union partners who did not comply with the consent requirement may not rely on the section in order to hold a bona fide third party to the transaction; only the bona fide third party may rely on the section: *Govender v. Maitin* 2008 (6) SA 64 (D).
1022. *Distillers Corporation Ltd v. Modise* 2001 (4) SA 1071 (O); *Broodie v. Maposa* 2018 (3) SA 129 (WCC).
1023. *Visser v. Hull* 2010 (1) SA 521 (WCC) para. 8.
1024. *Amalgamated Bank of South Africa Bpk v. Lydenburg Passasiersdienste* 1995 (3) SA 314 (T); *Bopape v. Moloto* 2000 (1) SA 383 (T); *Markram v. Scholtz* [2000] 4 All SA 452 (NC); *Visser v. Hull* 2010 (1) SA 521 (WCC).

civil union partner knew or ought reasonably to have known that consent would not be obtained and the joint estate suffered a loss as a result of the transaction.[1025]

Further, if such an order is essential for the protection of the interests in the joint estate of the spouse or civil union partner whose consent was not obtained, the court may suspend any power his or her spouse or civil union partner has in respect of the joint estate for a definite or indefinite period.[1026] The latter remedy is not restricted to instances where the consent requirement was not met. It can be invoked whenever suspension is essential for the protection of the interests of one of the spouses or civil union partners.

Another statutory remedy the spouse or civil union partner can invoke is requesting the court to order immediate division of the joint estate. The applicant must convince the court that his or her interests in the joint estate are being, or will probably be, seriously prejudiced by the conduct or proposed conduct of his or her spouse or civil union partner, and that no other person will be prejudiced by the order. The court may divide the joint estate in equal shares or on such other basis as it deems just. The court may also replace community of property with another matrimonial property system.[1027]

The spouse or civil union partner whose consent was not obtained also has common-law remedies at his or her disposal. If the transaction has not yet taken place and the object of the transaction is to fraudulently prejudice him or her, he or she can seek an interdict prohibiting the transaction.[1028] If a transaction has already occurred with the intention to fraudulently prejudice him or her and an asset has been transferred from the joint estate in consequence of the transaction, he or she has a right of recourse against his or her spouse or civil union partner on dissolution of the joint estate.[1029] Another option is to recover the alienated asset from the third party with the *actio Pauliana utilis*.[1030] However, it is unclear whether this remedy is available while the marriage or civil union lasts or, at any rate, while the joint estate remains undivided.[1031]

345. Special rules apply to litigation that is undertaken without the required consent. All third parties are protected regardless of whether they are bona or mala fide, because absence of the required consent does not affect the validity of legal proceedings. However, the spouse or civil union partner who litigates without the required consent may be punished by having a costs order made against him or her. If such an order is made, the court may order that the costs be recovered from his or her separate property. Insofar as his or her separate property is insufficient, the

1025. Section 15(9)(b).
1026. Section 16(1).
1027. Section 20(1) and (2).
1028. *Mundy v. Mundy* 1946 WLD 280; *Pickles v. Pickles* 1947 (3) SA 175 (W); *Laws v. Laws* 1972 (1) SA 321 (W); *Tel Peda Investigation Bureau (Pty) Ltd v. Laws* 1972 (2) SA 1 (T).
1029. *Cullammah v. Munean* 1941 NPD 163; *Ex parte Van Kraayenburg; Ex parte Ahlers* 1946 TPD 686; *Laws v. Laws* 1972 (1) SA 321 (W).
1030. *Pickles v. Pickles* 1947 (3) SA 175 (W); *Laws v. Laws* 1972 (1) SA 321 (W).
1031. In *Nel v. Cockcroft* 1972 (3) SA 592 (T) it was held that the action may only be instituted after dissolution of the marriage (or civil union), but this dictum has been justly criticized: *see*, e.g., *Reyneke v. Reyneke* 1990 (3) SA 927 (E); Hahlo, *The South African Law of Husband and Wife*, 195 n. 45; C.P. Joubert, *The Law of Donations and Trusts*, Annu. Surv. S. Afr. Law 122 (1972).

costs are recovered from the joint estate but an adjustment is effected in favour of the non-consenting spouse or civil union partner on division of the joint estate.[1032]

§3. THE CONSEQUENCES OF DIVORCE IN A MARRIAGE OR CIVIL UNION IN COMMUNITY OF PROPERTY

346. As indicated above, spouses and civil union partners who are getting divorced may arrange the financial consequences of the divorce in a settlement agreement. In the agreement, they may deviate from the normal consequences of termination of community of property, namely, equal division of the joint estate.[1033] If they are unable to reach agreement, the divorce order automatically operates as an order for equal division of the joint estate, unless forfeiture of patrimonial benefits is ordered by the court.

347. Any antenuptial contractual debts that are still outstanding after the divorce revert to the original debtor.[1034] As the debts became joint debts when the marriage or civil union was concluded, the original debtor ought to have a right of recourse against his or her former spouse or civil union partner if he or she settles the debt in full after the divorce.[1035]

Antenuptial delictual debts must also be claimed from the original debtor, but the original debtor has no right of recourse against his or her former spouse or civil union partner if he or she settles the debt in full after the divorce.[1036]

348. Contractual debts which were incurred during the subsistence of the marriage or civil union can be claimed in full from the spouse or civil union partner who originally incurred them, or half of each debt can be claimed from the original debtor and the other half from the other spouse or civil union partner.[1037] If the original debtor pays the debt in full, he or she has a right of recourse for half, as the debt was a joint liability.[1038] However, if one of the spouses or civil union partners possesses most of the assets of the former joint estate (e.g., because the court made an order for forfeiture of patrimonial benefits against the other spouse or civil union partner on divorce), the debt can be claimed in full from him or her.[1039]

1032. Section 17(2) and (3).

1033. *See* Part II, Ch. 2, §3 above.

1034. *Blatchford v. Blatchford's Executors* (1861) 1 EDC 365; *Thom v. Worthmann* 1962 (4) SA 83 (N).

1035. Voet, *Commentarius ad Pandectas*, 23.2.80; but *see Reis v. Executors of Gilloway* (1834) 1 Menz 186. Voet's view is preferred by modern authors: *see*, e.g., Erasmus, Van der Merwe & Van Wyk, *Lee and Honoré Family, Things and Succession*, para. 97(i); Hahlo, *The South African Law of Husband and Wife*, 182; Heaton & Kruger, *Family Law*, 69; M. de Jong & W. Pintens, *Default Matrimonial Property Regimes and the Principles of European Family Law – A European-South African Comparison (Part 2)*, J. S. Afr. Law 561 (2015).

1036. Van der Keessel, *Theses Selectae*, 94, 225.

1037. *Thom v. Worthmann* 1962 (4) SA 83 (N); *BP Southern Africa (Pty) Ltd v. Viljoen* 2002 (5) SA 630 (O).

1038. Voet, *Commentarius ad Pandectas*, 23.2.80; Van der Keessel, *Theses Selectae*, 225.

1039. *Maury (Edms) Bpk h/a Franelle Gordyn Boutique v. Erasmus* 1988 (2) SA 314 (O); *BP Southern Africa (Pty) Ltd v. Viljoen* 2002 (5) SA 630 (O).

Delictual debts must be claimed from the original debtor, and the original debtor has no right of recourse if he or she settles the debt in full.

§4. The Consequences of Death in a Marriage or Civil Union in Community of Property

349. In a marriage or civil union in community of property, the death of either of the spouses or civil union partners terminates the marriage or civil union as well as the community of property. The termination happens automatically by operation of the law.[1040] No court order is required to confirm the termination.

An executor winds up the joint estate in terms of the Administration of Estates Act 66 of 1965. Once all the debts have been settled, the executor delivers half the net balance of the joint estate to the surviving spouse or civil union partner. This half belongs to the surviving spouse or civil union partner because he or she owns it by virtue of the community of property that operated in the marriage or civil union; he or she does not inherit it.[1041] The other half devolves on the heirs of the deceased spouse or civil union partner.

350. As indicated above, it seems that not all customary marriages are dissolved by death.[1042] A surviving spouse who is a party to a customary marriage in community of property in which the sororate or levirate custom is applied can probably not claim half the joint estate, since he or she remains a party to an existing customary marriage. The community of property that operated between the deceased and the surviving spouse presumably continues between the surviving spouse and the substituted spouse.

§5. Alteration of the Matrimonial Property System

351. The parties to a marriage or civil union may change their matrimonial property system during the subsistence of their marriage or civil union if the court approves the change. In the case of a civil marriage, a civil union or a monogamous customary marriage that was concluded after the coming into operation of the Recognition of Customary Marriages Act 120 of 1998, the spouses or civil union partners must jointly apply to court for approval of a notarial contract that sets out the terms of the changed matrimonial property system.[1043] They must show that there are sound reasons for the proposed change; notice of the proposed change has been

1040. *See*, e.g., *Grimbeek v. The Master* 1926 CPD 183; *Joseph v. Joseph* 1951 (3) SA 776 (N); *Danielz v. De Wet* 2009 (6) SA 42 (C).

1041. *Estate Sayle v. Commissioner for Inland Revenue* 1945 AD 388. The surviving spouse does not have to quantify his or her share of the joint estate or lodge a claim against the estate: *Barnard v. Van der Merwe* 2012 (3) SA 304 (GNP).

1042. *See* Part II, Ch. 1, §2 above.

1043. Matrimonial Property Act 88 of 1984, s. 21(1); Civil Union Act 17 of 2006, s. 13; Recognition of Customary Marriages Act 120 of 1998, s. 7(5).

given to all their creditors; and no other person will be prejudiced by the change.[1044] What constitutes sound reasons for a change depends on the facts and circumstances of each case.[1045]

Spouses who entered into a customary marriage before the coming into operation of the Recognition of Customary Marriages Act have a similar mechanism at their disposal. They must also jointly apply to court for approval of a notarial contract setting out the change. If the marriage is polygynous, all wives must be joined in the proceedings. The court will only grant the application if it is satisfied that there are sound reasons for the proposed change; sufficient notice has been given to all the creditors to whom the spouses owe more than ZAR 500 (or such amount as the Minister of Justice and Correctional Services may determine in the *Government Gazette*); and no other person will be prejudiced by the proposed change.[1046]

352. Whether a matrimonial property system can be altered with retroactive effect is unclear. One division of the High Court has held that it can be done,[1047] while another has held that it cannot.[1048] Both decisions dealt with marriages in community of property. A third decision, by a different division of the High Court, dealt with introduction of the accrual system into a marriage that was subject to complete separation of property. In this case, the court held that the accrual system must be introduced from the beginning of the marriage; it cannot be introduced from the date of the court order.[1049] The implication of the decision is that retroactive alteration is compulsory if the matrimonial property system is changed to the accrual system.

353. Extra-judicial alteration of the spouses' matrimonial property system is invalid and unenforceable between the parties *inter se* and as against third parties.[1050] The same applies to extra-judicial alteration by civil union partners.[1051]

1044. Matrimonial Property Act 88 of 1984, s. 21(1).
1045. *Ex parte Engelbrecht* 1986 (2) SA 158 (NC); *Ex parte Lourens* 1986 (2) SA 291 (C).
1046. Recognition of Customary Marriages Act 120 of 1998, s. 7(4).
1047. *Ex parte Krös* 1986 (1) SA 642 (NC).
1048. *Ex parte Oosthuizen* 1990 (4) SA 15 (E).
1049. *Ex parte Burger* 1995 (1) SA 140 (D).
1050. *Honey v. Honey* 1992 (3) SA 609 (W); *SB v. RB* [2015] 2 All SA 232 (ECLD, George).
1051. Civil Union Act 17 of 2006, s. 13.

Chapter 4. Conventional Matrimonial Regimes

§1. Antenuptial Contract

354. As explained in the previous chapter, the primary matrimonial property system in South Africa is community of property. Spouses or civil union partners who do not want community of property to operate in their marriage or civil union may exclude it in an antenuptial contract. Parties who do not want to exclude community of property but want to exclude particular assets and/or liabilities from their joint estate may also enter into an antenuptial contract. Apart from dealing with the matrimonial property system, antenuptial contracts often include marriage or civil union settlements.[1052] Sometimes the parties create a trust, enter into an agreement about succession (*pactum successorium*),[1053] or govern their right of recourse in respect of expenses for household necessaries.[1054]

An antenuptial contract may contain any provision which is not impossible, contrary to good morals (*contra bonos mores*), inconsistent with public policy, or contrary to the law or the nature of marriage or a civil union.[1055] Thus, for example, a clause that the parties need not be faithful to each other or live together is null and void.[1056] So too is an agreement which is likely to encourage separation or divorce. However, the mere fact that an agreement is made in contemplation of a possible future separation or divorce does not mean that it is void, for '[i]t is the effect and not merely the fact of the agreement which must be assessed'.[1057] A clause in which one party waives his or her right to claim maintenance during the marriage and upon dissolution of the marriage is against public policy and unenforceable.[1058]

355. As the term suggests, an antenuptial contract must be concluded before the parties to the contract enter into a marriage or civil union with each other. The contract must also be registered in terms of the Deeds Registries Act 47 of 1937 within prescribed periods otherwise it does not bind third parties.[1059] An informal antenuptial contract is valid only as between the parties.[1060] However, the High Court may allow the spouses or civil union partners to formally execute and register their informal antenuptial contract after the conclusion of the marriage or civil union so that the contract can obtain validity as against third parties too.[1061]

1052. *See* Part III, Ch. 2 above.
1053. As a rule, a *pactum successorium* is invalid. A *pactum successorium* in an antenuptial contract is the only exception to this rule. *See* further Part IV, Ch. 3, §1 below.
1054. *See* Part III, Ch. 1, §2 above.
1055. Voet, *Commentarius ad Pandectas*, 23.4.15, 23.4.16, 23.4.19, 23.4.20; *Ex parte Wismer* 1950 (2) SA 195 (C).
1056. *Van Oosten v. Van Oosten* 1923 CPD 409.
1057. *Stembridge v. Stembridge* [1998] 2 All SA 4 (D).
1058. *ST v. CT* 2018 (5) SA 479 (SCA).
1059. Deeds Registries Act 47 of 1937, ss 86 and 87.
1060. *See, e.g., Steytler v. Dekkers* (1872) 2 Roscoe 102; *Aschen's Executrix v. Blythe* (1886) 4 SC 136; *Ex parte Spinazze* 1983 (4) SA 751 (T); *Odendaal v. Odendaal* [2002] 2 All SA 94 (W); *Schmitz v. Schmitz* [2015] 3 All SA 85 (KZD).
1061. Deeds Registries Act 47 of 1937, s. 88.

If a minor enters into an antenuptial contract, additional requirements must be complied with. As a minor cannot enter into a civil union,[1062] these requirements apply only to civil marriages and customary marriages. The minor must personally sign the contract,[1063] and he or she must have the consent of his or her guardian to enter into the contract. Although the Children's Act 38 of 2005 requires the consent of all the guardians of a minor for the minor's marriage,[1064] the Act is silent on the minor's antenuptial contract. Therefore, the general rule as set out in the Act applies, namely that any of the child's guardians may independently exercise guardianship in respect of the minor.[1065] If a minor has the requisite consent to marry but he or she does not have consent to enter into an antenuptial contract, the antenuptial contract is void and cannot be ratified or registered after the marriage has taken place.[1066]

356. An antenuptial contract does not lapse on dissolution of the marriage or civil union. Any provisions which have not yet been implemented, such as marriage or civil union settlements, must still be carried out. The antenuptial contract comes to an end only when all the obligations set out in it have been complied with.

§2. The Most Common Variations of Separation of Property

I. The Accrual System

A. General

357. As indicated in the previous chapter, the default system in a marriage out of community of property is the accrual system. In terms of the Matrimonial Property Act 88 of 1984, the accrual system applies to all marriages and all civil unions which are concluded out of community of property and out of community of profit and loss after the coming into operation of the Act (i.e., as from 1 November 1984), unless this system is expressly excluded in the couple's antenuptial contract.[1067]

358. The accrual system is very similar to the German system of *Zugewinngemeinschaft*. During the subsistence of the marriage or civil union, each party retains and controls his or her own estate, but on dissolution of the marriage or civil union the parties share equally in the growth their estates have shown during the subsistence of the marriage or civil union.

The sharing of the accrual is brought about by calculating the accrual in the estate of each party, deducting the smaller accrual from the larger accrual, and giving the

1062. *See* Part I, Ch. 3, §2 above.
1063. *Ex parte Potgieter* 1943 OPD 4.
1064. Section 18(3)(c)(i) read with s. 18(5).
1065. Section 18(4).
1066. *Edelstein v. Edelstein* 1952 (3) SA 1 (A); *Ex parte Du Toit* 1953 (4) SA 130 (O); *Ex parte Davis* 1957 (4) SA 594 (T). On the position if the minor does not have consent to marry, *see* below in this chapter.
1067. Section 2.

party whose estate shows the smaller accrual or no accrual at all a claim against the other party for half that amount. In other words, the claim is for an amount that is equal to half of the difference between the accrual of the respective estates.[1068] The accrual claim arises only on dissolution of the marriage or civil union, unless a court orders division of the accrual in terms of section 8 of the Matrimonial Property Act 88 of 1984 during the subsistence of the marriage or civil union.[1069]

359. As the accrual claim is for an *amount* that is equal to half of the difference between the accrual of the respective estates, neither party has any rights in respect of the property of the other.[1070] If the marriage or civil union is being dissolved by divorce, the parties can, naturally, agree in their settlement agreement that the party who has an accrual claim will receive property that is equal to the amount of the claim.[1071]

B. Calculating the Accrual

360. The accrual in the estate of each spouse or civil union partner is the amount by which the net value of his or her estate at the dissolution of the marriage or civil union exceeds the net value at the commencement of the marriage or civil union.[1072] The assets of an *inter vivos* discretionary trust that was created during the subsistence of the marriage may be taken into account if it is proved that a spouse transferred personal assets to the trust and dealt with them as if they were trust assets 'with the fraudulent or dishonest purpose' of avoiding the obligation to properly account for the accrual of the estate and thus to evade payment of the true amount of the other spouse's accrual claim.[1073] Certain assets are excluded from the estate for purposes of calculating the accrual. To calculate the accrual, one therefore deducts the net commencement value of the estate as well as the value of the assets which do not form part of the estate's accrual, from the net end value of the estate.

In the case of dissolution of the marriage by divorce, the net value of each spouse's estate for purposes of the accrual calculation must be determined upon divorce.[1074]

361. The Matrimonial Property Act 88 of 1984 prescribes a number of methods for proving the commencement or initial value of an estate. Firstly, the net commencement value may be declared in the parties' antenuptial contract or in a separate statement that is lodged either before or within six months of the date of the

1068. Section 3(1).
1069. On s. 8, *see* further below in this chapter.
1070. *Reeder v. Softline* 2001 (2) SA 844 (W); *RS v. MS* 2014 (2) SA 511 (GJ).
1071. On settlement agreements, *see* Part II, Ch. 2, §3 above.
1072. Section 4(1)(a).
1073. *REM v. VM* 2017 (3) SA 371 (SCA) para. 20. *See also Badenhorst v. Badenhorst* 2006 (2) SA 255 (SCA) where it was held that the value of trust assets may be taken into account to determine the value of the estate of one of the spouses if the trust is merely the alter ego of the particular spouse.
1074. *AB v. JB* 2016 (5) SA 211 (SCA); *ST v. CT* 2018 (5) SA 479 (SCA).

marriage or civil union.[1075] If the commencement value is not declared in either the antenuptial contract or a separate statement, it is deemed to be nil unless the opposite is proved. The net commencement value is also deemed to be nil if the liabilities of the spouse or civil union partner exceed his or her assets at the commencement of the marriage or civil union.[1076]

When the accrual is calculated on dissolution of the marriage or civil union, the net commencement value of each estate is adapted in accordance with the weighted average of the consumer price index as published from time to time in the *Government Gazette*.[1077]

362. In terms of the Matrimonial Property Act 88 of 1984, the following assets do not form part of the accrual:[1078]

(1) Non-patrimonial damages received during the subsistence of the marriage or civil union.
(2) Assets the spouses or civil union partners exclude in their antenuptial contract, as well as the proceeds of such assets and assets which replace them or are acquired with their proceeds. If a specific asset is excluded in the spouses' antenuptial contract, the value of the asset is irrelevant in the determination of the accrual; in other words, the asset is ignored for purposes of calculating the accrual and therefore does not form part of the net commencement or the net end value of the spouse's estate.[1079]
(3) Inheritances, legacies and donations received from a third party as well as the proceeds of such inheritances, legacies and donations, and assets which replace them or are acquired with their proceeds. However, the testator or donee may specify that an inheritance, legacy or donation must form part of the accrual of the estate of the recipient. In such event, the asset is not excluded when the accrual is calculated.
(4) Donations between the spouses or civil union partners while they are still alive.

1075. Section 6(1). If the value is declared in a separate statement, the statement must be signed by both parties; attested by a notary; and filed together with a copy of the parties' antenuptial contract in the protocol of the notary before whom the antenuptial contract was executed. The statement or antenuptial contract is prima facie proof of the commencement value of the estate: s. 6(3). The declared values are not binding and conclusive. Any interested party, including one of the spouses, may later prove the actual commencement value: *Thomas v. Thomas* [1999] 3 All SA 192 (NC); *TN v. NN* 2018 (4) SA 316 (WCC), but *see Olivier v. Olivier* 1998 (1) SA 550 (D).

1076. Section 6(4)(a) and (b).

1077. Section 4(1)(b)(iii). The consumer price index is published in the *Government Gazette* every month and is available by way of a historical table at http://www.statssa.gov.za/publications/P0141/CPIHistory.pdf, 24 Mar. 2019.

1078. Sections 4(1)(b)(i)–(ii), 5(1) and 5(2). The burden of proving that a particular asset is excluded falls on the person who alleges that the asset is excluded: *ST v. CT* 2018 (5) SA 479 (SCA). If excluded assets and included assets have become mixed, the owning spouse bears the burden of proving the extent of the exclusion: *ibid.*

1079. *Bath v. Bath* [2014] JOL 31724 (SCA).

Furthermore, in terms of a judgment of the Supreme Court of Appeal, the capitalized value of a living annuity from which a monthly income is derived cannot be taken into account in calculating the accrual, as a living annuity is not an asset in a spouse's estate.[1080]

C. Protection and Satisfaction of the Accrual Claim

363. As a rule, the accrual claim arises only on dissolution of the marriage or civil union. However, section 8 of the Matrimonial Property Act 88 of 1984 empowers the court to order division of the accrual during the subsistence of a marriage or civil union if the conduct or proposed conduct of one of the spouses or civil union partners seriously prejudices, or will probably seriously prejudice, the right of the other spouse or civil union partner to share in the accrual at the dissolution of the marriage or civil union, and no other person will be prejudiced by the order. The division may be done on whatever basis the court deems just.[1081] By making an unequal division of the accrual, the court can compensate the prejudiced spouse or civil union partner for loss suffered as a result of the conduct of the other spouse or civil union partner. The court may also order that the marriage or civil union will no longer be subject to the accrual system and will in future be subject to complete separation of property.[1082]

A spouse or civil union partner who will be prejudiced by the proposed conduct of his or her spouse or civil union partner can also seek an interdict to prohibit the proposed conduct.[1083] If assets have already been transferred to a third party with fraudulent intention to prejudice, the prejudiced spouse or civil union partner can attempt to recover the property from the third party with the *actio Pauliana utilis*.[1084]

364. When an accrual claim becomes due the court may, on application by the spouse or civil union partner against whom the claim operates, order that satisfaction of the claim be deferred. The deferment may be granted on any conditions the court deems just, such as the furnishing of security, payment by way of instalments, payment of interest, and delivery or transfer of specified assets.[1085] However, payment of the portion of a pension interest that has been assigned to the claimant may not be deferred, as the pension legislation entitles a spouse to immediate payment of the portion of the pension interest.[1086]

1080. *ST v. CT* 2018 (5) SA 479 (SCA).
1081. Section 8(1).
1082. Section 8(2).
1083. *Reeder v. Softline* 2001 (2) SA 844 (W) (*obiter*).
1084. *See*, e.g., Hahlo, *The South African Law of Husband and Wife*, 309; Heaton & Kruger, *Family Law*, 100; Himonga, *Marriage*, 301; A. van Aswegen *Transactions between a Spouse and a Third Party: The Effect of the Matrimonial Property Act 88 of 1984*, Mod. Businessman's Law 148 (1984).
1085. Matrimonial Property Act 88 of 1984, s. 10.
1086. *BS v. PS* 2018 (4) SA 400 (SCA). On pension interests, *see* Part 2, Ch. 2, § 3 above.

II. Complete Separation of Property

365. Complete separation of property refers to a marriage or civil union in which community of property, community of profit and loss, and the accrual system have been excluded. The effect of complete separation of property is that each of the parties retains the estate he or she had before the marriage or civil union as well as everything he or she acquires during the marriage or civil union.

III. Separation of Property with Retention of Community of Profit and Loss

366. In a marriage or civil union out of community of property with retention of community of profit and loss each party retains the assets and liabilities he or she has at the time of entering into the marriage or civil union. Donations, bequests and inheritances received during the subsistence of the marriage or civil union likewise remain the separate property of the party who receives them. However, because community of profit and loss is retained, all profit and loss arising during the marriage or civil union become joint profit and loss and constitute a joint estate of which each party owns an undivided half-share.

The main differences between this system and the accrual system are that in the case of community of profit and loss the parties share their postnuptial gains and losses and this sharing occurs during the subsistence of the marriage or civil union, while only profits are shared in terms of the accrual system and the sharing only takes place on dissolution of the marriage or civil union.

§3. The Proprietary Consequences of a Civil or Customary Marriage a Minor Concludes without the Necessary Consent

367. A marriage a minor concludes without the required consent is voidable.[1087] If the marriage is dissolved due to the lack of consent, the court may make any order it deems just with regard to the division of the parties' property.[1088] The position is less clear if the marriage is not set aside. Section 24(2) of the Matrimonial Property Act 88 of 1984 provides that 'the patrimonial consequences of the marriage are the same as if the minor were of age when the marriage was entered into and any antenuptial contract in terms of which the accrual system is included and which has been executed with a view to such a marriage, is deemed to have been validly executed'.[1089] It is clear that if the parties did not enter into an antenuptial contract, the primary matrimonial property system, namely community of property, applies. It is also clear that if the parties entered into an antenuptial contract that includes the accrual system, the antenuptial contract is valid. However, it is unclear what the

1087. *See* Part I, Ch. 3, §2 above.

1088. Matrimonial Property Act 88 of 1984, s. 24(1); Recognition of Customary Marriages Act 120 of 1998, s. 8(4)(a).

1089. Whether this section applies to a customary marriage a minor concluded without consent is unclear: Heaton & Kruger, *Family Law*, 227–228.

position is if the parties concluded an antenuptial contract which excludes the accrual system. Some authors are of the opinion that such an antenuptial contract must also be deemed to have been validly executed, while others submit that the antenuptial contract is invalid and the civil marriage in community of property.[1090] A third view is that the antenuptial contract is valid, but that the clause which excludes the accrual system is invalid, with the result that the marriage is subject to the accrual system.[1091] As a minor cannot enter into a civil union,[1092] the above rules apply only to civil and customary marriages.

§4. The Proprietary Consequences of Polygynous Customary Marriages

I. Marriages Concluded Before 15 November 2000

368. As indicated in the previous chapter, the rules that govern the matrimonial property system in a monogamous customary marriage are the same as those that apply to civil marriages and civil unions. The position is different in de facto polygynous customary marriages. The proprietary consequences of a polygynous customary marriage spouses concluded before the coming into operation of the Recognition of Customary Marriages Act 120 of 1998 are governed by customary law.[1093] In terms of the Constitutional Court's decision in *Ramuhovhi v. President of the Republic of South Africa*,[1094] this entails that the spouses have joint and equal ownership of, and joint and equal management and control over, their marital property. The husband and the wife of each house jointly exercise the rights relating to its house property and must do so in the best interests of the particular family unit. The husband and all his wives jointly exercise the rights relating to all family property and must do so in the best interests of the family constituted by all the houses.

II. Marriages Concluded After 15 November 2000

369. The proprietary consequences of a de facto polygynous customary marriage spouses concluded after the coming into operation of the Recognition of Customary Marriages Act 120 of 1998 are determined by way of a court-approved antenuptial contract. The Act requires that a husband who wants to marry another customary wife must draw up a contract that specifies which matrimonial property system will operate in his polygynous customary marriage. He must seek court approval of this contract before he enters into the additional customary marriage.[1095]

1090. *See*, e.g., Hahlo, *The South African Law of Husband and Wife*, 94, 265; J.D. Sinclair, *Introduction to the Matrimonial Property Act 1984* 61 (Juta & Co, Ltd 1984).
1091. Sinclair assisted by Heaton, *The Law of Marriage*, 376.
1092. *See* Part I, Ch. 3, §2 above.
1093. Recognition of Customary Marriages Act 120 of 1998, s. 7(1).
1094. 2018 (2) SA 1 (CC).
1095. Section 7(6).

If the husband's existing customary marriage is in community of property or subject to the accrual system, the court must terminate the matrimonial property system and effect a division of the property.[1096] In all applications, the court must ensure that the property is equitably distributed, and take into account all the relevant circumstances of the family groups that would be affected if the application were granted.[1097] All persons who have a sufficient interest in the matter and, in particular, the husband's present and future wives, must be joined in the proceedings.[1098]

The court may allow amendments to the proposed contract, grant an order subject to conditions or refuse the application if, in its opinion, any party's interests would not be sufficiently safeguarded by the proposed contract.[1099]

Failure to obtain a court-approved contract does not affect the validity of the marriage, since the requirement merely pertains to the spouses' matrimonial property system.[1100]

§5. The Consequences of Divorce in a Marriage or Civil Union Out of Community of Property

370. As indicated above, spouses and civil union partners who are getting divorced may arrange the financial consequences of their divorce in a settlement agreement. In the agreement, they may divide their property as they see fit. If they are unable to reach agreement and the accrual system operates in their marriage or civil union, the divorce order automatically operates as an order that the party with the smaller accrual or no accrual has an accrual claim against the other party, unless forfeiture of patrimonial benefits is ordered by the court. In some marriages that are subject to complete separation of property, the court has the power to order redistribution of assets.[1101]

§6. The Consequences of Death in a Marriage or Civil Union Out of Community of Property

371. The death of a spouse or civil union partner does not terminate the antenuptial contract of the parties if some of the clauses of the contract have not yet been complied with. Thus, for example, the survivor may claim marriage or civil union settlements that have not yet been delivered.

372. An executor winds up the deceased's estate in terms of the Administration of Estates Act 66 of 1965. The survivor must lodge any claims he or she has against

1096. Section 7(7)(a)(i).
1097. Section 7(7)(a)(ii) and (iii).
1098. Section 7(8).
1099. Section 7(7)(b).
1100. *MM v. MN* 2013 (4) SA 415 (CC).
1101. *See* Part II, Ch. 2, §3.

the deceased's estate with the executor, including a claim in terms of section 23 of the Matrimonial Property Act 88 of 1984 for excess contributions to the purchase of household necessaries.[1102]

In a marriage or civil union that is subject to the accrual system, the accrual of the estate of the deceased is determined before effect is given to any inheritances or donations which take effect on his or her death.[1103] Thus, accrual sharing takes place before the estate is distributed in terms of the rules of the Law of Succession.[1104] If the accrual of the survivor's estate is less than that of the deceased's estate, the survivor must lodge a quantified claim against the deceased's estate.[1105] If the accrual of the deceased's estate is less than that of the survivor's estate, the executor claims the deceased's share of the accrual from the survivor on behalf of the deceased's estate.

373. As indicated above, it seems that not all customary marriages are dissolved by death.[1106] Accrual sharing probably does not take place if the surviving spouse is a party to a customary marriage in which the sororate or levirate custom is applied, since the survivor remains a party to an existing customary marriage. The accrual system presumably continues between the surviving spouse and the substituted spouse.

§7. Alteration of the Matrimonial Property System

374. Spouses or civil union partners whose marriage or civil union is out of community of property may apply to court for permission to change their matrimonial property system.[1107]

1102. *See* Part III, Ch. 1, §2 above.
1103. Matrimonial Property Act 88 of 1984, s. 4(2).
1104. *Radebe v. Sosibo* 2011 (5) SA 51 (GSJ).
1105. *Barnard v. Van der Merwe* 2012 (3) SA 304 (GNP).
1106. *See* Part II, Ch. 1, §2 above.
1107. *See* further Part III, Ch. 3, §5 above.

Part IV. Succession Law

Introduction

375. The Law of Succession deals with the rules that regulate the devolution of the estate of a person (the deceased) upon death. It has two main branches, namely intestate succession (succession *ab intestato*) and testamentary or testate succession. Property may also pass upon a person's death in terms of a contract (*pactum successorium*) contained in an antenuptial contract.[1108]

376. The deceased's estate consists of all the assets and liabilities the deceased leaves behind at his or her death.[1109] Rights and duties of a purely personal nature, such as rights and duties under a contract of personal services, die with the deceased and do not form part of the estate.[1110] Other contractual obligations that are not purely personal are transmitted to the estate.[1111] The estate is therefore an aggregate of assets and liabilities. It does not have legal personality.[1112]

The deceased estate is represented by an executor who is appointed by the Master of the High Court in terms of the Administration of Estates Act 66 of 1965.[1113] The Master is tasked by the Administration of Estates Act to supervise the administration of the deceased estate. The Administration of Estates Act establishes a fund, the Guardian's Fund,[1114] into which the Master pays moneys received in terms of the Act.

377. After the liabilities of the estate have been settled by the executor from the assets of the deceased estate, the residue of the estate passes to the beneficiaries. Beneficiaries may be either heirs or legatees. A legatee inherits a legacy, which is a specific asset or a specific amount of money. A legatee is appointed in a will. Heirs can be appointed in a will or in terms of intestate succession. An heir inherits the

1108. *Ex parte Estate Executors Estate Everard* 1938 TPD 190. The *pactum successorium* is discussed in Ch. 3, §1 below in this part.
1109. B. de Clercq, M.C. Schoeman-Malan & P. de W. van der Spuy, *Deceased Estates* 1 (LexisNexis 11th ed. 2017).
1110. *Du Toit v. Miller, Terblanche & Zietsman* 1974 (4) SA 31 (C).
1111. South African law does not recognize a claim for wrongful death and the deceased estate consequently does not have a claim against a person who wrongfully caused the deceased's death for the loss suffered as a result of the death: *Lockhat's Estate v. North British & Mercantile Insurance Co Ltd* 1959 (3) SA 295 (A).
1112. *CIR v. MacNeillie's Estate* 1961 (3) SA 833 (A).
1113. Section 13.
1114. Chapter V of the Act.

whole or part of the estate or the residue of the estate. A testator may dispose of his or her whole estate by means of legacies.

378. The question of who owns a deceased estate in the period between the death of the deceased and the transfer of the assets to the beneficiaries has not yet been satisfactorily answered.[1115] Under the South African system of administration of estates, the beneficiaries do not become the owners of the property in the deceased estate immediately on the death of the deceased.[1116] On the death of the deceased, the beneficiaries merely acquire a vested (established or unconditional) personal right to claim delivery or transfer of the bequeathed benefits from the executor once the accounts have lain for inspection according to the requirements of the Administration of Estates Act 66 of 1965.[1117]

379. The first main branch of succession, namely intestate succession, identifies the heirs to a deceased estate when the deceased has failed to regulate the devolution of his or her property by means of a valid will or antenuptial contract, or where it is impossible to carry out the wishes of the deceased because the beneficiaries are, for example, unworthy to inherit, do not wish to inherit or are predeceased. A person can die completely intestate or only partly intestate.[1118] A person dies partly intestate when the will does not dispose of the whole estate or if a person appointed as heir is predeceased, cannot inherit, or refuses to inherit and no accrual to heirs or co-heirs takes place.[1119]

380. At present, the South African law of intestate succession is regulated by the Intestate Succession Act 81 of 1987.[1120] The intestate heirs of all intestate estates

---

1115. M.M. Corbett, G. Hofmeyer & E. Kahn, *The Law of Succession in South Africa* 16–17 (Juta Law 2d ed. 2002); M.J. de Waal & M.C. Schoeman-Malan, *Law of Succession* 11 (Juta 5th ed. 2015); N.J van der Merwe & C.J. Rowland, *Die Suid-Afrikaanse Erfreg* 8 et seq. (J.P. van der Walt en Seun (Edms) Bpk 6th ed. 1990); M.J. de Waal, *Testamentary Formalities in South Africa*, in *Comparative Succession Law, Volume I: Testamentary Formalities* 382 (K.G.C. Reid, M.J. de Waal & R. Zimmermann eds., Oxford University Press 2011). It can possibly be said that the executor becomes the owner. In *Van den Berg v. Coetzee* 2001 (4) SA 93 (T) 95 it was held that 'the executor does not step into the shoes of the deceased on his death; he does not succeed to the person of the deceased. He is simply required to administer and distribute the estate … '. However, in *Absa Bank v. Magiet* [2009] ZAWCHC 144, 10 Sept. 2009, (unreported), http://www.saflii.org/za/cases/ZAWCHC/2009/144.html, para. 14 it was held that 'even if it is accepted that the executor does not succeed to the *persona* of the deceased, the estate ultimately vests in the executor in the sense that the dominium and other rights and obligations of the estate reside in him'. *See also Mills v. Hoosen* 2010 (2) SA 316 (W) para. 12.

1116. *Greenberg v. Estate Greenberg* 1955 (3) SA 361 (A); *Commissioner, SARS v. Executor, Frith's Estate* 2001 (2) SA 261 (SCA).

1117. *Estate Smith v. Estate Follett* 1942 AD 364; *Greenberg v. Estate Greenberg* 1955 (3) SA 361 (A).

1118. *Brunsdon's Estate v. Brunsdon's Estate* 1920 CPD 159; *Havemann's Assignee v. Havemann's Executor* 1927 AD 473.

1119. Corbett, Hofmeyer & Kahn, *The Law of Succession in South Africa*, 562.

1120. South African intestate succession law has its historical roots in two intestate succession systems which operated in the province of Holland before codification, namely the *Aasdomsrecht* and the *Schependomsrecht*: Corbett, Hofmeyer & Kahn, *The Law of Succession in South Africa*, 563; Van der Merwe & Rowland, *Die Suid-Afrikaanse Erfreg* 22; M.J. de Waal, *Intestate Succession in*

are determined in terms of this Act and all intestate estates are administered in terms of the Administration of Estates Act 66 of 1965.[1121]

Prior to December 2000, there was a parallel system for the intestate estates of Blacks/Africans. The intestate estates of Black/African persons were subject to section 23 of the Black Administration Act 38 of 1927 and its accompanying regulations.[1122] This parallel system of intestate succession purported to give effect to the customary law of succession. It prescribed which estates were to devolve in terms of what the Act described as 'Black law and custom' and detailed the steps that had to be taken in the administration of those estates. Central to the customary law of succession is the principle of male primogeniture, in terms of which the eldest son of the head of the family is his heir. Women generally do not inherit in terms of customary law.[1123]

In December 2000, the Constitutional Court declared the separate system of administration for the intestate estates of Black persons, unconstitutional.[1124] A few years later the rule of male primogeniture as it applied to the inheritance of property in terms of customary law was also held to be inconsistent with the Constitution and declared invalid to the extent that it excluded or hindered women and children born of unmarried parents from inheriting property. The Constitutional Court held that as an interim solution, until Parliament adopted the necessary legislation, the Intestate Succession Act would be applied to all intestate estates. The court further ordered that all new estates were to be administered under the supervision of the Master of the High Court in terms of the Administration of Estates Act.[1125]

The Reform of Customary Law of Succession and Regulation of Related Matters Act 11 of 2009 was subsequently enacted to harmonize the customary and common law relating to intestate succession.[1126] The Act confirmed that the intestate estate

---

South Africa, in *Comparative Succession Law, Volume II: Intestate Succession* 250–256 (K.G.C. Reid, M.J. de Waal & R. Zimmermann eds., Oxford University Press 2015).

1121. If a person wants his or her estate to devolve in accordance with a specific religious system of inheritance (e.g., in terms of Islamic law of succession), the person can accomplish this by executing a will. On Islamic law of succession, *see* M. Abduroaf, *The Impact of South African Law on the Islamic Law of Succession*, Doctoral Thesis, Doctor of Laws, (University of Cape Town 2018); M. Abduroaf & N. Moosa, *Islamic Law Mode of Estate Distribution in South Africa*, in *The International Survey of Family Law* 457–479 (B. Atkin ed., Jordan Publishing 2016).

1122. Regulations for the Administration and Distribution of the Estates of Deceased Blacks (R200 in *G.G.* 10601 of 6 Feb. 1987).

1123. *See*, e.g., *Mthembu v. Letsela* 2000 (3) SA 867 (SCA) para. 8. *See also* De Waal, *Intestate Succession in South Africa*, 266.

1124. *Moseneke v. The Master* 2001 (2) SA 18 (CC). *See also Bhe v. Magistrate, Khayelitsha (Commission for Gender Equality as Amicus Curiae); Shibi v. Sithole; South African Human Rights Commission v. President of the Republic of South Africa* 2005 (1) SA 580 (CC).

1125. *Bhe v. Magistrate, Khayelitsha (Commission for Gender Equality as Amicus Curiae); Shibi v. Sithole; South African Human Rights Commission v. President of the Republic of South Africa* 2005 (1) SA 580 (CC); C. Rautenbach, *A Few Comments on the (Possible) Revival of the Customary Law Rule of Male Primogeniture: Can the Common-Law Principle of Freedom of Testation Come to its Rescue?*, in *South African Law of Succession and Trusts – The Past Meeting the Present and Thoughts for the Future* 132–160 (M. de Waal & M. Paleker eds., Juta & Co 2014).

1126. The Act came into operation on 20 Sep. 2010.

of any person, including a person who is subject to customary law, must devolve in terms of the Intestate Succession Act, but with certain modifications to accommodate customary law.[1127]

381. The second main branch of succession, namely testate succession, comes into play when the deceased (testator) left a valid will in which he or she provided how succession to his or her estate must take place.[1128] Testate succession is based on the principle of freedom of testation. This freedom is wide but not unlimited. A testator's wishes as expressed in a valid will must be carried out except in so far as the law places a limitation on freedom of testation. These limitations may be imposed by common law, by statute or by the Constitution.[1129]

All wills have to comply with the formalities required by the Wills Act 7 of 1953 in order to be valid. All testate estates are administered in terms of the Administration of Estates Act 66 of 1965.

1127. Section 2. The modifications include the following: polygyny is recognised; a person who is not a descendant in terms of the Intestate Succession Act, but who, during the deceased's lifetime, was accepted by the deceased in accordance with customary law as his or her own child, is considered to be a descendant; a woman, other than the deceased's spouse, with whom the deceased had entered into a union in accordance with customary law for the purpose of providing children for his spouse's house must, if she survives him, be regarded as a descendant of the deceased; and if the deceased was a woman who was married to another woman under customary law for the purpose of providing children for the deceased's house, that other woman must, if she survives the deceased, be regarded as a descendant of the deceased. *See* further J. Jamneck & C. Rautenbach (eds), *The Law of Succession in South Africa* (Oxford University Press Southern Africa 3rd ed. 2017), Ch. 15 for a discussion of the Reform of Customary Law of Succession and Regulation of Related Matters Act 11 of 2009. *See also* De Waal, *Intestate Succession in South Africa*, 267–268.

1128. The concept of a will is not found in customary law.

1129. The restrictions on freedom of testation are dealt with in Ch. 2, §7 below in this part.

Chapter 1. Intestate Succession

§1. The Opening of the Succession

382. Before the death of the deceased, the beneficiaries have no claim against the estate of the deceased. A beneficiary's personal claim against an executor in respect of his or her benefit arises when the estate 'falls open' in respect of the specific benefit. This 'falling open' of the estate is also referred to as *delatio*.[1130]

383. If a deceased dies without a valid will, the intestate heirs have to be determined at the date of his or her death.[1131] However, if a testator leaves a valid will but the provisions of the will (or some of them) fail and the estate (or part of it) consequently devolves *ab intestato*, the date on which the intestate heirs must be identified is the date of ultimate failure of the will.[1132]

I. Death

384. It is a prerequisite for succession that the owner of the estate must have died. The Director-General of the Department of Home Affairs is responsible for registering all deaths that occur in South Africa and for the issuing of official death certificates.[1133] An official death certificate is prima facie proof of the person's death.[1134]

II. Missing Persons and Absentees

385. If a person has disappeared and is thought to be dead but there is no body to prove the fact, the High Court may grant an order presuming the death of that person. Only once that has happened, may the estate be administered.[1135] Since the person in question could possibly still be alive, this situation constitutes an exception to the rule that a testator must be dead before succession can take place. For

1130. De Waal & Schoeman-Malan, *Law of Succession*, 7; Van der Merwe & Rowland, *Die Suid-Afrikaanse Erfreg*, 12.
1131. *Union Government (Minister of Finance) v. Olivier* 1916 AD 74; *Ramsumer v. The Master (NPD)* 1978 (4) SA 877 (N).
1132. *Harris v. Assumed Administrator, Estate MacGregor* 1987 (3) SA 563 (A).
1133. Births and Deaths Registration Act 51 of 1992, s. 22; Identification Act 68 of 1997, s. 13(1). *See* Part I, Ch. 2, §2 above.
1134. Births and Deaths Registration Act 51 of 1992, s. 28(2); Identification Act 68 of 1997, s. 13(1).
1135. *See*, e.g., *Re Beaglehole* 1908 TS 49; *Ex parte Alexander* 1965 (2) SA 608 (A); *Ex parte Govender* 1993 (3) SA 721 (D); *Ex parte Stoter* 1996 (4) SA 1299 (E). For a detailed discussion of the topic of missing persons and absentees, *see* Part I, Ch. 1, §3 above. *See also* M.C. Schoeman-Malan *Missing Persons – Current Tendencies* 81 J. Contemp. Roman-Dutch Law 218 (2018).

this reason, it is customary for the court to order that the estate of the missing person be divided among the heirs, subject to the furnishing of security that the estate will be restored to the person who has been presumed to be dead in the event of his or her reappearance.[1136]

Furthermore, although the court may not in a given case be prepared to make an order presuming a person's death, it may none the less order that the missing person's estate be administered and the property be divided amongst his or her heirs, provided that they furnish security for the return of the property, or its value, should the missing person reappear.[1137]

§2. THE HEIR

386. The heir is the person who succeeds to the whole or a portion of the net estate of a deceased person.[1138] Under South African law, the heir only inherits the assets of the estate; the liabilities do not devolve on him or her.[1139] The heir is not responsible for the administration of the estate – that function is fulfilled by the executor of the estate.[1140]

It should be noted that South African law does not have a system of forced heirship, although it does recognize maintenance claims against a deceased estate by dependent children and surviving spouses.[1141] Also, the rules regarding collation should be taken into consideration for both intestate and testate succession.[1142] Collation is a process whereby the inheritances of certain of the deceased's heirs are adjusted to take into consideration certain lifetime advances in the final distribution of the estate.[1143]

I. Capacity to Succeed

387. Capacity to inherit *ab intestato* is primarily based on blood relationship. However, the spouse of the deceased (which includes not only a spouse in terms of a civil marriage, but also a civil union partner, a spouse in a customary, Muslim or Hindu marriage, and a same-sex partner in a life partnership in which the partners have undertaken reciprocal duties of support) as well as adopted children, children born as a result of artificial insemination, children born in terms of a valid surrogacy agreement and, in the case of a deceased who is subject to customary law, a

1136. *Dempers and Van Ryneveld v. SA Mutual Life Insurance Society* (1908) 25 SC 162.
1137. *In re Cuthbert* 1932 NPD 615; *Ex parte Davids* 1948 (1) SA 1018 (W).
1138. Corbett, Hofmeyer & Kahn, *The Law of Succession in South Africa*, 4.
1139. Van der Merwe & Rowland, *Die Suid-Afrikaanse Erfreg*, 1.
1140. In terms of the Administration of Estates Act 66 of 1965.
1141. *See* De Waal, *Intestate Succession in South Africa*, 259. On maintenance, *see* further Part IV, Ch. 2, §7.
1142. De Waal, *Intestate Succession in South Africa*, 259.
1143. On collation, *see* Corbett, Hofmeyr & Kahn, *The Law of Succession in South Africa*, 21–30; Jamneck & Rautenbach (eds), *The Law of Succession in South Africa*, 217–228; De Waal & Schoeman-Malan, *Law of Succession*, 204–210.

person who during the lifetime of the deceased was accepted by the deceased in accordance with customary law as his or her own child, may also inherit *ab intestato*.[1144]

388. The beneficiary must be alive (or must have been conceived) at *delatio* (opening of the estate). A descendant who has been conceived when the estate falls open (usually at the death of the deceased) and who is subsequently born alive can benefit due to the application of the *nasciturus* fiction.[1145]

389. At common law, children born of unmarried parents could only inherit under certain circumstances.[1146] However, in terms of the Intestate Succession Act 81 of 1987 birth out of wedlock no longer affects the capacity of one blood relation to inherit *ab intestato* from another blood relation.[1147]

390. Because minors have legal capacity, they have capacity to inherit. However, because they do not have full capacity to act, their ability to enjoy their inheritance is limited until they come of age (i.e., when they turn 18).[1148] Movable property is received by the minor's guardian on behalf of the minor.[1149] Money is not paid to the guardian, but to the Guardian's Fund which is administered by the Master of the High Court.[1150] Immovable property is registered in the name of the minor,[1151] but administered by his or her guardian.[1152]

391. Mentally ill persons and prodigals have the capacity to inherit, but their ability to deal with their estates is limited.[1153]

392. A person who has been declared insolvent retains the capacity to inherit, but any property he or she inherits falls into the insolvent estate for the benefit of the creditors. However, the Supreme Court of Appeal has held that an insolvent may repudiate an inheritance, without causing any prejudice to creditors.[1154]

1144. *See* Ch. 1, §3 below in this part.
1145. *See* Part I, Ch. 1, §1 above.
1146. *See* De Waal, *Intestate Succession in South Africa*, 257.
1147. Section 1(2).
1148. *See* Part I, Ch. 1, §2 above on the difference between legal capacity and capacity to act, and Part I, Ch. 3 above on the capacity of a minor.
1149. Administration of Estates Act 66 of 1965, s. 43(1).
1150. *Ibid.*, s. 43(2) and (6) read with Ch. V.
1151. *Ibid.*, s. 39(1).
1152. *See also* Jamneck & Rautenbach (eds), *The Law of Succession in South Africa*, 108–109.
1153. *See* Part I, Ch. 1, §2 above.
1154. *Wessels v. De Jager* 2000 (4) SA 924 (SCA). According to the Supreme Court of Appeal, the heirs receive only a competence – and not a right – to inherit upon the death of the deceased. They only obtain a right once they accept the bequeathed benefit. Note that if a benefit is left to a beneficiary in a will, the testator may provide that if the beneficiary is insolvent at the time of the devolution, the beneficiary will forfeit the inheritance in favour of a named substitute: *Vorster v. Steyn* 1981 (2) SA 831 (O); Corbett, Hofmeyer & Kahn, *The Law of Succession in South Africa*, 137.

II. Commorientes

393. If several persons simultaneously lose their lives in the same disaster (*commorientes*), it may be important to determine which of them died first, in order to establish whether one inherited from the other. In terms of Roman-Dutch law, certain presumptions became operative when members of the same family were killed under circumstances which rendered it difficult to determine who had died first. However, the South African courts have refused to follow Roman-Dutch rules in this regard. Today, the general rule is that if it cannot be established without doubt who died first, no presumption of either simultaneous death or survival exists. In the absence of evidence to the contrary, the courts will find that *commorientes* died simultaneously.[1155]

III. Unworthiness to Succeed

A. *Introduction*

394. The cases of unworthiness discussed in this paragraph extend to both intestate and testate succession. There are also specific instances in which a person who is involved in the execution of a will is precluded from inheriting under that will. The latter instances are discussed in the chapter on testate succession.

395. A person may be disqualified from inheriting from a deceased because of conduct that makes him or her unworthy, in a legal sense, to inherit from the deceased.[1156] In general, a person is precluded from inheriting from the deceased if his or her conduct, aimed at the deceased, is against public policy or morally reprehensible.[1157]

The principle that no one should be permitted to benefit from his or her wrongful conduct should also be kept in mind.[1158] For example, in *L. Taylor v.*

1155. *See*, e.g., *Nepgen v. Van Dyk* 1940 EDL 123; *Ex parte Chodos* 1948 (4) SA 221 (N); *Ex parte Graham* 1963 (4) SA 145 (D). *See also* M.C. Schoeman-Malan, *Comparative Analysis of Commorientes – A South African Perspective: Part 1*, De Jure 50 36 (2017); M.C. Schoeman-Malan, *Comparative Analysis of Commorientes – A South African Perspective: Part 2*, 50 De Jure 378 (2017); M.C. Schoeman-Malan, *When Disaster Strikes – A Case Law Analysis of Simultaneous Deaths*, 38 Obiter 275 (2017).

1156. Corbett, Hofmeyer & Kahn, *The Law of Succession in South Africa*, 81. Unworthiness to inherit precludes the person from inheriting both *ab intestato* and under a will.

1157. *Taylor v. Pim* 1903 NLR 484 493.

1158. S. Barns & A. Thompson, *Reconsidering the Indignus Principle in the South African Law of Succession*, in *South African Law of Succession and Trusts – The Past Meeting the Present and Thoughts for the Future* 123–131 (M. de Waal & M. Paleker eds., Juta & Co 2014), argue that, in fact, the Roman-Dutch principle that 'no person may benefit from his or her own wrongdoing or benefit from what is punishable' is the overarching principle that should be applied where someone is to be disqualified from inheriting. The *indignus* principle referred to in *Taylor v. Pim* 1903 NLR 484, 'which holds that where a person's conduct so offends the notions of public policy, he or she may be deemed unworthy to take an inheritance', introduces vague policy principles that

A.E. Pim[1159] the court found that the defendant, who had cohabited with the deceased:

> was the cause of the deceased's fall from a virtuous and honourable life to a degraded and immoral one; that his conduct with her was adulterous; that he supplied her or allowed her to be supplied with intoxicating liquors at the time when their use was forbidden by her medical advisor, and that he did so at times when he could easily have prevented their use by the deceased had he so wished; that he neglected to provide her with medical attention … that while there he allowed her to have intoxicating liquors which caused her death; … and that in other respects his conduct was heartless and cruel … .

The court held that the defendant was unworthy to succeed as the deceased's heir. Similarly, in *Pillay v. Nagan*[1160] a person who had forged the will of the deceased was held not to be entitled to inherit *ab intestato* from the deceased.

The above instances of unworthiness do not form a *numerus clausus*. Other forms of conduct not discussed here, may also lead to unworthiness. In addition, it should be borne in mind that unworthiness is relative. Thus, a person may be unworthy of inheriting from one person, but worthy of inheriting from others.[1161]

396. Someone who is disqualified from inheriting from the deceased is not automatically excluded from inheriting; nor does the Master have the authority to exclude him or her.[1162] An order of court is required to exclude the beneficiary.[1163]

B. Person Who Caused the Death of the Deceased

397. A person who caused the death of the deceased is incapable of inheriting any benefit in the estate of the deceased. This is a principle of our common law which is derived from Roman law and is expressed in the maxim *de bloedige hand er neemt geen erffenis.*[1164] This principle is a subset of the overarching principle that no one should benefit from his or her own wrongdoing.[1165] Thus, a murderer is incapable of inheriting any benefit from his or her victim.[1166] However, it is not a general unworthiness that attaches to the murderer; it is only an unworthiness to inherit

---

could lead to 'startling outcomes' in the future. *See also* M.C. Schoeman-Malan, *Privaatregtelike Perspektief op Onwaardigheid om te Erf – die Uitwerking van Gesinsmoorde*, 10 LitNet Akademies 113 (2013).

1159. 1903 NLR 484 495.

1160. 2001 (1) SA 410 (D).

1161. Van der Merwe & Rowland, *Die Suid-Afrikaanse Erfreg*, 239.

1162. *Ferreira v. Die Meester* 2001 (3) SA 365 (O).

1163. Jamneck & Rautenbach (eds), *The Law of Succession in South Africa*, 114.

1164. Grotius, *Inleidinge tot de Hollandsche Rechts-geleerdheid*, 2.24.24, 2.28.42; *Ex parte Steenkamp and Steenkamp* 1952 (1) SA 744 (T).

1165. Barns & Thompson, *Reconsidering the Indignus Principle in the South African Law of Succession*, 123–131.

1166. *Ex parte Steenkamp and Steenkamp* 1952 (1) SA 744 (T); *Ex parte Wessels and Lubbe* 1954 (2) SA 225 (O).

from his or her victim. A murderer may therefore inherit intestate or testate from an heir or legatee of the person he or she has killed. This rule, that a killer is not precluded from inheriting from the heir of the victim, is subject to an exception. In *Ex parte Steenkamp and Steenkamp*[1167] it was held that a person who murdered the deceased's parent, child or spouse (so-called *coniunctissimi* of the deceased) may not inherit from the deceased. The reason is that murdering the parent, child or spouse of the deceased is regarded as a grave wrong to the deceased, as well as to the victim. However, the prohibition does not extend further than a parent, child or spouse. A person who murdered the deceased's grandparent, brother or grandchild is not invariably excluded by the murder. He or she will, however, be excluded if the result of the murder is directly to his or her benefit, for the law does not permit a person to be enriched by his or her own illegal act. There must, however, be a causal connection between the wrong and the enrichment.[1168]

398. The *bloedige hand* rule extends to a person who negligently caused the death of another. Although several South African writers have argued that the negligent killer should not be excluded from inheriting,[1169] the courts have held that 'principle and public policy' require that the maxim should apply to a person who negligently caused the death of another.[1170]

399. If the killing was justified, such as where a person acted in self-defence, the person is not disqualified from inheriting.[1171] If a person was mentally ill when he or she murdered the deceased, he or she retains the capacity to inherit from the deceased.[1172]

400. There is authority for the view that a spouse who married in community of property is entitled to receive half the joint estate by virtue of such community of property even if he or she murdered his or her spouse.[1173] However, in a more recent case the court held that it could, on the basis of public policy, declare the murderer's benefit from the joint estate forfeited.[1174] The *bloedige hand* rule has also been extended to disqualify a murderous spouse from receiving benefits from his or her victim's pension fund;[1175] and to exclude a spouse who hired a person to assault her

1167. 1952 (1) SA 744 (T).
1168. *Ex parte Steenkamp and Steenkamp* 1952 (1) SA 744 (T); *Nell v. Nell* 1976 (3) SA 700 (T).
1169. D.S.P. Cronjé & A. Roos, *Casebook on the Law of Succession / Erfregvonnisbundel* 188 (Unisa Press 4th ed. 2002); J.C. Sonnekus & J.C. van der Walt, *Die Nalatige Bloedige Hand – Voor die Hof én die Wetgewer*, J. S. Afr. Law 147 (1992); M.C. Schoeman, *Nalatige Doodsveroorsaking: Statutêre Hervorming van die Erfreg?*, 57 J. Contemp. Roman-Dutch Law 114 (1994). These authors argue that the maxim should apply only if the person's conduct is morally reprehensible.
1170. *L. Taylor v. A.E . Pim* (1903) 24 NLR 484; *Caldwell v. Erasmus* 1952 (4) SA 43 (T); *Casey v. The Master* 1992 (4) SA 505 (N).
1171. Corbett, Hofmeyer & Kahn, *The Law of Succession in South Africa*, 82.
1172. *Gafin v. Kavin* 1980 (3) SA 1104 (W); *Ex parte Meier* 1980 (3) SA 154 (T).
1173. *Ex parte Vonzell* 1953 (1) SA 122 (C); *Nell v. Nell* 1976 (3) SA 700 (T).
1174. *Leeb v. Leeb* [1999] 2 All SA 588 (N).
1175. *Makhanya v. Minister of Finance* 2001 (2) SA 1251 (D).

husband who later died as a result of the assault, from the proceeds of life insurance policies taken out by the husband on his own life.[1176]

§3. The System of Descent

I. The Classes of Heirs

401. Section 1 of the Intestate Succession Act 81 of 1987 determines the order of succession to a deceased's estate. In brief, the devolution of the estate follows the following order of priority: surviving spouse(s); children and grandchildren; parents; other members of the immediate family such as brothers and sisters; more distantly related family members; the State.

A. *Surviving Spouse(s) and Civil Union Partners*

402. In South African intestate succession law, a 'surviving spouse' includes not only the person to whom the deceased was married in a civil marriage. It also includes a civil union partner[1177] and a spouse in a customary marriage.[1178] As a result of judicial pronouncements, the term also includes a party to a monogamous[1179] or polygynous[1180] Muslim marriage, a party to a monogamous Hindu marriage,[1181] and a partner in a same-sex life partnership in which the partners undertook reciprocal duties of support.[1182] However, a heterosexual life partner does not qualify as a 'spouse'.[1183]

403. If a person dies intestate and is survived by a spouse but not by a descendant, the spouse inherits the entire intestate estate.[1184] Since customary marriages and certain religious marriages allow a husband to have more than one wife, it is

1176. *Danielz v. De Wet* 2009 (6) SA 42 (C). In *Marais v. Botha* 2009 JDR 0020 (C) para. 11 a spouse who was indicted on a charge of conspiracy to murder her deceased husband was denied the opportunity of being appointed as the executor of the deceased estate on the basis that it would be 'repugnant to all notions of justice and public policy'.
1177. Civil Union Act 17 of 2006, s. 13(1).
1178. *See* the definition of 'spouse' in s. 1 of the Reform of Customary Law of Succession and Regulation of Related Matters Act 11 of 2009. *See also* De Waal, *Intestate Succession in South Africa*, 265–268.
1179. *Daniels v. Campbell* 2004 (5) SA 331 (CC).
1180. *Hassam v. Jacobs* 2009 (5) SA 572 (CC); *Moosa v. Minister of Justice and Correctional Services* 2018 (5) SA 13 (CC).
1181. *Govender v. Ragavayah* 2009 (3) SA 178 (D). On the law relating to intestate succession in marriages under Muslim and Hindu law, *see* De Waal, *Intestate Succession in South Africa*, 268–271.
1182. *Gory v. Kolver (Starke Intervening)* 2007 (4) SA 97 (CC); *Laubscher v. Duplan* 2017 (2) SA 264 (CC).
1183. *Volks v. Robinson* 2005 (5) SA 446 (CC). On the discrepancy between the position of heterosexual and same-sex life partners, *see* Part II, Ch. 3, §3 above.
1184. Intestate Succession Act 81 of 1987, s. 1(1)(a). In other words, only a descendant can compete with a deceased's surviving spouse: *see* De Waal, *Intestate Succession in South Africa*, 260.

possible that a deceased may leave behind more than one spouse. In such event, the intestate estate is divided equally between all the spouses.[1185]

404. If the spouses were married in community of property, the joint estate is divided first before the rules of intestate succession are applied to the deceased's half of the joint estate.[1186] If the spouses were married out of community of property and the accrual system applied to the marriage, the principles of accrual sharing are applied to the intestate estate of the deceased before it is divided in terms of the rules of intestate succession. In other words, the amount of the accrual claim is either deducted from or added to the intestate estate before it is divided between the heirs.[1187]

B. Descendants

405. Descendants refer to all the lineal descendants of the deceased (children, grandchildren, etc.), and all the persons considered to be descendants in terms of the Reform of Customary Law of Succession and Regulation of Related Matters Act 11 of 2009. In terms of section 1 of this Act, a descendant includes a person who is not a descendant in terms of the Intestate Succession Act 81 of 1987, but whom the deceased accepted as his or her own child in accordance with customary law during his or her lifetime, and a woman in a substitute (sororate) customary marriage or a woman-to-woman customary marriage.[1188]

406. If a person dies intestate and is survived by a descendant or more than one descendant but not by a spouse, such descendant(s) inherit the entire intestate estate.[1189]

407. If a person dies intestate and is survived by a spouse or by more than one spouse and by a descendant or more than one descendant, the spouse(s) inherit either a child's share each of the intestate estate or a statutory amount determined by the Minister of Justice and Correctional Services (at present ZAR 250,000),[1190]

1185. Reform of Customary Law of Succession and Regulation of Related Matters Act 11 of 2009, s. 3(1).
1186. On community of property, *see* further Part III, Ch. 3, §2 above.
1187. On the accrual system, *see* further Part III, Ch. 4, §2 above.
1188. In terms of s. 2(2)(b) and (c) of the Reform of Customary Law of Succession and Regulation of Related Matters Act 11 of 2009, the following women are included as the deceased's descendants:

- a woman, other than the spouse of the deceased, with whom he had entered into a union in accordance with customary law for the purpose of providing children for his spouse's house must, if she survives him, be regarded as a descendant of the deceased;
- if the deceased was a woman who was married to another woman under customary law for the purpose of providing children for the deceased's house, that other woman must, if she survives the deceased, be regarded as a descendant of the deceased.

1189. Intestate Succession Act 81 of 1987, s. 1(1)(b).
1190. G.N. R921 in *G.G.* 38238 of 24 Nov. 2014.

whichever is the greater, and the descendants inherit the residue (if any) of the estate.[1191] A 'child's share' or a 'child's portion' is a statutory concept. In terms of the Intestate Succession Act 81 of 1987, a child's share is calculated as follows:[1192] the value of the intestate estate is divided by the number of children of the deceased who have either survived him or her or have predeceased him or her but are survived by their descendants, plus the number of spouses (which includes a woman in a substitute customary marriage or a woman-to-woman customary marriage[1193]).

The parents and siblings of the deceased are excluded from inheriting under intestate succession law if the deceased is survived by a spouse (or spouses) and/or descendants.

C. Ascendants and Collaterals

408. Ascendants refer to the ancestors of the deceased, that is, parents, grandparents et cetera. They only inherit if the deceased does not leave a spouse or descendants. Every group of parents and their descendants form a *parentela*. The deceased and his or her descendants form the first *parentela*. The parents of the deceased and their descendants are the second *parentela*. The third *parentela* consists of the grandparents of the deceased and their descendants. Members of the third *parentela* inherit *ab intestato* only if there are no members of the second *parentela*, and members of the second *parentela* inherit only if there are no members of the first *parentela*.

409. Collaterals refer to persons related to the deceased through at least one common ancestor, for example, brothers, sisters, and cousins. Collaterals are excluded from inheriting if the deceased leaves a spouse, descendants or both of his or her parents. However, if the deceased leaves no spouse or descendants and only

---

1191. Intestate Succession Act 81 of 1987, s. 1(1)(c).

1192. Section 1(4)(f):

> A child's portion, in relation to the intestate estate of the deceased, shall be calculated by dividing the monetary value of the estate by a number equal to the number of children of the deceased who have either survived the deceased or have died before the deceased but are survived by their descendants, plus the number of spouses and women referred to in paragraphs *(a)*, *(b)* and *(c)* of section 2(2) of the Reform of Customary Law of Succession and Regulation of Related Matters Act, 2008.

1193. Section 3(1) of the Reform of Customary Law of Succession and Regulation of Related Matters Act 11 of 2009. Some provisions of the Act consider a woman in a substitute customary marriage or a woman-to-woman customary marriage to be a descendant (s. 2(2)(b)), while others consider her to be a spouse (s. 3(1)). Jamneck & Rautenbach (eds), *The Law of Succession in South Africa*, 267 argue, correctly in our opinion, that these sections should not be interpreted to mean that a customary wife could qualify as both a spouse and a descendant when determining a child's portion. *See also* C. Rautenbach & M.M. Meyer, *Lost in Translation: Is a Spouse a Spouse or a Descendant (or both) in Terms of the Reform of Customary Law of Succession and Regulation of Related Matters Act?*, J. S. Afr. Law 149–160 (2012).

one parent, or leaves no parent at all, the descendants of the deceased parent(s) (who are collaterals of the deceased) can inherit.

In this regard, the provisions of the Intestate Succession Act 81 of 1987 are as follows: If a person dies intestate and is not survived by a spouse or descendant, but is survived by both of his or her parents, his or her parents inherit the intestate estate in equal shares.[1194]

If a person dies intestate and is not survived by a spouse or descendant, but is survived by one parent and descendants of the deceased parent, the surviving parent inherits half the intestate estate and the descendants of the deceased parent the other half. If there are no such descendants, the surviving parent takes the entire intestate estate.[1195]

If the deceased is not survived by a spouse, descendant or parent, but is survived by descendants of his or her deceased mother who are related to the deceased through her only, and by descendants of the deceased father who are related to the deceased through him only (i.e., half-brother(s) and half-sister(s)); or by descendants of his or her deceased parents who are related to the deceased through both such parents (i.e., full brother(s) and full sister(s)); or by half-brother(s) and half-sister(s) as well as by full brother(s) or full sister(s), the intestate estate is divided into two equal shares. The descendants related to the deceased through his or her deceased mother inherit half the estate and the descendants related to the deceased through the deceased father inherit the other half.[1196]

If the deceased is survived only by descendants of one of his or her deceased parents who are related to him or her through such parent alone, such descendants inherit the entire intestate estate.[1197] Half-blood relations in the second *parentela* therefore inherit to the exclusion of relations in the third *parentela.*

410. If there is nobody in the second *parentela* who can inherit from the deceased, the estate devolves on the third (or further) *parentela(e).* The Intestate Succession Act 81 of 1987 provides that if the deceased is not survived by a spouse, descendant, parent or descendant of a parent, his or her nearest blood relation(s) inherit the intestate estate in equal shares.[1198] This person may be a grandparent, an uncle or an aunt or even a more distant relation. For example, if the deceased is survived by one grandparent on his or her mother's side and two great-grandparents on his or her father's side, the grandparent inherits the entire intestate estate. If the deceased leaves one grandparent on his or her mother's side and two grandparents on his or her father's side, the three grandparents inherit the intestate estate in equal shares.[1199]

1194. Section 1(1)(d)(i).
1195. Section 1(1)(d)(ii).
1196. Section 1(1)(e)(i).
1197. Section 1(1)(e)(ii).
1198. Section 1(1)(f).
1199. *Ibid.*

II. Representation

411. Representation occurs when the place of an heir who cannot or does not wish to inherit is taken by his or her descendant(s). In relation to descendants of the deceased and descendants of a parent of the deceased (i.e., in the first and second *parentelae*), the division of the intestate estate takes place *per stirpes*[1200] and representation is allowed forever (*ad infinitum*).[1201] This means, for example, that if a deceased had three children, one of whom was predeceased but was survived by two children, the two surviving children of the deceased each takes one-third of the intestate estate and the two grandchildren inherit their predeceased parent's third in equal shares.

However, in the third and further *parentelae* the heirs inherit *per capita*,[1202] with the nearest blood relation(s) taking in equal shares.[1203]

412. In terms of South African common law, a person who was alive but refused to inherit or was disqualified from inheriting could not be represented by his or her descendants.[1204] Representation could only take place if the person was predeceased. Since October 1992, representation of a person who repudiates or is disqualified from inheriting has been allowed in terms of section 1(7) of the Intestate Succession Act 81 of 1987. This section is subject to section 1(6). Representation is therefore only allowed if subsection (6) is not applicable.[1205] In terms of subsection (6), if a descendant of a deceased person, who together with the surviving spouse of the deceased is entitled to a benefit from an intestate estate, renounces his or her right to receive such a benefit, the benefit vests in the surviving spouse. Subsection (7) provides that if a person is disqualified from being an intestate heir or if he or she renounces his or her right to be such an heir, any benefit which he or she would have received must devolve as if he or she had died immediately before the deceased died. This means that he or she can be represented by descendants.

The wording of subsection (6) only refers to intestate heirs who renounce (repudiate) their benefit. In other words, if an intestate heir who is a descendant of the deceased repudiates his or her intestate benefit, one first has to determine whether there is a surviving spouse. If there is, the spouse inherits the share of the descendant who repudiates, and such descendant cannot be represented by his or her descendants.[1206] It is only if there is no spouse or if the spouse is not entitled to

1200. Every descendant of the deceased who survives the deceased, or a predeceased descendant of the deceased who leaves living descendants, is a *stirps*.

1201. Intestate Succession Act 81 of 1987, s. 1(4)(a).

1202. An heir inherits *per capita* if he or she inherits according to the law of intestate succession on the ground of the degree of consanguinity in which he or she is related to the deceased. If more than one person is related to the deceased person in the same degree of consanguinity, each person inherits an equal share *ab intestato*.

1203. Intestate Succession Act 81 of 1987, s. 1(1)(f).

1204. The Intestate Succession Act 81 of 1987 initially contained a section that reflected this position, but it was deleted by the Law of Succession Amendment Act 43 of 1992.

1205. Subsections (6) and (7) were inserted into s. 1 of the Intestate Succession Act 81 of 1987 by the Law of Succession Amendment Act 43 of 1992.

1206. Section 1(7) enables a child (or more distant descendant) to repudiate an intestate benefit in favour of his or her surviving parent (or grandparent). If the deceased is survived by more than one

inherit (for instance, because the spouse is disqualified), that substitution by the descendants can take place in terms of subsection (7). However, a descendant who is disqualified from inheriting *ab intestato* can always be represented by his or her descendants.[1207]

III. Adoption, Artificial Insemination and Surrogacy

A. Adoption

413. The effect of adoption is that it terminates all rights and obligations between a child and the persons who were his or her parents before the adoption and between the child and the relatives of those parents, unless the child's step-parent or the life partner of the child's parent adopts the child.[1208] In the latter event, the adoption does not terminate the parental responsibilities and rights of the child's parent.[1209] Furthermore, the adopted child is for all purposes considered to be the child of the adoptive parent(s).[1210]

The Intestate Succession Act 81 of 1987 confirms this position by providing that an adopted child is deemed to be a descendant of his or her adoptive parents and not a descendant of his or her natural/biological parents, except in the case of a natural/biological parent who is also the adoptive parent of that child or was, at the time of the adoption, married to the child's adoptive parent.[1211] Thus, an adopted child can inherit from his or her adoptive parents and their relatives, but can no longer inherit from his or her natural parents, unless his or her biological father or his or her step-parent adopted him or her.[1212]

---

spouse, it is unclear whether repudiation by a descendant only favours the surviving spouse who is the parent of the repudiating child, or whether all the surviving spouses are entitled to share in the repudiated portion: J. Jamneck, *The Problematic Practical Application of Section 1(6) and 1(7) of the Intestate Succession Act under a New Dispensation*, 17 Potchefstroom Electron. Law J. 973 (2014).

1207. *See also* De Waal & Schoeman-Malan, *Law of Succession*, 33.
1208. Children's Act 38 of 2005, s. 242(1)(a) and (c).
1209. *Ibid.*, s. 242(2)(e).
1210. *Ibid.*, s. 242(3). On adoption, *see* further Part II. Ch. 5, §1 above.
1211. Intestate Succession Act 81 of 1987, s. 1(4)(e). In terms of s. 231(1)(c) and (d) of the Children's Act 38 of 2005, a step-parent and the biological father of a child born of unmarried parents may adopt the child.
1212. According to *Flynn v. Farr* 2009 (1) SA 584 (C), a child who was never legally adopted cannot be an intestate heir of the deceased, even if he or she was informally or de facto adopted by the deceased. This case confirms that in South African law a step-child has no right to inherit intestate from his or her step-parent: *see* De Waal, *Intestate Succession in South Africa*, 263. As indicated above, the position is different where the deceased was subject to customary law. A person who, during the lifetime of the deceased, was accepted by the deceased in accordance with customary law as his or her own child, may inherit *ab intestato* (*see* Part IV, Ch 1, §387).

B. Artificial Insemination

414. The Children's Act 38 of 2005 provides that a child who is born as a result of the artificial fertilization of a spouse using a donor gamete or donor gametes must for all purposes be regarded to be the spouses' child 'as if the gamete or gametes of those spouses had been used for such artificial fertilisation'.[1213] Thus, the child can inherit from the spouses who consented to the artificial fertilization and from their blood relations. As the biological contribution of the donor(s) is ignored the donor does not qualify as the child's biological parent with the result that the child cannot inherit from the donor or his or her blood relations. Furthermore, the Children's Act provides that no right, responsibility, duty or obligation arises between a child born of a woman as a result of artificial fertilization and any person whose gamete(s) were used to fertilize the woman, or between the child and the blood relations of that person, unless that person is the child's birth mother or the husband of the birth mother at the time of the fertilization.[1214] This provision also means that the child cannot inherit from the donor and his or her blood relations.

If the husband did not consent to the artificial insemination, he is not considered to be the parent of the child. In such event, the child can only inherit from his birth mother and her blood relations.

415. In the case of artificial fertilization of an unmarried woman, the child is for all purposes deemed to be the child of his or her unmarried birth mother.[1215] The child may therefore inherit from his or her unmarried mother. The child cannot inherit from the donor or the blood relations of the donor because the Children's Act provides that no right, responsibility, duty or obligation arises between the child and the donor or his or her blood relations.[1216]

416. A child who is born as a result of the artificial fertilization of one of the parties to a civil union, including of course a same-sex civil union, is treated exactly like a child who is born as a result of the artificial fertilization of a spouse who is a party to a civil marriage, since the Civil Union Act 17 of 2006 provides that a civil union has all the consequences of a civil marriage concluded in terms of the Marriage Act 25 of 1961.[1217]

C. Surrogacy

417. Chapter 19 of the Children's Act 38 of 2005 recognizes and regulates surrogacy. If the parties entered into a valid surrogacy agreement, any child born of a surrogate mother is for all purposes the child of the commissioning parent(s) from

1213. Children's Act 38 of 2005, s. 40(1)(a).
1214. Children's Act 38 of 2005, s. 40(3). Section 40(3) is subject to s. 296 which deals with surrogacy agreements. On the legal position of the child born as a result of a surrogacy agreement, *see* below in this chapter.
1215. Children's Act 38 of 2005, s. 40(2).
1216. Section 40(3). The section is subject to s. 296 which deals with surrogacy agreements.
1217. *See* Part II, Ch. 1, §1 above.

the moment of his or her birth.[1218] The child can therefore inherit *ab intestato* from his or her commissioning parents and their blood relations. Furthermore, the child has no claim of succession against the surrogate mother, her husband or partner or any of their relatives.[1219] If the surrogate motherhood agreement is invalid, the surrogate mother is for all purposes deemed to be the child's mother and the child has no relationship with the commissioning parent(s).[1220]

§4. The Rights of the State on the Bona Vacantia

418. If a person dies intestate without leaving any intestate heirs, South African common law stated that the state took the whole estate as *bona vacantia.*[1221] At present, the matter is regulated by the Administration of Estates Act 66 of 1965. It provides that if the intestate heirs are unknown or do not exist, the executor converts the intestate estate into money and, after paying the deceased's debts, places the proceeds in the Guardian's Fund.[1222] If nobody makes a legitimate claim to the estate within thirty years after the money has been paid into the Guardian's Fund, the intestate estate accrues to the state.[1223]

1218. Children's Act 38 of 2005, s. 297(1)(a).
1219. *Ibid.*, s. 297(1)(f).
1220. *Ibid.*, s. 297(2). On the effect of termination of a surrogacy agreement on the position of the child, *see* Heaton, *Law of Persons*, 51–52.
1221. *Ex parte Leeuw* (1905) 22 SC 340.
1222. Administration of Estates Act 66 of 1965, s. 35(13).
1223. *Ibid.*, s. 92.

Chapter 2. Testamentary Succession

§1. The Capacity to Make a Will

419. Three related issues are dealt with under this heading, namely testamentary capacity, factors undermining the testator's capacity to freely express his or her will, and the delegation of testamentary power.

I. Testamentary Capacity

420. The Wills Act 7 of 1953 governs the capacity to make a will. In terms of section 4 of this Act, every person of the age of 16 years or more may make a will, unless at the time of making the will the person is mentally incapable of appreciating the nature and effect of his or her act. The burden of proof that the person was mentally incapable at that time rests on the person making the allegation.[1224]

421. The age of majority is 18 years.[1225] However, in terms of the Wills Act 7 of 1953, a person has testamentary capacity at age 16. Persons of 16 and 17 years of age therefore do not need the assistance of their parents or guardians to make a will. Persons below the age of 16 cannot make a will – not even with the assistance of their parents or guardians.

422. Apart from the requirement that the person must be 16 or older, section 4 also requires that the testator must be able to appreciate the nature and effect of his or her actions at the time of making the will.[1226] The question whether someone is mentally capable of understanding the nature and effect of his or her actions is decided on the facts of each case. Mental incapacity may arise because the person is of unsound mind,[1227] or as a result of a disease or drunkenness.[1228] In the latter instance the person must have been so intoxicated that he or she was not in control of all his or her faculties when the will was made.[1229] By analogy, a person under the influence of drugs or hypnosis may also be mentally incapable of making a will.[1230]

1224. Wills Act 7 of 1953, s. 4. Section 4 is declaratory of the common law that was in place before the adoption of the Act. Consequently, common-law authority may be relied upon when interpreting this section.

1225. Children's Act 38 of 2005, s. 17.

1226. The testator must have the requisite capacity at the time the will is executed. The fact that he or she may have had the capacity at the time when the will was drafted is irrelevant: *Essop v. Mustapha and Essop* 1988 (4) SA 213 (D); *Geldenhuys v. Borman* 1990 (1) SA 161 (E).

1227. Voet, *Commentarius ad Pandectas*, 28.1.34. *See also* the discussion by F. du Toit, *Mental Capacity as an Element of Testamentary Capacity*, 122 S. Afr. Law J. 661 (2005).

1228. Voet, *Commentarius ad Pandectas*, 28.1.35.

1229. *Thirion v. Die Meester* 2001 (4) SA 1078 (T).

1230. On the effect of intoxication with alcohol or drugs, *see* further Part I, Ch. 7, §4 above.

The fact that a person is of old age and has reduced mental capacity does not necessarily exclude the person from making a will.[1231] Similarly, a person who was 'mentally retarded'[1232] and one who was incapable of managing his own affairs[1233] have been found to have the capacity to make a will.

What is required in order to satisfy the requirement that the testator must be able to appreciate the nature and effect of his or her actions, is the ability to understand and appreciate the testamentary act and its consequences.[1234] It has been held that this entails three things: the ability to appreciate the nature of the transaction itself, that is, the act of disposing of one's property to named beneficiaries after one's death; the ability to distinguish between potential heirs and to make a rational and reasoned decision as to their respective claims to the testator's assets; and the ability to appreciate in broad terms the nature, extent and value of the testator's estate.[1235]

A person who is mentally incapacitated may make a will, if it can be proved that the will was made during a lucid interval.[1236]

II. Factors Influencing Free Testamentary Expression

423. In order to make a valid will, the testator must have the serious intention to dispose of his or her property by will (*animus testandi*) and must be able to exercise that intention voluntarily.

424. Animus testandi is lacking if the testator signs the will under the mistaken belief that it is some other document. However, a mistake as to the reason for including a certain provision in the will does not invalidate that provision because a *falsa causa* (mistaken motive) has no legal consequences.[1237]

425. If it can be proved that a testator made a will because of fraud, duress or as a result of undue influence, the will is invalid since it does not reflect the testator's

1231. *Tregea v. Godart* 1939 AD 16; *Essop v. Mustapha and Essop* 1988 (4) SA 213 (D).

1232. *Spies v. Smith* 1957 (1) SA 539 (A).

1233. *Geldenhuys v. Borman* 1990 (1) SA 161 (E). *See also* J.C. Sonnekus, *Testeerbevoegdheid van 'n Handelingsonbevoegde*, J. S. Afr. Law 754 (1990); J.C. Sonnekus, *Testeerbevoegdheid, Herroeping van 'n Testament en Kuratele Sorg*, 15 Stellenbosch Law Rev. 450 (2004).

1234. *Tregea v. Godart* 1939 AD 16.

1235. *Katz v. Katz* [2004] 4 All SA 545 (C). *See also Strydom v. Strydom* 1953 (2) SA 799 (T); *Harlow v. Becker* 1988 (4) SA 213 (D); *Naidoo v. Crowhurst* [2010] 2 All SA 379 (WCC). *See also* M.C. Schoeman-Malan, *The Requirements and Test to Assess Testamentary Capacity (1)*, 78 J. Contemp. Roman-Dutch Law 604 (2015); M.C. Schoeman-Malan, *The Requirements and Test to Assess Testamentary Capacity (2)*, 79 J. Contemp. Roman-Dutch Law 69 (2016).

1236. Voet, *Commentarius ad Pandectas*, 28.1.34; *In re Kemp* (1844) 2 Menz 435. On mental illness and mental disability, *see* further Part I, Ch. 7, §1–§3 above.

1237. Corbett, Hofmeyr & Kahn, *The Law of Succession in South Africa*, 91.

own intention but that of somebody else.[1238] The pressure brought to bear on the testator must have been of such a nature that the will no longer conveyed the testator's intention.[1239]

III. Delegation of Testamentary Power

426. The general rule is that a testator must personally exercise his or her testamentary power and may not leave it to others to decide who will inherit under his or her will.[1240] However, there are exceptions to this rule.

The first exception relates to bequests for charitable purposes (*ad pias causas*). In the case of such bequests, the testator may authorize the administrator of the estate to nominate the beneficiaries.[1241] Secondly, the testator may authorize the bearer of an interim right to nominate the eventual beneficiaries, or to determine what each beneficiary is to receive or the manner in which they are to inherit. This is called a 'power of appointment'.[1242] A power of appointment may be given to the fiduciary in a *fideicommissum*, or to the usufructuary in a usufruct.[1243] Thirdly, a power of appointment may be granted to a trustee to appoint the trust beneficiaries.[1244] However, the trustee may not be given an unfettered discretion to appoint beneficiaries. The testator must designate a specific class of persons from whom the beneficiaries are to be appointed.[1245] This is referred to as a special or specific power of appointment.[1246]

§2. Different Types of Wills and Testamentary Formalities

I. Introduction

427. The Wills Act 7 of 1953, which came into operation on 1 January 1954, prescribes the formalities with which all wills made on or after 1 January 1954 must comply in order to be valid. Before 1954, various types of wills existed, such as underhand (statutory) wills, notarial wills and various privileged wills – for example, soldiers' wills and wills made in time of pestilence.[1247] The Wills Act repealed all existing provincial legislation, and prescribed uniform formalities in respect of wills executed on or after 1 January 1954. It also established the underhand form of will, as taken over from English law with its prescribed formalities, as

1238. *Spies v. Smith* 1957 (1) SA 539 (A).
1239. *Preller v. Jordaan* 1956 (1) SA 483 (A); *Spies v. Smith* 1957 (1) SA 532 (A); *Kirsten v. Bailey* 1976 (4) SA 108 (C).
1240. *Estate Watkins-Pitchford v. CIR* 1955 (2) SA 437 (A).
1241. *Ibid.*; *Ex parte Henderson* 1971 (4) SA 549 (D).
1242. Corbett, Hofmeyr & Kahn, *The Law of Succession in South Africa*, 357.
1243. *CIR v. Lukin's Estate* 1956 (1) SA 617 (A); *Estate Orpen v. Estate Atkinson* 1966 (4) SA 589 (A). The *fideicommissum* and usufruct are discussed below in this chapter.
1244. The trust is discussed below in this chapter.
1245. *Braun v. Blann and Botha* 1984 (2) SA 850 (A).
1246. De Waal & Schoeman-Malan, *Law of Succession*, 49.
1247. Van der Merwe & Rowland, *Die Suid-Afrikaanse Erfreg*, 132–145.

the only form of will in South Africa. Initially, the Act recognized one type of privileged will, namely a soldier's will. However, after sweeping changes to the Wills Act in 1992,[1248] only the underhand will remains.[1249] Thus, South Africa currently does not recognize any privileged wills.

428. After a testator's death, his or her will(s) must be lodged with the Master of the High Court.[1250] The Master may refuse to accept a document as a will if he or she is of the opinion that the document does not comply with the prescribed formalities.[1251] In such event, an interested party (such as the executor or a beneficiary in terms of the contested will) may approach the court to decide on the validity of the will. In the past, many wills were declared invalid because of non-compliance with section 2(1)(a) of the Wills Act 7 of 1953, which prescribes the formalities for a valid will, even if the non-compliance was only minor. This was the situation because section 2(1)(a) of the Wills Act did not give the Master a discretion to ignore minor mistakes in the formalities when considering the validity of the will. Over the years the courts were called upon to decide on the validity of wills where the Master had rejected them, sometimes because of purely technical shortcomings. These decisions were not always consistent.[1252] In 1992, the Wills Act was extensively amended after recommendations by the South African Law Commission.[1253] Of particular importance was the introduction of section 2(3), in terms of which a court may order the Master to accept a document that does not comply with all the prescribed formalities as a valid will if the court is satisfied that the document was drafted or executed by a person who has died since then, and who intended that document to be his or her will. Although the Act itself does not refer to this section as granting a power to condone non-compliance with formalities, most writers use this terminology when referring to section 2(3).[1254]

1248. By means of the Law of Succession Amendment Act 43 of 1992.
1249. According to De Waal, *Testamentary Formalities in South Africa*, 382, 'while the forms of will that were initially received into South African law were Roman-Dutch, the will that survived is essentially English in character'.
1250. Administration of Estates Act 66 of 1965, s. 8.
1251. *Ibid.*, s. 8(4).
1252. *See*, e.g., *The Leprosy Mission v. The Master* 1972 (4) SA 173 (C); *Kidwell v. The Master* 1983 (1) SA 509 (E); *Mellvill v. The Master* 1984 (3) SA 387 (C); *Jeffrey v. The Master* 1990 (4) SA 759 (N); *Ex parte Jackson: in re Estate Miller* 1991 (2) SA 586 (W); *Liebenberg v. The Master* 1992 (3) SA 57 (D); *Harpur v. Govindamall* 1993 (4) SA 751 (A).
1253. South African Law Commission, *Report on Review of the Law of Succession: Project 22*, (Government Printer 1991).
1254. *See*, e.g., Corbett, Hofmeyr & Kahn, *The Law of Succession in South Africa*, 52; De Waal & Schoeman-Malan, *Law of Succession*, 67; J.C. Sonnekus, *Kondoneringsbevoegdheid van Hof by Vormgebrekkige Testament'*, J. of S. Afr. Law 359 (1995); S. Cornelius, *Condonation of Electronic Documents in terms of Section 2(3) of the Wills Act 7 of 1953*, J. S. Afr. Law 208 (2003). It has also been called the 'rescue' provision of the Wills Act: M.C. Wood-Bodley, *MacDonald v. The Master: Computer Files and the 'Rescue' Provision of the Wills Act*, 121 S. Afr. Law J. 34 (2004). Section 2(3) is discussed in more detail in Ch. 2, §2 below in this part.

II. Formalities for the Execution and Amendment of Wills

A. Formalities for the Execution of Wills

429. The Wills Act 7 of 1953 Act does not define a will, but merely describes it in section 1 as 'including a codicil and any other testamentary writing'. In other words, a single set of formalities is prescribed in the Act for wills, codicils and other 'testamentary writings'. Therefore, no distinction is made between a will and a codicil, although the term 'codicil' usually refers to an addendum to a will.[1255]

Case law has determined that a testamentary writing is a document which describes any one of the three essential elements of a bequest, namely (1) the property bequeathed, (2) the extent of the interest bequeathed (such as ownership or usufruct) and (3) the beneficiary.[1256] If any one of these three elements appears in a document and the document reflects the testator's intent in respect of a bequest, such document is a 'testamentary writing'.

It has also been laid down in case law that any document in the nature of a testamentary writing incorporated into a will by reference must itself satisfy the formal requirements for a valid will.[1257] Hence, lists of assets for distribution, attached to a will, have no effect unless they too are executed in accordance with the formalities required for a valid will. Incorporation by reference, in terms of which an unattested document is given effect to if referred to in a will, is therefore not allowed in South African law.[1258]

430. Note that under South African law, a *donatio mortis causa* must also comply with testamentary formalities in order to be valid.[1259]

431. In terms of section 2(1)(a) of the Wills Act 7 of 1953, a will shall not be valid unless it complies with the formalities prescribed by this section. The formalities are intended *inter alia* to ensure the avoidance of fraud by the impersonation of testators and by misrepresentation to them of the nature of the documents put before them.[1260]

The formalities required in the execution of a will are:

1255. De Waal, *Testamentary Formalities in South Africa*, 385.
1256. *Ex parte Estate Davies* 1957 (3) SA 471 (N); *Oosthuizen v. Die Weesheer* 1974 (2) SA 434 (O).
1257. *Moses v. Abinader* 1951 (4) SA 537 (A).
1258. *Wessels v. Die Meester* [2007] ZASCA 17, 23 Mar. 2007, (unreported) http://www.saflii.org/za/cases/ZASCA/2007/17.html. *See also* De Waal, *Testamentary Formalities in South Africa*, 386.
1259. *Meyer v. Rudolph's Executors* 1918 AD 70; *Jordaan v. De Villiers* 1991 (4) SA 396 (C). *See* further Ch. 3, §1 below in this part.
1260. Corbett, Hofmeyr & Kahn, *The Law of Succession in South Africa*, 51. For a discussion of testamentary fraud, *see* M.C. Schoeman-Malan, *Fraud and Forgery of the Testator's Will or Signature: The Flight from Formalities to No Formalities*, J. S. Afr. Law 125–152 (2015).

(1) The will must be signed[1261] at its end by the testator or by some other person in the testator's presence and by his or her direction.[1262] (The person who signs on behalf of the testator is also referred to as an *amanuensis*.[1263]) A testator may sign the will by making a mark, such as a thumbprint or an X.[1264] If the testator signs the will by making a mark, or if an *amanuensis* signs the will, a prescribed certificate must be attached by a commissioner of oaths.[1265]

The testator must sign the will 'at the end thereof'. The meaning of this phrase is subject to different interpretations. Unfortunately, the 1992 amendments to the Act did not clarify the meaning of the phrase. A case in point is *Kidwell v. The Master.*[1266] In this case, an attestation clause was attached after the last paragraph of the will. The testator signed 17 cm below the attestation clause and 13 cm below the signatures of the witnesses. The court declared the will invalid on the ground that it had not been signed at the end. The court held that 'at the end thereof' means as close to the concluding words as possible. There was no suggestion of fraud in this case and the end result was that the testator's intention was defeated. As a result, this case has been criticized.[1267] The *Kidwell* case was decided before the adoption of section 2(3).[1268] If a similar case were to come before the courts today, section 2(3) could be used to rescue the will.

(2) Two or more competent witnesses must be present at the same time when the testator or the representative signs the will. As an alternative, the testator (and the *amanuensis* if applicable), must acknowledge the signature in the presence of the witnesses.[1269]

1261. The Electronic Communications and Transactions Act 25 of 2002 allows for the use of electronic signatures in certain circumstances. However, the Act specifically excludes wills from its ambit: s. 4(3) read with Sch. 1 and s. 4(4) read with Sch. 2. A will can therefore not be signed with an electronic signature. *See* De Waal, *Testamentary Formalities in South Africa*, 387; M. C. Wood-Bodley *Wills, Data Messages, and the Electronic Communications and Transactions Act*, 121 S. Afr. Law J. 526 (2004). If a testator leaves a will only in electronic format, the court may use its power under s. 2(3) to condone it. *See* De Waal, *Testamentary Formalities in South Africa*, 387 and §435 below.
1262. Wills Act 7 of 1953, s. 2(1)(a)(i).
1263. De Waal & Schoeman-Malan, *Law of Succession*, 58 n. 37; Jamneck & Rautenbach (eds), *The Law of Succession in South Africa*, 66.
1264. Section 1 of the Wills Act 7 of 1953 defines 'sign' as including 'the making of initials and, only in the case of a testator, the making of a mark … '. In *Ricketts v. Byrne* 2004 (6) SA 474 (C), printed letters were considered to be a mark, not a signature. A mark can be used by an illiterate, ill or ailing testator. *See* further M.C. Schoeman-Malan, *Assisting an Ailing Testator to Sign a Will*, 82 J. Contemp. Roman-Dutch Law 83 (2019) for a discussion of the statutory requirements that must be adhered to when a testator is too frail to sign his or her own will.
1265. Wills Act 7 of 1953, s. 2(1)(a)(v). The content of the certificate is discussed below in this chapter.
1266. 1983 (1) SA 509 (E).
1267. I.B. Murray, *Law of Succession (Including Administration of Estates)*, Annu. Surv. S. Afr. Law 254 (1983); D.S.P. Cronjé, *Kidwell v. The Master* 1983 1 SA 509 (OK) – *Ondertekening aan die End van 'n Testament*, 46 J. Contemp. Roman-Dutch Law 345 (1983); J.C. Sonnekus, '*Kidwell v. The Master* 1983 1 SA 509 (OK), J. S. Afr. Law 188 (1983).
1268. Section 2(3) is discussed below in this chapter.
1269. Wills Act 7 of 1953, s. 2(1)(a)(ii).

In order to be a competent witness, a person must be 14 years or older and be competent to give evidence in a court of law.[1270]

(3) The same witnesses who were present at the signing of the will by the testator or *amanuensis* must attest and sign[1271] the will in the presence of the testator, in each other's presence and, if the will is signed by an *amanuensis*, in the presence of the *amanuensis*.[1272] A witness may sign the will with an initial, but may not sign by making a mark.[1273] It is not prescribed where on the last page of the will the witnesses must sign the will, but in practice witnesses usually sign at the end of the page next to or below the testator's signature.[1274] They must sign after the testator has signed, since they are witnessing his or her signature.[1275] The witnesses need not know the contents of the will. They need not even know that they are witnessing a will. The only requirement is that they should know that they are witnessing the testator's signature, mark or initials, which the testator signed or acknowledged in their presence.[1276]

(4) If the will consists of more than one page, the testator (or the *amanuensis*) must also sign the other pages of the will.[1277] It is not prescribed where on the other pages the testator or the *amanuensis* must sign. In practice, the testator or *amanuensis* usually signs at the end of the other pages. The Act does not require that the witnesses must sign the other pages of the will, although this is usually done in practice.

(5) If the testator signs the will with a mark or if an *amanuensis* signs on behalf of the testator, a commissioner of oaths must attach a certificate to the will.[1278] In this certificate two matters must be stated, namely that the commissioner of oaths has satisfied himself or herself as to the identity of the testator and that the will is the will of the testator.[1279] The certifying officer must also state that he or she is signing as a commissioner of oaths.[1280] The commissioner of oaths

1270. Wills Act 7 of 1953, s. 1.

1271. The signing of the will also constitutes attesting the will. The Wills Act 7 of 1953 does not require anything more of the witness than that he or she should sign the will.

1272. Wills Act 7 of 1953, s. 2(1)(a)(iii).

1273. *Ibid*., s. 1.

1274. In *Liebenberg v. The Master* 1992 (3) SA 57 (D) the will was held to be valid although the witnesses had signed at the top of the last page.

1275. *Sterban v. Dixon* 1968 (1) SA 322 (C).

1276. *Ibid.*

1277. Wills Act 7 of 1953, s. 2(1)(a)(iv).

1278. *Ibid*., s. 2(1)(a)(v). *See* further M.C. Schoeman-Malan, *Assisting an Ailing Testator to Sign a Will*, 82 J. Contemp. Roman-Dutch Law 83 (2019).

1279. The commissioner of oaths need not use the exact words of the certificate. In *In re Jennett* 1976 (1) SA 580 (A) it was held that the object of s. 2(1)(a)(v) was to ensure that the document signed by the making of a mark was the will of the testator. This object can be realised without the exact words of the Act having to be used.

1280. In *Radley v. Stopforth* 1977 (2) SA 516 (A) it was held that the certifying officer must indicate his or her office as that of commissioner of oaths on the will. Failure to do so renders the will invalid. It is not sufficient to indicate the office as 'attorney', even though an attorney is ex officio a commissioner of oaths: *Jeffrey v. The Master* 1990 (4) SA 759 (N). The Wills Act 7 of 1953 contains a specimen certificate, but the specimen need not be used: *O'Conner v. The Master of the High Court* 1999 (4) SA 614 (NC).

may attach the certificate anywhere on the will. Each page of the will, excluding the page on which the certificate appears, must also be signed anywhere on the page by the commissioner of oaths. Further, the testator (or the *amanuensis*) and the witnesses must all sign the will in the presence of the commissioner of oaths and in each other's presence. The certificate must be made as soon as possible after the will has been signed. If the testator died after the will was properly signed but before the commissioner of oaths made or completed the prescribed certificate, the commissioner of oaths must, as soon as possible after the testator's death, make or complete his or her certificate and sign the other pages of the will.[1281]

432. The Act does not stipulate that the will should be dated. Nor does it require that an attestation clause be appended.

B. Formalities for the Amendment of Wills

433. Section 2(1)(b) of the Wills Act 7 of 1953 prescribes the formalities with which amendments to wills executed on or after 1 January 1954 must comply. An amendment is defined in the Act as a 'deletion, addition, alteration, or interlineation'.[1282] Deletion is defined as 'a deletion, cancellation or obliteration in whatever manner effected, excluding a deletion, cancellation or obliteration that contemplates the revocation of the entire will'.[1283] The revocation of an entire will is governed by the common law, which requires no formalities.[1284]

The formalities are only applicable if the amendments are made after the execution of the will. There are no statutory formality requirements for amendments to a will made before the execution of the will. However, the Act provides that any amendment made to a will shall be presumed, unless the contrary is proved, to have been made after the will was executed.[1285] It is therefore safer to treat pre-execution amendments like amendments made after execution of the will, since it may not be possible to establish after the testator's death that the amendment was in fact made before the execution of the will.[1286]

1281. Section 2(1)(a)(v) has been substantially changed by the Law of Succession Amendment Act 43 of 1992. Case law before 1992 on sub-s. (v) should therefore be treated with circumspection. Before 1992 the certificate had to be attached at the end of the will (this requirement created numerous problems: *see*, e.g., *Stemmet v. Die Meester* 1957 (3) SA 404 (C); *Volschenk v. Die Meester* 1958 (2) SA 363 (C); *Tshabalala v. Tshabalala* 1980 (1) SA 134 (O); *Philip v. The Master* 1980 (2) SA 934 (D)); it had to be attached at the same time as the signing of the will by the testator and the witnesses; and it could not be completed after the death of the testator (*Radley v. Stopforth* 1977 (2) SA 516 (A)). Furthermore, various classes of persons could act as certifying officers.

1282. Wills Act 7 of 1953, s. 1.

1283. *Ibid.*

1284. The revocation of wills is discussed below in this chapter.

1285. Wills Act 7 of 1953, s. 2(2).

1286. J. Jamneck, *Herroeping en Wysiging van Testamente*, 61 J. Contemp. Roman-Dutch Law 600 (1988).

434. The formalities for the amendment of a will are substantially the same as those that apply to the execution of a will: the amendment must be identified[1287] by the signature of the testator or an *amanuensis* in the presence of two or more competent witnesses who are present at the same time; the amendment must further be identified by the signatures of the same two witnesses, who must make their signatures in the presence of the testator (and the *amanuensis* if applicable) and in each other's presence; if the amendment is identified by the mark of the testator or by an *amanuensis*, a commissioner of oaths must attach a certificate on the will that certifies that he or she has satisfied himself or herself as to the identity of the testator and that the amendment has been made by or at the request of the testator; the amendment must be identified by the testator or the *amanuensis* and by the witnesses in each other's presence and in the presence of the commissioner of oaths; the certificate must be made as soon as possible after the will has been signed; and if the testator died after the amendment was identified but before the commissioner of oaths made the prescribed certificate, the commissioner of oaths must make or complete his or her certificate as soon as possible after the testator's death.[1288]

The Act does not specify where the certificate must be made on the will; nor does it require that the commissioner of oaths sign any pages of the will other than the one on which the certificate appears. The witnesses to the amendment need not be the same ones who were present at the execution of the will, since the amendment is a new act of testation.[1289]

III. Power of the Court to Condone Mistakes in the Formal Requirements: Section 2(3)

435. In terms of section 2(3) of the Wills Act 7 of 1953, if a court is satisfied that a document or the amendment of a document drafted or executed by a person who has died since the drafting or execution of the document, was intended to be his or her will or an amendment of the will, the court must order the Master to accept the document or the amended document as a will, even though it does not comply with all the formalities for the execution or amendment of wills prescribed by section 2(1)(a) and (b) of the Act.

The purpose of this section is not to do away with the formal requirements for the execution of a will. These requirements remain, but, as Corbett et al. point out, the court is 'given the power to make the order in question to avoid invalidity, the consequent frustration of the testator's intention and, frequently, inequitable

1287. The Wills Act 7 of 1953 does not define the word 'identify', but it has been suggested that attestation in the immediate vicinity of the amendment would be sufficient identification as the proximity of the signatures would show that they were appended in respect of the amendment in question: Corbett, Hofmeyr & Kahn, *The Law of Succession in South Africa*, 72; B. Beinart, *Testamentary Form and Capacity and the Wills Act, 1953*, 70 S. Afr. Law J. 280 (1953).

1288. Wills Act 7 of 1953, s. 2(1)(b)(i)–(v).

1289. Jamneck & Rautenbach (eds), *The Law of Succession in South Africa*, 77.

results'.[1290] These authors further emphasize that the legislature has stated requirements within the framework of which this purpose is to be served, and that the court is not granted a general discretion to condone non-compliance with the prescribed formalities.[1291]

436. Since the introduction of section 2(3) into the Wills Act 7 of 1953 in 1992, there has been a litany of cases dealing with the correct interpretation of the section. In brief, the case law has set the following requirements for employing the section to rescue a will that does not comply with all the prescribed formalities:

(1) There must be a written document.[1292] The document may be written by hand, typed on a typewriter, or typed on a computer. From case law it seems as if the electronic document need not have been printed before the deceased's death. In *MacDonald v. The Master*[1293] the document was created in electronic form on a computer and saved in a computer file. The electronic version of the document was printed only after the deceased's death. The court nevertheless accepted the document for purposes of section 2(3). In *Van der Merwe v. The Master*[1294] the Supreme Court of Appeal directed the Master to accept an email message containing the testator's unexecuted will, as the deceased's will.[1295] In case law, a note, an instruction to a bank, a letter to

1290. Corbett, Hofmeyr & Kahn, *The Law of Succession in South Africa*, 58–59.
1291. *Ibid.*, 59.
1292. De Waal & Schoeman-Malan, *Law of Succession*, 70. If a will is lost, the court has the power in terms of common law to order the Master to accept a copy or a reconstruction of the will as the valid will: *Ex parte Porter* 2010 (5) SA 546 (WCC). In *Haribans v. Haribans* [2011] ZAKZPHC 46, (unreported), http://www.saflii.org/za/cases/ZAKZPHC/2011/46.html) and *Hassan v. Mentor* [2012] ZAGPPHC 74, (unreported), http://www.saflii.org/cases/ZAGPPHC/2012/74.html, however, the court used s. 2(3) to order the Master to accept a copy of a duly executed lost will as a valid will, instead of using its common-law power. In *Yokwana v. Yokwana* [2013] ZAWCHC 22, (unreported), http://www.saflii.org/za/cases/ZAWCHC/2013/22.html, on the other hand, it was confirmed that the court must use its common-law power to accept a lost will. It was also held that an order in terms of s. 2(3) can only be made in respect of the original will (not in respect of a copy of the will). For a discussion of the application of s. 2(3) to a lost will, *see* Jamneck & Rautenbach (eds), *The Law of Succession in South Africa*, 86; De Waal & Schoeman-Malan, *Law of Succession*,74 n. 168; M.C. Wood-Bodley, *Lost Wills and Section 2(3) of the Wills Act* 132 S. Afr. Law J. 734 (2015).
1293. 2002 (5) SA 64 (O).
1294. 2010 (6) SA 544 (SCA).
1295. M.C. Schoeman-Malan et al., *Section 2(3) of the Wills Act 7 of 1953: A Retrospective and Critical Appraisal of Some Unresolved Issues*, in *South African Law of Succession and Trusts – The Past Meeting the Present and Thoughts for the Future* 101 (M. de Waal & M. Paleker eds., Juta & Co 2014), are of the opinion that an electronic document which cannot be converted to a hard-copy printed version, cannot be condoned, because a written document is required for purposes of an application in terms of s. 2(3). Their argument is based on the fact that the South African Law Commission, in its 1991 *Report on Review of the Law of Succession: Project 22*, paras 2.166–2.167, recommended that documents that are the subject of an application in terms of s. 2(3) must be contained in writing and that videotaped or recorded final wishes should not be considered as documents which can be rescued by s. 2(3). However, in our opinion, an electronic document containing text is contained in writing.

another person, an application form and an entry in a diary have all been accepted as a 'document' for purposes of this section.[1296]

(2) The document must have been drafted or executed by a person who has subsequently died.[1297] If the deceased person signed the will, he or she executed the will. Then, section 2(3) may be used to condone a defect in the remaining process of execution (such as that no witness, or only one witness, signed the will, or that the testator signed with a mark and the certificate of the commissioner of oaths is defective).[1298]

Section 2(3) can also be used to rescue the will if the deceased did not sign (execute) the will, but personally drafted it.[1299] The view that the deceased must have personally drafted the unsigned document was confirmed by the Supreme Court of Appeal in *Bekker v. Naude*.[1300] This means that an unsigned testamentary document that was drafted by a bank or an attorney cannot be rescued by section 2(3). As a result of this interpretation of section 2(3), the unexecuted wills of persons who cannot write, or who are blind or suffer from a physical defect that makes it difficult or impossible for them to make a will, cannot be condoned in terms of section 2(3). Paleker[1301] argues that section 2(3) unfairly discriminates against these persons and, since such discrimination is prohibited by section 9 of the Constitution, section 2(3) should be amended to provide for these persons. Another problem with the strict interpretation is that in the case of a joint will, only one of the parties to the will usually drafts the will. If the testator who wrote the will is the survivor, section 2(3) cannot be applied because the deceased did not draft the will.[1302]

1296. *Van Wetten v. Bosch* 2004 (1) SA 348 (SCA); *Smith v. Parsons* 2010 (4) SA 378 (SCA); *Mabika v. Mabika* [2011] ZAGPJHC 109, (unreported), http://www.saflii.org/za/cases/ZAGPJHC/2011/109.html.

1297. In *Theron v. The Master of the High Court* [2001] 3 All SA 507 (NC) the testator who made a mistake in the execution of the will, was still alive. In this case, two testators who were married to each other, made a joint will. The surviving testator inadvertently neglected to sign one of the pages of the will. The court held that s. 2(3) could be applied and accordingly directed the Master to accept the testamentary document as the joint will of the applicant and her late husband.

1298. *Mdulu v. Delarey* [1998] 1 All SA 435 (W); *Ex parte De Swardt* 1998 (2) SA 204 (C); *O'Conner v. The Master* 1999 (4) SA 614 (NC).

1299. In *Van der Merwe v. The Master* 2010 (6) SA 544 (SCA) the Supreme Court of Appeal accepted that the deceased had drafted his intended will, which was sent to the appellant (the sole beneficiary) in the form of an email. The court pointed out: 'The appellant provided proof that the document had been sent to him by the deceased via e-mail, lending the document an aura of authenticity. It is uncontested that the document still exists on the deceased's computer. Thus it is clear that the document was drafted by the deceased and that it had not been amended or deleted' (para. 17).

1300. 2003 (5) SA 173 (SCA). In *Bekker v. Naude* the deceased and his wife asked a bank to draft a will for them. The draft will was never signed by the parties. After the death of the deceased five years later, the wife brought an application in terms of s. 2(3), asking the court to order the Master to accept the draft will as the valid will of the deceased. The application was unsuccessful.

1301. M. Paleker, *Bekker v. Naude en Andere: The Supreme Court of Appeal Settles the Meaning of Drafted in Section 2(3) of the Wills Act, but Creates a Potential Constitutional Problem* 121 S. Afr. Law J. 27 (2004).

1302. J.C. Sonnekus, *Kondonering van Vormgebrekkige Testamente? Vergeet dit!*, 14 Stellenbosch Law Rev. 337 (2003).

(3) The deceased must have intended the document to be his or her will. It has been held that:

> [w]ritten instructions to an attorney or other adviser so as to enable the recipient to draft the testator's will are not intended by such testator to constitute his/her will albeit that they record the author's intended testamentary dispositions. Similarly, written advice to a third person as to how the author has disposed of his/her property in terms of his/her will or how he/she intends to dispose of it does not satisfy the third requirement of the section.[1303]

The facts of each case must be considered to ascertain the testator's intention.[1304] In *Van Wetten v. Bosch*[1305] the Supreme Court of Appeal ordered the Master to accept a handwritten letter by the deceased to his attorney as his will, because the deceased had contemplated suicide at the time when he had written the letter and had thus intended the letter to be his will.[1306] Similarly, in *Smith v. Parsons*[1307] the court made an order in terms of section 2(3) directing the Master to accept a letter the deceased had written to his life partner before committing suicide, as the will of the deceased.

1303. *Ex parte Maurice* 1995 (2) SA 713 (C) 716.

1304. *Back v. Master of the Supreme Court* [1996] 2 All SA 161 (C); *Ex parte Williams: In re Williams Estate* 2000 (4) SA 168 (T); *Van Wetten v. Bosch* 2004 (1) SA 348 (SCA).

1305. 2004 (1) SA 348 (SCA).

1306. The testator's intention as at the time of drafting the document is determinative: *see Van Wetten v. Bosch* 2004 (1) SA 348 (SCA); *De Reszke v. Maras* 2006 (2) SA 277 (SCA). According to the court in *Van Wetten v. Bosch*, the fact that the circumstances changed after the contested will was made is irrelevant in deciding what the intention of the deceased was at the time when he had drafted the will. The same applies to the conduct of the testator after he had made the will. Evidence as to subsequent conduct is relevant only insofar as it throws light on what was on the mind of the deceased at the time of making the contested will (para. 20). This position is similar to the situation where a testator makes a valid will and thereafter changes his or her mind as to the content of the will. If the testator does not change the will or revoke it before he or she dies, effect must be given to the content of the will at his or her death. The result of this approach is that the invalidly executed will has to be revoked by the testator if he or she no longer wants the document as his or her will. This is a rather anomalous situation: *see* M. C. Wood-Bodley *Tertius Bosch's Final over: Van Wetten v. Bosch*, 122 S. Afr. Law J. 52 (2005).

1307. 2010 (4) SA 378 (SCA). *See also Mitchell v. Wren* [2016] ZASCA 50, (unreported), http://www.saflii.org/za/cases/ZASCA/2016/50.html.

§3. CAPACITY TO BENEFIT UNDER A WILL

I. Introduction

437. As a general rule, any person, whether natural or juristic, whether born or unborn, and regardless of their general legal capacity,[1308] may take benefits conferred upon them by will.[1309] The capacity to take a benefit must exist at the time of vesting and when the beneficiary accepts the benefit.[1310]

438. At common law, certain persons, such as the deceased's murderer, are considered unworthy to inherit. Unworthiness to inherit is discussed in the previous chapter. The discussion is not repeated here.[1311]

The Wills Act 7 of 1953 excludes persons who participated in the execution of the deceased's will from succeeding to the estate of the deceased.[1312] The Act also contains general provisions dealing with the position of adopted and unborn children, children born of unmarried parents, and bequests to a class of beneficiaries.[1313] These provisions are dealt with next.

II. Statutory Provisions Dealing with the Capacity to Inherit under a Will

A. Adopted Children and Children Born of Unmarried Parents

439. The effect of adoption is that it terminates all rights and obligations between a child and the persons who were his or her parents before the adoption

1308. Minors have the capacity to inherit, but their ability to enjoy their inheritance is limited until they come of age. On the position of minors, *see* Part IV, Ch. 1, §2 above.

1309. Corbett, Hofmeyr & Kahn, *The Law of Succession in South Africa*, 79.

1310. *Ibid.*, 80. On vesting of a benefit, *see* below in this chapter.

1311. However, reference needs to be made to one common-law provision: In terms of Art. 12 of the Perpetual Edict of 1540, bequests of immovable property by a minor (at the time, a person younger than 25 years of age) to the minor's guardian, curator or administrator or to the children of these persons, or in favour of the minor's concubine were invalid. Whether this principle is still applicable in our law is unclear. In *Spies v. Smith* 1957 (1) SA 539 (A) the question was left open, but the court assumed that the article was part of South African law and applicable to minors (at that time, persons under the age of 21 years). It has been suggested that the rule will only be applied in cases where there has been undue influence: M.C. Schoeman-Malan, *Onbehoorlike Beinvloeding: Testeerbevoegdheid versus Testeervryheid*, 35 De Jure 333 (2002).

1312. Wills Act 7 of 1953, s. 4A.

1313. Section 2D of the Wills Act 7 of 1953 deals with the interpretation of the word 'child' or 'children' when used in a will in relation to adopted children, children born out of wedlock and children who form part of a class of beneficiaries. This section was inserted in the Wills Act in 1992 by the Law of Succession Amendment Act 43 of 1992 and is therefore not applicable to the will of a testator who died before the commencement of the 1992 Act: *see Harvey v. Crawford* 2019 (2) SA 153 (SCA).

and between the child and the relatives of those parents, unless the child's step-parent or the life partner of the child's parent adopts the child.[1314] Furthermore, the adopted child is for all purposes considered to be the child of the adoptive parent(s).[1315]

Section 2D(1)(a) of the Wills Act 7 of 1953 confirms this position by providing that for the purposes of the interpretation of a will, unless otherwise indicated in the will, an adopted child must be regarded as having been born of his or her adoptive parents, and, in determining his or her relationship to the testator or another person for the purposes of a will, he or she must be regarded as the child of his or her adoptive parents, and not of his or her biological/natural parents. An exception applies in the case of a biological parent who is also the adoptive parent of the child or was, at the time of the adoption, married to the child's adoptive parent.[1316] Thus, if a testator intends to exclude adopted relations, he or she has to make that intention clear in the will otherwise a reference to 'children' will be interpreted to include adopted children.

440. Section 2D(1)(b) of the Wills Act 7 of 1953 provides that when a will is interpreted, the fact that a person was born out of wedlock (is a child born of unmarried parents) must be ignored when his or her relationship to the testator or another person is determined. Thus, if the word 'children' is used in a will, it will be interpreted to include children born of unmarried parents, unless the testator clearly indicates that they should be excluded.

B. The Unborn Child and Class Bequests

441. A testator may nominate beneficiaries who will be born only after the will has been made or after the testator has died. However, the beneficiary must be alive or must at least have been conceived at the moment when the bequeathed benefit vests in him or her. In terms of the common law, a beneficiary who has been conceived when the estate falls open and who is subsequently born alive, can benefit due to the application of the *nasciturus* fiction.[1317]

442. In terms of the common law, if the beneficiaries in a will were not appointed as individuals but as members of a class, for example, 'my grandchildren' or 'my brother's children', it was very difficult to determine whether only those members of the class who had already been conceived at the testator's death could inherit, or whether members who were subsequently conceived should also be considered.[1318] If children conceived after the testator's death could also inherit,

---

1314. Children's Act 38 of 2005, s. 242(1)(a), (c) and 242(2)(e).
1315. *Ibid.*, s. 242(3). On adoption, *see* further Part II. Ch. 5, §1 above.
1316. In terms of s. 231(1)(c) and (d) of the Children's Act 38 of 2005, a step-parent and the biological father of a child born of unmarried parents may adopt the child.
1317. *See* Part I, Ch. 1, §1 above.
1318. In *Wentzel v. Brink's Executors* (1892) 9 SC 328, *Ex parte Estate Cronjé* 1941 CPD 123 and *Reichenberg v. Bader* 1977 (2) SA 1045 (W) the courts held that children born after the testator's

it meant that the estate would only fall open after the birth of the last beneficiary; in the meantime the estate could not be wound up.

Section 2D(1)(c) of the Wills Act 7 of 1953 addresses this situation. It provides that, unless otherwise indicated in the will, any benefit allocated to a person's children or to the members of a class of persons, vests in such children or in those members of the class of persons who are alive at the time of the devolution of the estate or who had already been conceived at that time and who are later born alive. If a testator wants to benefit children conceived after the devolution of the estate, his or her intention to this effect has to be made clear in the will in order to negate the application of section 2D(1)(c).

C. Persons Taking Part in the Execution of a Will

443. In terms of the Wills Act 7 of 1953, a person who signs the will as a witness or an *amanuensis*, or who writes out the will or any part of it in his or her own handwriting, and the spouse of such person at the time of the execution of the will, are disqualified from inheriting any benefit under the will.[1319]

The Act provides for exceptions to this general rule. Firstly, the court may declare the writer, witness or *amanuensis* or his or her spouse competent to receive a benefit under the will if it is satisfied that the person or his or her spouse did not defraud or unduly influence the testator in the execution of the will.[1320] Secondly, such a person or his or her spouse is not disqualified from receiving a benefit under the will if he or she would have inherited intestate had the testator died intestate. However, the person or his or her spouse is not entitled to receive more than he or she would have received had the deceased died intestate.[1321] Thirdly, a witness or his or her spouse is not disqualified from inheriting under the will if the will was signed by at least two other competent witnesses who do not receive any benefit under the will.[1322]

444. The nomination in a will of a person as executor, trustee or guardian is regarded as a benefit to be received by such person under that will.[1323] The above rules therefore apply to such person as well. If he or she signs as a witness, writes out the will or signs as *amanuensis*, the nomination is invalid, unless one of the exceptions applies.

---

death could inherit. In contrast, in, e.g., *Ex parte Chapman* 1975 (1) SA 441 (O), *Ex parte Standard Bank of SA: in re Estate Martin* 1977 (3) SA 750 (W) and *Smit v. Estate Smit* 1982 (4) SA 529 (C) the wills in question were interpreted to benefit only members of the class who were alive at the time of the testator's death. *See also* J. D'Almaine & F.N. Zaal *Inheritance Rights for Posthumously Procreated Children: A Growing Challenge for the Law* 21 Potchefstroom Electron. Law J. 1 (2018).

1319. Section 4A(1).
1320. Section 4A(2)(a).
1321. Section 4A(2)(b).
1322. Section 4A(2)(c).
1323. Wills Act 7 of 1953, s. 4A(3).

The prohibition on the writer's receiving a benefit also applies to the surviving testator who wrote a mutual or joint will in his or her own handwriting.[1324]

§4. The Joint Will

I. Introduction

445. A joint will is a single document in which two or more testators set out their respective wills. Joint wills are frequently executed by persons married in community of property. However, it is not required that the testators should be married in this manner or that they should be married at all.[1325] If the testators confer benefits on each other in the joint will, the joint will is also known as a mutual will. All mutual wills are joint wills, but not all joint wills are mutual wills.

Joint wills must comply with the same formalities as other wills. A joint will may be valid in respect of one testator, but invalid in respect of the other.[1326] This will, for example, be the case if only one of the testators signed the will. The rules as to capacity to benefit under a will also apply to joint wills. It is therefore not advisable that one of the testators to a mutual will write the will, because if the writer of the will is the survivor, he or she will ordinarily not be able to inherit under the will.[1327]

A joint will must be read as the separate wills of the testators involved.[1328] Technically, there are as many separate wills in the same document as there are testators. If the testators are married in community of property, the stipulations made by each spouse relate only to his or her share of the joint estate. If they are married out of community of property, the stipulations made by each testator relate only to his or her separate estate. Each testator is at liberty to revoke or alter his or her will without the knowledge or collaboration of the co-testator during the co-testator's lifetime or after the co-testator's death, and he or she is not, by doing so, precluded from taking a benefit that has been left to him or her in the will of the co-testator,[1329] unless the joint will effected massing.[1330]

II. Joint Wills, Election and Massing

446. The surviving testator in a joint will may not revoke or alter his or her will after the death of the co-testator if massing occurred and the surviving testator has

1324. *Van Rensburg v. Van Rensburg* 1963 (1) SA 505 (A).
1325. *Estate Koopmans v. Estate De Wet* 1912 CPD 1061.
1326. *Ex parte Maurice* 1995 (2) SA 713 (C).
1327. Corbett, Hofmeyr & Kahn, *The Law of Succession in South Africa*, 35.
1328. *Rhode v. Stubbs* 2005 (5) SA 104 (SCA).
1329. Corbett, Hofmeyr & Kahn, *The Law of Succession in South Africa*, 436–437.
1330. Massing is discussed immediately below.

accepted a benefit under the will of the first-dying testator.[1331] This is in keeping with the general principle of election as applied to testamentary benefits.[1332]

'Election' has to take place when a testator leaves a benefit to a beneficiary and simultaneously imposes a burden on him or her. The beneficiary is put to an election; in other words, he or she has to make a choice: He or she may accept the benefit (adiation), but must then also carry out the provisions of the will that impose obligations on him or her; a person who wishes to accept part of a will must accept the whole will insofar as its terms are intended to apply to him or her. Alternatively, the beneficiary may reject any provision which he or she dislikes (repudiation), but then he or she may not accept any benefit under the will. In other words, a beneficiary under a will may not accept or repudiate conditionally.[1333] Election plays a pivotal role in massing.

447. Massing takes place when the whole or portions of the estates of various testators are consolidated into one economic unit for the purposes of a testamentary disposition by the testators jointly, leaving a limited beneficial interest in the estate (such as a usufruct or *fideicommissum*[1334]) to the survivor, which benefit the survivor accepts upon the death of the first-dying testator. For massing to be effective, one testator must have disposed of both his or her own estate (or part of his or her estate) and the estate (or part of the estate) of the other testator *and* the surviving testator must have accepted a benefit under the will.[1335]

Massing is often found in wills in South Africa, particularly in joint or mutual wills of couples married in community of property, but it is not limited to such wills.

An example of massing is the following: Two testators married in community of property provide in their joint will that their children must inherit their farm whilst the surviving testator must receive a usufruct over the farm. If the surviving testator accepts the usufruct upon the death of the first-dying testator, massing takes place.[1336] The survivor gives up ownership of his or her half-share of the farm in exchange for a usufruct over the entire farm. However, if the survivor rejects the usufruct, he or she retains ownership of his or her half of the farm, and the will of the first-dying operates only in respect of his or her share of the estate.

In terms of the common law, the ultimate beneficiaries (the children in the above example) acquired a real right in respect of the first-dying testator's share of the massed estate and a personal right to the survivor's share once the surviving testator had adiated.[1337] However, section 37 of the Administration of Estates Act 66 of 1965 changed this situation. This section provides that the ultimate beneficiaries of

1331. *See*, e.g., *The Receiver of Revenue v. C.H. Hancke* 1915 AD 64; *Holmes' Executor v. Rawbone* 1954 (3) SA 703 (A); *Rampathy v. Krumm* 1978 (4) SA 935 (D).
1332. Corbett, Hofmeyr & Kahn, *The Law of Succession in South Africa*, 437.
1333. *Watson v. Burchell* (1891) 9 SC 2; *Van der Merwe v. Van der Merwe's Executrix* 1921 TPD 9.
1334. These concepts are discussed below in this chapter.
1335. *Rhode v. Stubbs* 2005 (5) SA 104 (SCA); *Theart v. Scheibert* [2012] 4 All SA 278 (SCA).
1336. *Ibid.*
1337. *Rosenberg v. Dry's Executors* 1911 AD 679; *The Receiver of Revenue v. C.H. Hancke* 1915 AD 64.

the massed estate obtain the same rights in respect of the survivor's share of the massed estate as they do, according to the will, in respect of the property of the first-dying testator.

The survivor's incapacity to make a new will applies only to the portion of the joint estate that has been massed. Thus, if massing relates to only a portion of the joint estate, the survivor may make a will dealing with the portion of the estate that has not been massed. Likewise, the survivor is entitled to dispose by will of assets acquired after the death of the first-dying testator.[1338]

Once the surviving testator has accepted the bequeathed benefit under the joint will which effects massing, he or she cannot subsequently make an independent will which is in conflict with the provisions of the joint will. Since massing restricts the freedom of testation of the surviving testator there is a presumption against massing. Thus, if there is any reasonable doubt as to the testator's intention to create massing, the court will hold that massing was not intended.[1339]

§5. Revocation and Revival of Wills

I. Revocation of a Will

A. Introduction

448. Revocation of wills is not regulated by the Wills Act 7 of 1953; thus, the common law rules still apply.[1340] The Wills Act does, however, contain one provision relating to revocation of wills, namely section 2A which was inserted into the Act by the Law of Succession Amendment Act 43 of 1992. This section empowers the court to condone certain acts of revocation that were not recognized at common law.[1341]

A will is a unilateral legal act which consists of the testator's declaration of intention. It becomes effective only on the death of the testator. Consequently, the will is revocable by the testator at any stage until the moment of his or her death,[1342] unless massing is involved.[1343] Provisions contained in an antenuptial contract that take effect only on the death of one of the parties, can also not be departed from unilaterally. An agreement by the testator not to revoke his or her will is invalid.[1344]

1338. *Joubert v. Ruddock* 1968 (1) SA 95 (E).
1339. *Rhode v. Stubbs* 2005 (5) SA 104 (SCA); *Theart v. Scheibert* [2012] 4 All SA 278 (SCA).
1340. *Senekal v. Meyer* 1975 (3) SA 372 (T).
1341. Section 2A is discussed below in this chapter.
1342. *Digesta* 34.4.4; *Crookes v. Watson* 1956 (1) SA 277 (A).
1343. On massing, *see* above in this chapter.
1344. *SA Association v. Mostert* 1869 Buch 231. The situation is different if the parties to an antenuptial contract included testamentary provisions in the antenuptial contract; they are bound by those provisions and one of the parties may not revoke the provisions without the consent of the other party: *Ex parte Executors Estate Everard* 1938 TPD 190.

In order to revoke a will, there must be an act of revocation accompanied by the intention to revoke (*animus revocandi*) on the part of the testator. Thus, a will cannot be revoked orally[1345] or by mistake.[1346]

In South Africa, a change in the testator's status after making a will, for example through marriage or the birth of children, does not result in the automatic revocation of the person's will. However, in terms of the Wills Act 7 of 1953, a person's divorce or the annulment of his or her marriage does have a temporary influence on some of the provisions of his or her will, as is explained below in this chapter.

B. Revocation by a Subsequent Will, Codicil or Antenuptial Contract

449. A will may be revoked expressly or tacitly by means of a later will or codicil. A later will expressly revokes an earlier will if it contains a revocatory clause (*clausula revocatoria*).[1347] Even if it does not contain a revocatory clause, it still revokes the earlier will if its provisions are in conflict with those of the earlier will. If a testator leaves various wills on his or her death, the wills must all be read together and reconciled as far as possible. However, if the wills cannot be reconciled, effect is given to the latest will and the previous wills are considered as having been revoked insofar as they are in conflict with the latest will.[1348]

450. An unmarried testator may also expressly revoke his or her will by means of a subsequent antenuptial contract.[1349]

C. Revocation by Destruction

451. In terms of the common law, a will may be revoked expressly by its deliberate destruction by either the testator or someone else duly authorized to do so by the testator.[1350] Acts of destruction include burning the will, tearing it up, deleting

1345. Grotius, *Inleidinge tot de Hollandsche Rechts-geleerdheid*, 2.24.10; Voet, *Commentarius ad Pandectas*, 28.3.1.8; *Louw v. Engelbrecht* 1979 (4) SA 841 (O).

1346. *Ex parte Lutchman* 1951 (1) SA 125 (T).

1347. *Re Estate Whiting* 1910 TPD 527.

1348. Voet, *Commentarius ad Pandectas*, 28.3.3; *Re Estate Whiting* 1910 TPD 527; *In re Estate Marks* 1921 TPD 180. *Pienaar v. Master of the Free State High Court, Bloemfontein* 2011 (6) SA 338 (SCA) provides an example of a situation where the later will and the first will could not be read together. The court affirmed *Price v. The Master* 1982 (3) SA 301 (N) 304 where it was held that 'where there are two wills, which to some extent contain similar provisions, but are in effect different, and each of the wills deal[s] with the entire estate, then they cannot stand together and the later will must be construed as having impliedly revoked the earlier': *Pienaar v. Master of the Free State High Court, Bloemfontein* para. 14.

1349. Voet, *Commentarius ad Pandectas*, 23.4.65.

1350. A person holding a general power of attorney may not destroy a will on behalf of the testator; the person must have express authority to do so: *Clarke v. Executors of Castray & Beale* (1902) 19 SC 498.

the testator's signature,[1351] writing 'cancelled' on the pages of the will,[1352] and destroying the duplicate of the original will where the original 'lay beyond the reach of the testator's revoking hand'.[1353]

The will may be destroyed wholly (*in toto*) or only in part (*pro tanto*). If only part of the will has been revoked, the remaining portion remains valid as long as it is intelligible on its own without reference to the deleted part.[1354] Should that not be possible in the circumstances, the conclusion will be drawn that the testator intended to revoke the entire will.[1355]

If a testator cancels only part of his or her will, the cancellation may constitute either a 'deletion' or a 'revocation'. If it is considered a deletion, the formalities for the amendment of wills have to be complied with,[1356] while no formalities are required for a revocation.

452. The act of destruction must be accompanied by the *animus revocandi* on the part of the testator. If the will is destroyed by someone else without the testator's knowledge or consent, or if the testator destroys the will while mentally ill, drugged, drunk or delirious, it cannot be said that the will was destroyed *animo revocandi*. The content of a will that was destroyed in error can be proved by referring to a copy of the will or, in the absence of a copy, by evidence from other sources.[1357]

453. In terms of the common law, several legal presumptions come into play when the court has to consider whether a will has been revoked by the testator. Firstly, if the testator destroyed a will, it is rebuttably presumed that he or she destroyed the will with the intention of revoking it.[1358] Secondly, if a will which was in the testator's possession cannot be found after his or her death, a rebuttable presumption operates that the testator destroyed the will with the intention of revoking it.[1359] However, no such rebuttable presumption operates if the will was in a third person's possession. Thirdly, if a will was drawn up in duplicate and the copy or duplicate which was in the testator's possession cannot be found after his or her death, it is rebuttably presumed that the testator destroyed the will with the *animus revocandi*.[1360] This rebuttable presumption does not apply, however, if both copies were in the testator's possession and only one copy is found after his death.[1361] This

1351. *Fram v. Fram's Executrix* 1947 (1) SA 787 (W).
1352. *Senekal v. Meyer* 1975 (3) SA 372 (T).
1353. *Marais v. The Master* 1984 (4) SA 288 (D) 294.
1354. Voet, *Commentarius ad Pandectas*, 28.4.3; *In re Lloyd* (1895) 12 SC 117.
1355. Corbett, Hofmeyr & Kahn, *The Law of Succession in South Africa*, 97–98.
1356. *See* above in this chapter.
1357. *Nell v. Talbot* 1972 (1) SA 207 (D).
1358. Voet, *Commentarius ad Pandectas*, 28.4.4; *In re Beresford* (1883) 2 SC 303; *Nelson v. Currey* (1886) 4 SC 355; *Wynne v. Estate Wynne* (1908) 25 SC 951.
1359. *Ibid. See also* M.C. Wood-Bodley *Wills Lost whilst in the Testator's Possession – Rebutting the Presumption of Revocation*, 133 S. Afr. Law J. 731 (2016).
1360. *Nelson v. Currey* (1886) 4 SC 355.
1361. Voet, *Commentarius ad Pandectas*, 28.4.1.

rebuttable presumption that the testator has destroyed his or her will with the *animus revocandi* also falls away if it is proved that the testator destroyed his or her will in a thoughtless moment, by mistake, or in a moment of rage, drunkenness or mental illness.[1362]

The rebuttal of the presumption depends on the particular circumstances of each specific case. In other words, the presumption may be rebutted by the facts.[1363]

454. In terms of the Administration of Estates Act 66 of 1965, the Master must ignore these common-law presumptions concerning the revocation of a will when he or she makes a decision about acceptance of a will.[1364] The Master may also accept a duplicate of the original will if the original cannot be found.[1365] The reason for this provision is that the Master is not in a position to consider evidence in regard to the presumption – this is the task of the courts. Interested parties who want to rely on these presumptions must take the Master's decision to accept the will to court, where they may present evidence of the facts regarding the possible revocation of the will.

D. Court's Power of Condonation at Revocation

455. Section 2A of the Wills Act 7 of 1953 empowers the court to condone certain acts of revocation which were not recognized in terms of the common law. This section empowers the court to declare a will, or part of it, to have been revoked if the court is satisfied that the testator intended to revoke the will, or part of it, provided that the revocation is apparent from the appearance of the will itself or from another document. In terms of this section, the intention to revoke the will can be made clear by the testator or by someone on his or her behalf, by writing on the will itself, performing another act in relation to the will which is apparent on the face of the will, or by drafting another document from which such intention is evident.[1366]

In this regard, the basic question is whether the testator intended to revoke the will, and not whether the particular act is a recognized act of revocation. The power to condone the revocation of a will is conferred upon the courts, notwithstanding the fact that the act of revocation, or the document from which the revocation is evident, does not comply with the necessary formalities. The only prerequisite is that the act of revocation should be evident from a document or on the face of the will. Oral revocation is therefore still impermissible.[1367] Examples of acts of revocation

1362. *Van Niekerk v. Van Niekerk* (1898) 15 SC 229; *In re Bain* 1912 NPD 258.
1363. *Ex parte Slade* 1922 TPD 220; *Ex parte Lutchman* 1951 (1) SA 125 (T).
1364. Administration of Estates Act 66 of 1965, s. 8(4A).
1365. *Ibid.*, s. 8(4B).
1366. *See Webster v. The Master* 1996 (1) SA 34 (D); *Olivier v. Die Meester: In re Boedel Wyle Olivier* 1997 (1) SA 836 (T); *Henwick v. The Master* 1997 (2) SA 326 (C) for examples of the application of s. 2A.
1367. *Mdlulu v. Delarey* [1998] 1 All SA 434 (W).

under this section would include the testator's writing on a separate piece of paper that he or she revokes his or her will, or the testator's instructing his or her attorney to tear up the will.[1368]

E. Conditional Revocation or the Doctrine of Dependant Relative Revocation

456. A testator's intention to revoke a will may be dependent on a condition or a supposition, for example, that a later will has been validly executed. If the condition is not fulfilled or the supposition turns out to be incorrect, the revocation does not have any legal effect, as the necessary *animus revocandi* was lacking. South African courts apply the 'doctrine of dependent relative revocation' in this regard. This doctrine originated from English law, but has been accepted in South African case law as being part and parcel of South African law.[1369] In *Raabe v. The Master,*[1370] the court, per Trengove J, warned that although the doctrine of dependent relative revocation may be useful:

> it is not a magic formula. This doctrine, as I understand it, is not a statement of legal rules and principles. It is simply a convenient method of reasoning to be applied in cases where the true intention of a testator, who has performed what appears to be an act of revocation, has to be determined.

F. Effect of Divorce on a Will

457. Section 2B of the Wills Act 7 of 1953 applies if a marriage between a testator and his or her former spouse is dissolved by divorce or annulment by a court: If the testator dies within three months after the divorce or annulment, the will must be implemented as if the former spouse had died before the date of the dissolution of the marriage. The effect of this provision is that the former spouse does not inherit under the testator's will if the testator dies within the three-month period. However, the former spouse does inherit if it is apparent from the will that the testator intended the former spouse to benefit, notwithstanding the dissolution of the marriage.[1371]

It must be noted that section 2B does not revoke the will and also has no effect on any other provisions of the will apart from the provisions dealing with the former spouse. Also, if the testator dies more than three months after the divorce or annulment, this section does not apply and the former spouse can inherit under the will.

1368. *See also Roos v. Saaiman* 2018 (6) SA 279 (GP).
1369. *Davis v. Steel and Eriksen* 1949 (3) SA 177 (W); *Le Roux v. Le Roux* 1963 (4) SA 273 (C).
1370. 1971 (1) SA 780 (T) 785.
1371. *See Louw v. Kock* 2017 (3) SA 62 (WCC); M.C. Wood-Bodley, *Wills, Divorce, and the Provisions of Section 2B of the Wills Act: Louw NO v Kock*, 135 S. Afr. Law J. 418 (2018).

II. Revival of a Revoked Will

458. Revival of a will occurs when a previously revoked will is once more given legal force at a later stage. The Wills Act 7 of 1953 does not contain any provisions regarding the revival of revoked wills and we must therefore consult case law to establish the relevant principles.

Early on, case law at provincial level established that a revoked will can only be revived if it has not physically been destroyed and is still available, and that a revoked will cannot be revived orally or by means of a non-testamentary act.[1372] It was also established that a will that was revoked in a subsequent will, does not automatically revive when the second will is revoked, for example, if the second will is destroyed by the testator with the intention of revoking it. This is the position even if the testator destroyed the second will with the express intention of thereby reviving the revoked will.[1373] It was also held that a later will may breathe life into an earlier will, provided that the earlier will was validly executed.[1374] Re-execution of the revoked will was not required for its revival, but it was required that there should be proof in a testamentary instrument that the former will had been acknowledged as the last will of the deceased.[1375] It was further required that a reviving document existed and that this document had been executed in accordance with testamentary formalities.[1376]

The Appellate Division (now the Supreme Court of Appeal) considered the issue of revival of revoked wills in 1951 in *Moses v. Abinader*.[1377] After this decision the law regarding revival of revoked wills was in an uncertain state, because the judges in *Moses v. Abinader* were not in agreement whether a revoked will had to be re-executed in order to be revived.

More recently, the Supreme Court of Appeal re-visited the issue of revival in *Wessels v. Die Meester*.[1378] The court held that re-execution of a revoked will was not necessary for its revival. The revoked will can be revived by a subsequent will in which the intention to revive the revoked will is made clear. Both the revoked will and the reviving will must have been validly executed.[1379]

1372. *In re Estate Marks* 1921 TPD 180; *Ex parte Estate Gillespie* 1943 CPD 58; *Fram v. Fram's Executrix* 1947 (1) SA 787 (W).
1373. *Fram v. Fram's Executrix* 1947 (1) SA 787 (W); *Le Roux v. Le Roux* 1963 (4) SA 273 (C).
1374. *Van Reenen v. Board of Executors* 1876 Buch 44.
1375. *In re Estate Marks* 1921 TPD 180; *Wood v. Estate Fawcus* 1935 CPD 350.
1376. *Ex parte Estate Gillespie* 1943 CPD 58.
1377. 1951 (4) SA 537 (A).
1378. *Wessels v. Die Meester* [2007] ZASCA 17, 23 Mar. 2007, (unreported) http://www.saflii.org/za/cases/ZASCA/2007/17.html.
1379. Paragraph 22.

§6. FREEDOM OF TESTATION

459. South African law recognizes freedom of testation or the right of an individual to dispose of his or her property on his or her death as he or she pleases.[1380] In principle, a testator has complete freedom of testation, and the courts are compelled to give effect to a testamentary disposition in a valid will, provided the disposition is not illegal, *contra bonos mores* or too vague and uncertain to be given effect to.[1381] Nevertheless, this freedom is not absolute and a few limitations are imposed by common law and by statute.[1382]

460. The Constitution also has an influence on the principle of freedom of testation. Section 25(1) of the Constitution (the 'property clause') guarantees the right not to be deprived of one's property except in terms of law of general application, which law may not permit arbitrary deprivation of property. This right is said to include the right to dispose of one's property during one's lifetime or at one's death. Interpreted thus, section 25(1) guarantees the institution of succession as well as the principle of freedom of testation that supports it.[1383] In *BoE Trust Ltd*,[1384] the Supreme Court of Appeal agreed with this view. It further held that 'not to give due recognition to freedom of testation, will … also fly in the face of the founding constitutional principle of human dignity. The right to dignity allows the living, and the dying, the peace of mind of knowing that their last wishes would be respected after they have passed away'.[1385]

If the principle of freedom of testation clashes with the constitutional value of non-discrimination, freedom of testation has to give way in cases that involve the creation of a trust with a public character.[1386] In *Curators, Emma Smith Educational Fund v. University of Kwazulu-Natal*[1387] the Supreme Court of Appeal held that:

> the constitutional imperative to remove racially restrictive clauses that conflict with public policy from the conditions of an educational trust intended to benefit prospective students in need and administered by a publicly funded educational institution such as the University, takes precedence over freedom of

1380. Corbett, Hofmeyr & Kahn, *The Law of Succession in South Africa*, 39; Van der Merwe & Rowland, *Die Suid-Afrikaanse Erfreg*, 612.
1381. Van der Merwe & Rowland, *Die Suid-Afrikaanse Erfreg*, 612.
1382. *See* Part IV, Ch. 2, §7 below.
1383. De Waal & Schoeman-Malan, *Law of Succession*, 4; *Minister of Education v. Syfrets Trust Ltd* 2006 (4) SA 205 (C) para. 18
1384. 2013 (3) SA 236 (SCA).
1385. Paragraph 26. *See also Harvey v. Crawford* 2019 (2) SA 153 (SCA). *See* further K. Lehman, *Testamentary Freedom versus Testamentary Duty: In Search of a Better Balance*, in *South African Law of Succession and Trusts – The Past Meeting the Present and Thoughts for the Future* 10 (M. de Waal & M. Paleker eds., Juta & Co 2014).
1386. Where the relevant provision does not introduce a public element, testamentary freedom may outweigh the right to equality. In *King v. De Jager* 2017 (6) SA 527 (WCC) a *fideicommissum* that only benefited male descendants was upheld. The court held that in the particular circumstances the limitation of the female descendants' right to equality was reasonable and justifiable given the importance accorded to the right to freedom of testation.
1387. 2010 (6) SA 518 (SCA).

testation, particularly given the fundamental values of our Constitution and the constitutional imperative to move away from our racially divided past.

Removing racially restrictive conditions from the provisions of a trust in these circumstances therefore did not amount to unlawful deprivation of property.[1388]

In this case, a testator created a trust with the object of providing bursaries for white South African women who needed financial support for a tertiary education. The court applied section 13 of the Trust Property Control Act 57 of 1988 which empowers a court to vary trust provisions that have consequences which the founder of the trust did not contemplate and which, *inter alia*, hamper the achievement of the objects of the founder or are in conflict with the public interest. The court held that the particular provision which restricted potential beneficiaries along racial lines violated public policy since it infringed the constitutional right to equality. The provision also prevented the realization of the testator's intention to entrust a university with administering the bursary programme, since universities, having an obligation to apply public policy, cannot administer funds with racially restrictive conditions and, as publicly funded institutions, cannot be associated with racially discriminatory practices.[1389]

In *Minister of Education v. Syfrets Trust Ltd*[1390] the court also varied the provisions of a trust by removing a condition that unfairly discriminated against certain racial groups, religious groups and women. The court held that the testamentary provisions in question constituted unfair discrimination and, as such, were contrary to public policy as reflected in the foundational constitutional values of non-racialism, non-sexism and equality. The court was empowered, in terms of the existing principles of the common law, to order variation of the trust deed in question by deleting the offending provisions from the will.[1391]

In *BoE Trust Ltd*,[1392] the Supreme Court of Appeal refused to uphold an appeal against the decision of the High Court not to remove racially restrictive conditions. In this case, a testamentary trust provided for the provision of bursaries to assist white South African students who had completed an MSc degree in Organic Chemistry at a South African university and were planning to complete their studies with a doctorate degree at a university in Europe or Britain. The testator had been advised that this provision would possibly not be given effect to due to its discriminatory nature. The testator, however, chose not to remove the word 'white'. Instead, she provided that, should it become impossible for the trustees to carry out the terms of the trust, the income generated by the trust had to be used to provide donations to a number of charitable organizations. The trustees of the trust were unable to find a university that was willing to accept the bursary bequest, because of the racial selection criterion. They applied to the court for the removal of the word 'white'. The court held that the High Court was correct in finding that the bursary bequest was rendered impossible as a result of the universities' stance and that effect should

1388. Paragraph 42.
1389. Paragraphs 39–40 and 43.
1390. 2006 (4) SA 205 (C).
1391. Paragraph 47. *See also Board of Executors v. Benjamin Godlieb Heydenrych Testamentary Trust* 2012 (4) SA 103 (WCC) which abided by the decisions in *Emma Smith* and *Syfrets*.
1392. 2013 (3) SA 236 (SCA) para. 26.

therefore be given to the alternative disposition expressly provided for in the will. The trust income had to go to the charitable organizations. The court held that the testator's wishes had to be given effect to, because 'the enshrined rights to dignity and property demand it'.[1393]

§7. Restrictions on Freedom of Testation

I. Introduction

461. As indicated above, apart from a few exceptions, which are dealt with below, a testator is free to dispose of his or her estate as he or she wishes and the court must enforce the provisions of the will in accordance with the principle *voluntas testatoris servanda est*. The High Court has no general authority to consent to alterations to the testator's will in contradiction of the testator's express intention.[1394] Even if all the beneficiaries agree to it, the court may not change the binding clauses of a will.[1395] However, the High Court has inherent jurisdiction to delete an aspect that was inserted into the will by the drafter by mistake.[1396] The court may even add words to a will by way of rectification if this is necessary to give effect to the wishes of the testator.[1397] If the circumstances since the making of a will have changed to such a degree that it would have been impossible for the testator to have foreseen them, the court also has the authority to deviate from the terms of the will.[1398]

II. Impossible, Illegal, Vague and Uncertain Conditions and Conditions that Are *Contra Bonos Mores*

462. Conditions that are impossible to give effect to or are illegal, vague or uncertain, are taken as *pro non scripto* and the beneficiary inherits the benefit free of the particular condition, provided that, after the deletion of the condition, a rational bequest remains which can be carried out.[1399]

463. Likewise, the courts do not enforce conditions in a will which are considered to be *contra bonos mores*. Conditions which may be considered to be against

1393. *Ibid.*, para. 29. For a discussion of these cases, *see* C. Rautenbach, *A Few Comments on the (Possible) Revival of the Customary Law Rule of Male Primogeniture: Can the Common-Law Principle of Freedom of Testation Come to its Rescue?*, in *South African Law of Succession and Trusts – The Past Meeting the Present and Thoughts for the Future* 132–160 (M. de Waal & M. Paleker eds., Juta & Co 2014).

1394. *Ex parte Loewenthal* 1939 TPD 250; *Jewish Colonial Trust v. Estate Nathan* 1940 AD 163; *Jewish Colonial Trust v. Estate Nathan* 1967 (4) SA 397 (N); *Ex parte Kruger* 1976 (1) SA 609 (O).

1395. *Bydawell v. Chapman* 1953 (3) SA 514 (A); *Ex parte Watling* 1982 (1) SA 936 (C).

1396. *Rens v. Esselen* 1957 (4) SA 8 (W).

1397. *Ex parte Van der Spuy* 1966 (3) SA 169 (T); *Ex parte Dison* 1968 (3) SA 268 (W).

1398. *Ex parte Sidelsky* 1983 (4) SA 598 (C).

1399. *Grusd v. Grusd* 1946 AD 465; *Levy v. Schwartz* 1948 (4) SA 930 (W); *Aaronson v. Estate Hart* 1950 1 SA 539 (A).

the good morals of society are those that prohibit the beneficiary from marrying or force the beneficiary to live in a certain place or to change his or her lifestyle, religion or political affiliation, to name but a few.[1400] These conditions interfere with the fundamental rights of the individuals concerned.[1401]

464. A testator may not leave a benefit to a beneficiary who has never been married on the condition that the beneficiary remains unmarried. Such a condition is *contra bonos mores* since it encourages the beneficiary to continue in the unmarried state.[1402]

If the purpose of a condition is to destroy an existing marriage, the condition is null and void.[1403] Note that it is the object – not the effect – which is important.[1404] Thus, if the outcome of a bequest is that a marriage breaks down without this having been the testator's intention, the bequest is valid.

465. To date, the courts have upheld conditions prohibiting beneficiaries from marrying members of a particular religion, race or nationality,[1405] provided the condition was not considered too vague.[1406] However, it is suggested that these conditions will in future be considered as *contra bonos mores*. The Constitution places an obligation on the courts to develop the common law to promote the spirit, purport and objects of the Bill of Rights.[1407] The *boni mores* will in future also be informed by the constitutional values of non-racialism, non-sexism and equality.[1408]

466. In the past, the courts have upheld conditions which required someone to live in a certain place or on a certain property.[1409] However, given that freedom of movement is a fundamental right under the Constitution,[1410] this type of provision could now be considered *contra bonos mores*.[1411]

1400. De Waal & Schoeman-Malan, *Law of Succession*, 135; Jamneck & Rautenbach (eds), *The Law of Succession in South Africa*, 132.
1401. In terms of s. 9(4) read with s. 9(3) of the Constitution, no one may, directly or indirectly, discriminate unfairly against anyone on the basis of race, gender, sex, pregnancy, marital status, ethnic or social origin, colour, sexual orientation, age, disability, religion, conscience, belief, culture, language or birth.
1402. Voet, *Commentarius ad Pandectas*, 28.7.12, 14; *Aronson v. Estate Hart* 1950 (1) SA 539 (A); *De Wayer v. SPCA Johannesburg* 1963 (1) SA 71 (T). It has been held that it is not *contra bonos mores* to prohibit someone who has been married before from marrying again (Voet, *Commentarius ad Pandectas*, 28.7.13; *Ex parte Gitelson* 1949 (2) SA 881 (O)). It is doubtful whether this type of condition will in future pass constitutional scrutiny.
1403. *Levy v. Schwartz* 1948 (4) SA 930 (W); *Ex parte Isaacs* 1964 (4) SA 606 (GW); *Ex parte St Clair Lynn* 1980 (3) SA 163 (W); *Oosthuizen v. Bank Windhoek* 1991 (1) SA 849 (Nm).
1404. *Ex parte Swanevelder* 1949 (1) SA 733 (O); *Ex parte Higgs: In re Estate Rangasami* 1969 (1) SA 56 (D); *Barclays Bank DC and O v. Anderson* 1959 (2) SA 478 (T).
1405. *Aronson v. Estate Hart* 1950 (1) SA 539 (A); *Standard Bank of SA Ltd v. Betts Brown* 1958 (3) SA 713 (N); *Ex parte Administrator Estate Sandler* 1976 (4) SA 930 (C).
1406. *Wasserzug v. Administrators Estate Nathan* 1944 TPD 369; *Ex parte Haworth* 1946 CPD 679.
1407. Constitution, s. 39(2).
1408. *See* para. 459 above. *See also* Corbett, Hofmeyr & Kahn, *The Law of Succession in South Africa*, 133–134; De Waal & Schoeman-Malan, 136–1393.
1409. *Ex parte Kock* 1952 (2) SA 502 (C); *Ex parte Higgs: In re Estate Rangasami* 1969 (1) SA 56 (D).
1410. Section 21.
1411. Jamneck & Rautenbach (eds), *The Law of Succession in South Africa*, 131–132.

467. Whenever a prohibition is created, another person must be appointed in whose favour the prohibition operates, otherwise the prohibition is a *nudum praeceptum* (nude prohibition) and will not be enforced.[1412]

III. Maintenance of Children and the Surviving Spouse or Civil Union Partner

468. A testator may disinherit his or her spouse and children. However, South African law grants these parties a maintenance claim against the deceased estate in certain circumstances. These claims indirectly limit the testator's freedom of testation.

A. *Maintenance of Children*

469. In terms of the common law, a deceased estate may be liable for maintenance of the deceased's children.[1413] The obligation to maintain the child ends when the child is able to support himself or herself,[1414] but may continue after the child has become a major.[1415] The claim is subordinate to the claims of creditors,[1416] but ranks above that of heirs and legatees.[1417]

B. *Maintenance of the Surviving Spouse or Civil Union Partner*

470. If a marriage or civil union is terminated by death, the survivor may claim maintenance from the estate of the deceased in terms of the Maintenance of Surviving Spouses Act 27 of 1990 if he or she is unable to provide for his or her reasonable maintenance needs[1418] from his or her own means and earnings.[1419] In this context, the word 'spouse' has been judicially interpreted to include a party to a

1412. *Aronson v. Estate Hart* 1950 (1) SA 539 (A); *Barnett v. Estate Scherescheswke* 1957 (3) SA 679 (C).
1413. *See*, e.g., *Carelse v. Estate De Vries* (1906) 23 SC 532; *Spies' Executors v. Beyers* 1908 TS 473; *Secretary for Inland Revenue v. Brey* 1980 (1) SA 472 (A); *Lambrakis v. Santam* 2000 (3) SA 1098 (W). On a parent's duty to support his or her child, *see* Part II, Ch. 6, §2 above.
1414. *Carelse v. Estate De Vries* (1906) 23 SC 532; *Glazer v. Glazer* 1963 (4) SA 694 (A).
1415. *Hoffman v. Herdan* 1982 (2) SA 274 (T); *Ex parte Jacobs* 1982 (2) SA 276 (O).
1416. *Ritchken's Executors v. Ritchken* 1924 WLD 17; *In re Estate Visser* 1948 (3) SA 1129 (C).
1417. *Davis' Tutor v. Estate Davis* 1925 WLD 168; *Goldman v. Executor Estate Goldman* 1937 WLD 64; *Ex parte Estate Pitt-Kennedy* 1946 NPD 776.
1418. *See Oshry v. Feldman* 2010 (6) SA 19 (SCA).
1419. Section 2(1). For a full discussion of this topic, *see* Part III, Ch. 1, §5 above.

monogamous[1420] or polygynous[1421] Muslim marriage, and a partner in a same-sex life partnership in which the partners had undertaken reciprocal duties of support.[1422]

IV. Other Limitations

471. In terms of the Pension Funds Act 24 of 1956, a benefit payable by a pension fund in respect of a deceased member does not form part of the member's estate.[1423] The testator may therefore not decide how this benefit should devolve after his or her death. The Act prescribes how the benefit has to be dealt with.

472. In terms of both the common law and the Immovable Property (Removal or Modification of Restrictions) Act 94 of 1965, the court has a limited power to alter or remove restrictions on immovable property imposed by a testator. In terms of the common law, the court has the jurisdiction to authorize, where applicable, the sale or exchange of fideicommissary[1424] property for reasons of necessity (*ob causam necessarium*)[1425] or if all the fideicommissaries have consented to the alienation and such alienation is to their advantage.[1426] The court will also authorise the exchange and substitution of fideicommissary property if it benefits the fideicommissary heirs.[1427]

In terms of the Immovable Property (Removal or Modification of Restrictions) Act, the court has the power to remove or modify burdens, such as *fideicommissa*, on immovable property. In terms of section 2, the court may remove or modify a restriction if the removal or modification will benefit the beneficiaries. Section 3 provides that if the court finds that the shares of the immovable property are too small for beneficial occupation, that beneficial use is prevented by a prohibition against subdivision, or that circumstances have arisen which the maker of the will or document did not foresee, it may remove or modify such restriction or make another order that seems just.[1428]

473. The testator's capacity to restrict the alienability of land by means of long-term provisions, such as long-term *fideicommissa*, is also limited by the Immovable Property (Removal or Modification of Restrictions) Act 94 of 1965, because he or

1420. *Daniels v. Campbell* 2004 (5) SA 331 (CC).
1421. *Hassam v. Jacobs* [2008] 4 All SA 350 (C).
1422. *Gory v. Kolver (Starke Intervening)* 2007 (4) SA 97 (CC); *Laubscher v. Duplan* 2017 (2) SA 264 (CC). On the position of heterosexual life partners, *see* Part II, Ch. 3, §3 above.
1423. Section 37C.
1424. The *fideicommissum* is discussed below in this chapter.
1425. *Ex parte Strauss* 1949 (3) SA 929 (O).
1426. *Ex parte Kruger* 1976 (1) SA 609 (O).
1427. *Ex parte Botha* 1952 (2) SA 224 (O).
1428. *See*, e.g., *Ex parte Wallace* 1970 (1) SA 103 (NC) where the court, in considering what amounts to 'public interest', held it not to be in the public interest to compel people to carry on an activity, in this case farming, for which they had no inclination or desire and thus to prevent them from doing what they really wanted to.

she may not place a restriction on alienation which lasts longer than the Act prescribes. At common law there was no limitation as to the number of successive fideicommissaries the testator could provide for. The Act limits the number of successive fideicommissaries to two substitutions. The second successive fideicommissary becomes full owner free of the *fideicommissum*.[1429]

474. The court also has the power to authorize the amendment of trust provisions,[1430] both under the common law and in terms of the Trust Property Control Act 57 of 1988. The court's power to vary trust provisions in terms of the common law is limited. The court may sanction the variation of trust provisions for reasons of necessity or if there has been a change of circumstances, unforeseen by the founder, which would lead to frustration of the testator's intention if the trust instrument were not amended.[1431]

Section 13 of the Trust Property Control Act extends the power of the court to vary trust provisions. The section applies if a trust instrument contains any provision which brings about consequences which, in the opinion of the court, the founder of the trust did not contemplate or foresee and which hamper the achievement of the objectives of the founder, prejudice the interests of the beneficiaries, or are in conflict with public interest. In these circumstances, the court may, on the application of the trustee or any person who in the opinion of the court has a sufficient interest in the trust property, delete or vary any such provision or make any order in respect of the provision which it deems just.[1432] Such order may include an order in terms of which trust property is substituted for other property and an order terminating the trust.

475. Other statutory provisions which affect a testator's freedom of testation are the Subdivision of Agricultural Land Act 70 of 1970,[1433] the Mineral and Petroleum Resources Development Act 28 of 2002[1434] and the Close Corporations Act 69 of 1984.[1435]

§8. Content of a Will

476. By their very nature, wills may vary greatly in content, since a testator is entitled to dispose of his or her estate as he or she wishes. Testators may use any

1429. Sections 6–8.
1430. The trust is discussed in Part IV, Ch. 2, §8 below.
1431. *Ex parte Jewish Colonial Trust Ltd: In re Estate Nathan* 1967 (4) SA 397 (N); *Webb v. Marquard* 1981 (2) SA 43 (C); *Ex parte Watling* 1982 (1) SA 936 (C); *Ex parte Sidelsky* 1983 (4) SA 598 (C).
1432. *Curators, Emma Smith Educational Fund v. University of Kwazulu-Natal* 2010 (6) SA 518 (SCA); *Ex parte President of the Conference of the Methodist Church of Southern Africa: In re William Marsh Will Trust* 1993 (2) SA 697 (C).
1433. Sections 3–5.
1434. Section 11.
1435. Section 35.

words they want as long as their intention can be ascertained with reasonable certainty. The law does not prescribe formulas to be used.[1436] It is thus not possible to discuss all aspects of the possible content of wills, but a few typical ways in which testamentary bequests usually occur in practice are briefly referred to.[1437]

I. Conditions and Time Clauses

477. The beneficiary's claim against the executor arises at the moment of *delatio* (when the estate 'falls open'). This moment is also referred to as the moment when the beneficiary's right becomes vested or the moment of *dies cedit. Dies cedit* must be distinguished from *dies venit*, which is the moment the right becomes enforceable. These two moments can occur simultaneously, or *dies venit* may be postponed to a date after *dies cedit*, for example, if the testator attaches a suspensive time clause to a benefit. *Dies cedit* usually occurs at the death of the testator, unless the testator has postponed it by attaching a suspensive condition to the benefit. Naturally, if *dies cedit* is postponed, *dies venit* is also postponed.[1438]

478. From the foregoing it is evident that the testator may make a benefit conditional, that is to say, subject to the fulfilment of a suspensive condition.[1439] In such event, the vesting of the benefit in the beneficiary is dependent on the fulfilment of an uncertain, future event. *Dies cedit* is postponed until the fulfilment of the condition. If the suspensive condition is not fulfilled, the bequeathed benefit does not vest in the beneficiary.[1440] This means that the particular bequest falls away and might accrue to other inheritances in accordance with the right of accrual,[1441] devolve by intestate succession, or fall into the remainder of the testator's inheritance, depending on the circumstances.

A benefit may also be subject to a resolutive condition. A resolutive condition does not postpone *dies cedit* or the vesting of the benefit in the beneficiary, but the possibility exists that, if the resolutive condition is fulfilled, the beneficiary will lose the vested right which he or she has. In such event, the testator must have appointed another beneficiary to take the benefit otherwise the condition is considered a *nudum praeceptum* and is disregarded.[1442]

1436. In other words, there are no internal formalities. *See* De Waal, *Testamentary Formalities in South Africa*, 382.

1437. According to De Waal, *Testamentary Formalities in South Africa*, 382 'the vast majority of typical testamentary institutions and provisions originate from Roman law and were received as such into Dutch law and later South African law'.

1438. De Waal & Schoeman-Malan, *Law of Succession*, 8.

1439. A condition may not be impossible, vague, uncertain, illegal or *contra bonos mores*. In this regard, *see* further above in this chapter.

1440. Voet, *Commentarius ad Pandectas*, 28.7.32, 36.2.2; *Smith v. Estate Smith* 1949 (1) SA 534 (A).

1441. The right of accrual is discussed below in this chapter.

1442. *Ex parte Sieberhagen* 1946 CPD 83; *Jewish Colonial Trust Ltd. v. Estate Nathan* 1949 AD 163.

479. A benefit may also be subject to a time clause, that is, subject to a certain future event. A time clause may be suspensive or resolutive. In the case of a suspensive time clause, the beneficiary is appointed as from a certain date. A time clause does not have any effect on the vesting of the benefit in the beneficiary, and vesting (*dies cedit*) usually takes place at the death of the testator. However, the beneficiary will only be able to enjoy the benefit from the specified date, that is, *dies venit* is postponed until a future date.[1443]

In the case of a resolutive time clause, the beneficiary is instituted up to a certain day. When the day arrives, the beneficiary has to hand over the property to the appointed heirs or, in the absence of appointed heirs, to heirs *ab intestato.*[1444]

II. Modus

480. A modus is a qualification added to a testamentary disposition, in terms of which the person who is benefitted is required and bound to devote the property he or she receives, or its value, in whole or in part to a specific purpose.[1445] The modus does not make the bequest conditional and therefore has no influence on the time when the bequeathed benefit vests.[1446] As soon as the beneficiary accepts the bequeathed benefit, a personal obligation arises, in consequence of which he or she is bound to carry out the modus.[1447] However, if the modus is impossible, illegal or *contra bonos mores*, it is void and is considered to be *pro non scripto.*[1448]

III. Substitution

481. Substitution takes place when a testator appoints a beneficiary to inherit a benefit and, at the same time, appoints another beneficiary to take the place of the first-mentioned beneficiary when a particular event occurs, such as the death of the appointed beneficiary. Substitution may take one of two forms: direct substitution or fideicommissary substitution.[1449]

482. In a direct substitution, a testator nominates a beneficiary to take a benefit and also nominates an alternative beneficiary to take the same benefit in the event

1443. Voet, *Commentarius ad Pandectas*, 36.2.3; *Fuller's Estate v. Fuller* 1949 (3) SA 570 (N).
1444. Voet, *Commentarius ad Pandectas*, 38.7.32; *Smith v. Estate Smith* 1949 (1) SA 534 (A).
1445. For a comprehensive discussion of this topic, *see* Corbett, Hofmeyr & Kahn, *The Law of Succession in South Africa*, 337–341; J. Jamneck, *The Modus in Modern South African Succession Law*, in *South African Law of Succession and Trusts – The Past Meeting the Present and Thoughts for the Future* 104–122 (M. de Waal & M. Paleker eds., Juta & Co 2014).
1446. Voet, *Commentarius ad Pandectas*, 35.1.12; *Jewish Colonial Trust Ltd v. Estate Nathan* 1940 AD 163.
1447. *Ex parte Strümpfer* 1945 OPD 268; *Ex parte Esterhuyse* 1971 (4) SA 261 (O); *Wessels v. D.A. Wessels en Seuns (Edms) Bpk* 1987 (3) SA 530 (T); *Kommissaris van Binnelandse Inkomste v. Van Blommenstein* 1999 (2) SA 367 (SCA).
1448. Voet, *Commentarius ad Pandectas*, 35.1.13; *Marks v. Estate Gluckman* 1946 AD 289.
1449. For a comprehensive discussion of this topic, see Corbett, Hofmeyr & Kahn, 199–221.

that the first-mentioned beneficiary cannot, or does not wish to, take the benefit. In other words, a direct substitution is one in which two or more beneficiaries are instituted in the alternative.[1450]

In one instance, direct substitution is implied *ex lege*. Section 2C(2) of the Wills Act 7 of 1953 provides that if a testator appoints a descendant as a beneficiary and that descendant predeceases the testator or is disqualified from inheriting, the instituted descendant is directly substituted by his or her descendants. If a descendant renounces his or her benefit, his or her descendants may also directly substitute him or her, provided that the testator did not leave behind a spouse who is jointly entitled to a testamentary benefit together with the descendant. If there is such a spouse, the benefit accrues to the spouse in terms of section 2C(1).[1451]

483. Fideicommissary substitution occurs where a testator directs in his or her will that, after his or her death, a series of successors (heirs or legatees) are to inherit his or her whole estate, part of it or specific assets, so that the benefit passes from one successor to another. The different successors thus inherit the same benefit one after the other. A fideicommissary substitution is used to create a *fideicommissum*. The first successor is called the fiduciary (*fiduciarius*) and every beneficiary to whom the bequeathed benefit must be transferred after a certain time or upon the fulfilment of a certain condition is called a fideicommissary (*fideicommissarius*).

According to case law, a *fideicommissum* is implied if the testator leaves benefits to his or her descendant and provides that if the descendant dies without children (a *si sine liberis decesserit* clause), a third party must inherit. It is inferred that the testator intended to create a tacit *fideicommissum* in favour of the descendants referred to in the *si sine liberis decesserit* clause, provided they are direct descendants of the testator.[1452] Thus, if the testator's descendant dies and leaves descendants, they inherit as fideicommissary substitutes and the third party does not inherit.

IV. *Fideicommissum*

484. In a *fideicommissum*, the testator leaves property (almost always material, corporeal things) to a fiduciary, subject to the burden of the fiduciary having to hand

---

1450. *Greeff v. Estate Greeff* 1957 (2) SA 269 (A).

1451. Section 2C(1) provides as follows:

> If any descendant of a testator, excluding a minor or mentally ill descendant, who, together with the surviving spouse of the testator, is entitled to a benefit in terms of a will renounces his right to receive such a benefit, such a benefit shall vest in the surviving spouse.

In *Moosa v. Minister of Justice and Correctional Services* 2018 (5) SA 13 (CC) a declaration of constitutional invalidity of this section by the Western Cape, Cape Town division of the High Court was confirmed, because the definition of 'surviving spouse' excluded spouses in polygamous Muslim marriages. The court held that the following words should be read into the section: 'For the purposes of this sub-section, a "surviving spouse" includes every husband and wife of a monogamous and polygamous Muslim marriage solemnised under the religion of Islam.'

1452. *Du Plessis v. Strauss* 1988 (2) SA 105 (A).

it over in full ownership to a fideicommissary at a certain time or upon the fulfilment of a condition.[1453] A *fideicommissum* may also be created *inter vivos* by means of a gift or a contract.[1454]

The testator may provide for a series of successive fideicommissaries. However, the Immovable Property (Removal or Modification of Restrictions) Act 94 of 1965 limits the number of successive fideicommissaries to two substitutions.[1455]

The fiduciary is normally the owner of the property. However, the fiduciary does not have full ownership since he or she may not alienate or encumber the fiduciary property, as the property must be delivered to the *fideicommissarius* when the fiduciary's interest is terminated.

485. In the case of the *fideicommissum residui*, however, the fiduciary has the power of alienation. In a *fideicommissum residui*, property is left to a beneficiary subject to the condition that as much of it as may be left at the time of the beneficiary's death, is to devolve upon another person. It is thus inherent in the concept of a *fideicommissum residui* that the fiduciary has the power to alienate the fideicommissary property during his or her lifetime and that the fideicommissary will only receive whatever remains upon the termination of that interest. The beneficiary may nevertheless not alienate more than three-quarters of the estate – the other quarter must be left for the fideicommissary, unless the testator's intention clearly indicates otherwise.[1456]

V. Usufruct

486. A usufruct occurs if a testator bequeaths ownership of property to one person (the *dominus* or 'remainder person') and the right to possess, use and enjoy the property to someone else (the usufructuary).[1457] The usufructuary must use the property in such a manner that its character is preserved.[1458] When the usufruct is terminated, the property must be passed to the owner.[1459] A usufruct may be created by will or *inter vivos*.[1460]

1453. *Union Government v. De Kock* 1918 AD 22; *British South Africa Company v. Bulawayo Municipality* 1919 AD 48; *Erasmus N.O. v. Estate Late Booysen* 2014 (4) SA 1 (SCA).
1454. *British South Africa Company v. Bulawayo Municipality* 1919 AD 48; *Ex parte Nell* 1963 (1) SA 754 (A); *Crookes v. Watson* 1956 (1) SA 277 (A).
1455. *See* above in this chapter.
1456. The three-quarters limitation was introduced by the *Novella* 108, a statute of Justinian dating from the sixth century AD.
1457. For a comprehensive discussion of this topic, *see* Corbett, Hofmeyr & Kahn, *The Law of Succession in South Africa*, 366–386. *See also* Ch. 3, §2 below.
1458. Voet, *Commentarius ad Pandectas*, 7.1.3; *Brunsdon's Estate v. Brunsdon's Estate* 1920 CPD 159.
1459. *Brunsdon's Estate v. Brunsdon's Estate* 1920 CPD 159.
1460. Voet, *Commentarius ad Pandectas*, 7.1.7; *Master v. African Mines Corporation Ltd* 1907 TS 925; *Ex parte Geldenhuys* 1926 OPD 155.

A usufruct is classed as a personal servitude and, as such, attaches to a particular person and cannot be passed on to another person.[1461]

VI. Trusts

487. A trust is established when one person (the trust founder) hands over property to another (the trustee), who has to take control of the property and administer it for an impersonal purpose or for the benefit of yet another person or persons (the trust beneficiary or beneficiaries).[1462] The underlying principle of a trust is that the trustee is entitled to ownership and/or control of property, not for his or her own benefit but for the benefit of another party.[1463] In other words, the trustee may have no beneficial interest in the trust property. The trustee is usually the owner of the trust property, but South African law also recognizes the trust where the beneficiary is the owner of the trust property.[1464]

488. Modern South African law received the concept of the trust from English law. An administrator who managed the property of others was known in Roman-Dutch law, but the trust was unknown in Roman-Dutch law. This legal concept originated in English law and was adopted in South African law through custom when British settlers began to use the trust in their wills and contracts in the nineteenth century.[1465] However, South African law did not adopt the content of English trust law, despite our usage of the English legal terms 'trust' and 'trustee'.[1466] South African trust law was developed by the courts. Another step in the development of the South African law of trusts was the adoption of the Trust Property Control Act 57 of 1988.[1467]

489. A trust may be created in a will (*mortis causa*) or among living persons (*inter vivos*). The trust *inter vivos* falls within the realm of contract law.[1468] Case

1461. Deeds Registries Act 47 of 1937, s. 66. *See Troksie v. Liquidator of RSD Construction CC* [2015] ZAGPPHC 321, 8 May 2015, (unreported), http://www.saflii.org/za/cases/ZAGPPHC/2015/321.html.

1462. For a comprehensive discussion of trusts, *see* E. Cameron, M. de Waal & P. Solomon, *Honoré's South African Law of Trusts* (Juta 6th ed. 2018) (*in toto*); F. du Toit, B.S. Smith & A. van der Linde, *Fundamentals of South African Trust Law* (LexisNexis, 2018) (*in toto*). *See also* Ch. 3, §2 below and the relevant monograph in this series.

1463. The core concept of a trust is the separation of ownership or control from enjoyment: *see Land and Agricultural Bank of South Africa v. Parker* 2005 (2) SA 77 (SCA). *See also* Du Toit, Smith & Van der Linde, *Fundamentals of South African Trust Law*, 2.

1464. *Schaumberg v. Stark* 1956 (4) SA 462 (A). *See also Braun v. Blann and Botha* 1984 (2) SA 850 (A).

1465. De Waal & Schoeman-Malan, *Law of Succession*, 167; Du Toit, Smith & Van der Linde, *Fundamentals of South African Trust Law*, 20–21. On the history of South Africa, including the British occupations, *see* General Introduction, §1 above.

1466. *Lucas' Trustee v. Ismail and Amod* 1905 TS 239; *Estate Kemp v. McDonald's Trustee* 1915 AD 491; *Braun v. Blann and Botha* 1984 (2) SA 850 (A).

1467. *See* Du Toit, Smith & Van der Linde, *Fundamentals of South African Trust Law*, 20–26 on the development of trust law in South Africa by the courts, the legislature and legal scholars.

1468. *See* Part IV, Ch. 2, §2 below.

law initially equated the trust *mortis causa* with a special type of *fideicommissum*,[1469] but in *Braun v. Blann and Botha*[1470] it was held that the testamentary trust is a legal institution sui generis. Case law has also established that a trust is not a juristic person with separate legal personality.[1471] However, a trust estate, comprising of an accumulation of assets and liabilities, is a separate entity from the estate of the founder, the trustee and the beneficiaries.[1472]

490. In order for a trust to be created, it must appear from the trust instrument that the testator intended to create a trust; the intention must be expressed in a way that creates a binding obligation to set up a trust; the trust founder must indicate the trust property with reasonable certainty; the trust object or trust beneficiaries must be indicated with reasonable certainty; and the trust object must be lawful.[1473] The trust may be created for the benefit of specific beneficiaries or for an impersonal object.[1474] A trust does not fail for want of a trustee. If no trustee is designated, or if the designated trustee does not wish to accept his or her office, the High Court or the Master[1475] will appoint a trustee in order to give effect to the trust.[1476]

491. A trust created for a charitable purpose is treated more benevolently than other trusts. The courts uphold these types of trusts as far as possible and do not allow them to fail on the ground that vague language renders the extent of their application unclear or because the objectives of the trust are stated in broad terms.[1477] Furthermore, in terms of the *cy près* doctrine, if a trust that evidences a general charitable intent becomes invalid, impossible or impractical to administer

1469. *Estate Kemp v. McDonald's Trustee* 1915 AD 491.
1470. 1984 (2) SA 850 (A).
1471. *CIR v. MacNeillie's Estate* 1961 (3) SA 833 (A); *Commissioner for Inland Revenue v. Friedman* 1993 (1) SA 353 (A); *Land and Agricultural Bank of South Africa v. Parker* 2005 (2) SA 77 (SCA); *Lupacchini v. Minister of Safety and Security* [2011] 1 All SA 138 (SCA); *Standard Bank of South Africa Limited v. Swanepoel* 2015 (5) SA 77 (SCA). However, in some respects the trust is treated as if it has a legal personality separate from the trustee: An *inter vivos* trust may be a beneficiary in a will (*Kohlberg v. Burnett* 1986 (3) SA 12 (A)); a trust fund is considered to be a 'person' for income tax purposes (Income Tax Act 58 of 1962, s. 1); upon sequestration of a trust, the trust is considered to be a debtor in the usual sense of the word within the meaning of s. 2 of the Insolvency Act 24 of 1936); immovable property may be registered in the name of a trust (Deeds Registries Act 47 of 1937, s. 102). *See* further M.J. de Waal, *Anomalieë in die Suid-Afrikaanse Trustreg*, 56 J. Contemp. Roman-Dutch Law 1 (1993).
1472. *Land and Agricultural Bank of South Africa v. Parker* 2005 (2) SA 77 (SCA); *Raath v. Nel* 2012 (5) SA 273 (SCA).
1473. Cameron, De Waal & Solomon, *Honoré's South African Law of Trusts*, 135–204; Du Toit, Smith & Van der Linde, *Fundamentals of South African Trust Law*, 51–59. *See also* M.J. de Waal, *The Abuse of the Trust (or: "Going Behind the Trust Form") The South African Experience with Some Comparative Perspectives*, 76 Rabel J. Comp. Int. Private Law 1084 (2012).
1474. Corbett, Hofmeyr & Kahn, *The Law of Succession in South Africa*, 394–399.
1475. In terms of s. 7(1) of the Trust Property Control Act 57 of 1988.
1476. *Land and Agricultural Bank of South Africa v. Parker* 2005 (2) SA 77 (SCA).
1477. *Estate Villet v. Estate Villet* 1939 CPD 152; *Ex parte Henderson* 1971 (4) SA 549 (D). *See also* Du Toit, Smith & Van der Linde, *Fundamentals of South African Trust Law*, 205–206.

as directed, the court will permit a change in the dispositive provisions to accomplish a general charitable intent that resembles the original intent as closely as is possible.[1478]

492. The Trust Property Control Act 57 of 1988 regulates the administration of trust property by trustees where the trusts have not been established orally, but by means of trust instruments.[1479] From the definition of a trust in this Act, it is evident that the legislature recognizes both the trust where the trustee is the owner of trust property, and the trust where the beneficiary is the owner of the trust property. The second type of trust is also referred to as a *bewind* trust.[1480]

493. The trustee is appointed in accordance with the provisions of the trust instrument.[1481] Before the trustee may start to act as a trustee, the Master must issue letters of authority to the trustee.[1482] The trustee must provide security for the faithful performance of his or her duties as trustee, unless exempted in the trust instrument.[1483] The trustee must give effect to the provisions of the trust deed; in other words, he or she must administer the trust assets in such a manner that the purpose of the trust, namely to benefit a personal or impersonal beneficiary, is realized. The trustee must exercise his or her own discretion as to the best way of achieving the purpose of the trust, but must act with the care, diligence and skill which can reasonably be expected of a person who manages the affairs of another.[1484] This general duty of the trustee to administer the trust assets for the benefit of the beneficiaries gives rise to a few more specific duties. These duties attach to the office of trustee by operation of law, that is, either in terms of the common law or by virtue of the Trust Property Control Act 57 of 1988.

The trustee must keep the trust assets separate from his or her own property.[1485] The trust property does not form part of the trustee's insolvent estate should the trustee's personal estate become insolvent.[1486]

1478. *Truter v. Die Administrateur, Kaapprovinsie* 1978 (3) SA 489 (C). *See* further Cameron, De Waal & Solomon, *Honoré's South African Law of Trusts*, 544–555.

1479. A trust instrument is defined in s. 1 of Act 57 of 1988 as a written agreement, testamentary writing or a court order according to which a trust was created.

1480. *Schaumberg v. Stark* 1956 (4) SA 462 (A).

1481. On the appointment of the trustee, *see* Cameron, De Waal & Solomon, *Honoré's South African Law of Trusts*, 210–243.

1482. Trust Property Control Act 57 of 1988, s. 6(1) and (2); *Simplex (Pty) Ltd v. Van der Merwe* 1996 (1) SA 111 (W); *Lupacchini v. Minister of Safety and Security* 2010 (6) SA 457 (SCA); *Hyde Construction CC v. Deuchar Family Trust* 2015 (5) SA 388 (WCC). *See also* Cameron, De Waal & Solomon, *Honoré's South African Law of Trusts*, 110, 249–259.

1483. The trustee's duty to give security is recognised by common law and regulated by the Trust Property Control Act s. 6(2). *See* further Cameron, De Waal & Solomon, *Honoré's South African Law of Trusts*, 279–302.

1484. Trust Property Control Act 57 of 1988, s. 9(1).

1485. Trust Property Control Act 57 of 1988, ss 10 and 11. *See also* Du Toit, Smith & Van der Linde, *Fundamentals of South African Trust Law*, 3, 167–176.

1486. Trust Property Control Act 57 of 1988, s. 12.

Trusteeship is a quasi public office[1487] and the trustee must account to the Master for the proper administration of the trust property.[1488] The trustee can be removed by the High Court[1489] or the Master[1490] for failing to comply with his or her duties. The trustee is entitled to reasonable remuneration for services rendered.[1491]

494. The beneficiary has a personal right against the trustee to receive the income or capital due to him or her under the trust. This personal right entitles the beneficiary to sue the trustee for compliance with the trust provisions if the trustee fails to carry out his or her duties.[1492] The beneficiary may also approach the court for relief if the beneficiary feels aggrieved by any action of the Master in terms of the Trust Property Control Act 57 of 1988.[1493]

495. As indicated above in this chapter, the court may vary trust provisions in certain situations.[1494]

VII. The Right of Accrual

496. The right of accrual (*ius accrescendi*) is the right of an heir or legatee to inherit those bequeathed benefits which a co-heir or co-legatee refuses to inherit or is incompetent to inherit.[1495] Accrual can also operate where one of the co-beneficiaries has predeceased the testator. Accrual does not take place if the testator has nominated a substitute to inherit in the place of a beneficiary who is unable to take or who repudiates the benefit. If accrual does not operate, the benefit either falls back into the residue of the estate (in the case of a legacy) to be inherited by the heir, or (in the case of an inheritance) devolves on the intestate heirs. Whether or not accrual must take place, depends on the intention of the testator. If the testator did not make his or her intention clear, certain indications (*coniecturae*) are taken into consideration in deciding whether or not accrual must take place.

The most important indication is the wording which the testator used in appointing the beneficiaries in his or her will. If the testator joined together the bequests to

1487. Cameron, De Waal & Solomon, *Honoré's South African Law of Trusts*, 69, 207. *See also Land and Agricultural Bank of South Africa v. Parker* 2005 (2) SA 77 (SCA).

1488. Trust Property Control Act 57 of 1988, s. 16. At common law, the trustee must also account to the beneficiaries and co-trustees. *See* further Cameron, De Waal & Solomon, *Honoré's South African Law of Trusts*, 393–397.

1489. Trust Property Control Act 57 of 1988, s. 20(1). *See Tijmstra v. Blunt-Mackenzie* 2002 (1) SA 459 (T) for some of the circumstances in which a trustee can be removed by the court.

1490. Trust Property Control Act 57 of 1988, s. 20(2).

1491. Trust Property Control Act 57 of 1988, s. 22. *See* further Cameron, De Waal & Solomon, *Honoré's South African Law of Trusts*, 409–423.

1492. Trust Property Control Act 57 of 1988, s. 19. *See* further Cameron, De Waal & Solomon, *Honoré's South African Law of Trusts*, 425–462.

1493. Trust Property Control Act 57 of 1988, s. 23. *See also Gross v. Pentz* 1996 (4) SA 617 (A).

1494. On variation of trust provisions by the court, *see* Du Toit, Smith & Van der Linde, *Fundamentals of South African Trust Law*, 67–73; Cameron, De Waal & Solomon, *Honoré's South African Law of Trusts*, 516–563.

1495. For a comprehensive discussion of this topic, see Corbett, Hofmeyr & Kahn, 243–258. See also De Waal & Schoeman-Malan, 199–203.

various beneficiaries in some way, the manner in which the interests were joined can indicate whether or not the testator intended accrual to take place. Essentially, there are three ways in which bequests to beneficiaries may be joined together. They are called joinder *re tantum*, joinder *re et verbis*, and joinder *verbis tantum*.

Joinder *re tantum (*or joinder *re*) occurs when the testator bequeaths the same thing (or benefit) to two or more persons in different bequests in the will. The interests of the beneficiaries are joined by the thing alone. The inference is that the testator intended that accrual must take place in such circumstances, unless the will reveals a contrary intention.[1496]

Joinder *re et verbis* occurs when the testator, in a single bequest, bequeaths the same benefit to two or more beneficiaries without allocating specific shares to each of them. The interests of the beneficiaries are joined by the thing and by the words. Again, the inference is that the testator intended accrual to take place, unless the will reveals a contrary intention.[1497]

In a joinder *verbis tantum* the testator, in a single bequest, bequeaths the same benefit to two or more beneficiaries, but allocates specific shares to each beneficiary (e.g., one-third to A and two-thirds to B). Traditionally, it was held that the effect of a bequest *verbis tantum* is to create a presumption against accrual, but that a contrary intention could be proved. It was therefore presumed that the testator intended to exclude the right of accrual.[1498] However, more recently the courts have held that the mere fact that a joinder is *verbis tantum* does not automatically mean that accrual does not take place, but that the focus should be on the testator's probable intention.[1499]

497. The legislature provided for a form of statutory accrual in section 2C(1) of the Wills Act 7 of 1953.[1500]

§9. Interpretation of a Will

I. General Principles

498. A testator may personally draft a will or approach a professional person, such as an attorney or a bank official, to draft the will on his or her behalf. The wording of a will drafted by a lay person is often unclear and ambiguous.[1501] Even if the will was drafted by a professional person, the meaning of certain provisions may be unclear. After the death of the testator, the will must be interpreted without the benefit of the testator's input. If there is any obscurity or ambiguity in the will,

1496. *Steenkamp v. De Villiers* (1893) 10 SC 56; *Barnett v. Estate Schereschewske* 1957 (3) SA 679 (C); *Ex parte Parker: In re Estate Parker* 1968 (1) SA 253 (C).
1497. *Steenkamp v. De Villiers* (1893) 10 SC 56; *Labuschagne v. Schoeman* 1915 CPD 19.
1498. *Winstanley v. Barrow* 1937 AD 75.
1499. *Lello v. Dales* 1971 (2) SA 330 (A); *Griessel v. Bankorp Trust Bpk* 1990 (2) SA 328 (O).
1500. This section is referred to in the discussion of direct substitution above in this chapter.
1501. *See*, e.g., *Raubenheimer v. Raubenheimer* 2012 (5) SA 290 (SCA).

it is the task of the High Court to interpret the will. The onus of proving that a will is obscure or ambiguous rests on the person who alleges this.[1502]

499. The main principle in the interpretation of wills is that the testator's intention, as it appears from the words used in the will, must be ascertained.[1503] This means that in interpreting the will the aim is not to determine the meaning of the words of the will detached from the testator's intention, but rather to determine what the testator meant by using those words.[1504] It further means that effect cannot be given to a possible intention on the part of the testator that has not been embodied in the words he or she used in the will in question.[1505]

The first step is to determine the testator's intention as it appears from the will read as a whole.[1506] All clauses must be read together and interpreted in accordance with the general scheme of the will.[1507] The dominant clause must be given overriding effect throughout the will.[1508]

The court must give the ordinary grammatical and everyday meaning to words which they had at the time of the making of the will, unless it appears from the context that the testator used the words in a different sense.[1509] Technical words must be interpreted to have their technical meaning, unless it is apparent from the context of the will that the testator used them in another sense.[1510] If words have a technical as well as an ordinary meaning, they must be given their ordinary meaning, unless it is clear from the will that the technical meaning is intended.[1511] If the same word occurs more than once in the will, it is presumed that the testator used it in the same sense every time, unless the opposite is apparent from the will.[1512] If a word or expression in a will is capable of bearing more than one meaning, the court must attach to it the meaning which will render the will valid rather than invalid, or according to which it will make sense instead of nonsense, or according to which the beneficiaries will benefit rather than be placed under an obligation.[1513] Where contradictory words, expressions or provisions appear in a will, an attempt must be

1502. *Gentle v. Ebden's Executors* 1913 AD 118.
1503. *Robertson v. Robertson's Executor* 1914 AD 503; *Gordon's Bay Estates v. Smuts* 1923 AD 160; *Cuming v. Cuming* 1945 AD 201; *Campbell v. Daly* 1988 (4) SA 714 (T); *Will v. The Master* 1991 (1) SA 206 (C).
1504. *Robertson v. Robertson's Executor* 1914 AD 503; *Cuming v. Cuming* 1945 AD 201.
1505. *Cuming v. Cuming* 1945 AD 201; *Leiman v. Ostroff* 1954 (4) SA 1004 (A).
1506. *Kemp's Estate v. MacDonald's Trustee* 1915 AD 491; *Raubenheimer v. Raubenheimer* 2012 (5) SA 290 (SCA) para. 22.
1507. *Lello v. Dales* 1971 (2) SA 330 (A); *Cronje v. Kruger* 1985 (2) SA 812 (A).
1508. *Ex parte Melle* 1954 (2) SA 329 (A); *Schaumberg v. Stark* 1956 (4) SA 462 (A); *Raubenheimer v. Raubenheimer* 2012 (5) SA 290 (SCA) para. 18.
1509. Voet, *Commentarius ad Pandectas*, 28.7.30, 34.5.4, 36.1.25; *Troitz v. Trotsky's Executrix* 1924 WLD 53.
1510. *Hofmeyer v. De Wet* 1869 Buch 317; *De Jager v. De Jager* 1 Buch AC 440; *Raubenheimer v. Raubenheimer* 2012 (5) SA 290 (SCA) paras 17–19.
1511. *Troitz v. Trotsky's Executrix* 1924 WLD 53.
1512. *Wood v. Petrie* 1923 AD 420; *Ex parte Malan* 1951 (3) SA 715 (O).
1513. Voet, *Commentarius ad Pandectas*, 28.7.30; 34.5.4; *Brown v. Estate Dickinson* 1919 AD 457.

made to reconcile them with one another or with the general intention of the testator as it appears from the will read as a whole.[1514] If it is completely impossible to bring about such reconciliation, both of the conflicting words, expressions or provisions must be held *pro non scripto*.[1515]

If a will is partly printed and partly typed and there is a contradiction between the typed part and the printed part, the typed part receives precedence.[1516]

500. In determining the intention of the testator from the will, the will may be supplemented by admissible evidence.[1517] 'Armchair evidence' is always admissible. It refers to evidence that places the court in the 'armchair' of the testator at the time of the making of the will and includes evidence of all the relevant facts and circumstances which were known to the testator.[1518] This includes evidence about the testator's age, state of health, life expectancy, habits, level of education, social position and family structure; the nature and size of the estate at the time of the drafting of the will; the circumstances under which the will was drawn up; and the knowledge and expertise of the person who drafted the will.[1519] Evidence about facts, people, property and circumstances affected by the will is also admissible. An example is evidence that identifies the persons or property referred to in the will.[1520] Extrinsic evidence may also be led to clarify the meaning of what the testator has written, for example, if a beneficiary was referred to by a nickname or reference was made to 'my wife' but the testator was not legally married.[1521] Patent as well as latent ambiguities may be cleared up by evidence.[1522] For example, if the testator appoints a specific charity as beneficiary, but it turns out that there is no charity by that specific name, although there are two charities with names that almost match the description in the will, evidence may be led to clarify the testator's intention.[1523]

If the intention of the testator is clear from the will, extrinsic evidence is not admissible to show that the testator had a different intention.[1524]

501. The courts cannot make a will for a testator or change the devolution of the estate as directed in the will. As indicated above in this chapter, a court may amend the provisions of a will only in very limited circumstances.

However, a court may rectify mistakes in a will. If a testator obviously made a mistake in the will, the court is competent to correct the mistake in accordance with the testator's general intention as it appears from the will as a whole.[1525] Clerical

1514. *Lombard v. Engelbrecht* (1908) 25 SC 519.
1515. Voet, *Commentarius ad Pandectas*, 34.5.4; *Smith v. Smith* 1913 CPD 869.
1516. *Taylor v. The Master* 1980 (4) SA 414 (T).
1517. *Gordon's Bay Estates v. Smuts* 1923 AD 160.
1518. *Cuming v. Cuming* 1945 AD 201; *Lello v. Dales* 1971 (2) SA 330 (A).
1519. Corbett, Hofmeyr & Kahn, *The Law of Succession in South Africa*, 468; *Raubenheimer v. Raubenheimer* 2012 (5) SA 290 (SCA) para. 17.
1520. *Cuming v. Cuming* 1945 AD 201; *Dison v. Hoffmann* 1979 (4) SA 1004 (A).
1521. Corbett, Hofmeyr & Kahn, *The Law of Succession in South Africa*, 469.
1522. *Ibid.*
1523. *Ex parte Eksekuteure Boedel Malherbe* 1957 (4) SA 704 (C).
1524. *Aubrey-Smith v. Hofmeyr* 1973 (1) SA 655 (C).
1525. *Ex parte Estate Allison* 1933 WLD 36.

mistakes may also be corrected.[1526] The court is competent to delete an aspect which has been inserted into a will by mistake.[1527] Words may also be added in order to complete a sentence or to give effect to the testator's intention if the testator obviously omitted words.[1528]

II. Presumptions

502. If a court is unable to ascertain the testator's intention in the light of the general principles, it may make use of certain presumptions.[1529] These presumptions are inferences based on common sense and the experience of centuries as to what testators usually mean when they use a certain phrase or word.[1530]

The following are some of the most important presumptions from the common law:[1531]

(1) Although, in South African law, a person may die partly testate and partly intestate, it is presumed that if a will has been made, the testator wished to dispose of all his or her assets in the will and therefore wished to die testate.[1532]
(2) It is presumed that a testator did not wish to disinherit his or her children or descendants, but intended to benefit them all equally.[1533]
(3) If the testator was in possession of his or her will, but it cannot be found after his or her death, it is presumed that he or she destroyed it with the *animus revocandi*.[1534]
(4) If a testator was co-owner of joint property, it is presumed that the testator wished to dispose of only his or her share of the property in the will.[1535]
(5) It is presumed that a joint will contains the separate wills of the co-testators and that each testator wished to dispose of only his or her own assets. Consequently, a presumption against massing operates.[1536]
(6) It is presumed that beneficiaries acquire vested rights under the will at the testator's death.[1537]

1526. *Botha v. The Master* 1976 (3) SA 597 (E).
1527. *Rens v. Esselen* 1957 (4) SA 8 (T).
1528. *Harter v. Epstein* 1953 (1) SA 287 (A); *Will v. The Master* 1991 (1) SA 206 (C); *Hotz v. Goodman* 1994 (2) SA 186 (C); *Henriques v. Giles* 2010 (6) SA 51 (SCA).
1529. *Havemann's Assignee v. Havemann's Executor* 1927 AD 473.
1530. Corbett, Hofmeyr & Kahn, *The Law of Succession in South Africa*, 506.
1531. The statutory presumptions introduced by the Wills Act 7 of 1953 are discussed in Part IV, Ch. 2, §3 above.
1532. *Brunsdon's Estate v. Brunsdon's Estate* 1920 CPD 159; *Haveman's Assignee v. Havemann's Executors* 1927 AD 473.
1533. Voet, *Commentarius ad Pandectas*, 36.1.17; *Ex parte Van Nieuwenhuyzen* 1954 (2) SA 336 (T); *Schaeffer and Nagel v. Estate Petzall* 1966 (3) SA 769 (W); *Erasmus v. Estate Late Booysen* 2014 (4) SA 1 (SCA) para. 24.
1534. *Nelson v. Currey* (1886) 4 SC 355; *Wynne v. Estate Wynne* (1908) 25 SC 951.
1535. *Receiver of Revenue v. Hancke* 1915 AD 64 73.
1536. *Rohm v. The Master* 1950 (1) SA 135 (SR); *D' Oyly-John v. Lousada* 1957 (1) SA 368 (N).
1537. *Estate Cato v. Estate Cato* 1915 AD 290; *McEwan's Estate v. McEwan's Estate* 1933 CPD 489.

(7) A presumption in favour of direct substitution and against fideicommissary substitution operates in cases of reasonable doubt.[1538]
(8) If assets are left to a beneficiary, it is presumed that he or she has been left full ownership of the assets.[1539]

1538. *Van Zyl v. Van Zyl* 1951 (3) SA 288 (A).
1539. *Brits v. Hopkinson* 1923 AD 492.

Chapter 3. Acts *Inter Vivos* Relating to the Estate

§1. Donatio Mortis Causa and Pactum Successorium

503. Upon the death of a testator, a beneficiary may acquire rights to the property of the deceased under the provisions of a *donatio mortis causa* or a *pactum successorium* contained in an antenuptial contract.

504. A *donatio mortis causa* is a gift or donation made in contemplation of the death of the donor.[1540] It must comply with the testamentary formalities in order to be valid.[1541] It is revocable by the donor until his or her death, and the property vests in the donee only on the death of the donor. The fact that the donation may be revoked until the death of the testator is important, because it means that a *donatio mortis causa* does not restrict the testator's freedom of testation. If the donee dies before the donor, the gift is revoked. If the donor has not delivered the gift before his or her death, the donee has a claim against the donor's estate for the gift.

505. A *pactum successorium*[1542] is an agreement between two parties purporting to regulate the devolution of the estate (or part of the estate) of one or both of them after the death of the party or parties. In general, *pacta successoria* are invalid under South African law since they restrict a person's freedom of testation and evade the formality requirements for wills.[1543] An exception is allowed, however, in that a *pactum successorium* may be included in an antenuptial contract.[1544]

In *Radebe v. Sosibo*,[1545] Satchwell J was of the opinion that in order to be valid a succession clause in an antenuptial contract must comply with the prescribed formalities for wills. However, before this case was decided, the general view was that a succession clause in an antenuptial contract is not a testamentary disposition and therefore does not have to comply with testamentary formalities.[1546] For this reason, the opinion of commentators on this aspect of *Radebe v. Sosibo* is that it is not correct.[1547]

1540. *Meyer v. Rudolph's Executors* 1918 AD 70.

1541. *Meyer v. Rudolph's Executors* 1918 AD 70; *Jordaan v. De Villiers* 1991 (4) SA 396 (C); *Radebe v. Sosibo* 2011 (5) SA 51 (GSJ).

1542. *See also* De Waal & Schoeman-Malan, *Law of Succession*, 211–218; Jamneck & Rautenbach (eds), *The Law of Succession in South Africa*, 251–261.

1543. *Borman en De Vos v. Potgietersrusse Tabakkorporasie Bpk.* 1976 (3) SA 488 (A); *Erasmus v. Havenga* 1979 (3) SA 1253 (T); *Jubelius v. Griessel* 1988 (2) SA 610 (C).

1544. *Ex parte Executors Estate Everard* 1938 TPD 190; *Radebe v. Sosibo* 2011 (5) SA 51 (GSJ).

1545. *Radebe v. Sosibo* 2011 (5) SA 51 (GSJ).

1546. Van der Merwe & Rowland, *Die Suid-Afrikaanse Erfreg*, 592; Jamneck & Rautenbach (eds), *The Law of Succession in South Africa*, 261; Rautenbach C. & A. van der Linde. *The Requirements for a Valid Pactum Successorium in an Antenuptial Contract: The Curious Case of Radebe v. Sosibo NO*, 129 S. Afr. Law J. 24 (2012).

1547. Rautenbach & van der Linde, *The Requirements for a Valid Pactum Successorium in an Antenuptial Contract*, 24; De Waal & Schoeman-Malan, *Law of Succession*, 218; Jamneck & Rautenbach (eds), *The Law of Succession in South Africa*, 261.

§2. Estate Planning

I. Introduction

506. Estate planning refers to planning measures that are taken during a person's lifetime but come into effect only after his or her death. Estate planning forms part of the wider concept of financial planning, which include measures which come into effect before the person's death. The purpose of financial planning is to provide for the short- and long-term financial needs of a person and to see to it that the person's particular concerns are met after his or her death.[1548]

507. In terms of the Estate Duty Act 45 of 1955, estate duty is levied on the net value of the deceased estate.[1549] At present, the rate is 20% on the first ZAR 30 million and 25% above ZAR 30 million. However, the first ZAR 3.5 million of the estate is exempt from estate duty.[1550] (This amount is increased from time to time to keep up with inflation.) If the deceased's spouse is the sole heir of the estate, no estate duty is payable because a deduction of the bequest to the spouse is allowed in terms of the Act.[1551]

In order to reduce the amount of estate duty payable, estate planners may put measures in place during a person's lifetime which peg the growth of his or her estate or reduce the value of the estate. The growth of the estate can be pegged by means of, for example, a trust. The value of the estate can be reduced *inter alia* by means of donations.

II. *Inter Vivos* Donations

508. A person may reduce the value of his or her estate by donating some of his or her assets to family members. However, in order to prevent the evasion of estate duty, donations tax is levied in terms of the Income Tax Act 58 of 1962.[1552] At present, the rate is 20% on donations less than ZAR 30 million, and 25% on donations exceeding ZAR 30 million.[1553] The first ZAR 100,000 that an individual donates per annum is exempt from donations tax.[1554] (This amount is increased from time to time to keep up with inflation.)

1548. W. Abrie, C.R. Graham & A. van der Linde, *Estate and Financial Planning* 6 (ProPlus Publishers, 2003). *See also* M. Botha et al., *Estate Planning and Fiduciary Services Guide* 209–247 (LexisNexis 2016).

1549. Estate Duty Act 45 of 1955, s. 2(1). The net estate value refers to the amount that remains after deducting all allowable deductions (including a given amount of R3.5 million).

1550. Section 4A.

1551. Section 4(q). For a detailed discussion of estate duty, *see* M.L. Stein, *Estate Duty: Principles and Planning* (LexisNexis 4th ed. 2011). *See also* De Clercq, Schoeman-Malan & Van der Spuy, *Deceased Estates*, 145–182; Cameron, De Waal & Solomon, *Honoré's South African Law of Trusts*, 695–713.

1552. Income Tax Act 58 of 1962, ss. 54–64. *See also* Cameron, De Waal & Solomon, *Honoré's South African Law of Trusts*, 688–695.

1553. Section 64.

1554. Section 56(2)(b).

Certain donations are exempt from donations tax, for example, donations between spouses.[1555] However, if assets are transferred from one spouse to another for purposes of avoiding income tax, the donor is nevertheless taxed on income derived from the donated property.[1556] Also excluded from donations tax are donations in terms of a *donatio mortis causa*[1557] and donations in terms of which the donee will not obtain any benefit until the death of the donor.[1558] However, although excluded from donations tax, the latter two types of donations are taxed in terms of the Estate Duty Act 45 of 1955, since property donated in this way is deemed to be property in the deceased estate for purposes of calculating estate duty.[1559] A bona fide contribution made by a donor towards the maintenance of any person also qualifies for exemption, limited to what the Commissioner considers reasonable.[1560]

If property is sold for consideration that the Commissioner of Inland Revenue considers to be inadequate, the property is deemed to have been donated.[1561]

III. Trusts

509. The type of trust that is created in a will (trust *mortis causa*) comes into effect after the death of the testator. This type of trust is often used to protect beneficiaries from themselves. For example, property or money left to minors is frequently placed in a trust to be administered by the trustee for the benefit of the beneficiaries until they reach the age specified by the trust founder in the trust document (the will).

510. South African law also recognizes the trust *inter vivos*. In South African law, this type of trust is equated with a contract for the benefit of a third party (a *stipulatio alteri*).[1562] According to our courts' interpretation, a contract comes into being between the founder and the trustee. The donor agrees to donate property to a trust. The trustee undertakes to control the trust assets (the donation) in accordance with the deed for the benefit of a third party (the beneficiary). The beneficiary is not a party to the contract; nor does he or she have any right against the trustee in terms of the contract. However, as soon as the third party (beneficiary) accepts the benefit, he or she obtains a claim against the trustee. As a result, the trust cannot be rescinded without his or her co-operation. The practical effect of this construction is that a trust *inter vivos* remains revocable until it has been accepted by a beneficiary.[1563]

1555. Section 56(1)(b).
1556. Section 7(2)(a).
1557. Section 56(1)(c).
1558. Income Tax Act 58 of 1962, s. 56(1)(d).
1559. Estate Duty Act 45 of 1955, s. 3(3)(b).
1560. Income Tax Act 58 of 1962, s. 56(2)(c)
1561. *Ibid.*, s. 58(1).
1562. *CIR v. Estate Crewe* 1943 AD 656; *Crookes v. Watson* 1956 (1) SA 277 (A). *See also* Du Toit, Smith & Van der Linde, *Fundamentals of South African Trust Law*, 28–30.
1563. *See Potgieter v. Potgieter* 2012 (1) SA 637 (SCA) para. 18.

511. Trusts *inter vivos* can be used to provide care to the founder and his or her beneficiaries. The trust founder may appoint himself or herself as the income beneficiary of a trust, and his or her children as the capital beneficiaries. If the trust founder becomes incapable of managing his or her affairs, there is no need to appoint a curator for him or her since the trustee already administers the property on his or her behalf. After the death of the founder, the capital beneficiaries receive their benefits from the trust.[1564]

Inter vivos trusts can also be used to protect assets. For example, a founder may have a dependant who is unable to manage money. The trust founder may want to help the dependant financially, but does not trust him or her to manage the money. The money may be placed in a trust to be administered for the benefit of the dependant.

A trust can also be used to peg the value of an estate in order to minimize the estate duty that is payable on the death of the deceased. In such circumstances, the money would usually not be donated to the trust, as the donor (trust founder) would incur liability for donations tax. However, the trust founder may lend the trust money to purchase assets. The loan remains an asset in the estate of the trust founder, but it does not increase in value over the years as other property might do.[1565]

IV. Insurance Contracts

512. Life insurance contracts are common in South Africa. The normal life insurance policy is a contract between the insurance company and the insured in terms of which the insurance company undertakes to pay a sum of money when a certain risk event occurs. In return, the insured pays a recurrent premium to the company. The risk event is usually the death or disability of the person insured. The company undertakes to pay the money to the insured person, his or her estate, or persons nominated by him or her as beneficiaries.[1566]

These contracts are not testamentary in character and need not comply with the testamentary formalities.

V. Usufruct

513. Although a usufruct is usually created in a will, it may also be created *inter vivos*.[1567] A person can use a usufruct to protect property that he or she intends to use for the benefit of more than one beneficiary.[1568] For example, a testator may want to provide for his or spouse after his or her death without having to transfer ownership of his or her property to the spouse, since he or she also wants to provide

1564. Abrie, Graham & Van der Linde, *Estate and Financial Planning*, 148.
1565. *Ibid.*, 194.
1566. *Ibid.*, 62.
1567. Voet, *Commentarius ad Pandectas*, 7.1.7; *Master v. African Mines Corporation Ltd* 1907 TS 925; *Ex parte Geldenhuys* 1926 OPD 155. *See also* Ch. 2 §8 Content of Wills above in this part.
1568. The usufruct is discussed in Part IV, Ch. 2, §8 above.

for his or her descendants after the death of the surviving spouse. The testator may anticipate that the surviving spouse would not leave the property to his or her children. In such event, the testator may leave the usufruct of the property to his or her surviving spouse and bare ownership to his or her children. The surviving spouse is entitled to the income derived from the property during his or her lifetime, but cannot sell or encumber the property. After the death of the surviving spouse the children receive full ownership of the property.[1569] The same result may be achieved by means of a trust, but a trust is more expensive to administer and may therefore not be acceptable to the testator.

A usufruct can also be used in conjunction with a trust to reduce the value of an estate for estate duty purposes.[1570]

1569. Corbett, Hofmeyr & Kahn, *The Law of Succession in South Africa*, 366–367.
1570. For more detail, *see* Abrie, Graham & Van der Linde, *Estate and Financial Planning*, 211–213.

Chapter 4. Acquisition and Administration of the Estate

514. As previously indicated,[1571] the deceased estate is represented by an executor who is appointed by the Master of the High Court in terms of the Administration of Estates Act 66 of 1965.[1572] The Master is tasked by the Act to supervise the administration of the deceased estate.

515. The Administration of Estates Act 66 of 1965 prescribes the basic procedure for administration of deceased estates. The procedure is the same irrespective of whether the deceased died intestate or testate.[1573]

The first step after the death of a person who leaves property or a will is the submission of a death notice to the Master.[1574] The death notice must be accompanied by a death certificate. The duty of preparing the death notice rests on the surviving spouse, the nearest relative or the person in control of the premises where the death occurred. The notice must be sent within fourteen days after the death of the deceased. The notice must give information as to the deceased's date and place of birth; the deceased's surviving spouse and descendants, if any; whether the deceased left property; and whether he or she left a will.[1575] If any details cannot be supplied by the person signing the death notice, they can be supplied later by the executor.[1576]

The person who is in possession of the testator's will must hand the will in at the Master's Office.[1577] The Master registers the will in a register of wills.[1578] Registration by the Master does not mean that the will is recognized as valid. The determination of the ultimate validity of every will rests with the High Court.[1579]

A person who is in possession of any property or documents of the deceased at the time of his or her death must retain the documents or property until an executor has been appointed.[1580]

The testator may nominate an executor in his or her will.[1581] A lay person, such as the deceased's surviving spouse, may be nominated as executor. In such event, the testator usually gives the executor the right of assumption, that is, the right to use another person as executor to help him or her to wind up the estate.[1582] In the case of an intestate estate (where an executor was not nominated by will), the Master will appoint a person whom he or she deems fit and proper to be an executor of

1571. *See* the Introduction to this part.
1572. Section 13.
1573. For a detailed description of this process, *see* De Clercq, Schoeman-Malan & Van der Spuy, *Deceased Estates*, 87 et seq.
1574. Administration of Estates Act 66 of 1965, s. 7(1).
1575. De Clercq, Schoeman-Malan & Van der Spuy, *Deceased Estates*, 95.
1576. In practice, the executor usually completes the death notice as part of his or her preliminary duties before receiving his or her letters of executorship. The executor also compiles a preliminary list of assets to be handed in at the Master's Office together with the will.
1577. Section 8(1).
1578. Section 8(3).
1579. Section 8(4).
1580. Section 11(1).
1581. Section 14(1).
1582. Section 15(1).

the deceased estate.[1583] Corporations may also be appointed as executors.[1584] In the case of a small estate, where the value of the estate does not exceed a certain amount,[1585] the Master may dispense with the appointment of an executor and give directions as to how the estate must be liquidated and distributed.[1586]

The executor must formally accept the appointment. If he or she does so, letters of executorship are issued to him or her.[1587] In the case of a corporation, the letters of executorship are issued to a director or another officer of the corporation.[1588] In principle, an executor must provide security for the proper performance of his or her functions. However, the testator may exempt the executor from giving security. The parent, spouse or child of the deceased is automatically exempted.[1589]

After accepting the appointment as executor, the executor must take all the property, books and documents of the estate into his or her possession and control them.[1590] He or she must compile an inventory of all the assets of the estate, showing their estimated value, and submit it to the Master.[1591]

The executor must open a bank account in the name of the estate as soon as he or she has ZAR 1,000 or more in estate moneys in his or her possession.[1592] The Master must be informed of the opening of the account and all estate money must be deposited into the account. Failure to do so is a crime and conviction results in the removal of the executor.[1593]

The executor must ascertain who the creditors are and get them to submit their claims. This is done by advertising the fact of the deceased's death and calling on creditors to submit their claims within a certain time. This notice takes the form of an advertisement in the *Government Gazette* and a newspaper.[1594]

The executor must assess the solvency or otherwise of the estate.[1595] He or she must compile a liquidation and distribution account and submit it to the Master for inspection within six months after the letters of executorship have been issued.[1596] This account must indicate how the creditors will be paid and how the residue of the estate will be distributed between the beneficiaries. In the liquidation and distribution account the executor has to list all the assets in the estate, together with their valuations. Also listed are all creditors and the amounts owing to them. The

1583. Section 18.
1584. Section 16.
1585. This amount is determined by the Minister of Justice and Correctional Services by notice in the *Government Gazette*. At present the amount is ZAR 250 000: G.N. R920 in *G.G.* 38238 of 24 Nov. 2014.
1586. Administration of Estates Act 66 of 1965, s. 18(3). The advantages of this process are that no executor's fee needs to be paid and that a liquidation and distribution account need not be compiled, making the process much quicker.
1587. Sections 14(1), 15(1), 16(1), 18(1).
1588. Section 16.
1589. Section 23.
1590. Section 26(1).
1591. Section 27(1).
1592. Section 28(1).
1593. Sections 28(1) and 102(1)(i).
1594. Section 29(1).
1595. If the estate is insolvent, the procedure for dealing with the estate is also set out in the Administration of Estates Act 66 of 1965, s. 34.
1596. Section 35(1).

executor has to state exactly how and to whom the assets in the estate are to be distributed. This account must lie open to the public for inspection (in the Master's Office) for a certain period of time to afford anyone who has any objections to the account an opportunity to make them known.[1597] The fact that the account is lying open for inspection must be advertised in the *Government Gazette* as well as a newspaper. If anyone objects to the account, the Master considers the objections and may order the executor to correct or amend the account accordingly.[1598] Normally, the amended account must again lie for inspection. If the Master overrules the objection, an appeal lies to the High Court.[1599]

Once the account has finally lain for inspection for the proper period and no further objections have been upheld, the executor must forthwith pay the creditors and beneficiaries in the estate in accordance with the account.[1600]

If the executor is unable to distribute money in the estate to beneficiaries within two months after finalizing the account, the moneys must be paid to the Master in order to be deposited into the Guardian's Fund.[1601]

After the executor has performed all his or her duties, he or she is entitled to be discharged.[1602]

516. The executor is in a fiduciary relationship with the estate. The common law places a duty on persons in a position of trust to disclose any personal interest they may have in any transaction which is carried out as part of their fiduciary duties. They may not reap any secret profits. Any purchase of estate property by the executor or by certain members of his or her family or other persons connected with him or her is void in terms of the Administration of Estates Act 66 of 1965, unless the Master or the court assents to or confirms the purchase.[1603]

517. The executor is entitled to remuneration. A specific rate is prescribed in the Act, but the testator is also entitled to determine the remuneration in his or her will.[1604] The executor's fee is paid from the estate. A Master's fee is also payable by the estate.

518. Funeral arrangements are in the hands of the deceased's family. Directions by the deceased in his or her will or any other document in this regard must be observed insofar as they are lawful, permissible and possible.[1605] Funeral expenses are paid by the estate.[1606]

1597. Section 35(5).
1598. Section 35(9).
1599. Section 35(10).
1600. Section 35(12).
1601. Section 35(13). Ch. V of the Act establishes this Fund.
1602. Section 56.
1603. Section 49.
1604. Section 51.
1605. *Mankahla v. Matiwane* 1989 (2) SA 920 (Ck).
1606. Administration of Estates Act 66 of 1956, s. 11(1)(b).

Selected Bibliography

Abrie, W., C.R. Graham & A. van der Linde. *Estate and Financial Planning*. Pretoria: ProPlus Publishers, 2003.

Abduroaf, M. *The Impact of South African Law on the Islamic Law of Succession*. Doctoral Thesis. Doctor of Laws. University of Cape Town, 2018.

Abduroaf, M. & Moosa, N. 'Islamic Law Mode of Estate Distribution in South Africa'. In *The International Survey of Family Law*, edited by B. Atkin. Bristol: Jordan Publishing, 2016.

Banoobhai, W. & S. Hoctor. 'The Court's Power to Compel DNA Testing in Paternity Disputes – LB v. YD 2009 5 SA 463 (T)'. *Obiter* 30 (2009): 791–802.

Barns, S. & A. Thompson. 'Reconsidering the Indignus Principle in the South African Law of Succession'. In *South African Law of Succession and Trusts: The Past Meeting the Present and Thoughts for the Future*, edited by M. de Waal & M. Paleker. Claremont: Juta, 2014.

Barratt, A. (ed.). *Law of Persons and the Family*. 2nd ed. Cape Town: Pearson Education South Africa, 2017.

Beinart, B. 'Testamentary Form and Capacity and the Wills Act, 1953'. *South African Law Journal* 70 (1953): 280–298.

Bekker, J. & G. van Niekerk. '*Gumede v. President of the Republic of South Africa*: Harmonisation, or the Creation of New Marriage Laws in South Africa?'. *SA Public Law* 24 (2009): 206–222.

Bennett, T.W. *Human Rights and African Customary Law under the South African Constitution*. Cape Town: Juta, 1995.

Boezaart, T. *Law of Persons*. 6th ed. Claremont: Juta, 2016.

Bolowana, A. 'Constitutional Court Reserves Judgment on Corporal Punishment Matter'. http://www.sabcnews.com/sabcnews/constitutional-court-reserves-judgement-on-corporal-punishment-matter/, 6 Feb. 2019.

Botha, M. et al., *Estate Planning and Fiduciary Services Guide*. Durban: LexisNexis, 2016.

Cameron, E., M. de Waal & P. Solomon. *Honoré's South African Law of Trusts*. 6th ed. Cape Town: Juta, 2018.

Central Intelligence Agency. 'Urbanization'. https://www.cia.gov/library/publications/the-world-factbook/geos/sf.html, 30 Jan. 2019.

Clark, B. 'Domicile'. In *Boberg's Law of Persons and the Family*. 2nd ed., edited by B. van Heerden, A. Cockrell & R. Keightley. Kenwyn: Juta & Co, Ltd, 1999.

Selected Bibliography

Cockrell, A. 'Capacity to Litigate'. In *Boberg's Law of Persons and the Family*. 2nd ed., edited by B. van Heerden, A. Cockrell & R. Keightley. Kenwyn: Juta & Co, Ltd, 1999.

Cockrell, A. 'Capacity to Perform Juristic Acts: Contracts'. In *Boberg's Law of Persons and the Family*. 2nd ed., edited by B. van Heerden, A. Cockrell & R. Keightley. Kenwyn: Juta & Co, Ltd, 1999.

Corbett, M.M., G. Hofmeyr & E. Kahn. *The Law of Succession in South Africa*. 2nd ed. Lansdowne: Juta Law, 2002.

Cornelius, S. 'Condonation of Electronic Documents in terms of Section 2(3) of the Wills Act 7 of 1953'. *Journal of South African Law* (2003): 208–211.

Corpus Iuris Civilis: Editio Decima Octava Lucis Ope Expressa. vol. I. *Institutiones*. Investigated by P. Kruger. *Digesta* investigated by T. Mommsen and re-investigated by P. Krueger. Berlin: Weidmannsche Verlagsbuchhandlung, 1965.

Corpus Iuris Civilis: Editio Stereotypa Septima. vol. II. *Codex Iustinianus*. Investigated by P. Krueger. Berlin: Weidmannsche Verlagsbuchhandlung, 1900.

Corpus Iuris Civilis: Editio Stereotypa Septima. vol. III. *Novellae*. Investigated by R. Schoell. Work of Schoell Interrrupted by Death. Completed by G. Kroll. Berlin, Weidmannsche Verlagsbuchhandlung, 1904.

Cronjé, D.S.P. '*Kidwell v. The Master* 1983 1 SA 509 (OK) – Ondertekening aan die End van 'n Testament'. *Journal of Contemporary Roman-Dutch Law* 46 (1983): 345–349.

Cronjé, D.S.P. & A. Roos. *Casebook on the Law of Succession/Erfregvonnisbundel*. 4th ed. Pretoria: Unisa Press, 2002.

Curran, E. & E. Bonthuys. 'Customary Law and Domestic Violence in Rural South African Communities: Notes and Comments'. *South African Journal on Human Rights* 21 (2005): 607–635.

D'Almaine, J. & F.N. Zaal. 'Inheritance Rights for Posthumously Procreated Children: A Growing Challenge for the Law'. *Potchefstroom Electronic Law Journal* 21 (2018): 1–30.

De Jong, M. & W. Pintens, 'Default Matrimonial Property Regimes and the Principles of European Family Law – A European-South African Comparison (Part 2)'. *Journal of South African Law* (2015): 551–566.

De Clercq, B., M.C. Schoeman-Malan & P. de W. van der Spuy. *Deceased Estates*. 11th ed. Durban: LexisNexis, 2017.

De Ru, H. 'A Historical Perspective on the Recognition of Same-sex Unions in South Africa'. *Fundamina* 19 (2013): 221–250.

De Waal, M. 'Anomalieë in die Suid-Afrikaanse Trustreg'. *Journal of Contemporary Roman-Dutch Law* 56 (1993): 1–10.

De Waal, M.J. 'Intestate Succession in South Africa'. In *Comparative Succession Law, Volume II: Intestate Succession*, edited by K.G.C. Reid, M.J. de Waal & R. Zimmermann. Oxford: Oxford University Press, 2015.

De Waal, M.J. 'Testamentary Formalities in South Africa'. In *Comparative Succession Law, Volume I: Testamentary Formalities*, edited by K.G.C. Reid, M.J. de Waal & R. Zimmermann. Oxford: Oxford University Press, 2011.

De Waal, M.J. 'The Abuse of the Trust (or: "Going Behind the Trust Form") The South African Experience with Some Comparative Perspectives'. *The Rabel Journal of Comparative and International Private Law* 76 (2012): 1078-1100.

De Waal, M.J. 'The Law of Succession and the Bill of Rights'. In *Bill of Rights Compendium*. Consulting eds Y. Mokgoro & P. Tlakula. Loose-leaf. Durban: LexisNexis, 1998.

De Waal, M.J. & M.C. Schoeman-Malan. *Law of Succession*. 5th ed. Cape Town: Juta, 2015.

De Wet, J.C. & A.H. van Wyk. *Die Suid-Afrikaanse Kontraktereg en Handelsreg: Volume I: Kontraktereg*. 5th ed. Durban: Butterworths, 1992.

Department of Justice and Constitutional Development. 'Community Courts'. http: //www.justice.gov.za/about/sa-courts.html, 30 Jan. 2019.

Devenish, G.E. *Interpretation of Statutes*. Kenwyn: Juta, 1992.

Du Bois, F. 'Sources of Law: Common Law and Precedent'. In *Wille's Principles of South African Law*, 9th ed., edited by F. du Bois. Cape Town: Juta & Co, 2007.

Du Plessis, J. *The South African Law of Unjustified Enrichment*. Claremont: Juta, 2012.

Du Plessis, L. *Reinterpretation of Statutes*. Durban: Butterworths, 2002.

Du Toit, F. 'Mental Capacity as an Element of Testamentary Capacity'. *South African Law Journal* 122 (2005): 661–683.

Du Toit, F., B.S. Smith & A. van der Linde. *Fundamentals of South African Trust Law*. Durban: LexisNexis, 2018.

Edwards, A.B. *The History of South African Law – An Outline*. Durban: Butterworths, 1996.

Erasmus, H.J., C.G. van der Merwe & A.H. van Wyk. *Lee and Honoré Family, Things and Succession*. 2nd ed. Durban: Butterworths, 1983.

Forsyth, C. *Private International Law: The Roman-Dutch Law Including the Jurisdiction of the High Courts*. 5th ed. Lansdowne: Juta, 2012.

Gallinetti, J. & J. Loffell. 'Foster Care'. In *Commentary on the Children's Act*, edited by C.J. Davel & A.M. Skelton. Loose-leaf. Claremont: Juta & Co, Ltd, 2007.

Giliomee, H. *The Afrikaners: Biography of a People*. Cape Town: Tafelberg, 2003.

Grotius, H. *Inleidinge tot de Hollandsche Rechts-geleerdheid with Notes by S.J. Fockema Andreae*. 3rd ed., edited by L.J. van Apeldoorn. Arnhem: S Gouda Quint, 1926.

Hahlo, H.R. & E. Kahn. *South Africa: The Development of Its Laws and Constitution*. London: Stevens & Sons Limited, 1960.

Hahlo, H.R. *The South African Law of Husband and Wife*. 5th ed. Cape Town: Juta, 1985.

Hall, K. & Z. Mokomane. 'The Shape of Children's Families and Households: A Demographic Overview'. In *2018 South African Child Gauge*, edited by K. Hall et al. Cape Town: Children's Institute, 2018.

Hall, K. & W. Sambu. 'Demography of South Africa's Children'. In *2017 South African Child Gauge*, edited by L. Jamieson, L. Berry & L. Lake. Cape Town: Children's Institute, 2017.

Heaton, J. 'Mental and Physical Disability; Prodigality'. In *Boberg's Law of Persons and the Family*. 2nd ed., edited by B. van Heerden, A. Cockrell & R. Keightley. Kenwyn: Juta & Co, Ltd, 1999.

Heaton, J. 'Parental Responsibilities and Rights'. In *Commentary on the Children's Act*, edited by C.J. Davel & A.M. Skelton, loose-leaf. Claremont: Juta & Co, Ltd, 2007.

Heaton, J. *South African Law of Persons*. 5th ed. Durban: LexisNexis, 2017.

Heaton, J. 'The Concept of Capacity'. In *Boberg's Law of Persons and the Family*. 2nd ed. edited by B. van Heerden, A. Cockrell & R. Keightley. Kenwyn: Juta & Co, Ltd, 1999.

Heaton, J. 'The Concepts of Status and Capacity: A Jurisprudential Excursus'. In *Boberg's Law of Persons and the Family*. 2nd ed., edited by B. van Heerden, A. Cockrell & R. Keightley. Kenwyn: Juta & Co, Ltd, 1999.

Heaton, J. 'The Law of Persons and Family Law'. *Annual Survey of South African Law* (2015): 393–434.

Heaton, J. 'The Proprietary Consequences of Divorce'. In *The Law of Divorce and Dissolution of Life Partnerships in South Africa*, edited by J. Heaton. Cape Town: Juta, 2014.

Heaton, J & H. Kruger *South African Family Law*. 4th ed. Durban: LexisNexis, 2015.

Himonga, C. 'Children (Minors)'. In *Wille's Principles of South African Law*. 9th ed., edited by F. du Bois. Cape Town: Juta & Co, 2007.

Himonga, C. 'Marriage'. In *Wille's Principles of South African Law*. 9th ed., edited by F. du Bois. Cape Town: Juta & Co, 2007.

Himonga, C. 'Persons and Family: Introduction'. In *Wille's Principles of South African Law*. 9th ed., edited by F. du Bois. Cape Town: Juta & Co, 2007.

Himonga, C. 'The Advancement of African Women's Rights in the First Decade of Democracy in South Africa: The Reform of the Customary Law of Marriage and Succession'. *Acta Juridica* (2005): 82–107.

Himonga, C. & T. Nhlapo (eds). *African Customary Law in South Africa. Post-Apartheid and Living Law Perspectives*. Cape Town: Oxford University Press Southern Africa, 2014.

Hoexter Commission. *Fifth and Final Report RP 78/1983 Commission of Inquiry into the Structure and Functioning of the Courts*. Pretoria: Government Printer, 1983.

Horn, J.G. & A.M. Janse van Rensburg, 'Practical Implications of the Recognition of Customary Marriages'. *Journal for Juridical Science* 27 (2002): 54–69.

Humby, T., L. Kotzé & A. du Plessis (eds). *Introduction to Law and Legal Skills in South Africa*. Cape Town: Oxford University Press Southern Africa, 2012.

Hunt, P.M.A. 'Error in the Contract of Marriage'. *South African Law Journal* 80 (1963): 94–126.

International Monetary Fund. 'Country Groups Information'. https://www.imf.org/external/pubs/ft/weo/2018/02/weodata/weoselagr.aspx, 30 Jan. 2019.

Jamneck, J. 'Herroeping en Wysiging van Testamente'. *Journal of Contemporary Roman-Dutch Law* 61 (1998): 600–608.

Jamneck, J. 'The Modus in Modern South African Succession Law'. In *South African Law of Succession and Trusts: The Past Meeting the Present and Thoughts for the Future*, edited by M. de Waal & M. Paleker. Claremont: Juta, 2014.

Jamneck, J. 'The Problematic Practical Application of Section 1(6) and 1(7) of the Intestate Succession Act under a New Dispensation'. *Potchefstroom Electronic Law Journal* 17, no. 3 (2014): 973–997.

Jamneck, J. & C. Rautenbach (eds). *The Law of Succession in South Africa.* 3rd ed. Cape Town: Oxford University Press Southern Africa, 2017.

Jansen, R-M. 'Family Law'. In *Introduction to Legal Pluralism in South Africa.* 4th ed., edited by C. Rautenbach & J.C. Bekker. Durban: LexisNexis, 2014.

Johnson, R.W. *South Africa: The First Man, The Last Nation.* London: Weidenfeld & Nicolson, 2004.

Joubert, C.P. 'The Law of Donations and Trusts'. *Annual Survey of South African Law* (1972): 121–124.

Kahn, E. *The South African Law of Domicile of Natural Persons.* Cape Town: Juta, 1972.

Kalula, S.Z. et al., 'Profile and Management of Patients at a Memory Clinic'. *South African Medical Journal* 100 (2010): 449–451.

Keightley, R. 'Nationality'. In *Boberg's Law of Persons and the Family*. 2nd ed., edited by B. van Heerden, A. Cockrell & R. Keightley. Kenwyn: Juta & Co, Ltd, 1999.

Keightley, R. 'The Child's Right to a Nationality and the Acquisition of Citizenship in South African Law'. *South African Journal on Human Rights* 14 (1998): 411–429.

Kleyn, D. et al. *Beginner's Guide for Law Students*, 5th ed. (Claremont: Juta Law, 2018).

Kruger, H. & A. Skelton (eds). *The Law of Persons in South Africa.* 2nd ed. Cape Town: Oxford University Press Southern Africa, 2018.

Lehman, K. 'Testamentary Freedom versus Testamentary Duty: In Search of a Better Balance'. In *South African Law of Succession and Trusts: The Past Meeting the Present and Thoughts for the Future*, edited by M. de Waal & M. Paleker. Claremont: Juta, 2014.

Lue-Dugmore, M., V. Karth, & J. Redpath. 'Petty Crimes that Matter: Evaluating the Western Cape Community Courts'. *SA Crime Quarterly* no. 15 Mar. 2005: 27–34.

Marais, D. *South Africa: Constitutional Development: A Multi-Disciplinary Approach.* Revised 2nd ed. Halfway House: Southern Book Publishers, 1993.

Meintjies, H. et al., 'Orphans of the AIDS Epidemic? The Extent, Nature and Circumstances of Child-Headed Households in South Africa'. *AIDS Care* 22 (2010): 40–49.

Mofokeng, L.L. *Legal Pluralism in South Africa: Aspects of African Customary, Muslim and Hindu Family Law.* Pretoria: Van Schaik Publishers, 2009.

Murray, I.B. 'Law of Succession (Including Administration of Estates)'. *Annual Survey of South African Law* (1983): 254–267.

Olivier, N.J.J. 'Law of Delict'. In *Introduction to Legal Pluralism in South Africa.* 4th ed., edited by C. Rautenbach & J.C. Bekker. Durban: LexisNexis, 2014.

Olivier, N.J.J. et al., 'Indigenous Law'. In *Law of South Africa*. vol. 32. 2nd ed., edited by founding ed. W.A. Joubert. planning ed. J.A. Faris. Durban: LexisNexis, 2009.

Oomen, B. 'Traditional Woman-to-Woman Marriages and the Recognition of Customary Marriages Act'. *Journal of Contemporary Roman-Dutch Law* 63 (2000): 274–282.

Paleker, M. '*Bekker v. Naude en Andere*: The Supreme Court of Appeal Settles the Meaning of Drafted in S 2(3) of the Wills Act, but Creates a Potential Constitutional Problem'. *South African Law Journal* 121 (2004): 27–33.

Palmer, A. 'The Best Interests Criterion: An Overview of Its Application in Custody Decisions Relating to Divorce in the Period 1985–1995'. In *Children's Rights*, edited by R. Keightley. Kenwyn: Juta & Co, Ltd, 1996.

Rautenbach C. 'A Few Comments on the (Possible) Revival of the Customary Law Rule of Male Primogeniture: Can the Common-Law Principle of Freedom of Testation Come to its Rescue?'. In *South African Law of Succession and Trusts: The Past Meeting the Present and Thoughts for the Future*, edited by M. de Waal & M. Paleker. Claremont: Juta, 2014.

Rautenbach, C. 'The Phenomenon of Legal Pluralism'. In *Introduction to Legal Pluralism in South Africa*. 4th ed., edited by C. Rautenbach & J.C. Bekker. Durban: LexisNexis, 2014.

Rautenbach C. & M.M. Meyer. 'Lost in Translation: Is a Spouse a Spouse or a Descendant (or Both) in Terms of the Reform of Customary Law of Succession and Regulation of Related Matters Act?'. *Journal of South African Law* (2012): 149–160.

Rautenbach C. & A. van der Linde. 'The Requirements for a Valid *Pactum Successorium* in an Antenuptial Contract: The Curious Case of *Radebe v. Sosibo NO*'. *South African Law Journal* 129 (2012): 22–32.

Schoeman, M.C. 'Nalatige Doodsveroorsaking: Satutêre Hervorming van die Erfreg?'. *Journal of Contemporary Roman-Dutch Law* 57 (1994): 114–121.

Schoeman-Malan, M.C. 'Assisting an Ailing Testator to Sign a Will'. *Journal of Contemporary Roman-Dutch Law* 82 (2019): 83–101.

Schoeman-Malan, M.C. 'Comparative Analysis of Commorientes – A South African Perspective: Part 1'. *De Jure* 50 (2017): 36–59.

Schoeman-Malan, M.C. 'Comparative Analysis of Commorientes – A South African Perspective: Part 2'. *De Jure* 50 (2017): 378–395.

Schoeman-Malan, M.C. 'Fraud and Forgery of the Testator's Will or Signature: the Flight from Formalities to no Formalities'. *Journal of South African Law* (2015): 125–152.

Schoeman-Malan M.C. 'Missing Persons – Current Tendencies'. *Journal of Contemporary Roman-Dutch Law* 81 (2018): 218–238.

Schoeman-Malan, M.C. 'Onbehoorlike Beïnvloeding: Testeerbevoegdheid versus Testeervryheid'. *De Jure* 35 (2002): 333–341.

Schoeman-Malan, M.C. 'Privaatregtelike Perspektief op Onwaardigheid om te Erf – die Uitwerking van Gesinsmoorde'. *LitNet Akademies* 10 (2013): 113–175.

Schoeman-Malan, M.C. 'The Requirements and Test to Assess Testamentary Capacity (1)'. *Journal of Contemporary Roman-Dutch Law* 78 (2015): 604–621.

Schoeman-Malan, M.C. 'The Requirements and Test to Assess Testamentary Capacity (2)'. *Journal of Contemporary Roman-Dutch Law* 79 (2016): 69–84.

Schoeman-Malan, M.C. 'When Disaster Strikes – A Case Law Analysis of Simultaneous Deaths'. *Obiter* 38 (2017): 275–295.

Schoeman-Malan, M.C. et al., 'Section 2(3) of the Wills Act 7 of 1953: A Retrospective and Critical Appraisal of Some Unresolved Issues'. In *South African Law of Succession and Trusts: The Past Meeting the Present and Thoughts for the Future*, edited by M. de Waal & M. Paleker. Claremont: Juta, 2014.

Scholtens, J.E. 'Sterility or Impotence?'. *South African Law Journal* 78 (1961): 159–170.

Sinclair, J.D. *Introduction to the Matrimonial Property Act 1984*. Cape Town: Juta & Co, Ltd, 1984.

Sinclair J.D. assisted by J. Heaton. *The Law of Marriage*. vol. 1. Kenwyn: Juta, 1996.

Sloth-Nielsen, J. 'Realising Children's Rights to Legal Representation and to be Heard in Judicial Proceedings: An Update'. *South African Journal on Human Rights* 24 (2008): 495–524.

Smith, B. 'Intestate Succession and Surviving Heterosexual Life Partners: Using the Jurist's "Laboratory" to Resolve the Ostensible Impasse that Exists After *Volks v Robinson*'. *South African Law Journal* 133 (2016): 284–315.

Sonnekus, J.C. '*Kidwell v. The Master* 1983 1 SA 509 (OK)'. *Journal of South African Law* (1983): 188–193.

Sonnekus, J.C. 'Kondonering van Vormgebrekkige Testamente? Vergeet dit!'. *Stellenbosch Law Review* 14 (2003): 337–348.

Sonnekus, J.C. 'Kondoneringsbevoegdheid van Hof by Vormgebrekkige Testament'. *Journal of South African Law* (1995): 359–365.

Sonnekus, J.C. 'Testeerbevoegdheid, Herroeping van 'n Testament en Kuratele Sorg'. *Stellenbosch Law Review* 15 (2004): 450–463.

Sonnekus, J.C. 'Testeerbevoegdheid van 'n Handelingsonbevoegde'. *Journal of South African Law* (1990): 754–762.

Sonnekus, J.C. & J.C. van der Walt. 'Die Nalatige Bloedige Hand – Voor die Hof én die Wetgewer'. *Journal of South African Law* (1992): 147–153.

South African Law Commission. *Report on Domicile: Project 60*. Pretoria: Government Printer, 1990.

South African Law Commission. *Report on Review of the Law of Succession: Project 22*. Pretoria: Government Printer, 1991.

South African Law Commission. *Report Pertaining to Matrimonial Property Law with Special Reference to the Matrimonial Affairs Act, 1953, the Status of the Married Woman, and the Law of Succession in so far as it Affects the Spouses RP26/1982*. Pretoria: Government Printer, 1982.

South African Law Reform Commission. 'Current Investigations'. http://www.justice.gov.za/salrc/projects.htm, 31 Jan. 2019.

South African Law Reform Commission. *Project 118 Report on Domestic Partnerships*. Pretoria: Government Printer, 2006.

Spiro, E. 'Domicile in South African Law'. *Acta Juridica* (1962): 62–75.

Spiro, E. *Law of Parent and Child*. 4th ed. Cape Town: Juta, 1985.

Spiro, E. 'Marriage Without the Requisite Permission of the Minister of the Interior'. *Journal of Contemporary Roman-Dutch Law* 33 (1960): 5–10.

Statistics South Africa. *Community Survey 2016 in Brief, Report 03-01-06*. Pretoria: Statistics South Africa, 2016.

Statistics South Africa. 'Consumer Price Index History'. http://www.statssa.gov.za/publications/P0141/CPIHistory.pdf, 24 Mar. 2019.

Statistics South Africa. 'Mid-Year Population Estimates, 2018, P0302'. http://www.statssa.gov.za/publications/P0302/P03022018.pdf, 24 Mar. 2019.

Statistics South Africa. *Quarterly Labour Force Survey, Quarter 3, 2018, P0211*. Pretoria: Statistics South Africa: 2018.

Statistics South Africa. 'Statistical Release P0301.4, Census 2011'. http://www.statssa.gov.za/publications/P03014/P030142011.pdf, 30 Jan. 2019.

Statistics South Africa. *Survey of Activities of Young People, 2015, P0212*. Pretoria: Statistics South Africa, 2015.

Stein, M.L. *Estate Duty: Principles and Planning*. 4th ed. Durban: LexisNexis, 2011.

Tibane E. (ed.). 'History'. *2017/18 South Africa Yearbook*. 25th ed. Pretoria: Government Communication and Information Service, 2018.

Tibane E. (ed.). 'Justice and Correctional Services'. *2017/18 South Africa Yearbook*. 25th ed. Pretoria: Government Communication and Information Service, 2018.

Tibane E. (ed.). 'Land and Its People'. *2017/18 South Africa Yearbook*. 25th ed. Pretoria: Government Communication and Information Service, 2018.

United Nations Development Programme. 'Human Development Indices and Indicators: 2018 Statistical Update. Briefing Note for Countries on the 2018 Statistical Update'. http://www.hdr.undp.org/sites/all/themes/hdr_theme/country-notes/ZAF.pdf, 30 Jan. 2019.

Van Aswegen, A. 'Transactions Between a Spouse and a Third Party: The Effect of the Matrimonial Property Act 88 of 1984'. *Modern Businessman's Law* (1984): 140–148.

Van den Heever, F.P. *Breach of Promise and Seduction in South African Law*. Cape Town: Juta & Co, Ltd, 1954.

Van der Keessel, D.G. *Praelectiones Iuris Hodierni ad Hugonia Grotii Introductionem ad Iurisprudentiam Hollandicam*, Translated by H.L. Gonin in Consultation with D. Pont under the title *Voorlesinge oor die Hedendaagse Reg na Aanleiding van De Groot se "Inleiding tot de Hollandse Rechtsgeleerdheyd": D.G. van der Keessel*, edited by P. van Warmelo, L.I. Coertze & H.L. Gonin. Amsterdam: AA Balkema, 1961–1975.

Van der Keessel, D.G. *Theses Selectae Juris Hollandici et Zelandici*. Amsterdam: F Muller, 1860.

Van der Merwe, N.J. & C.J. Rowland. *Die Suid-Afrikaanse Erfreg*. 6th ed. Pretoria: J.P. van der Walt en Seun (Edms) Bpk, 1990.

Van Leeuwen, S. *Censura Forensis*. Lugduni in Batavis: S Luchtmans and C Haak, 1741.

Van Leeuwen, S. *Het Rooms-Hollands-Regt with Notes by C.W. Decker and J. Ten Houten*. Amsterdam: Hendrik en de Wed van Dirk Boom, vol. I. 1780, vol. II. 1783.

Visser, D. *Unjustified Enrichment*. Wetton: Juta, 2008.

Voet, J. *Commentarius ad Pandectas*, Translated with Explanatory Notes and Notes of All South African Cases by P. Gane Under the Title *The Selective Voet Being the Commentary on the Pandects [Paris Edition of 1829] by Johannes Voet [1647–1713] and the Supplement to That Work by Johannes van der Linden [1756–1835]*. Beach Grove: Butterworth & Co. (Africa) Ltd, 1956.

Vorster, L.P. 'Traditional Leadership in South Africa, Marriages and Succession'. *Obiter* 20 (1999): 75–91.

Wood-Bodley, M.C. 'Lost Wills and Section 2(3) of the Wills Act'. *South African Law Journal* 132 (2015): 734-747.

Wood-Bodley, M.C. '*MacDonald v. The Master*: Computer Files and the "Rescue" Provision of the Wills Act'. *South African Law Journal* 121 (2004): 34–43.

Wood-Bodley, M. C. 'Tertius Bosch's Final Over: *Van Wetten v Bosch*'. *South African Law Journal* 122 (2005): 52–58.

Wood-Bodley, M.C. 'Wills, Data Messages, and the Electronic Communications and Transactions Act'. *South African Law Journal* 121 (2004): 526–528.

Wood-Bodley, M.C. 'Wills, Divorce, and the Provisions of Section 2B of the Wills Act: *Louw NO v Kock*'. *South African Law Journal* 135 (2018): 418–432.

Wood-Bodley, M.C. 'Wills Lost whilst in the Testator's Possession – Rebutting the Presumption of Revocation'. *South African Law Journal* 133 (2016): 731–744.

Worden, N. *The Making of Modern South Africa: Conquest, Segregation and Apartheid*. 3rd ed. Malden: Blackwell Publishing, 2000.

Zaal, N. & C. Matthias. 'Alternative Care'. In *Commentary on the Children's Act*, edited by C.J. Davel & A.M. Skelton. Loose-leaf. Claremont: Juta & Co, Ltd, 2007.

Selected Bibliography

Index

The numbers here refer to paragraph numbers.

Index

Index

Made in the USA
Monee, IL
18 October 2026

66041407R10157